Shades of Difference

Shades of Difference

Mythologies of Skin Color in Early Modern England

SUJATA IYENGAR

PENN

University of Pennsylvania Press

Philadelphia

10   9   8   7   6   5   4   3   2   1

Published by
University of Pennsylvania Press
Philadelphia, Pennsylvania 19104-4011

Library of Congress Cataloging-in-Publication Data

Iyengar, Sujata.
    Shades of difference : mythologies of skin color in early modern
England / Sujata Iyengar.
        p.   cm.
    ISBN 0-8122-3832-X (acid-free paper)
    Includes bibliographical references and index.
    1. English literature—Early modern, 1500–1700—History and criticism. 2. Race in
literature. 3. Literature and society—England—History—16th century. 4. Literature
and society—England—History—17th century. 5. Human skin color—Social aspects—
England. 6. Difference (Psychology) in literature. 7. Human skin color in literature.
8. Mythology in literature. 9. Blacks in literature. 10. England—Race relations—
History—16th century. 11. England—Race relations—History—17th century.
PR428.R35 I94   2004
820.9′3552—dc22   2004052022

For Richard and Kavya,
with love

Contents

Abbreviations

Ado	Shakespeare, *Much Ado About Nothing*
AH	Heliodorus, trans. Underdowne, *Aethiopian Historie*
Ant.	Shakespeare, *Antony and Cleopatra*
APC	Cavendish, *Assaulted and Pursued Chastity*
AS	Barnfield, *The Teares of an Affectionate Shepheard*
AYL	Shakespeare, *As You Like It*
Beauty	Jonson, ed. Orgel, *Masque of Beauty*
Bishops'	Bishops' Bible
Blackness	Jonson, ed. Orgel, *Masque of Blackness*
BW	Cavendish, *Blazing World*
CMC	Middleton, *Chaste Maid in Cheapside*
DP	Musaeus, trans. Chapman, *Divine Poem of Musaeus*
ES	Heliodorus, trans. Morgan, *Ethiopian Story*
FE	Lisle, *Fair Ethiopian*
FQ	Spenser, ed. Hamilton, *The Faerie Queene*
Geneva	Geneva Bible
GM	Jonson, ed. Orgel, *The Gipsies Metamorphosed*
Ham.	Shakespeare, *Hamlet*
HDA	Africanus, trans. Pory, *History and Description of Africa*
Histoire	Heliodorus, trans. Amyot, *Histoire Aethiopique*
HL	Marlowe, *Hero and Leander*
HLC	Chapman, *Hero and Leander Completed*
Irish	Jonson, *Workes, Irish Masque at Court*
KJV	King James Version of the Bible
Lanthorn	Dekker, *Lanthorn and Candlelight*
LC	Shakespeare, *A Lover's Complaint*
LD	Brereton, ed., *Lusts Dominion*
Memorable	Chapman, *Memorable Masque*
MM	Shakespeare, *Measure for Measure*
MND	Shakespeare, *A Midsummer Night's Dream*

MV	Shakespeare, *The Merchant of Venice*
NSRV	New Standard Revised Version of the Bible
PE	Browne, *Pseudodoxia Epidemica*
Per.	Shakespeare, *Pericles*
PN	Hakluyt, ed., *Principal Navigations*
R2	Shakespeare, *Richard II*
Rom.	Shakespeare, *Romeo and Juliet*
SD	Gough, *Strange Discovery*
SG	Middleton and Rowley, *The Spanish Gypsy*
Tem.	Shakespeare, *The Tempest*
Tit.	Shakespeare, *Titus Andronicus*
TN	Shakespeare, *Twelfth Night*
TNK	Shakespeare and Fletcher, *The Two Noble Kinsmen*
TT	Middleton, *The Triumphs of Truth*
Ven.	Shakespeare, *Venus and Adonis*
View	Spenser, *View of the Present State of Ireland*
WD	Webster, ed. Luckyj, *The White Devil*
WE	*The White Ethiopian*
WT	Shakespeare, *The Winter's Tale*
2H4	Shakespeare, *Henry IV, Part Two*

Introduction

This book argues that we can only understand the early modern relationships among "race," embodiment, and skin color in their multiple contexts—historical, geographical, and literary. But unlike work that tries to find a specific historical or disciplinary point for the emergence of race as a color-coded classification, mine insists that the terms *race* and *racialism* cannot and should not be treated as pure or hermetic categories. Instead, I wish to maintain conversations among early modern culture texts, between historical and material contexts, and between various early modern ways of figuring difference (bodily, cultural, and social). I resist the imposition of a straightforward historical trajectory "toward" racialism or "toward" color-prejudice. In particular, I suggest that *literary* affiliations (the compulsion of narrative, the longing of lyric, the agendas of masque, and the escape of romance) entangle with variable concepts of skin color and emergent racial distinctions.

Moving through the early modern curriculum or *paideia*—from the learned professions of religion, medicine, and law to popular and practical sources of knowledge about the world such as rogue literature and travel narrative—I distinguish the early modern characteristics, interests, and intentions of cultural fields that engage skin color and human differences, and examine their significance for conventional literary genres, ranging from sixteenth-century epyllion to seventeenth-century lyric and Restoration prose romance. Each of these early modern discourses inherits and produces its own assumptions and language about skin color—and these early modern representations of racial difference, I maintain, at once create and interrogate the assumptions about race, skin color, and gender that we live with today. While these mythologies fail to translate in any simple way to our own structures of feeling, this book aims to make the strangeness of early modern racialized discourse familiar, without losing its distinctiveness.

Take, for example, early modern travel narrative (perhaps the sharpest pressure point for competing beliefs about human divisions and variation), which gives us richly conflicting uses of the word *race*. The ambiguous marginal note, "The Negroes race their skinnes," beside

William Towerson's account of ritual scarification in what is now Ghana ostensibly uses "race" in its sense of to mark or to scar, to *raze*, as his body text makes clear: "the most part of them have their skin of their bodies raced with diuers workes, in maner of a leather Jerkin."[1] At the same time, the use of the word "Negroes"—a term that takes dark or "black" skin to constitute the defining characteristic of an imagined nation or group—ensures that "the Negroes'" skins are "raced" in two senses. They bear the marks of their own cultural affiliation and the gaze of a distancing colonial eye.

Or—to take another instance—let us turn to stage play, to an example from Shakespeare's *Measure for Measure* (*MM*), whose use of the word "race" again seems at first to have little or nothing to do with the discourse of skin color. Gloating over Isabella, Angelo declares, "Now I give my sensual race the rein" (*MM*, 2.4.160).[2] OED glosses this rare and obsolete usage as one's "natural or inherited disposition"; figuratively, Angelo's illicit fantasy of sexual possession evokes the frenzied racehorses of desire held in check by the inadequate bridle of virtue.[3] Angelo additionally, however, associates his "sensual race" with dirt, pollution, and blackening. No one will believe Isabella, Angelo threatens, because of Angelo's "unsoiled name"; she herself will "smell of calumny" unless she "lay[s] by all . . . prolixious blushes" (2.4.163), the modest signs of continence thought in the period to belong only to the white-skinned (a belief to which I will return throughout this book). From her very first entrance Isabella has been associated with "fair" (1.4.24) skin whose "cheek-roses" proclaim her virginity (1.4.16). And again, the richness of meaning within Angelo's words points to a characteristic of its genre. In drama—Shakespearean drama in particular—conflicts occur not only between but also within characters. The revelation of Angelo's "race" reveals, as the Duke has predicted, "what our seemers be" (1.3.54); in this most metadramatic of plays, Angelo himself is an actor. Angelo's "sensual race" is something essential or innate, but at the same time individuated, specific to him.

Race and Genre

The structure of my project reflects my desire to engage texts and bodies, fictions and fact, in dialogue. It concerns itself with what Renaissance scholar Rosalie Colie called "The Resources of Kind"—the early modern *copia* that classifies, multiplies, subdivides, and recreates the genres and modes of literature, and that claims "mixed genre [as] a mode of *thought* as well as poetry."[4] Moreover, I concur with Alastair Fowler's assertion that, although the sheer range of the *paideia* in inclusive genre systems such as Julius Caesar Scaliger's suggests the absence of boundaries between the literary and the nonliterary, many early modern genre-critics (including Scaliger and Sidney) distinguish between fictional and nonfictional modes, between "poesy" and didacticism, between delight and instruction. Jonathan Crewe identifies this invest-ment in forms or kinds as "the continuing holds they exercise, the fas-cinations they exert," phrases that testify to the power of kind at once to "limit" and to attract writers and readers.[5] "Kind" contains within itself the idea of reproduction, both sexual and figurative. "To work one's kind" is to generate offspring.[6] Daydreaming Gonzalo imagines a commonwealth where "Nature should bring forth, / Of it[s] own kind, all foison" (*Tem.*, 2.1.163–64). Similarly, kinds of literature give birth to other kinds; epigram and lyric marry to beget the sonnet—what Colie calls a "counter-genre"—while courtly dancing and public stage play join hands in the masque.[7] Like races or tribes, kinds of literature expand into larger and more diffuse versions of themselves; Colie in-terprets the essay as the adage writ large, and I address in later chapters the flowering of romance from travelers' tales. "Kind," of course, evokes in the Renaissance not only generic forms but also human distinc-tions—skin color, gender, and social status. Elizabeth I's famous edict expelling "blackamoores" dismisses them as a strange "kinde of people."[8] Women are the "female kind."[9] Malvolio is "a kind of a puritan" (*TN*, 2.3.140). And just as generic kinds in the period generate, recreate, and redefine themselves, so, I will argue, does the language of race and skin color.

My model for understanding the development of racialism from ethnic prejudice and mythologies of color, and its literary affiliations and impli-cations, comes from Raymond Williams's account of social change in *Marxism and Literature*, and his classification of "residual," "dominant," and "emergent" "structures of feeling." He uses the phrase *structures of feeling* in preference to the term *ideology* because he wishes to point out the places where seemingly explicit, overtly political institutions and seemingly hidden, private beliefs overlap. At any time, Williams argues, all three elements—residual, dominant, and emergent—coexist: "no mode of production and therefore no dominant social order and there-fore no dominant culture ever in reality includes or exhausts all human practice, human energy and human intention."[10] This statement is not "wishful theory," to borrow Jonathan Dollimore's useful phrase[11]; it is an affirmative version of history—but one that's nonetheless true. In Williams's model the dominant structure of feeling is *always* tempered by residual structures from the previous generation, and emergent ones from the one ahead. A residual structure of feeling can remain in play for years, even centuries, after its moment has passed, and become dom-inant again when it is revived as politically expedient.

This book employs Williams's model to examine the forms and practices of both kinds of kind—human variation and literary genre. The alignment of various nonsystematic xenophobias—mythologies of color, nationality, religion, class, and gender—into a coherent mythology of race is an emergent structure of feeling in the sixteenth century, a structure of feeling that grows stronger throughout the seventeenth century and that becomes dominant during the eighteenth. Genres accompany residual meanings from the past; mixed genres sometimes indicate emergent ideologies. To return to my earlier example of the masque as a mixed genre: courtly dancing celebrates social graces, the elegance of courtship, and the forms and services of aristorcracy; it merges with stage play and civic pageant, demotic in tone and feel, to produce the masque, a form peculiarly suited to, say, King James's revival of the theory of Divine Right and his modernization of old practices to suit contemporary political ends.

Structures of Critical Feeling

The historiography of race and slavery itself follows Williams's model. The terms and discourse of race studies shift and change according to the discipline or discourse employed (science, postcolonialism, ecology) and according to emergent and residual structures of feeling within our own culture (the Civil Rights movement, Afrocentrism, feminism). Theorists of race and historians of slavery have historically been divided on the following questions: (1) did slavery cause modern racialism, or did racialism inevitably lead to slavery? (2) is racial difference essential, fundamental, ineluctable, or is it socially constructed, contingent, and the result of historical accident? (3) are colonized cultures and marginalized groups totally engulfed by the dominant culture or do they retain idiosyncratic or hybrid "subcultures" that remain distinctively their own? Winthrop Jordan explained what he called the "abasement of the Negro" and the institution of slavery as cause and effect (slavers entrapped black Africans because they already despised and demonized them), but Peter Fryer argues that it was only because of slavery's economic power that a coherent system of racialism came into being.[12] Kwame Anthony Appiah and Henry Louis Gates argue that race is a social fiction, and demolish the old anthropological model that divided humankind into the three subspecies, Negroid, Mongoloid and Caucasoid.[13] Taking the social constructivist argument a step further, Theodore Allen blames the institution of slavery for beginning the process that his books call "the invention of the white race": in other words, racialism became a convenient justification for an increasingly profitable, but controversial, trade.[14]

Allen, Gates and Appiah regard "race" as a solely cultural fiction. But some prominent black scholars, such as W. E. B. Du Bois, Frantz Fanon, and, most recently, Molefi Kete Asante, have proclaimed a theory of "negritude," or essential Black (in upper case) identity to be reclaimed and reaffirmed, insisting that race is a necessary and useful category despite its use by white slavers and supremacists to justify the subjugation of darker-skinned peoples.[15] Fanon had justified his belief in negritude by arguing that the white establishment overwhelmed the consciousness of black men, and that racial accommodation was impossible; his supporters often advocated separatism, voluntary segregation, as the only option for black people wishing to live with minds and bodies free from colonial oppression. Other black thinkers, however, argue that it is not necessary to essentialize Blackness in order to develop what bell hooks calls an "oppositional gaze" or consciousness—an identity politics based on shared historical circumstances.[16] Lani Guinier and Gerald Torres's proposal of "political race" would incorporate likeminded believers of every background into a coalition united by their desire for political change.[17] Gayatri Chakravorty Spivak's critique of the liberal subject includes her suggestion that groups adopt a "strategic essentialism" in order to exert agency.[18] Homi Bhabha has suggested that "hybrid" identities in colonial settings can provide a way for oppressed peoples to interrogate and coopt the dominant culture.[19]

The concept of "hybridity" has proven enormously influential not only among African American, Afro-British, and postcolonial scholars, but also among literary critics in more traditional fields. Some scholars of early modern England have in recent years critiqued "hybridity" as a model that encourages us to read history with a comfortable sense of irony and discourages us from alleviating the institutional structures of racism that still exist today. Alan Sinfield, for example, queries the extent to which hybridity in itself provided a meaningful challenge to colonialism or patriarchy, and Ania Loomba argues that the specific *context* of so-called hybrid activities will determine whether or not these activities are subversive.[20] As will be clear from my mixture of past and present tense, to a certain extent these debates are themselves historical, as residual scholarly analyses gave way in the nineteen-sixties to the decentered subject and antiessentialist drive of emergent poststructuralist praxis. Critical thinkers considering race and colonialism in the new millennium tend to recognize that the institution of slavery and the discourse of racialism at once mutually interrogate and reinforce one another.

I rehearse these three phases in African, African American, and postcolonial studies here in part because the scholarship of early modern race has developed along similar lines. Peter Erickson's article "The Moment of Race in Renaissance Studies" distinguishes between two distinct "phases" or waves of Renaissance race studies. The first, in the

1960s, resulted from "individual interest or effort"; the second, in the 1990s, treated race as "a major organizing category for the period as a whole."[21] We can place both "phases" into larger political and social structures of feeling. The 1960s brought the Civil Rights movement in the U.S.A. and a corresponding interest in the African and Afro-Caribbean presence in Britain. In the 1980s, the immediate racism of Thatcher's Britain engendered new work on Black British cultural studies and on subcultures in the UK.[22] The 1990s saw the rise of so-called "identity politics" in the United States, coupled with an increase in the number of African and Ethnic Studies programs in the academy. Current work on early modern race studies focuses upon the material *process* of racialization, ranging from the origins of "English" identities to studies of travel, trade, labor relations, and reevaluations of the role of climate theory in early modern understandings of skin color.[23]

Just as we can historicize the first phase of early modern race studies in light of these changing political and academic contexts, so we can consider current work in light of late twentieth- and early twenty-first-century discoveries about the origins and nature of the human, in different disciplines and genres—genetics, biological anthropology, archaeology, and history. The Human Genome Project established that what we call race— a term that for us is inextricably linked to skin color—is a social category, not a biological one: "Although frequencies for different states of a gene [alleles] differ among races, we have found no 'race genes'— that is, states fixed in certain races and absent from all others."[24] Sub-Saharan Africans demonstrate the greatest variation within alleles. Some biological anthropologists have taken this African diversity as proof that all human beings today share a common ancestor who left Africa only 200,000 years ago—a nanosecond in what Shakespeare's Prospero calls the "dark backward and abysm" of evolutionary time (*Tem.*, 1.2.50). Genetic variations among human beings, even within isolated populations such as Icelanders, are not enough to constitute subspecies, let alone separate species or races. Furthermore, genetic differences between two individuals in a single population may display greater variation than between two individuals from different populations, and such distinctions do not seem to correlate with pigmentation.[25] "World historian" and biologist Jared Diamond likewise refutes racialism and its associated hierarchies through his present-day climatological explanation for the varying rates of scientific "development" and discovery on different continents. Dismissing myths of racial superiority, he explains Eurasia's premodern advantage as the stretch of East-West zones that shared the same climate, which enabled large domestic animals (and their germs), scientific and military inventions, crops, languages, and culture to cross vast expanses of land with relative ease and to flourish there.[26]

The Renaissance scholars now writing about race do not usually forge connections between these developments in the social sciences and their own studies in literary and intellectual history. But it is easy to see their work as part of this wide-ranging interrogation of the old category *race* and its discontents, together with another aspect of twenty-first century living—the global market. Reinterpretations of early modern climate theory resonate with Diamond's ecological approach to world history and human migration. Excavations of "British" genealogies and the animal-human divide pick up our contemporary obsessions with genetic inheritance. Explorations of labor, travel, and freedom in the Renaissance mirror current concerns about European Renaissance cultures in a global context.

My own work attends closely to material contexts and discursive networks, refracting the black/white (or, in Kim Hall's more historically resonant formulation in *Things of Darkness*, dark/fair) binary through a prism that displays its colors.[27] I explore bodily differences in parallel, moving both "top down" and "bottom up" through the historical and literary record. I examine, as it were, individual genetic variation in discourse—Renaissance "counter-texts," popular accounts of corporeal differences that evoke mythologies of color as well as myths of race, and the ways in which these works interrogate each other. I am not denying the importance of racial distinctions in everyday life, either in the present day or in the early modern period: on the contrary, the concept of race has been used both as a weapon against marginalized groups and as a tool for their survival and growth, just as genre or discipline has been pressed into service too (think of the relative weight we give to a philosopher's thoughts on race versus those of a geneticist). Imtiaz Habib's helpful formulation in *Shakespeare and Race* suggests that race is both an epistemology and an ontology—that is, both a way of knowing or of organizing knowledge, and a state of being—an imaginary category with real consequences, an intellectual fiction and an experiential fact.[28] Genre, similarly, exists in a quantum state, both there and not-there, a convenient but imaginary way of dividing up a world of words, a system responsive to human needs and desires (the demands of science, the compulsion for romance). We cannot generate overarching statements of early modern beliefs about skin color and human differences without taking account of the disciplinary and literary affiliations that shape them.

A Case Study: The Curse of Cham

Depending upon what discourse we examine, blackness may or may not appear as a distinct taxonomic division, a situation I investigate at greater length in Chapter Three. For now, I offer as an example of my approach a comparison of perhaps the two most widely discussed treatments of blackness in Renaissance race studies: George Best's notorious commentary on the book of Genesis (1578), printed in Hakluyt's *Principal Navigations* (*PN*, 1598–1600), and Sir Thomas Browne's essay "On the Blacknesse of Negroes," from *Pseudodoxia Epidemica* (*PE*, 1646).[29] Both writers refute heliotropism—the belief that dark skin was caused by the sun's rays; both writers seem unaware of the pernicious argument, used in later centuries to justify African enslavement, that Noah cursed his son Cham and his descendants with perpetual servitude. Yet I shall show that their differing motives and experiences, and the consequences of their generic decisions, indicate the conflict between a residual mythology of color and an emergent myth of race.

Having encountered South Americans, East Indians, and Moluccan Islanders, all of whom, despite living "under the Equinoctiall . . . are not blacke, but tauney and white, with long haire uncurled as wee haue," Best questions the theory that the sun's heat causes blackness and tightly curled hair (*PN*, 7:261). He speculates instead that such characteristics proceed from a "natural infection" or hereditary taint. As further proof of this, he adduces the example of "an Ethiopian as blacke as a cole" who married "a faire English woman" and yet "begat a sonne . . . as blacke as the father" (7:262). Nowadays we know of course that two people of different skin tones or other physical differences can produce a child that resembles one, either, or neither of them. Classical theories of conception, long familiar to the Renaissance, attributed the conferral of form or appearance to the father, and of matter or substance to the mother (incorporating a common pun on the Latin word for mother, *mater*). But both classical and early modern observers realized that skin color could not be reducible to either form or matter, since black parents of either sex did not reliably produce dark-skinned offspring. Pliny recounts the birth of "the famous boxer Nicaeus, whose mother was the offspring of adultery with an Ethiopian but had a complexion no different from that of other women, whereas Nicaeus himself reproduced his Ethiopian grandfather."[30] And in a fictional example from Shakespeare's *Titus Andronicus* (1592), Aaron, a black Moor, sires a dark-skinned babe through a union with the white-skinned Tamora. At the same time, Aaron suggests exchanging the child with the infant of Muly, his countryman. Muly's infant, like Aaron's, is the offspring of a black father and a white mother, but unlike Aaron's child, is fair-skinned (*Tit.*, 4.2.152–54).[31]

To explain such phenomena, Best mixes genre, moving from travel narrative into biblical exegesis. He repeats the story that Noah's three sons, Shem, Cham, and Japheth, colonized Asia, Africa, and Europe respectively after the flood. Since, he argues, everyone presently on the "whole earth . . . must needes come of the off-spring" of one of these sons, "all three being white, and their wiues also, by course of nature should have . . . brought foorth white children" (*PN*, 7:264). Instead, however, Cham and his wife disobeyed Cham's father by having sexual intercourse, "for the which wicked and detestable fact" Cham begot a son called Chus, "who not onely it selfe, but all his posteritie after him should bee so blacke and lothsome . . . and of this blacke and cursed Chus came all these blacke Moores which are in Africa" (7:264). Having identified black skin with Noah's curse, Best concludes that blackness must be an "infection of blood" (7:264), transmitted through "lineall discent" from father to child (7:263). Best's account links black skin to polluted and polluting "sexual transgression," implicitly associating the Ethiopian father in England and his "faire" wife with the sexual disobedience of Cham and his spouse in the Ark.[32] Its mixed modes mimic its fears about sexual commixture, the horrifying fantasy of racial pollution.

The narrative's motives, like its genre, are also mixed. Its ostensible goal, like Browne's, is to correct a common error, but this curiosity and thirst for knowledge is far from disinterested, characterized instead by the desire for mastery of the seas and climate typical of travel narrative. The descriptive and inductive ("I myself have seen," "hair uncurled as we have") mutates into the didactic and deductive ("must needes come"). This generic or modal shift accompanies a movement from neutral to derogatory, as the "coal-black" Ethiopian in England becomes a descendant of the "blacke and cursed" Moors in Africa.

Recalling Colie's analysis of the Renaissance essay as an outgrowth of emblem or adage, we can now read Browne's essay on blackness as a scientific rewriting or response to the well-worn Renaissance chestnut, "to wash an Ethiop white," signifying impossibility. Having distinguished between the dark skins of sunburned Europeans, "Artificial Negroes, or Gypsies," and those of the Africans or "True Negroes," Browne maintains, like Best, that there appears to be little or no correlation between exposure to the sun and the darkness of Africans' skin, arguing that the Africans' blackness must be "spermatical," passed from father to child. In contrast to Best, however, Browne denies the exegetical tradition that explained black skin as a divine or patriarchal curse. He very sensibly observes that there is no reason to consider black skin a "curse": "if we seriously consult the definitions of beauty, and exactly perpend what wise men determine thereof, we shall not apprehend a curse, or any deformity therein" (*PE*, 3:245).

Like earlier medical writers, Browne conflates sperm or seed with the embryo itself, believing that sperm contained a "homunculus" or miniature human being that was already complete. At the same time, he cannot believe that the sperm (the "seed") of black men is darker than that of white ones (another popular belief). On the contrary, sperm is "in its naturals white," but blackness is an "accident" in the scholastic sense: a cover or "efflorescence" created by the natural processes of birth that "shadow" the essential whiteness of the embryo. This process, he continues, means that "not only their legitimate and timely births, but their abortions are also dusky, before they have felt the scorch and fervor of the Sun" (3:242). Browne's early empiricism (his observation of fetuses and of semen) encourages him to draw a subtle but meaningful distinction. Blackness is not essential, although it is inherited; it is an "accident," a "dusky" cover for the Africans' natural whiteness. Blackness gilds the "out-side" of essentially white men.

Note that although the essay as a form privileges authority or *ethos*, Browne admits defeat; his conclusion is no conclusion at all. "Efflorescence" describes both a flowering or completion (an association that leads him to discuss "abortions" or untimely births) and the chemical crystallization of fine, powdery particles on the surface of a substance when water is removed from it, "the separation of parts," as Browne puts it. Blackness is an external crust, but also a decoration, like a flower— worthy of wonder rather than open to analysis. Blackness remains opaque to him, undercutting the mastery inherent in the essay form (even as it continues to fetishize blackness *as* mysterious and unknown, as Kim Hall has observed).[33]

Both Best and Browne question a generally held belief about blackness. Neither espouses polygenesis—the belief that people with different skin colors had completely separate origins. To do so would contradict the word of the Bible, and in fact, Browne explicitly states that "Negroes" descend from "the seed of Adam," just like Englishmen, Chinamen, Guinea Moors, and all the inhabitants of the world (*PE*, 3:240). Most important, neither connects black skin, or the divine curse, with slavery; such a connection does not become standard until the end of the seventeenth century. Even the connection of Cham with Africa is contentious in the Renaissance. William Bourne's *Treasure for Trauailers* (1578) derives the Africans from Shem, not from Cham, arguing that Shem "dyd inhabite the partes of Africa," Cham, "the partes of Asia," and Japhet, "Europe, and . . . the great Ilande Atlantida [Atlantis], nowe called America."[34] Bourne's compendium of useful travel information (instructions in navigation, mathematics, shipbuilding, and meteorology) briskly dismisses as "vayne and contentious arguments" the belief that "there were any more Adams than one, or any more Noyes [Noahs] the[n] one."[35]

Best's hybrid or mixed form of travel narrative and Browne's "abort[ive]" essay can suggest how loose mythologies of color became a systematic mythology of race. The demise of the heliotropic or sunburn theory of blackness is caused not only by observation (Browne's early scientific method) but also by early modern travel and new methods of generating wealth and work. There existed in the Renaissance a hitherto overlooked, residual relationship between labor and skin color, one that was transformed into the more familiar connections epitomized by the curse of Cham by travel, labor, and the new science. Those who were suntanned worked, voyaged, or spent extended periods outdoors, such as the "sunne-burnt pilgrim," the "sun-tand slave" who manned ancient galleys, or the "tawnie" gardener with "sunne-burnt hands."[36] With the establishment of plantations in Barbados, this residual connection between skin color and outdoor, manual work (through the figure of sunburn or suntan) becomes an emergent myth linking dark skin and other physical features to an inherited destiny to slave labor on the one hand and to species difference on the other. Consider the sailor Dionise Settle's words when he encounters dark-skinned Inuit in his search for the Northwest Passage in 1577. He comments in surprise that despite the climate's cold darkness, the Inuits' "colour is not much unlike the Sunne burnt countrey man, who laboureth daily in the Sunne for his living" (*PN*, 7:224). Settle's words domesticate the strange and evoke English hierarchies of rank and region. Travel narrative, biblical exegesis, and scientific treatise foreground this shift differently. Without surveying the differing motives, experiences, and forms of Best, Browne, and others, these gradual transformations would remain invisible.

Parts and Chapters

This book's three parts, "Ethiopian Histories," "Whiteness Visible," and "Travail Narratives," thus attempt to engage in dialogue with each other and with various early modern structures of feeling: mythologies of color and myths of race, "new" discoveries and "ancient" literature. Part I, "Ethiopian Histories," considers the Renaissance transmission of two ancient texts, one classical, one biblical, and their changing representations of blackness in fiction and lyric, before ending with a comparison of the Irish and the Ethiopian in the early modern colonial imagination. Chapter 1, "Pictures of Andromeda Naked," tracks the ways in which the sexual and racial ambiguities in Heliodorus's ancient Greek romance, *Aithiopika* or "Ethiopian Story," and in early modern mythographies of Ethiopia harden into essential notions of racial difference in seventeenth-century adaptations of Heliodorus's *fabula.* I argue in Chapter 2, "Thirteen Ways of Looking at a Black Bride," that exegetical and literary interpretations of the "black" bride in the biblical Song of Songs shift from reading her negritude as a sign of her Ethiopian origin to dismissing her blackness as purely literary rather than literal. This shift corresponds, I suggest, to a growing African presence in Britain and to the transformation of the "ancient rhyme" of the sonnet tradition to the new, scientific—called by Samuel Johnson "metaphysical"—poetry. Chapter 3, "Masquing Race," concludes this part of the book by examining two groups who, although not usually called "black" in the period, nonetheless seem to constitute "races," in our modern sense, in the Renaissance—the Irish and the (Native) Americans. Looking at the Jacobean court masque and its colonial and regal agendas proselytizing for the "plantation" of Ireland, the economic conquest of sub-Saharan Africa, and the religious conversion of Virginians, I contend that the status and meanings of blackness as an epithet alter according to their political, geographical, and literary contexts.

The next part of the book, "Whiteness Visible," suggests that reading skin explicitly called "white" or "fair" is in the Renaissance a hermeneutic enterprise akin to literary criticism. "Heroic Blushing," Chapter 4, engages moral treatises that both stigmatize and praise the blush with early modern epyllia. These erotic narrative poems use the figure of a fluctuating blush to evoke sexual freedom, moral indeterminacy, and the enthusiasm of lyric, and the notion of fixed blackness or pallor to trope sexual constraint, race, and the compulsion of narrative. Chapter 5, "Blackface and Blushface," maintains that what I call "blushface" makeup and the strictures against it in anticosmetic and antifeminist tracts highlight the emphasis in stage plays on cosmetics as racial or gender prosthetics on the one hand and indices of meta-theatrical illusion on the other. Chapter 6, "Whiteness as Sexual Difference," further analyzes pallor as a metaphor that breaks down distinctions of sex and the direction of sexual desire altogether. In Elizabethan homoerotic verse, excessively pallid, "green," or "white" skin unites young men and women in their suffering from what medical texts call "greensickness," satirizing heteroerotic pairings and teasingly allowing the possibility of same-sex desire.

My final part, "Travail Narratives," mobilizes two of the meanings of "travail" in the period, as hard labor on the one hand and as travel or voyaging on the other. Chapter 7 reads the statutes established against the Gypsies (the so-called "Artificial Negroes" of the chapter's title) in Jacobean England in the context of popular "cony-catching" pamphlets and drama. Where legislators and the writers of rogue literature castigate Gypsies as illicit or unlicensed laborers (arguing that they are in effect unemployed and unemployable, unauthorized actors or performers), I find that masque and stage play foreground the relations between the suspiciously playful work of the wandering Gypsy and the invisible labor of the artist. Chapter 8, "Suntanned Slaves," contrasts the association of dark skin with gold in the city pageant before investigating the ways ethnographic accounts turn the black bodies of Africans themselves into currency. The first English slavers to return from the Senegambia produce tribal ethnographies that rapidly produce what I argue is already a version of racialism—a hierarchical ordering of human beings that depends upon skin color and labor, especially slavery. The final chapter of this part, Chapter 9, allows me to return to where I began, with an encounter between romance and historiography that, to adapt de Certeau, is also an encounter with the Other. "Experiments of Colors" glances ahead to the Restoration and the scientific revolution, when, I suggest, the connections between personal autonomy and embodiment become increasingly restrictive in light of the growing prominence of the slave trade and polygenetic theories of black inferiority imported from the American colonies. Reading prose romance alongside theories of color and light from the scientific revolution, I speculate that the world of romance offers a literary escape from the emerging cultural hierarchies of gender and pigmentation—the social fiction of race. *Shades of Difference* concludes with a brief "Afterword" about a contemporary interpretation of race—digital artist Nancy Burson's "Human Race Machine."

Keywords

In a book concerned with "shades of difference" in so many senses, it is particularly important that my terms be exact. Out of context, Hamlet's first words, "A little more than kin, and less than kind" (*Ham.,* 1.2.64–65), could serve as a working definition for "race" in the early modern period. "Race" in the Renaissance connotes a little more than mere "kin" or family ties on the one hand, a little more than skin color or physical appearance on the other, but in either case a little less than the differences of "kind" or species difference that eighteenth- and nineteenth-century taxonomists believed to indicate the existence of biologically distinct human subspecies. This book therefore employs our term "race" in both what Margo Hendricks has suggested is the word's most common Shakespearean sense—family origin or lineage—and its emergent reference to inherited physical differences (most importantly, pigmentation, and secondarily other characteristics such as facial features or hair type) associated with ancestry in a particular geographical area.[37]

Fryer defines "racism" as the historical conflation of three sets of beliefs: (1) the unthinking connection of blackness with sin, (2) the ugly association of Africans with apes (linked to the claim that Africans shared characteristics with animals), and (3) the pseudoscientific doctrine of polygenesis (the assumption that diverse groups of human beings sprang from separate origins). He contrasts early "race-prejudice" with a later, consistent, "mythology of race."[38] Fryer's terms, however, presuppose a belief in distinct races and thus have limited application in the sixteenth and early seventeenth centuries in England, where perceived physical differences and accusations of savagery, bestiality, and moral turpitude are leveled against different populations and individuals with varying reference to skin color. But during the course of the seventeenth century race became the justification for the slave trade and for Britain's expanding empire. We need to locate the manufacture of race historically, in the context of Britain's incipient involvement in the slave trade and of an increasing division of labor between male and female, rural and urban, free and forced.

I therefore use "racialism" to refer to the mistaken notion that such visible differences demonstrated speciation, like the differences between cats and dogs, that such supposed species could be ranked hierarchically, and that they should not intermarry. My term "mythologies of color" describes the complex of early modern beliefs surrounding the significance of skin of all perceived shades—white, black, red, green, brown, yellow, and transparent. I call immigrants to early modern Britain "strangers," as they would have been called at the time, as well as by the modern name "foreigners" (in early modern England this word is used primarily by the inhabitants of one county or shire to refer to people from another English county). Similarly, I adopt for the sixteenth and early seventeenth centuries the phrase "ethnic prejudice" to refer to the tribal xenophobia, often related to religious or national prejudice rather than to skin color, that was directed against groups perceived as foreign in early modern England. Stuart Hall's well-known definition of "ethnicity" acknowledges the historical contingencies not only of events but also of the language we use and have used to define particular categories:

The term "ethnicity" acknowledges the place of history, language, and culture in the construction of subjectivity and identity, as well as the fact that all discourse is placed, positioned, situated, and all knowledge is contextual. Representation is possible only because enunciation is always produced within codes which have a history, a position within the discursive formations of a particular space and time.[39]

But I wish also to retain the Renaissance associations of the word "ethnick": "a heathen . . . or Pagan, one that knoweth not God."[40] Adding to Stuart Hall's discussion an awareness of the word's early modern sense of religious exclusion allows us to track the development of taxonomies of racial difference and skin color through the sixteenth and seventeenth centuries.

These terms—like the concepts they evoke—cannot and should not be "pure" or situated safely in the past. Later chapters employ the term "caste" to refer to hierarchies based upon vocations to which one is only "called" by the accident of birth. I also appropriate the nineteenth-century coinage, "miscegenation," or its Renaissance equivalent, "commixture," to characterize the fear that sexual pollution or unhealthy mixing would occur if humans belonging to different races were to produce children together. Such beliefs drove the anthropological division of humanity into distinct races or subspecies, Caucasian, Mongol, Negro, Malay, and American, an increasingly complicated scheme of racial classification that would dominate scientific and humanistic thinking about human societies from the eighteenth to the twentieth centuries. Racial thinking begins to color not only the growing colonialism of the early modern period and its engagement with literature but also the representation of Britons and of their slaves. Through the sixteenth and seventeenth centuries ethnic prejudice and mythologies of color decline in favor of racialism and the fear of miscegenation.

I have called this book a dialogue, but perhaps better even than "dialogue" would be the term "polyphony": "the plurality of consciousness-centers not reduced to a single ideological common denominator."[41] Let me reiterate that I do not wish to construct an overarching narrative, a just-so story, about why and how race and racialism came to exist and to figure so largely in our lives. Early modern ethnic prejudice, xenophobia, and color prejudice, pernicious though they were, comprised a different structure of feeling from modern pseudoscientific racialism. We can by all means point out the existence of, and the preconditions for, racialism and color prejudice, but we should also acknowledge the competing structures of feeling that battle it, reinforce it, and (in the Renaissance) are ultimately quashed by it. Otherwise, we end up creating a version of history that is static and closed, rather than dynamic and open, a history that cannot take account of change and multiplicity. At the same time, one of the goals of a racially informed Renaissance literary criticism should be to open up the study of race and encourage us to realize that protoracialized rhetoric is omnipresent in early modern texts, even in those without any "black" characters. For racial difference—its existence and its significance—is not a constant. Notions of essential bodily variation, purity, and hierarchy emerge at different points in history, and they intersect in the twenty-first century with issues of gender, class, sexuality, power, aesthetics, and American academic politics. A racially informed Renaissance criticism should therefore simultaneously be a *feminist* criticism, a *materialist* criticism, a *queer* criticism, a *new historicist* criticism, a *formal* criticism, and an *interventionist* one. We cannot escape from our own mythologies of color, but we can continue to reimagine them, with the help of the shifting stories of the past.

I
Ethiopian Histories

Chapter 1

Pictures of Andromeda Naked

Heliodorus's Greek romance, *Aithiopika* or *Ethiopian Story* (*ES*, 230–275 CE), has obsessed scholars and critics in three historical periods: the English Renaissance, the Harlem Renaissance, and our own era.[1] It narrates the difficulty of reading the body, in particular, that of its heroine, Chariclea, born fair-skinned to the dark-skinned King Hydaspes and Queen Persina of Ethiopia because her mother gazed upon a religious icon—a picture of their white-skinned ancestress and deity Andromeda—during conception. Secretly exposed at birth by Persina (who fears the imputation of adultery), raised by a succession of foster fathers, during the course of the novel Chariclea falls in love with a young Thessalian, Theagenes, and eventually returns to Ethiopia, where her royal father fails to recognize her and attempts to sacrifice the lovers to the gods. In a dramatic recognition scene, the oral testimony of her Ethiopian foster father, the written account of Persina's letter, the physical evidence of the jewels, signet ring, and swaddling clothes left with the baby, the painted proof of the picture, and the bodily evidence of Chariclea's birthmark finally convince Hydaspes that this fair-skinned Greek girl is indeed his daughter. The romance concludes with the lovers' marriage and the abolition of all human sacrifice in Ethiopia.

Three moments stand out particularly within the *Aithiopika* as challenges to stable methods of reading the body and its heredity. The religious oracle informing Theagenes and Chariclea of their Ethiopian destiny, Persina's explanatory letter to Chariclea, with its description of the picture of Andromeda, and Chariclea's birthmark, the final proof of her Ethiopian and royal heritage, all undermine seemingly transparent differences of skin color and sex. Even the heroine whose picture Chariclea supposedly resembles, Andromeda, turns out to be racially ambiguous, both black- and white-skinned, in classical and early modern accounts. In this chapter I compare the treatment of these episodes in early modern translations and adaptations of Chariclea's story: Thomas Underdowne's *Æthiopian Historie* (*AH*, 1569); William Lisle's *The Faire Ethiopian* (*FE*, 1631); the anonymous, unpublished Caroline play *The*

White Ethiopian (*WE*); Jacques Amyot's French *Histoire Aethiopique* (*Histoire*, 1559), and John Gough's *The Strange Discovery* (*SD*, 1640).[2]

Underdowne's lively translation, the first in English, was probably used by Shakespeare (who refers to the *Aithiopika* in *Twelfth Night*), Philip and Mary Sidney (whose revised *Arcadia* borrows its embedded narrative structure and some specific plot points from Heliodorus's romance), and possibly Abraham Fraunce. Both Amyot and Underdowne intend a translation that is explicitly accurate or "perfect" and implicitly timeless, "a patterne," like *Morte Darthur* and *Amadis de Gaule*, as Underdowne's preface to the 1587 edition maintains (*AH*, A2v–A3r). Both translators, however, locate their story firmly in their own sixteenth-century worlds, betraying contemporary beliefs about magical conceptions, fantastic kingdoms, and unlikely coincidences. The seventeenth-century adaptations, too, lie open to close literary readings with broad cultural resonances surrounding their treatment of race, skin, and sex.

Chariclea's increasing pallor in these versions corresponds to new and fluctuating ways of understanding gender and inherited physical characteristics, including skin color, in the early modern period. Thomas Laqueur has argued that early modern culture imagined male and female existing on a single bodily continuum, and gender as a potentially mutable category. At the same time, medical writers such as Helkiah Crooke challenged the old one-sex model and reinterpreted Galen to argue for the prevalence of two separate and distinct genders. Crooke insists in *Microcosmographia* (1615) that sexual difference is not "essentiall" but "accidental," and that women are perfect in their own sex, but his categories are fixed and unchanging.[3] Race, as we have seen and will continue to see, is likewise under scrutiny. Heliodorus provides a bodily hermeneutics that is independent of skin color. Instead, he depends upon an understanding of race both as an inherited "genos" or lineage and as a social category—a race that can only come into existence once it is recognized. But seventeenth-century versions of his novel find the blackness of the Ethiopian royal family to be problematic. Underdowne maintains, with Heliodorus, that Chariclea's sex and origins are indeterminate for most of the novel, until materialized through her actions. Chariclea's translation to Africa makes her black; falling in love makes her female and heterosexual. But Lisle and Gough strive to diminish the radical ambiguity of Heliodorus's novel. Their adaptations stabilize Chariclea's sex and race through her heredity rather than through her actions, asserting her social rank and forcing it to match her skin tone by retroactively blanching her parents—and Chariclea herself.

This shift in understanding skin color corresponds to a generic transformation. Underdowne, following Heliodorus, maintains that "art can breake nature" (*AH*, M3r)—a fundamental tenet of romantic wonder. Renaissance adaptations of Heliodorus foreground the ways in which early modern culture begins to regard Chariclea's pallor and her parents' darkness as the most miraculous or romantic paradox of Heliodorus's plot, more fabulous than even the other unlikely events of the romance, including shipwrecks, oracles, human sacrifice, and infants restored after exposure. The treatments of Chariclea's story, and Crooke's and others' explanations of skin color, mingle residual mythologies of color—classical myths of Ethiopian princes and princesses, travelers' tales about Ethiopian religious practices, theories of "maternal impression"—with emergent medical explanations of heredity and pseudoscientific understandings of race as biological inheritance.

Reading the *Aithiopika*

A modern critic explains the novel's appeal to African American writers, arguing that it offers alternative cultural models and a different literary lineage by overturning "The valence of the skin colours familiar from America . . . [T]he aristocracy is black, and it is the white body which shows up as aberrant . . . cast out and ultimately subjected through battering and enslavement to control."[4] Another similarly claims that the *Aithiopika* renders whiteness both spectacular and spectacularly unwanted.[5] Some commentators argue that any supposed blackening or Ethiopianizing of Chariclea and Theagenes represents rather a blanching or Hellenization of the Ethiopians (symbolized by the latter's ultimate abolition of human sacrifice, seemingly as a direct result of their encounter with the Hellenized Chariclea and the Greek-born Theagenes).[6] As Arthur Heiserman observes, the novel counters this suggestion by satirizing the superstition of "Delphian Apollo," epitomized by Chariclea's "foolish" Greek foster father Charicles.[7] In addition, Chariclea does not plead against the custom of human sacrifice in itself but merely that she, as a royal daughter, should not be its victim. The motion against human sacrifice comes from the thoroughly Ethiopian Sisimithres, Chariclea's first foster father, who is "black as [he] could be" (*ES*, 403) and who, with his fellow gymnosophists ("naked sages"), urges both the king and the Ethiopian people against religious murder. Sacrifice, he argues, whether human or animal, is "barbaric . . . nor do we believe that is pleasing to the divinity" (*ES*, 565). The gymnosophists were traditionally based in India, but Heliodorus draws upon Philostratus's account of a group of Ethiopian sages who brought gymnosophist teachings back to Ethiopia to emphasize not a Greek but an Eastern tradition of respect for human and animal life.[8]

These religious traditions not only prohibit the taking of life but also urge its active preservation. This is why, says Sisimithres, he saved the exposed infant Chariclea in the first place: "once a soul had taken human form it would have been a sin for me to pass it by in its hour of peril—this is the sole precept of the naked sages of my country, to whose teaching I had recently been admitted" (*ES*, 404). Sisimithres later argues that class, caste, and color should have no bearing on justice when Hydaspes objects to hearing out Chariclea. Hydaspes's objections are twofold: first, her rank (she is a slave and a prisoner, while he is a king), and second, her supposed origin (she is a foreigner, and not, he says, protected by Ethiopian law). "'For a wise man,' retort[s] Sisimithres, 'a person's character is as important as the color of his face in reaching a judgment'" (*ES*, 566).

Brigitte Egger observes that the *Aithiopika* challenges our assumptions about heredity by questioning the meaning of fatherhood.[9] Each of Chariclea's foster fathers represents a different aspect of paternity. Hydaspes, her biological father, is the king who begets her but does not know of her survival. Sisimithres, her first foster father, is the compassionate Ethiopian gymnosophist who rescues her from exposure. Charicles, her adoptive father, is the childless Greek priest who names her "Chariclea" after himself, raises her to adulthood, and tries to arrange her marriage to his nephew. Calasiris, her spiritual father, is the wise Egyptian divine who reveals to her the secret of her birth and encourages her to flee to Ethiopia with Theagenes. Of all Chariclea's foster fathers, only Sisimithres is "the ideal sage"; both Charicles and Calasiris prove to be inadequate fathers, Charicles because he is weak and Calasiris because he is devious.[10] Only Sisimithres and the Ethiopian gymnosophist tradition he represents can provide a model for an Ethiopia that is "Utopia."[11]

So deep is the author's sympathetic identification with a utopian Ethiopia that some classicists believe that Heliodorus may himself have been a Hellenized black African.[12] Even skeptics (who argue that the author is more likely to have been a Phoenician from Syria, bilingual in Greek and "a Semitic language") observe that this writer's self-chosen name means "gift of the sun."[13] The author concludes with a description of his own genealogy from "the clan of descendants of the Sun" in order to connect his own heliocentric cult with the sun-worshipping Ethiopians and the peace-loving gymnosophists (*ES*, 588). In the following sections, I discuss the oracle, the letter, and the birthmark in detail, beginning with Morgan's standard English translation and comparing it to early modern appropriations.

Reading the Oracle

The mysterious Delphic oracle in the *Aithiopika* pronounces:

One who starts in grace and ends in glory, another goddess-born:
Of these I bid you have regard, O Delphi!
Leaving my temple here and cleaving Ocean's swelling tides,
To the black land of the sun will they travel,
Where they will reap the reward of those whose lives are passed in virtue:
A crown of white on brows of black. (*ES*, 409)

Chariclea's name means "Glorious Grace," Theagenes's, "Goddess-begotten."[14] Ethiopia may be "black," in an epithet transferred from its Ethiopian population or from its parched terrain, and called "the land of the sun" because of its proximity to the equator and its fierce climate. A 1961 translation gives "they shall win and wear . . . A white coronal from darkling brows," retaining the participle but transferring its blackness from the winners to the losers, implying that the coronal or crown is given to the lovers at the Ethiopians' expense, and alluding to Chariclea's being "in the dark," as it were, about her own origins.[15] Selden argues that the final Greek line of the oracle translates literally as "a white crown shall be affixed on blackening brows," employing the present participle, *melainomenon* (μελαινομενον), *blackening*, to indicate, as John Hilton writes, "at the very least the recognition of the indeterminacy of race."[16] The indirect structure of the story further emphasizes race as a social, rather than a biological, function. At one point in Book Two, during Calasiris's account of Chariclea's childhood, we are hearing a narrative embedded "at three removes, as Cnemon hears from Calasiris what Charicles had told him he had heard from [Sisimithres]."[17] Chariclea and Theagenes begin the romance as white Greeks and finish it as black Ethiopians through an illuminating story glimpsed through a glass darkly, rather than directly.

Renaissance texts vary in their recognition of the oracular and colored ambiguity of this passage. Underdowne translates the oracle as simply

Yee men of Delphi singe of her,
And Goddes ofspringe praye:
Who nowe in grace beginnes to growe,
But fame shal ende her daies.
Who leavinge these my Temples here,
And passinge surginge streames:
Shall come at length to Countrie scortche,
with Phebus blasinge beames

Where they as recompences due
That vertues rare doo gaine:
In time to come ere it belonge,
White Miters shall obtaine. (*AH*, K2r)

"Miter" is the literal translation of the Latin *mitra* and Greek μιτρα, ancient tiara or headcovering, but its first meaning for an early modern audience is as a Christian symbol: a sign of episcopal rank, the high hat of a bishop. In heraldry, the miter replaces the helmet in the arms of episcopal sees.[18] Just as Heliodorus connects his own contemporary sun cult to the ancient Ethiopian belief system, so his translator Underdowne links Christian religious hierarchy to the sun worshippers in Ethiopia.

Although Renaissance writers link the African continent at large with paganism or pantheism (like that practiced by the Moorish king converted from sun worship to Christianity in Thomas Middleton's *Triumphs of Truth* [*TT*, 1613]), Ethiopia is a special instance, connected by both patristic and medieval tradition to Christianity. As my next chapter considers at greater length, Origen and other patristic commentators describe the bride in the biblical Song of Songs as Ethiopian. Origen finds examples of biblical "Ethiopians" in order to prove that what he calls "an Ethiopian beauty" is necessary for divine grace.[19] Having suggested that nowhere in the Pentateuch is Moses as lavishly praised as after taking an Ethiopian woman for his wife (Num. 12), he identifies the bride with the Christian "queen of the south . . . [Sheba, who] came from the uttermost parts of the earth to hear the wisdom of Solomon" (Matt. 12:42). Next he praises Ebed'melech, the Ethiopian eunuch who rescues the prophet Jeremiah from prison (Jer. 38 and 39), and quotes Isaiah, "*Ethiopia shall get her hands in first with God.* It is well said that she shall get in first; for . . . Ethiopia [has] been healed while Israel is still sick."[20] Like St. Jerome, he points out that while Jeremiah asks a seemingly rhetorical question, "Can the Ethiop change his skin, or the leopard his spots?" (Jer. 13:23), through Christ both these things can and will happen. Ethiopians represent the peoples of "the ends of the earth," the most distant part of the known world, the farthest extent to which Jesus's power may stretch.[21]

Underdowne's "white miters" evoke a mythical Ethiopian realm that combines the biblical "ends of the earth" and the medieval kingdom ruled by the Christian King Prester ("Presbyter") John: "in the early fourteenth century the realm of the mysterious Prester John was first identified with Ethiopia in the [lost] treatise of Giovanni da Carignano."[22] The account of Francisco Alvares (printed in 1540), a priest sent on a Portuguese mission in 1520 to Prester John's kingdom, made extravagant claims for the legendary ruler's Christian piety. Prester

John's refusal to marry a non-Christian and to practice polygamy so angered the Moorish kings surrounding his empire that they attacked him every year.[23] Upon learning that the Portuguese ambassadors could not conduct religious services because they lacked a suitable tent, Prester John sent them a magnificent pavilion—on condition that they say Mass every day.[24] Prester John would sit majestically mantled in his throne "as they paint God the Father on the wall"; during Lent, his hairshirted monks and nuns would sit neck-deep in a huge tank of water, for penance.[25]

The myth was first popularized in England by Sir John Mandeville. (The 1582 publication of Mandeville's *Voyages* identifies Prester John as "Emperour of Inde" rather than ruler of Ethiopia, but the denomination of India and Ethiopia as "Inde the greater" and "Inde the less" goes back at least as far as Herodotus.[26]) John Pory expands his translation of Leo Africanus's *History and Description of Africa* (*HDA*, 1600) in order to include a description of Prester John's empire and includes a translation of part of Alvares's ethnography.[27] Pory derives the Abyssinians from "the sonne of *Salomon*, which (as they say) he begot of the Queen of *Saba*," and from this son's attendants, and concludes that such a lineage is believable because the Ethiopians still practice "the Iewish ceremonies of circumcision, [and] obseruing of the sabaoth . . . likewise they abhorre swines flesh and certaine other meates, which they call vncleane" (*HDA*, B1v). Abraham Hartwell's translation of Lopez's *Description of the Kingdome of Congo* (1597) similarly emphasizes the Ethiopians' observance of "the Lawe of the Hebrewes" alongside Marian ritual.[28] Prester John's subjects are "of diuers colours, as white, blacke, and a middle colour betweene both," and uphold rigid sumptuary laws, "according to the seuerall degrees of men."[29] A country with a single religion and varying skin tones must be regulated, it seems, by rank, an order later adopted by Margaret Cavendish for her *Blazing World*, as we will see in Chapter 9. Pory earlier claims that the Ethiopians' adherence to rank is extreme, leading to idolatrous king worship. The result of such a "strange and stately kinde of gouernement" is to "abase his subiects, whom the Prete used like slaues" (*HDA*, B2v). The account concurs that the Prester keeps both "the noble and great" and "those of meaner qualitie" "in most base seruitude . . . in treating them rather like slaues, then subjects" (*HDA*, 2I1r). The argument that Africans suffered from a "servile" or slave-like condition even *before* their transportation to England or Barbados resurfaced at the end of the century, as I discuss at greater length in Chapter 8.

Underdowne emphasizes his lovers' merit ("recompences due" and "virtues rare") and retroactively Christianizes the Ethiopians to justify, in the world of romance, the absolutist monarchy to be inherited by

Theagenes and Chariclea. The lovers will serve as religious rather than political leaders. The oracle's prophecy in Underdowne connects the religious practices of ancient Ethiopia, and its extravagant performance of royalty, with those of the Christian church, while simultaneously retaining Heliodorus's references to the cult of the sun.

In addition to emphasizing the Christian overtones of "Miters," Underdowne makes explicit the connection between blackness and Phoebus with the phrase, "Countrie scortche, with Phebus blasinge beames." In Greek mythology, Phaëthon, the unruly son of the sun god Phoebus, attempted to drive his father's chariot across the sky only to engineer a series of climatological disasters when the horses ran amok, melting the polar icecaps and burning the Ethiopians permanently "blacke and swart."[30] Zeus shot down his headlong career at the request of the crop goddess Ceres. Renaissance mythographers associate Phaëthon with excess of all kinds, linking him to Prometheus and Icarus, mythological overreachers who, in the words of Phaëthon's epitaph, "although [they] chaunst to slide, / Yet that [they] gave a proud attempt it cannot be denide."[31] Underdowne is not alone in fusing the two Ethiopian rulers, the Christian Prester John and the overreaching pagan Phaëthon. The character Senapo, Christian king of Ethiopia in Canto Thirty-Three of Lodovico Ariosto's *Orlando Furioso* (1532), has been punished with blindness and starvation for attempting to scale the mountain at whose summit lies the historical location of Paradise. Sir John Harington's translation (1591) confirms that "We call [this king] Prester John or Prester Jany," but glosses the king as if he were Phaëthon, one of those

young carelesse men, that being left rich by their parents or else advaunced (unworthily in their owne consciences) to some extraordinarie fortunes, straight in conceits begin to despise the devine providence (as Senapo assaulted Paradise) and dispute with their prophane tongues not against this or that religion but against all religion.[32]

The episode recalls the classical punishment of Prometheus, who stole fire from the gods, and the Biblical scattering of the builders of the tower of Babel.

The myth of Phaëthon is reversed in the first French translation of the *Aithiopika*. Where the story of Phaëthon envisions a nation originally created white and later burned black—a narrative that, as Kim Hall points out, treats blackness as the result of a cataclysm or natural disaster, a connection iterated, I would add, in the curse of Cham or in the Marlovian mythopoeia that imagines, "Since Heroes time, hath halfe the world beene blacke"[33]—the prophecy in Amyot imagines that whiteness conceals fundamentally dark skins, to be revealed through the workings of oracular romance. Amyot figures the "lovely crowns" of Theagenes and Chariclea "both enclosed with white" ("leurs beaux chefz tous deux de blanche enceincte" [*Histoire*, Fv]).[34] Their blackness hides beneath their white headdresses, like an infant struggling to be born (the pun on *enceinte* meaning "enclosed" and "pregnant" is present even in early modern French).[35]

In contrast, Lisle's Jacobean versification of Chariclea's story returns to the myth of an original whiteness, imagining blackness and religious differences crowning or covering the lovers' whiteness when "their tanned temples [are] crowned with Turban white" (*FE*, G4r). The "turban" is a telling particular, and worth unpacking in some detail. It alludes to seventeenth-century images of Islam, in particular to fears of Ottoman expansion and capture of English prisoners. At the end of the sixteenth century, English travelers saw Turkey for themselves for the first time, returning home to write treatises in awe of what they believed to be the Turks' military expertise and social organization on the one hand and of their ferocious (or "barbarous") destruction of earlier civilizations (the classical and the Byzantine) on the other. Edward Webbe (1590) opposes Turks to Christians in his account of his forced service in the Turkish army: "against this Prester John, I went with the Turkes power, and was then their maister Gunner in the hold."[36] Francis Knight's memoir of *Seaven Yeares Slaverie Vnder the Turkes of Argeire* (1640) expresses outrage at the "inhumane and diabollical" treatment of Christian galley slaves and at the "renegadoes" (Muslim descendants of converted Christians) who help the Turks to capture them.[37] Its frontispiece depicts a turbaned Turk whipping a bleeding, manacled "Christian slave" (Figure 1). The book begins by castigating the "sonnes of Christians" who, "forced to abuses," "professe the new Religion, priding themselves in Turkish ceremonies, and in a faith once execrable unto them; whereto, not confidence but vice invokes them."

The semiotics of the turban engage in emergent categories of race and ethnicity. Although early modern travel narratives initially associate the turban with both Judaism and Islam, the garment rapidly came to be associated primarily with Persia and Turkey. French geographer Nicholas Nicolay (1585) relates that Jews are compelled by the Great Turk to wear yellow turbans, Persians wear red ones to distinguish themselves from Turks, Turks usually wear white, and those who claim to be kin to Mohammed, green.[38] The turban could also become the focus of political anxieties. Upon the return of Sir Robert Sherley to England in 1609, elaborate negotiations ensued over his turban, which he had customized with a huge crucifix in place of the usual Muslim crescent. First the hostage, then the relative by marriage, and finally the ambassador of Shah Abbas of Persia, Sherley found himself in a quandary in his audience with King James. Removing the turban would prove an insult to Islam and to the shah; retaining it would offend the king, before whom subjects were required to appear bareheaded. Samuel Chew summarizes the contradictory accounts as to how Sherley settled the matter; on at least one occasion, he expeditiously doffed his turban for an instant before immediately resuming it again.[39]

Lisle's ethnic crossing converts coronets or crowns, signs of English royalty, into the exotic Eastern "Turban" that shines whitely in contrast to the newly darkened brows of Theagenes and Chariclea. His pale lovers have become tanned or made tawny by the sun (again, like Chariclea's mythical Ethiopian ancestors, burned black by Phaëthon's fatal charge). Unlike those travelers who allegedly converted to Islam by force, however, Theagenes and Chariclea effect a voluntary conversion on the

The manner of Turkish tyrannie over Christian slaves.

Figure 1. Turbaned Turk scourging a manacled Christian slave. Francis Knight, *Seaven Yeares Slaverie Vnder the Turkes of Argeire* (1640), frontispiece. Reproduced by permission of the Folger Shakespeare Library.

king—from sun worship and human sacrifice to a religion that evokes barbarous opulence rather than savage primitivism. Lisle refers once more to the "turban" at the very end of his narrative, when the reunited lovers celebrate the fulfillment of the prophecy by wearing "The white silke Turban with the Blackmore Crowne" (*FE*, Bbv) combining pallor with negritude just as their "tanned temples" did.

The Caroline manuscript play *The White Ethiopian* perhaps comes closest to Heliodorus's ambiguous register by prophesying:

Goe to ye zone where downright rayes
Make ye earth smoake by parching dayes,
Rewards of virtues shall be found
White garlands on the blacker ground (fo. 36)

—imagining a comparative racial category in a dramatization that, as we shall see, foregrounds the story's references to negritude and pallor. These Ethiopians are twice blackened, once by Phaëthon and once more by the oracle. The sun's rays parallel the white garlands, just as the "blacker ground" figures both the lovers' bodies and the scorched equatorial earth.

Reading the Letter

The mysterious oracle is partly explained by the hieroglyphic letter written by Persina, left with her exposed child and deciphered by the canny priest Calasiris. Persina's letter describes Chariclea's conception. Initially shocked by her daughter's "skin of gleaming white, something quite foreign to Ethiopians," Persina quickly understands

the reason: during your father's intimacy with me the painting had presented me with the image of Andromeda . . . depicted stark naked, for Perseus was in the very act of releasing her from the rocks, and [it] had unfortunately shaped the embryo to her exact likeness. (*ES*, 432–33)

Heliodorus's Ethiopians descend from the line of Perseus through his union with Andromeda, a famous story retold in these fictional palace frescoes and widely disseminated in the early modern period through mythographies such as Natalis Comes's *Mythologiae* (1551) or Hyginus's *Fabularum Liber* (1535, rpt. 1608). Cassiopeia, wife of Cepheus, King of Ethiopia, boasted that her daughter Andromeda's beauty (in Appollodorus's version, her own beauty) rivaled the Nereids'. An angry Neptune sent a monster to terrorize Ethiopia and required that Andromeda be exposed to the sea-beast (in some versions, the oracle of Ammon makes the demand). Seeing Andromeda chained to the rock as he flew above Ethiopia, Perseus fell in love with her. Aided by his winged sandals, a gift from Mercury, Perseus uncoupled the links that bound the princess, slew the dragon, and married Andromeda. Some versions of the myth include Cepheus's collusion against Perseus with a rival suitor and this suitor's ultimate defeat. A popular play by Euripides, now extant only in fragments, translated the lovers, and Andromeda's parents, to the heavens, where they became constellations.[40]

Persina's account of Chariclea's generation alludes to a theory attributing the appearance of a child to its mother's impressions or thoughts at the time of conception (compare the folk belief, still present today, that a baby's birth- or strawberry mark indicates that its mother experienced a fright during pregnancy). Pliny extends this power of impression to both parents: "a thought suddenly flitting across the mind of either parent is supposed to produce likeness or to cause a combination of features."[41] Gazing upon Andromeda's fair, naked body during the act of love, Persina conceives a child who resembles not herself or her husband, but the picture.

Underdowne's Persina explains, "because I looked upon the picture of Andromeda naked, while my husbande had to doo with me (for then he first broughte her from the rocke, had by mishappe ingendred presently a thing like to her)" (*AH*, Or). Note the elision of time and the confusion of Persina's pronouns; she identifies herself with the nude, fettered, and passive Andromeda, Hydaspes with the weaponed, mobile, and active Perseus, reenacting an ancient encounter ("then [when] he [Perseus] first brought her from the rock, [I] had by mishappe ingendred presently a thing like to her"). In describing lovemaking as "my husbande had to doo with me" twice within two pages, Underdowne's Persina implies a detachment or even distaste for Hydaspes's embraces. While many ancient and early modern accounts of reproduction, including those of Avicenna, Jacob Rüff, and Lazare Rivière, claimed that female orgasm during heterosexual coupling was necessary for conception to occur, others refute the assertion. Crooke concedes that conception may occur without pleasure (though such women, he argues, have "ill affected wombes" [Bb5v]) and Nicholas Fontanus observes in 1652 that women's "unspeakable pleasure . . . conduceth little or nothing to conception."[42] I return to these debates in Chapter 6, but for now remain within the *Aithiopika*. Either Persina conceives without pleasure, or her true interest hangs on the walls, in the "picture of Andromeda naked," in her imagination. Even though Persina is not guilty of physical infidelity, her same-sex fantasy (or at least, her interest in icon worship) competes with her affection for her husband. In Underdowne's text, the color of Persina's child demonstrates the fluidity of biological race, nationality, and the direction of sexual desire.

The plot of Heliodorus's novel thus demands an Andromeda depicted in chains, unclothed, whose bare skin, like Chariclea's, is "gleaming white" despite her Ethiopian origin. The Andromeda myth is an important inter-text for the novel, and for the Renaissance; it is worth considering at some length. Writing about nineteenth-century English reworkings of the Andromeda myth, Adrienne Munich argues that the very structure of the story encodes a gendered and racial allegory. The Victorian paintings Munich interprets render Andromeda naked and shackled, a combination that Munich identifies as "pornographic": "Perseus saves Andromeda, then keeps her for sexual and dynastic purposes; obligated to her rescuer, she can neither rescue herself nor refuse his offer of marriage."[43]

The Greeks may have seen it differently. Although most Greek pottery lay undiscovered during the early modern period, it is worth considering these classical representations briefly to give ourselves a sense of aesthetic and social alternatives, other ways of representing the story and its somatic distinctions. Greek vase painting usually observes a convention representing women as fair-skinned, men as dark-skinned, using the color of the clay, or white paint over it, for female skin, and black-figure ("a silhouette with the inner details drawn on the black glaze with some fine incising tool") for male.[44] Typically, vase painters render Ethiopian origin through facial features and hair-type rather than through skin color. Andromeda appears "gleaming white," like Chariclea, and with Greek features (the so-called Grecian nose, thin lips, and straight hair) in contrast to those of the Ethiopian attendants (broad nose, full lips, and curled hair) who surround her.[45] A Corinthian amphora depicts a clothed Andromeda, arms not manacled but full of rocks, helping a nude Perseus to throw stones at the monster, participating fully in her own rescue and that of her kingdom.[46] Other vase paintings show Andromeda wearing Amazonian garments, or flowing robes, in contrast to Perseus, painted or carved nude in order to display his athleticism.[47]

The transmission of classical literature in the early modern period is more reliable than that of other forms of art. Ovid, the most important source for the early moderns, usually comments upon the darkness of Andromeda's skin to observe that her skin color presented no obstacle to Perseus's love. "Perseus loved the daughter of Cepheus, Andromeda, who was dark with the color of her native land," he observes in the *Heroides*, as part of Sappho's defense of her own tawny complexion.[48] Otho Vaenius's *Amorum Emblemata* (*Emblemes of Love*) (1608) includes this Ovidian tag in defense of Andromeda's "brown" beauty. The motto "brown beries are sweet of taste" appears alongside an engraving praising "the lovely brown" above "the fayrest whyte" not because of its temperate color but because it draws the eye to observe grace or feature rather than color.[49] It repeats in capitals the Virgilian tag "alba ligustra cadunt, uaccinia nigra leguntur," "white privet flowers fall while black berries are gathered," that, as we shall see in Chapter 6, also inspires Richard Barnfield's paean to blackness in *The Teares of an Affectionate Shepherd* (1592).[50]

The verse attached to Vaenius's emblem reads:

Cupid not alwayes doth, shoot at the fayrest whyte,
But at the lovely brown, most often drawes his bow,
Good gesture and fyne grace, he hath the skill to know,
Delighting for to chuse, the cause of his delight.[51]

The emblem itself seems to depict something different from the text: a brown Cupid (shaded with crosshatching) aims at a whyte, or target, who is his white twin, pierced to the heart with love for the darker archer (Figure 2).[52] Other emblems make clear the reasons for the reversal. One depicts two cupids shooting at each other simultaneously, with the tag, "A wished warre": since love's wounds are mutual, it does not matter whether the brown or the white cupid shoots.[53] Another presents one

Figure 2. "Brown beries are sweet of taste." Otho Vaenius [Otto Van Veen], *Amorum Emblemata [Emblemes of Love]* (1608), 173. Reproduced by permission of the Huntington Library.

Cupid shooting his arrow at another, on whose breast is drawn a target; since "the lovers hart is Cupids whyte," both lovers are at once hunter and hunted.[54] Vaenius's motto describes "brown beries," but the slippage between "brown beries" and "black" or Ethiopian women is implicit in the epigram. Andromeda is *fusca*, usually translated as "dark" or "brown." Her "native land" is Ethiopia in the *Metamorphoses*, but the "black Indies" in the *Ars Amatoria*.[55] Her parents Cepheus and Cassiopeia are the rulers of Ethiopia, during the sixteenth and seventeenth centuries considered the home of the blackest people in the world. In addition, claims the *Ars Amatoria*, "Nor was Andromeda's color objected to by [Perseus], he who wore moving wings on his twin feet."[56] In other classical sources, Andromeda fluctuates from the light-skinned maiden described by Philostratus and Achilles Tatius to the ambiguous heroine of Euripides's lost drama. Euripides's editors claim that he contrasts his heroine's creamy skin with the brown hues of her friends who compose the chorus, but Dilke asserts that the Euripidean fragments are inconclusive.[57]

All these classical sources, visual and written, present Andromeda as clothed—with the exception of Heliodorus. Given the dearth of classical images of Andromeda naked, there are two contradictory explanations for Persina's picture. Either Heliodorus is referring to a tradition that has not survived, perhaps because such erotic paintings were fragile frescoes on bedroom walls (as, indeed, the *Aithiopika* describes), or he emphasizes Andromeda's nudity precisely because such images were rare or nonexistent, enhancing Ethiopia's status as a fabulous realm and the *Aithiopika*'s fictiveness. Although, as we have seen, Ovid mentions neither Andromeda's clothing nor lack thereof, and comments on her dark skin, early modern engravings seem inspired by Heliodorus, presenting a white, chained, and naked Andromeda. Plate 40 of Antonio Tempesta's widely disseminated illustrations for Ovid's *Metamorphoses* (1606) displays Perseus, with spear and shield, mounted on Pegasus in the middle left-hand side of the image, robe billowing out behind him, Pegasus's tail billowing likewise. The sea-monster, in the lower left-hand side of the print, has a dog's head, scales, claws, and long curling tail. A pale Andromeda, spread-eagled, round breasts facing the viewer, face turned away to the monster, lies chained on the rock, which takes up the right-hand side of the image (Figure 3). The motto reads, "Perseus occisa bellua Andromedam liberat" ("Having slain the monster, Perseus frees Andromeda.") A Dutch engraving from 1615, accompanying Johannes Florianus's translation, likewise presents a naked Andromeda, arms apart, breasts and genitals displayed to the viewer.[58] George Sandys's illustrated translation of *Metamorphoses* includes a white-skinned, naked Andromeda in the distant background of the frontispiece to Book IV, in which her story is told.

These well-known illustrations demonstrate Andromeda's passivity by stripping and chaining the heroine; moreover, in a translation of the *Ars Amatoria* attributed to Thomas Heywood, *Loves Schoole* (pub. 1640), her sexual subjugation is linked to dark skin. This author modifies Ovid to exaggerate Andromeda's physical and national differences and to titillate the reader with an anti-blazon of her body. This Perseus "among the Negrees [sic] sought, / And faire Andromade from Inde brought"; this Indian, Negroid Andromeda "was belly sides and backe, /To Perseus seene, he did not terme her blacke."[59] "Belly sides and backe," a deliberately vulgar catalogue of unpoetic parts, turns the blazon into an auction; like a prize pig, Andromeda has been seen naked and found to be worthy of her price.[60]

Andromeda is meant to breed a new and "likely Race" in George Chapman's *Andromeda Liberata* (1614), written to commemorate the marriage of Frances Howard and Robert Carr.[61] Mingling neoplatonic paean with

Figure 3. "Having slain the monster, Perseus frees Andromeda." Antonio Tempesta, Ovid's *Metamorphoses* (1606), Plate 40. Reproduced by permission of the Bodleian Library.

a dynastic and pornographic emphasis on Andromeda's subjection, it replaces Andromeda's nakedness at the rock with a lubricious interlude in which the heroine helplessly attempts to flee. Instead, she is captured and revealed by her own beauty and the hunger of the natural world to see, expose, and penetrate it. The winds "pursue, / And with enamoured sighes, her parts assaile" (B2v) as if they are trying to enter her body, holding her "by the vaile" (B4r) as the sun "all inuasion seekes" (B4v) like a jealous and angry lover. As she tries to hide in a bush,

Her breasts (laid out) show'd all enflamed sights
Loue, lie a sunning, twixt two Crysolites:
Her naked wrists showde, as if through the skie,
A hand were thrust, to signe the Deitie. (B4v)

"[L]aid out," as if to eat, to "all enflamed sights," as if in invitation, her breasts themselves are "Crysolites," like transparent prisms, focusing the rays of the sun, building a glass conservatory for Cupid to sunbathe in. So pellucid is her body that her "naked wrists" seem to appear from nowhere, through a skyey void. Her wrists and hands appear like suppliants, "to signe the Deitie," as if she is praying. A long neoplatonic interlude emphasizes the mutuality of Perseus's and Andromeda's love, the ways in which they recreate each other. With Perseus's mind and Andromeda's beauty, Chapman argues, "Where both Sex graces, met as in their Mirror"; their union unites the best of both sexes (C3r). Finally, Chapman reasserts Perseus's dynastic motives in marrying: "with her life, the life of likely Race / Was chiefe end of his action" (Ev).

Heliodorus's Andromeda does, indeed, engender a new "Race": Persina worries that she will be accused of adultery because of her baby's color, that nobody will believe her fantastic explanation. Hydaspes's angry skepticism in the final scene lasts an embarrassingly long time: Terence Cave argues that Hydaspes's disbelief, even when faced with letters, tokens, and the picture of Andromeda, suggests the inadequacy of empirical proof.[62] Heiserman cogently observes that Heliodorus's heroine seems to be providing readers with a self-consciously literary display of "Four of Aristotle's five sorts of recognition scenes" from the *Poetics*: tokens (bodily, decorative, and written); self-revelation; stagy contrivance; and finally inference, in order to illustrate a sustained parallel between artistic and divine creation and power.[63] Presented with artistic and literary evidence, Hydaspes, like Shakespeare's Leontes, must "awake [his] faith" (*WT*, 5.3.95). Life imitates art, or, as Calasiris puts it in a different context, "Art can breake nature," a *sententia* so apt for this novel that Underdowne found it worthy of marginal signposting (*AH*, M3r).

Crooke maintains that this fracture of nature by art is essential for maternal impression to occur. Like other early modern medical writers, he maintains a skeptical belief in maternal impressions, concluding that such phenomena did occur but explaining at length how "extraordinary" such influence over the "formative faculty" of the seed or embryo must be. Crooke's extraordinary medical histories focus upon skin color and hair texture. Adducing Galen's advice to "an Aethyopian that hee might beget a white and beautifull childe, to set at his beds feete a faire picture, uppon which his wife might wistly looke in the time of her conception" (Dd5v), Crooke counters those who do not believe such an effect possible:

what will [they] say to that white woman who attentively fixing her eyes upon the picture of an Aethiopian brought foorth a blacke childe? What to her that brought forth a hayrie child by looking often upon the picture of S. Iohn Baptist cloathed in Cammels haire? (Dd6r)

Usually, explains Crooke, the formative faculty naturally draws the embryo to resemble "Particular" forms of its father or mother (depending upon whose seed is stronger). Less frequently, the embryo will resemble its grandparents, and rarely, the "Universall" form of mankind (in which case the child looks like a human being, but resembles no member of its family).

Under the extraordinary circumstances of maternal impression, however, "Imagination or Cogitation," "more noble" than even the power of men to confer form, "setteth a new seale uppon the tender and soft nature of the childe" (Dd6r). The image of the seal imprinting upon the wax-soft, malleable child makes it clear that skin color, like hirsutism or other aspects of physical appearance, pertains to form and to the masculine, rather than to matter and to the feminine. Crooke deliberately chooses images of extreme variations in color and texture. The "fair picture" before the dark Ethiopian couple, the "picture of an Aethiopian" before the "white woman," and the icon of John the Baptist "cloathed in Cammels haire" before the smooth mother-to-be all emphasize the power of maternal impression, since it can make seeming opposites resemble each other. At the same time, Crooke implies that the very disparity of the images might be what enables the impression to take hold: had the contrast between picture and viewer been less pronounced, the impression might not have been deep enough to alter the form of the child. Thus their seeming binarism is misleading; however striking variations in skin color and texture may seem, they do not alter the basic "species" or "kind" of the child, its humanity.

The final phrase of Persina's account in Underdowne reverses the subjectivity of the child and the picture ("had by mishappe ingendred presently a thing [Chariclea] like to her [Andromeda]"). The embryo is a "thing" engendered, an object that resembles a living creature, the picture, which earns the pronoun "her." The picture of Andromeda is alive, as if the heroine herself begets Chariclea, exerting a posthumous power over reproduction, reversing the structure of coerced dynastic coupling that Munich finds inherent in the myth. If Andromeda generates Chariclea, she also contradicts a common early modern definition of sex difference that finds "a man, to be a creature begetting in another, a woman a Creature begetting in herselfe."[64] The accident of Chariclea's birth and her miraculous restoration in Underdowne thus demonstrate the power of art or literature to create, break down, and restore categories of classification: black/white, Ethiopian/foreign, chaste/adulterous, male/female. Art continues to break nature.

If Underdowne emphasizes art's power over nature, then the Caroline author of *The White Ethiopian* turns the materials of literary production into living signs of revelation. Having revised his adaptation, originally composed in a mixture of blank verse and couplets, to put it entirely into couplets, he intensified the play's references to blackness. The original, early seventeenth-century *White Ethiopian* superscribes Persina as "Queen of Ethiopia" in her letter, but the revised version adds: "Compelled by the most severest law / Of keeping reputation makes my inke / Blacker then is my skin or eyes that winke" (*WE*, fo. 48v). This interpolation associates blackness with secrecy and darkness but also, paradoxically, with literary discovery. This text interests itself in relative degrees of blackness and pallor, and the role of the sun and sun worship in both creating blackness (through tanning, and through the original fall of Phaëthon) and illuminating it. Persina conceives when "the King was warmed . . . in a summer roome" (*WE*, fo. 49), as if the sun had impregnated her, like Spenser's Chrysogonee (*FQ*, 3.6.5–9). Thus when Persina writes, "The sunne so black a crime had seldom seen," she spots the full irony of her situation: the white child threatens to *blacken* Persina's reputation for a crime that is not adulterously *black* at all.

Reading the Body: Blood, Sweat, and Tears

Just as race and desire prove ambiguous, comparative, so Heliodorus's *Aithiopika* additionally links the process of racial crossing with the sexing of Chariclea. Chariclea's white body misleads observers, a false witness to her national and genetic origins, but truthfully testifies to her gender. Yet her insistence on maintaining her virginity leads both her adoptive and biological fathers to diagnose her as physically and mentally ill because, they claim, she will not acknowledge sexual desire for men and "realize that she was born a woman," or "know her sex."[65] "Sex" to us means both sexual difference and sexual intercourse; for Chariclea's fathers, sexual intercourse, or the desire for it, *defines* sexual difference.

Since Chariclea steadfastly refuses to confess her love for Theagenes, her bodily responses become a substitute for the words she will not speak. It is only when she falls in love with Theagenes and agrees, at least theoretically, to surrender her pathological virginity that she begins her translation from white to black. Moreover, this surrender is never uttered outright by Chariclea (as Selden, Egger, and others observe) but narrated for her, first by Calasiris and finally by Persina. Approached directly by Calasiris, urged to confess her feelings for Theagenes, Chariclea still cannot talk; Calasiris must pronounce, "Theagenes has captured your heart at first sight" (*ES*, 435). Similarly, at the very end of the romance, threatened by torture, Chariclea still cannot speak her love, but confesses it to Persina behind the scenes. Only when Persina tells Hydaspes and the assembled crowd that Chariclea and Theagenes are affianced is Theagenes saved from ritual sacrifice and Chariclea cleared of the imputation of insanity.

Although Chariclea's words are constrained, her body is eloquent. When she first sees Theagenes at the temple, she blushes at the sight of him and grows pale as her love takes root. Her somatic response to Calasiris's interrogation is to kiss his hand, weeping, and to break into "rivers of perspiration" (*ES*, 435). For an Elizabethan and seventeenth-century audience, blushing is racially coded, a mark of fairness, sexual desire, and shame. As my Chapter 4 discusses at length, early modern moral philosophers and anticosmetic pamphleteers argued that shame and morality could not exist without visible blushes, and that therefore black and dark-skinned peoples, who did not seem to redden, did not experience shame. Heliodorus, in contrast, offers his readers various kinds of body language—blushing and bodily fluids—ways of reading the body that are independent of skin color. Chariclea sheds tears when Charicles calls in Calasiris to diagnose what ails her, sweats copiously when Calasiris discovers her secret love and reveals her Ethiopian heritage, and boasts a revelatory birthmark. Heliodorus even makes blackness compatible with blushing. Chariclea continues to blush after she crosses racial lines and the white garland sits upon her black/blackening/blacker brow, when Hydaspes asks her to describe her relationship with Theagenes (*ES*, 572). Likewise, Hydaspes's nephew and chosen match for Chariclea (a parallel to Charicles's chosen groom, who is also a nephew), blushes deeply enough that "even in his black skin he could not conceal the blush that suffused his countenance" (*ES*, 575).

Amyot and Underdowne, our sixteenth-century translators, faithfully represent Chariclea's blushes, palings, weepings, and transudations. At their first meeting, Theagenes and Chariclea display "five hundred countenances . . . in shorte time, and the changinge of all kinde of coloure" (*AH*, Lv), "in infinite varieties" ("en infinie sortes" [*Histoire*, F5r]). When

Calasiris first goes to the languishing Chariclea, "vanquished by affection . . . the bewtie of her colour was gonne out of her face, and the heate therof, was quenched with teares, as if it had ben with water" (*AH*, M1v). By the time Calasiris finishes speaking, Chariclea's bodily reaction is more pronounced, and the heat has returned to her body: "she was in a grete swette" (*AH*, O2v), so that "the sweat ran down her whole body" ("la sueur luy couloit par tout le corps") [*Histoire*, H3r]). James Sandford's *Amorous and Tragical Tales* (1567) translates only this episode from the *Aithiopika* in which the heroine's ailment becomes explicit, including both pallor and other physical manifestations as signs of love: "hir eyes swell and rise up, and hir looke set awry, hir face pale, not complaining in hir heart."[66] *The White Ethiopian* transfers the "teares" to the servants watching over the lovesick Chariclea and to her grieving father (*WE*, fo. 42v), but later includes Chariclea's colorful and watery responses to Calasiris simultaneously, so that its heroine issues "a lake of sweat" "with many a blush" (*WE*, fo. 51v).

Gough and Lisle, however, alter the spiritual character and corporeal manifestation of Chariclea's love. In Gough's play, Theagenes and Chariclea, in an elaborate (and unplayable) stage direction, "blush'd and then became pale again" (*SD*, E1v). They blush at first sight, and then blush no more, as if pallor, rather than color, is the sign of love. Chariclea demonstrates her lovesickness not by changing color but by lying on her bed (*SD*, E3v). Gough replaces her excessive reluctance to utter her love by making her state baldly, "I love Theagenes" (*SD*, G3r). Her later blushes and perspiration in the Greek story appear instead as color on the cheeks of her embarrassed mother, whose angry husband enquires, "What meaneth this, Persina, that thy blood / Thus comes and goes, and that thy countenance / Weaves such an alteration?" (*SD*, L4v). Blushes here are signs of sexual shame, associated with "alteration" and the threat of female fickleness, adultery, or deceit ("weaving"). Persina may be blushing from the consciousness of guilt or of innocence, or she may not be blushing at all, her color merely the rhetorical one of Hydaspes's anger, an insoluble problem we shall encounter with Shakespeare's *Much Ado About Nothing* in Chapter 5. Persina may be blushing from guilt, because she committed adultery (with a man in the flesh, or with the picture of Andromeda in the mind); remorse, because she exposed her child; innocent shame, because the old anxieties that she will be suspected of adultery have arisen again; or joy at her reunion with her long-lost daughter. In contrast, Chariclea's emotions are easier to read: once she has confessed her love for Theagenes, she is free from shame and thus from blushing.

But blushing demonstrates innocence for Lisle's Chariclea, whose cheeks stain with "sudden blushing die" (*FE*, K2v) at the revelation of her love. The copious sweat that marks her discovery in earlier versions of the story becomes a fungible flow that could be decorous, valuable, feminine tears: "Her colour's gone, her all-delighting grace / With pearly show'r allayed" (*FE*, H4r). Like Shakespeare's black-skinned Moor Aaron, who calls white "a treacherous hue, that will betray with blushing / The close enacts and counsels of thy heart" (*Tit.*, 4.2.117–18), Hydaspes sees the ability to change color by blushing as evidence of insurmountable biological difference. Chariclea's "color, now so peregrine," he says, proves that she "can be none of mine" (*FE*, Z2r). Lisle's King and Queen emphasize their blackness and their fundamental difference from Chariclea by describing themselves not as rulers of "Ethiopia" but as king and queen of "Blackmoreland" (*FE*, I4r), a metonym that avoids the Christian associations of "Ethiopia." Like the "tanned Turbans" of Lisle's oracle, his king and queen link Africa to an Islamic rather than a Christian tradition. They see themselves as a "Blackmore paire" in contrast to this child "so beautiful and faire," a rhyming couplet and hidden pun that intensifies their negritude (they are *more black* than Chariclea, and, as rulers of "Black-more" land, live among *more blacks*, in a scorching climate that makes them yet *more black* with every day that passes).

Reading the Body: Marks and Scars

Hydaspes's and Persina's identities are fixed, whereas Chariclea's remains subject to confirmation and reconfirmation throughout the novel, through code names, passwords and physical tokens. Chariclea's token is her ring, but Theagenes's is a scar on his knee obtained pursuing a boar, like the scar of Odysseus that first confirms Eurykleia's suspicion that her former nursling has returned. Ironically, neither code names nor physical tokens convince Theagenes and Hydaspes: both depend upon bodily attributes. Theagenes recognizes "the brilliance of [Chariclea's] eyes" (*ES*, 494), and the most compelling physical proof of Chariclea's identity, the true confirmation of her "parentage and descent" (*ES*, 569), proves to be the "sign of her race"[67]: her birthmark.

Comparing our modern, our sixteenth-century, and seventeenth-century translations, we see the birthmark become more than the typical trope of Greek romance. Instead, it functions as a mark of racial singularity. A stippled "ring of ebony staining the ivory of her arm" (*ES*, 569), the birthmark recalls in its shape the magic ring with its insignia *Pantarbe* or Fear-no-ill, a courtship gift from Hydaspes that Persina hides with her baby, and the sun, the Ethiopian deity. Walter Stephens suggests that the birthmark doubles the signet ring as "Hydaspes' mark or seal of sexual possession," adding that the mark's resemblance to "a circle and an omicron" predicts "Chariclea's 'odyssey,' her circular wanderings from Ethiopia to Greece and Egypt and back to Ethiopia."[68] We might also recall the exchange of rings, explicitly equated with female sexual chastity, in *The Merchant of Venice*, and a husband's anxiety about "keeping safe [a wife's] ring" that concludes the play (*MV*, 5.1.307).

Not only the shape of the birthmark matters, but also its contrast to Chariclea's skin in its darkness and unusual mottling. Amyot's translation is close to many modern versions, imagining "a black mark, which was like a small piece of perfectly smooth ebony, staining her white arm shining like ivory" ("un sein noir, qui estoit comme une petite pièce d'Hebene toute ronde, tachant son bras blanc et poly comme Yvoire" [*Histoire*, T6v]). The participial phrase dangles slightly in both Amyot's translation and my own, allowing Chariclea's arm to glow like ivory in contrast to the mark even as the dark mole gleams like ivory in contrast to the arm. Underdowne conveys the mole's mottling but little else, adding a confusing reference to elephants: "Cariclia uncovered her lefte arme, and aboute it there was in a manner a mole, muche like to the strakes, that Elephantes have" (*AH*, Mm2v). His Latin source reads: "Nudavit illis Chariclia sinistram, et erate quasi ebenus quaedam, in circuitu brachium tanquam elephantem maculans,"[69] "Chariclea exposed her left arm, and there was something there like ebony, in a circle around her arm, spotting the ivory" (my translation). Presumably Underdowne misunderstood *elephantem maculans* to mean "spotted elephant," although *elephantem* agrees with *brachium* ("arm") and is clearly a metonym for "ivory."

Underdowne's error imagines the ring *surrounding* Chariclea's arm ("aboute it"), humanizes her with the down-to-earth word "mole," and vividly picks up on the striking stripes or stains on Chariclea's arm. Hilton proposes that the streaky birthmark presents Chariclea as two-toned and therefore divine, like the Goddess Isis. The converse is true, I would suggest; Chariclea's pied beauty makes her human in its imperfection. Think, anachronistically, of Nathaniel Hawthorne's short story *The Birth-mark*, where the little red hand upon the otherwise perfect face of the protagonist's wife proves to be "the bond by which an angelic spirit kept itself in union with a mortal frame . . . that sole token of human imperfection,"[70] or, historically, of classical and seventeenth-century fashions that recommended the wearing of artificial beauty spots to ward off the evil eye. The birthmark distinguishes the living Chariclea from the "picture of Andromeda naked," the religious image that she so strongly resembles.

Amyot turns the birthmark into a jewel, and Chariclea into another artifact (transforming her back into a picture, or a deity) by smoothing the rough stripes on the speckled mole. Hilton argues that the mole's dappled surface not only allies Chariclea's mark with Odysseus's streaky scar but also evokes, because of Sisimithres's "reference to 'race' (γενοσ) [genos]," an inherited "mottled skin or melanoma."[71] What proves Chariclea's Ethiopian identity is not the mark's uniform blackness, or a perceived similarity to the dark skin of her people, but its idiosyncratic streakiness, its difference from her own skin and from most Ethiopians'. Sisimithres seems to be emphasizing the predominance of race (understood as *genos*) as rank and kinship (her royalty), rather than as skin color and national identity.

Gough's treatment of the long recognition scene comes closest of our texts to associating Chariclea's journey with the Hellenization, and effective blanching, of Ethiopia, while pallor similarly makes rank visible in a literal sense in Lisle's poem. Gough's Hydaspes, hostile to the idea of Chariclea's miraculous birth, which is "against all humane sence, and reason naturall" (*SD*, M2r), bizarrely uses the common Renaissance adage signifying impossibility, "to wash the Ethiop white," to express his own difficulty in believing Sisimithres and Persina's story. "You strive to wash me white an Aethiopian in hindering this sacrifice," he exclaims, connecting his Ethiopianness with his eagerness to perform human sacrifice (*SD*, M2v).[72] Since he does not, ultimately, sacrifice his daughter, are viewers to conclude that the "strange discovery" of Chariclea's birth and his newfound reluctance to perform religious murder has indeed "washed him white"?

Lisle's blushing Chariclea displays her fairness even through her birthmark, which is not black but "blue . . . / . . . like azure ring / On pollish't Iu'rie" (*FE*, Z2v). The references to blue and azure associate Chariclea with "blue blood" or royalty, another early modern way of displaying whiteness. The "azure ring" is a royal seal, but one that demonstrates her absolute difference from her parents, the "Blackemore paire"; she cannot be touched or stained with even the slightest hint of blackness. One could include the strange appearance of the "curle-head black-boy" at the end of Book Ten, who serenades the lovers on the "Irish harp," as part of this blanching. The boy's tutor, famous Zanzibar, "trauelled as far / As th'Isle of Britain" to learn his skill (*FE*, Bbv): if Chariclea and Theagenes are like the royal English, the Ethiopians, it seems, are like the servile Irish, a comparison I explore at greater length in Chapter Three.

Lisle distinguishes his white heroine from her black parents even after her birth has been proven and explained; Gough allows Chariclea to wash her Ethiopian father white and make her mother blush (differently put, *to change color*). Where Underdowne faithfully avers that "art can breake nature," or even that nature itself can produce—through the magic of maternal impression and the power of romantic invention—a child who does not resemble its parents and whose sex and race are indeterminate for most of the novel, later adaptations strive to diminish Chariclea's color-coded crossings and conversions according to various early modern mythologies of color. In so doing, they betray a desire for a world in which skin color is stable and readable as a sign of ethnic origin, moral character, and sexual chastity, a desire shared by early modern exegetes and poetic translators of the biblical Song of Songs.

Chapter 2

Thirteen Ways of Looking at a Black Bride

I continue to explore the transmission of ancient texts—and their negotiations among skin color, inherited characteristics, and religious belief—in early modern English culture by turning now to a Hebrew
poem, the biblical Song of Songs, Canticles, or Song of Solomon. Like
the *Aithiopika*, the Song displays a heroine whose skin color is ambiguously related to her rank, her beauty, and her national origin. In the
King James Version (KJV, 1611), she describes herself thus:

I am black, but comely, O ye daughters of Jerusalem, as the tents of Kedar, as the
curtains of Solomon.
Look not upon me, because I am black, because the sun hath looked upon me:
my mother's children were angry with me; they made me the keeper of the vineyards: but mine own vineyard have I not kept.[1]

These verses raised a perplexing series of questions for early modern
translators and poets, questions that continue to puzzle commentators
today. Is the speaker excusing or celebrating her blackness? Should we
translate her self-description as *black*, *dark*, or *brown*? Is her supposed
blackness a reference to skin color, and if so, does her skin color reflect
a particular national or geographical origin? Is she as "black as the tents
of Kedar" because she comes from Kedar, in Arabia, or is the comparison purely a metaphor, with no geographical association or foreign origin implied?

Early modern responses to these questions in exegeses and poetic
translations of the Song function, I will argue, as a prehistory to early
modern anti-Petrarchan lyric—in particular, to the startling reversals
of the Shakespearean sonnet. Exegetes commented upon the Song as
though it were a narrative of conversion from "black" or sinful to "fair"
or pure, with discrete events, characters, and conclusions. In the Geneva
Bible (Geneva, 1560), the bride's conversion from black to white represents the triumph of faith over works. Protestant churchmen oppose the
bride's black beauty to the painted beauties, dependent upon concealment and cosmetics, that they identify with the Catholic church. The
Bishops' Bible (Bishops', 1568) calls her "blacke . . . but fayre" to express

the paradox of Anglicanism, neither decorated like the Catholic church, nor plain, like the Protestant sects in Geneva. And in Elizabethan and early Jacobean tracts, her blackness is usually a sign of her "Aethiopian" origin and therefore considered an emblem of Anglican tolerance.[2]

Like twentieth-century poets and translators of the Song, however, early modern secular poets did not necessarily read the Song as a narrative poem, but as a lyric or even a series of lyrics, with obscure episodes, shape-shifting characters, and irresolution. When we read the Song in this way, rather than as a story, the progress from black to fair is by no means straightforward; it celebrates an ongoing moment of conflict rather than a chronological transformation. Responsive both to debates about the role of poetry and the symbolic in religious life on the one hand, and to the new influx of African slaves to Britain on the other, the discourse of biblical exegesis on the subject of "racial" difference thus forms the residual matter in the production of English lyric poetry. The sonnets of Edward Herbert and Shakespeare, I will conclude, figure the supposed conversion of the black bride as a continuing battle between narrative and lyric itself.

The Narrative

Over centuries of commentary, scholars have read this mysterious book as a collection of unrelated love lyrics; an erotic poem about the sexual awakening of a Hebrew girl and her lover; a drama starring King Solomon, his black bride (often called "the Shulamite" or Queen of Sheba), and a rival lover; a praise poem, or an allegory of the love of the soul for God. It has been read mystically, allegorically, erotically, philologically, anthropologically, poetically, and politically.[3] Early modern commentators on the Song followed Aquinas's model of four-fold biblical interpretation, finding a historical or literal level that chronicled actual historical events, and three allegorical or mystical levels.[4] On the typological level, the historical personages of the Old Testament prefigured those of the New; on the anagogical level, the events described shadowed the history of the Christian church and the day of Judgment; on the moral or tropological level, the story allegorized the relationship of the individual Christian soul with Christ. The three allegorical levels were often confused, but on the literal level, Tudor and Stuart commentators read the Song as a narrative or a marriage song, and, lacking documentary evidence to prove the contrary, assumed that the Song was certainly *about*, and probably *by*, King Solomon himself.

The Song in Geneva, Bishops', and KJV has the same narrative structure, a divine love story in which King Solomon woos the bride. First, the bride claims she is "black" or unworthy, ill-used by her brothers who make her tend another's vine, but asserts her desirability ("but comely," KJV, 1:5–6). The bridegroom praises her and calls her "fair" (KJV, 1:15) and promises to come to her that night, but when he arrives at the door she tarries in opening it and when she finally flings open the door he "had withdrawn himself, and was gone" (KJV, 5:6). "Sick of love," the bride wanders the streets, "wounded" by the watchmen who guard the door, beseeching the "daughters of Jerusalem" to find her love, whom she describes as "white and ruddy, the chiefest among ten thousand" (KJV, 5:6–10). Reunited, the lovers wander in the "wilderness" and return to the city, the bride adjuring her friends not to awaken her lover until he is ready (KJV, 8:5, 8:4).

Explanations for the bride's self-description as black in the early modern period varied on all four levels, literal, typological, anagogical, and tropological. Linda Van Norden finds sixteen commentaries between 1549 and 1675 that identify the bride with the Church, blackened by nearly a dozen different afflictions.[5] With the benefit of a wider body of later scholarship and more sophisticated research tools, I have found more than twenty commentaries between 1549 and 1662 alone.[6] These treatises offer an even more dizzying array of explanations for the bride's blackness: affliction, Anglicanism, antiquity, apostasy, Arabian origin, blindness, bruising, chastisements, church troubles, conversion, corruption, damnation, dawn, defection of Solomon, deformity, devilry, dispersal of the ten tribes, division of the kingdom, Egyptian origin, election, Ethiopian origin, Ethiopian supremacy over Israel, fall of Rehoboam, foolishness, frailty, Gentiles, history, horror, humility, idolatry, illusion, infirmity, iniquity, menstruation, mourning, original sin, outward appearance, persecution, punishment, recidivism, recusancy, sorrow, stoning to death, subjugation to a tyrannous king, suffering, sunburn, terror, tribulation, tricks of the Catholic church and Islam, vileness, virginity, weakness of the flesh, wealth (spiritual *and* material), and works.

Most of the commentaries combine several types of explanation at once, like Antonio Brucioli's (1598). Brucioli interprets the bride as a figure for the Christian soul, with her blackness a sign of sin (on the moral level). On a literal level, her blackness slips between being a bodily characteristic (she is vile and humble in her black body, he suggests) and merely a mote in the eye of the beholder (she is black only to fools, but fair to wise men). Most important to Brucioli, however, is her status on the anagogical level, as a reminder of the end of the world and the perils of eternal punishment. He associates blackness with a temporary, earthly, bodily state of being, fairness with "eternall and everlasting goods" and heavenly permanence.[7] The most redemptive aspect of blackness for him is its association with humility and with mortality; blackness reminds Christians that earthly life is temporary, while heavenly life is immortal.

In arguing that blackness is a sign of a temporary state of being, Brucioli contradicts other theories of color, such as heraldry, which identify black or "sable" as "the auncientest emongst colours" and as a sign of permanence, constancy, and antiquity.[8] Gervase Markham's *Poem of Poems* (1596) refers to heraldic theories of color only to break down the association of black with permanence by calling the bride's "Sable tinckture" "decaying old." Markham praises not the bride's age but "youths features," the renewal of faith that the bridegroom's arrival brings.[9] "[T]inckture" suggests paint or gilding, and a few lines later, Markham compresses references to paint, along with several alternative Renaissance explanations for blackness (allegorical as well as physical), in a single stanza:

Disdaine me not because of blacke attaint,
For why the scorching sunne hath kist my brow,
And with his eieballs, on my cheeks doth paint,
What sinne-inflicting nature doth alow
Through the corruption of her broken vow.[10]

The bride is black because of dirt ("blacke attaint"), sunburn ("scorching sunne"), cosmetics ("paint"), "sinne," decay ("corruption"), and recusancy ("broken vow"). Markham implies that, if the bride were free from sin and fallen human "nature," the sun could not have painted her with sunburn; the image of the sun kissing and painting her with his eyeballs is perhaps deliberately grotesque.

"Ethiopian Beauty"

British Renaissance divines most consistently claimed the poem represented Christ's marriage with the church, in particular, with the Church of England. They developed this reading from that of the church fathers, notably Origen, whose commentaries and homilies on the Song were translated by St. Jerome. Subsequently edited by Desiderius Erasmus and republished along with Jerome's Bible (the Vulgate) in the sixteenth century, Origen's commentaries on the Song went through several editions.[11] He took the bride to figure the Church of the Gentiles and the bridegroom to figure Christ. The so-called "Origenist heresy" denied any literal or historical level of meaning to the Song, treating it as though it were *only* about the Gentiles and Christ, but Origen himself does not deny the historical level. In particular, he insists that it is the very blackness of the bride in Canticles that renders her beautiful and, as I observed in my previous chapter, he finds examples of biblical "Ethiopians" such as Moses' Ethiopian wife (Num. 12:1), the Queen of Sheba or "the queen of the South" (Matt. 12:42), Ebed'melech, the saintly Ethiopian eunuch (Jer. 38 and 39), and the Ethiopian governor baptized by Philip (Acts 8:26), to prove his point. We may recall that Origen repeats Jerome's Christian gloss on Jeremiah's rhetorical question, "Can the Ethiopian change his skin, or the leopard his spots?" (Jer. 13:23), and argues that Christ enables both these metamorphoses, converting the proverb itself from an allegory of incorrigibility into one of regeneration.

Origen argues that the black bride in the Song of Songs is beautiful in both her physical, dark-skinned body and, once Christ has bleached away her sins, in her soul. He imagines her uttering a spirited defense of her beauty:

I am indeed black, O daughters of Jerusalem, in that I cannot claim descent from famous men, neither have I received the enlightenment of Moses's Law. But I have my own beauty, all the same. For in me too there is that primal thing, the Image of God wherein I was created, and, coming now to the Word of God, I have received my beauty. . . . I am black indeed by reason of my lowly origin; but I am beautiful through penitence and faith.[12]

Origen ventriloquizes the bride's blackness as beautiful because it represents the "primal . . . Image of God," spirit rather than flesh, transformed by the word of God; he evokes theological and classical commentaries that consider blackness an emblem of Chaos, as the "darkness" that precedes the "light" at the Creation.[13]

Origen is at first careful to distinguish between the pejorative *metaphor* implicit in the charge of "blackness" that the daughters of Jerusalem bring against the bride, and her physical body, which he insists possesses both "natural beauty" and "that which is acquired by practice."[14] He seems to take the bride's conversion, from dark to light-skinned, to apply to a purely spiritual state, explaining that she is "black" with sin, as we all are, and burnt by the "sun of justice," "black" in the eyes of the daughters of Jerusalem because she is a Gentile and cannot claim the blood of the Fathers. In this he contradicts the Jewish tradition that reads the bride as Israel and her blackness as the metaphorical rendering of her sufferings as a slave in Egypt.[15]

A modern commentator points out that "by dint of some fancy exegetical footwork, Origen . . . undermine[s] his own positive approach to the theology of negritude."[16] At one point Origen denies that the bride's skin color is a "natural blackness" from the sun's brightness, such as the Ethiopians transmit to their offspring, and calls her negritude instead the result of the burning of the "sun of justice." The sun of justice can both blacken and blanch sinners' skins, but neither of these effects is natural, neither color innate. It darkens believers when they sin but bleaches them when they repent. Origen also associates "blackness" with

Christian humility and constancy, because, he believes, its hue remains constant while lighter skins blush or grow pale, an argument that, as we shall see in later chapters, Shakespeare's Aaron in *Titus Andronicus* and Barnfield's Daphnis in *The Affectionate Shepheard* both repeat. The bride's Ethiopian origins remain important, however; after purification and repentance, "your soul will indeed be black because of your old sins, but your penitence will give it something of what I may call an Ethiopian beauty."[17]

An "Ethiopian beauty" is a mark of special redemption. For Origen, the bride's Ethiopian blackness is beautiful because it marks her necessary difference from the daughters of Jerusalem. In marrying an Ethiopian, Solomon opens the kingdom of the Jews to foreigners, an act of exogamy that prefigures Christ's extending grace to the Gentiles as well as to the Jews. The Ethiopian bride becomes not just a convert but the means by which others are brought to Christ. Origen explicitly identifies color prejudice with what he calls an outdated Jewish tradition rather than the Christian, reading Aaron's dislike of Moses's Ethiopian wife as the typological precursor of the Jews' refusal to convert:

Let the Aaron of the Jewish priesthood murmur, and let the Mary of their synagogue murmur too . . . *Ethiopia shall get her hands in first with God.* It is well said that she shall get in first; for . . . Ethiopia [has] been healed while Israel is still sick.[18]

As we shall see, Renaissance commentators concur with Origen's view that the Song praises Ethiopia over Israel, and share his hostility to Jews, but they primarily interpret "Ethiopia" as a reference to the British church, "healed" while the Church of Rome "is still sick." The reformed Protestant church becomes the bride who is called "black" by the Catholic church but who in fact is the "whitest" of all because of her purification by God. The association of the black bride and the true church establishes a link between the Englishman and the Ethiopian bride: "Ethiopia shall get her hands in first with God."[19]

Melainophobia

There are three major problems in translating Song 1:5–6: (1) Is the bride black *and* comely, or black *but* comely? (2) Is she black, blackish, brown, brownish, tawny, swart, dusky, dark, or some combination thereof? (3) Is her dark skin evidence of a particular geographic or national origin, or is her blackness the temporary result of a suntan? Let us take these questions in order.

Origen gives Song 1:5 as "Nigra sum & speciosa filiæ Hierusalem, ut tabernacula cedar: ut pelles Solomonis," "I am black *and* lovely, daughters of Jerusalem, as the tents of Kedar: as the hangings of Solomon."[20] The Vulgate, however, gives "nigra sum sed formosa," "I am black *but* comely."[21] We might call these two options emphatic blackness versus exculpatory blackness. As Frank Snowden observes, the Septuagint and the early Patristic writings give *and*.[22] Most modern translations likewise give "black and beautiful" for the Hebrew.[23] Blackness is here a *condition* of beauty, not a contrast with it. The four major Renaissance English translations, however—Geneva, Bishops', KJV, and the Catholic Rheims-Douai—all treat the bride's blackness as a contradiction, a surprise, in the context of her beauty and desirability. The translators of the Douai Bible believed that the Latin Vulgate was closer to God's word than the Septuagint and so followed it strictly. The Protestant translators, however, boasted of their return to "the original Greek and Ebrue" (Geneva, subtitle). Why then replace "and" with "but"?

Marvin Pope dismisses the Protestant preference for *but* over *and* as what he calls "melainophobia," or fear of blackness. But according to Ariel and Chana Bloch, the variations between *but* and *and* spring from a genuine ambiguity in the Hebrew, "where the conjunctive *ve-* may be used either in its common meaning 'and' or in an adversative sense."[24] They conclude that the bride may be either excusing her blackness or emphasizing it as a sign of her beauty. While the Blochs concede that both interpretations of the bride's blackness are possible, Marcia Falk argues that "the Hebrew conjunction w^e-[sic] means 'and' far more commonly than 'but'; the standard translations are based on the unfortunate assumption that blackness and beauty are contradictory."[25] In their translation itself, Bloch and Bloch agree with Falk, rendering the phrase as "dark . . . and beautiful," regarding the bride's statement of blackness as emphatic rather than exculpatory.[26]

But the next verse raises a second series of questions, this time about not only the tone of the bride's statement but about the degree of her blackness. In "Look not on me because I am black" (KJV, 1:6), the Hebrew word for "black" (šəḥôrāh) is slightly different (šəḥārḥōreth)— a hapax legomenon, or unique usage in the Hebrew Bible (the Song of Songs has the highest rate of hapax legomena in this corpus).[27] Some readers take the change to indicate a diminution of the bride's blackness. Jerome translates the second "black" as *fusca*, "dark" or "brown," in contrast to *nigra*, "black," in the previous verse; Henry Ainsworth (1623) gives "brown" and NRSV gives "dark" where it gave "black" before.[28] Others, however, read the second "black" as at least as strong as the first, if not stronger. The Septuagint gives "black" as in the previous verse,[29] Geneva "blacke," Bishops' "so blacke," KJV "black." The Blochs retain their first translation, "dark," and Falk gives "black as the light before dawn."[30]

While Pope notes that Hebrew lexicographers usually distinguish between two similar-sounding words (šḥr I and šḥr II) that mean "dark" and "dawn" respectively, Falk argues that there is a deliberate pun at work that expresses the paradox of darkness that comes from the sun, the source of light.[31] John Robotham had argued the same thing in 1652:

The Hebrew word here translated *blacke*, signifieth *blacknesse, or darknesse*: and therefore the Hebrew word *Mishchar* is taken from the same roote, which signifieth the *morning*, or the day-dawning, *because of the blacknesse or darknesse* thereof.[32]

Falk uses this paradox of dark or black light to translate the bride's words triumphantly: "Yes, I am black! and radiant—."[33] Blackness for Falk is a poetic device expressing mystery and magnificence, and she reads the references to Kedar and to Solomon's curtains as "parallel," both expressing concealed, dark beauty.[34]

NRSV, in contrast, takes the references to the bride's blackness and to Kedar as allusions to the bride's dark skin, which it interprets as a sign of a particular ethnic origin: "The new bride is *dark* because she is from *Kedar* in northern Arabia, where a tribe lived that was linked with Abraham's son, Ishmael" (NRSV, 1:5n.). Origen likewise takes the bride's blackness to be a reference to her dark skin, although he argues that she is Ethiopian rather than Arabian. NRSV, Origen and Falk all describe the bride's blackness as emphatic, but for Falk it is a primarily poetic device to convey mystery, not an accurate description of her skin. The bride's blackness may be beautiful, but she is not necessarily a foreigner. Kedar and Solomon are not references to actual places or historical figures, but metaphors that evoke a sense of opulence. Like Falk, the Blochs emphasize the bride's blackness, and the allusions to Kedar and Solomon as poetic devices that evoke romantic associations, rather than as statements of ethnic origin or historical fact. They call the bride's darkness "sunburned skin . . . associated with a lower social status, a fair complexion being the mark of those who could afford not to work outdoors," and explain the "tents of Kedar" as a reference to the tents of "nomadic Bedouin . . . typically woven from the wool of black goats."[35] They read "Solomon's tapestries" as a reference to his kingly splendor, so that "black" qualifies the reference to Kedar (they find a pun on Kedar and *qdr*, the root of the verb "to be black") and "beautiful" the tapestries.[36] Such metaphors are orientalizing, in Edward Said's sense, because they use allusions to an exotic, foreign part of the world purely to evoke a contrast and to assert the bride's fundamental similarity to the daughters of Jerusalem, which is concealed by her superficial blackness.[37]

"blacke . . . therwithall comlier"

These debates about the tone of the bride's self-assessment, the degree of her blackness, and its significance, were current in translations of the Song throughout the Renaissance. Henoch Clapham's translation of the Song (1603) describes the bride as "blacke (o ye daughters of Jerushalem) and to be desired."[38] This is a literal translation of Martin Luther's "Nigra sum, sed desiderabilis, filiae Hierusalem" in his brief comments on the Song in 1539.[39] As Kim Hall observes, Ainsworth's translation "includes both the phrases 'I am black, and comely' and 'I am black, but am pleasing-comly.'"[40] Ainsworth explains the "opposition" thus: "as *blackness* is in the colour and skin; so *comelines* is in the parts, features and proportion of the body."[41] The distinction he makes between skin color and shapeliness possibly comes from the Vulgate, which gives *formosa*, well formed or comely, rather than *pulchra*, beautiful, in the bride's praise.

Dudley Fenner's translation of the Song of Songs (1587) words the bride's beauty and her defense more strongly than Ainsworth's, declaring:

Be it that I am blacke,
howe be it so as I
O daughters of Jerusalem
am therwithall comlier.
Graunt that like to the Tentes
Of Kedar I remaine,
Yet like I am to those that dwell
in Solomon's curtayne.[42]

Fenner carefully glosses "howe be it so as" to show us the meaning of the original Hebrew, which he gives as "and, or notwithstanding." We might wonder whether his lengthy circumlocution arises from the uncomfortable exigencies of Poulter's Measure; indeed, thirteen lines after "how be it so as," Fenner has to introduce the awkward "Or for because that I" instead of the straightforward "or because I" that the sense requires. Common Meter, Poulter's Measure, or even old-fashioned "fourteeners" need not, however, be quite so heavy-handed. Drayton used fourteeners mellifluously four years later to translate the same verse:

Ye daughters of Ierusalem, although that browne I bee,
Than arras rich or cedars fruits I seemelier am to see:
Disdaine me not, although I be not passing faire,
For why, the glowing sunny raies discolloured haue my laire.[43]

Her "laire" may be her "leer" or "appearance," or perhaps her "dwelling-place."

Yet Fenner is not simply a bad poet. While Drayton sacrifices accuracy to euphony, turning the guttural "black" into "browne," the harsh "Kedars tentes" into the lushly evocative "cedars fruits," and removing the reference to Solomon, Fenner valiantly attempts to turn the Song into verse and remain true to his Hebrew. "How be it so as" attempts to keep both meanings, *and* as well as *notwithstanding*, in circulation, along with the opposing attitudes towards black beauty that each term implies. Black *and* comely gives each term equal weight, does not assume that blackness precludes beauty, and even hints that blackness is part of the bride's charm. Black and *notwithstanding* comely excuses the bride's negritude by weighing her beauty against her skin tone. Even *notwithstanding*, however, maintains a certain vagueness; during the sixteenth century it is used not just to mean "in spite of" but also like a Latin ablative absolute, to indicate a syntactical relationship between two terms[44]: "Being black, I am comely," might be an apt equivalent. Fenner employs a similar ambiguity with "Therwithall" (glossed "ident.," that is, the same as above). OED gives "therewithal" as meaning first "in addition to."[45] In fact the comparative "comlier" suggests a degree of causation: the bride's blackness, which Fenner equates both with Ethiopian origin and with sin, makes her all the more beautiful in the eyes of her beloved.[46]

Fenner's notes upon his translation, however, qualify his description of her as all the "comlier" for her blackness by describing the "principall places of beautie" as "both cheekes and necke . . . adorned with ornamentes of the Spirit, as gratiouse, as rewes of precious stones, or gergeous collers of great price."[47] His translation demonstrates an encounter between the residual religious myth of black religious conversion and the emergent early modern connection between blackness and material wealth. His bride's blackness is beautiful because it sets off her jewels all the better (just as Shakespeare's Juliet shines "like a rich jewel in an Ethiop's ear" [*Rom.*, 1.5.46] next to the other Capulet ladies). Heraldry is again illuminating: the combination of "Argent, and . . . Sable," silver and black, in heraldry is called "Most fairest," because "Argent will be seene in the darkest place that is, and contrariwise, Sable will bee seene in the most clearest light that may be."[48]

And when Fenner characterizes the bride's adornments, rather than her body, as attractive, he prefigures the ways in which African house servants in England would over the course of the next century be kept and treated as beautiful household furniture. The slave trade had begun in the 1440s, when Portuguese merchants, claiming they wanted to "save" the Africans they met by converting them to Christianity, kidnapped 235 people from Guinea (one of whom became a Franciscan friar). England at first held a good reputation among the Guineans, who distinguished between the Portuguese and Spanish, who came to kidnap them, and the English merchants, who came to look for gold. In 1555, five men traveled from Ghana to England. John Lok's well-known contemporary account refers to them as "blacke slaues" (the marginal gloss, "fiue blacke Moores") (*PN*, 6:176), but Towerson suggests that they were translators employed to enlist African support for the British against the Portuguese, who had established a trading monopoly on the Ivory Coast (6:200).[49] Towerson's account admits that the men had been carried away "perforce" (6:205), but reassures an indignant compatriot that the men will return as soon as their English is adequate:

he demaunded why we had not brought againe their men, which the last yeere we tooke away . . . .we made him answere, that they were in England well used, and were there kept till they could speake the language, and then they should be brought againe to be a helpe to Englishmen in this Countrey. (6:200)

Upon their return to Ghana "with much joy" on the part of "the people . . . specially one of their brothers wives, and one of their aunts" (6:218), they did indeed act as intermediaries between their countrymen and the English, convincing them that it was safe to trade metal with the English ships. Peter Fraser finds further evidence of their free status in Lok's narrative as a whole, which emphasizes gold and ivory as the valuable commodities to be found in Africa, not the bodies of Africans themselves, and the Africans' "wary" skill in trading.[50]

The 1560s saw John Hawkins's three slaving voyages; despite their overall failure, there is evidence of a black presence in Tudor England from the second half of the sixteenth century onward, one large enough to cause Elizabeth some consternation. Africans brought to Britain during the 1590s served as living pawns exchanged between the English and the Spanish in their long hot-and-cold war. On July 11, 1596, the queen wrote a now infamous "open letter to the Lord Maiour of London" complaining that "there are of late divers blackmoores brought into this realme, of which kinde of people there are allready here to manie."[51] Such people, she continues, take work away from native-born Englishmen, who then "for want of service and meanes to sett them on work fall to idlenesse and to great extremytie." She urges the bearer, Edward Banes, to deport the ten "blackmoores" recently brought to London by Sir Thomas Baskervile.[52] On the eighteenth, the Queen issued "an open warrant" to the Lord Mayor and other "publicke officers" requiring them to help Lubeck merchant Casper van Senden "to take up [89] blackamoores here in this realme and to transport them into Spaine and Portugall." Fryer calls this an "astute" political move rather than an attack of blind xenophobia; the queen had already arranged to exchange Africans for 89 imprisoned Englishmen set free by Van Senden "at his owne cost and chearges."[53]

Seeming to anticipate some opposition, Elizabeth urges three kinds of nationalism on her Londoners in order to convince them to give up their servants. First, she describes the duty of a subject to the monarch ("her Majesty's good pleasure"), and second, the duty of a host to a guest and "stranger," twice in the same document (the "charitable affection" of Van Senden to the imprisoned Englishmen, despite "being a stranger" and "the good deserving of the stranger towardes her Majesty's subjectes"). Third and most important, she urges (again, more than once) the duty of one Christian to another. "Christian people . . . perishe for want of service"; reluctant masters "shall doe charitably and like Christians rather to be served by their owne contrymen," she insists.[54] At the turn of the century, the queen trotted out the Christian motive once more when she renewed Van Senden's license for "taking such Negroes and blackamoors to be transported" out of the realm. In 1601, Elizabeth engages ethnic or religious prejudice, blaming them not only for taking jobs and food from native Britons, but also "for that the most of them are infidels having no understanding of Christ or his Gospel." Such arguments may not have been effective, since the letter concludes with a threat to recalcitrant masters: "if they shall eftsoons willfully and obstinately refuse, we pray you to certify their names to us, to the end her majesty may take such further course therein as it shall seem best in her princely wisdom."[55]

Afro-Britons in London suffered a dubious legal status (as I shall discuss in Chapter 8), neither slave nor free, paid for their labor yet liable to deportation on political grounds. They might have served in the fields of entertainment, trade, interpreting, or sex-work. Parish records in London note servants, musicians, and a "black sailor," and some scholars even identify the so-called "Dark Lady" of Shakespeare's *Sonnets* with the "Lucy Negro" named in the Gray's Inn Christmas Revels of 1594 as the "Abbess de Clerkenwell," or London Madam.[56] But later in the early modern period the body of the black slave herself, rather than her decorations, becomes part of a meretricious display of conspicuous consumption. By the turn of the century, an African in Britain presented, as Kim Hall has argued, "'an object in the midst of other objects'": chained in gold, with silver "collars riveted round their necks," portrayed as expensive jewels and adorned with the same, but captive nonetheless—a sinister light upon Fenner's description of black beauty in terms of "collers" or "preciouse stones."[57] Compare, too, Knevet's 1662 decasyllables that define the bride's black comeliness negatively, with "no blemish or deformed spot," as if she is being advertised, and adorn her in what seem to be literal trappings: "rich jewels set in rows," and chains of gold.[58]

"metamorphocall toyes"

Fenner's account implicitly distinguishes between the use of paint or cosmetics on "cheekes and necke" that we will encounter in the next section
of this book, "Whiteness Visible," and the use of ornament or decoration; the one conceals its wealth through deception, the other displays it
through ostentation. His praise of ornamentation might seem to contradict the Protestant movement away from statues and decorations. But
the position of the Song as a book of *poetry* (the "poem of poems," as
Markham calls it) made it central to debates about the function of ornamentation, allegory, and poetry itself for Protestant, Anglican, and Catholic divines, as well as for poets and writers. These debates interpreted
the bride's black beauty as a defense of a particular kind of ornamentation: Genevan blackness against Roman paint. Lewalski, John Pendergast,
and others have examined these debates within Protestantism, and concluded that just because there was a strand of Protestant rhetoric that
dismissed ornamentation, that did not mean that Protestant writers and
preachers ceased to use it altogether. All that the distrust of ornament
meant was that images could be used in the service of religion, as long
as they were recognized as *signs* rather than as referents, rendered meaningful for their relation to symbolism (especially biblical symbolism) rather
than as symbols themselves.[59] Thus Fenner's insistence that the bride wears
"ornaments of the Spirit" tries to reconcile the sensual and sensory beauty
of the Song with his Protestant dislike of decoration. Hill points out that
Fenner, exiled from Britain for his youthful beliefs, carefully "consign[s]
'the ornaments of scarlet, fine linen, silk gold, organs, copes, surplices
. . . to the Babylonian strumpet,'" that is, the Roman Catholic church.[60]

   In choosing the Song for his text, Fenner was asserting its rightful
place in the canon; he spends several pages justifying its inclusion to
those who consider it to be only a love poem. In praising the bride's
ornaments, he was asserting the right of the Protestant church to use
images, ornamentation, and allegory. Other Protestants treat the Song
as a test case for the value of poetry itself. Jud Smith (1585) contrasts
the poetry of the Song to the popular, secular "metamorphocall toyes"
of Chaucer and Ovid.[61] Smith claims that a reader who wishes to find
real poetry and a story of spiritual rather than physical metamorphosis,
should turn to the biblical Song of Songs rather than to the Ovidian
myth of Actaeon. In *Sions Sonets* (1625), Francis Quarles justifies both
the content of poetry and its form, praising the bride's mouth for uttering "Sacred Poesie," which he glosses as "Divine harmonie":

Thy lips (my dearest Spouse) are the full Treasures
Of Sacred Poesie, whose heavenly measures

Ravish with joy the willing heart, that heares,
But strike a deafenesse in rebellious eares:
Thy wordes, like Milke and Honie, doe require
The season'd Soule, with profit and delight.[62]

Poetry is the combination of words and music in "heavenly measures"
(D2r), the perfect way of instructing through delight. Christopher
Jelinger (1641) argues that, given that the Pope presents a "glistering,
and glorious . . . rose" to the Catholics every year, it is a Protestant minister's duty to do the same, by offering a sermon on the Song of Songs.[63]
The Song, he continues, comes between Proverbs and Ecclesiastes because Proverbs indicates the moral life, Ecclesiastes the natural, and
Song, the contemplative; the way of reaching the contemplative life is
through "mysterie," or poetry.[64] Joshua Sprigg's commentary on the
Song (1648) calls rhyme a symbol of divine harmony and the peaceful
coexistence of different churches, ages, and human souls; "God makes
one time or age to Rhime to another, one Christians heart, condition,
temptations to Rhime to another." [65] Metaphor, likewise, is a divine gift,
"not only meat but sauce" to the Scriptures.[66]

"bitter notis"

Given the centrality of the Song and its rich symbolism for debates at the
heart of the schism between Catholic and Reformed churches, the marginal glosses interpreting the text in Geneva and Bishops' were areas of
religious warfare. When "an English lady" gave James VI of Scotland a
copy of Geneva, he complained that the notes were "very partial, untrue,
seditious, and savouring too much of dangerous conceits."[67] The Geneva
commentators interpret the bride's delay in opening the door to the
bridegroom, his subsequent absence, and her sorrow, as the Catholic
church's ultimate disappointment in finding that works alone will not
lead to salvation. "The spouse . . . shall not finde [Christ] if she thinke
to anoint him with her good workes," explain the annotations on "I rose
up to open to my wellbeloved, and mine hands did droppe downe
myrrhe, and my fingers pure myrrhe upon the handels of the barre"
(Geneva, 5:5). Similarly, "the watchmen" who "smote and wounded" the
seeking bride are "false teachers, which wounde ye conscience with their
traditions" (5:7). Compare the NRSV on the same verse: it turns the
bride's sloth in opening the door into bathos, a purely mechanical failure, when the bride's fingers slip upon the bolt because her hands "drip
. . . with myrrh" and "the king . . . becomes impatient as she tries to slide
the bolt and admit him" (NRSV, 5:5n.).

The Geneva glosses to the Song regard the relationship between the bride and bridegroom not as the marriage of Israel and Yahweh, as the Jewish interpreters had suggested, but as the marriage of the true (Protestant) church with Christ. The marginal notes interpret "blacke . . . but comelie" as "The Church confesseth her spots and sinne, but hathe confidence in ye favour of Christ." This seems like a mild example of the opinionated Calvinistic glosses that James found so objectionable, but its bias is clear nonetheless. "Confidence in ye favour of Christ" is a call to arms; tropologically, the Song was interpreted as the union of the Christian soul with Christ, but the Geneva Song insists that such a union can be effected only through faith and individual election (Christ's "favour"), not through works.

This Protestant emphasis on faith over works is anticipated by the figure of the black and comely bride in William Baldwin's verse translation of the Song (1549):

Why I am blacke an other cause there is:
My mothers sonnes (for Eva is mother of all)
Fel out with me, the cause wherof is this:
I damne my wurkes, on Christes mercies I call.[68]

Baldwin dedicated his translation to Edward VI, whose Protestant sympathies were well known. This bride is a vocal advocate of Protestantism and is blackened both by the calumnies of her brothers and by her works, which prevent her from having faith in Christ and being saved. When she receives Christ in faith, she becomes "fayre" and "beautified" by him.[69]

Geneva's translation of the Song separates "blacke" and "comelie" by the address to the daughters of Jerusalem, emphasizing the bride's blackness before qualifying it:

I am blacke, o daughters of Jerusalem, but comelie, as the frutes of Kedar, & as the curtines of Salomon.
Regarde ye me not because I am blacke: for the sunne hathe looked upon me. The sonnes of my mother were angrie against me: thei made me the keper of the vines: but I kept not mine own vine. (Geneva, 1:4–5)

It gives "frutes of Kedar" rather than "tents of Kedar," emphasizing the supposed lineage of Kedar from Ishmael, "of whome came the Arabians [that] dwelt in tents" (Geneva, 1:4). Elizabeth detested the Geneva Bible as much as James did, and requested that *her* Authorized Version, Bishops', should follow Coverdale's Great Bible (1539), Henry VIII's Authorized Version, as far as possible and avoid "bitter notis vppon any text . . . Lightnes[,] or obscenitie."[70] In practice, Bishops' "for the most part . . . happily reprinted the Great Bible text with, now and then, a revision introduced from the Geneva Bible."[71] In comparison to Geneva, Bishops' often seems wordy and profuse, and the Song is no exception:

I am blacke (O ye daughters of Hierusalem) but yet fayre and well favoured, like as the tentes of the Cedarenes, and as the hangings of Solomon.
Marvaile not at mee that I am so blacke, for why? the Sunne hath shined upon me: my mothers children have evill will at me: they made me the keeper of the vineyards, but mine owne vineyarde have I not kept. (Bishops', 1:4–5)

Gerald Hammond, with some justification, calls Bishops' "either a lazy and ill-informed collation . . . or . . . the work of third-rate scholars and second-rate writers."[72] But Bishops' prolixity in this instance is no accident but the deliberate representation of a specific political position. Bishops' emphasizes more strongly the paradox of the bride's beauty by doubling "but" and "yet" and by pairing "blacke" with "fayre." Black and fair are opposites, but it is through the union of these two opposites that the Elizabethan church can flourish. As many of the commentaries maintain, the Anglican church's strength and righteousness derived from its balance. The "Elizabethan settlement" supposedly steered a "via media" or middle way between the extreme Protestant belief in redemption through faith and election alone and the Roman Catholic belief in redemption through works and ritual alone.[73] Bishops' notes to the Song gloss "the flowres are come up" (Bishops', 2:12) as good works, and "the voyce of the turtle dove" as the voice of the Holy Spirit, in a combination of faith and works. When the bridegroom abandons the bride in 5:6, he does so not because the Church has sinned but because "he would stirre up in them a greater desire of him." There is a more direct statement of ecumenism in 6:8: "there are threescore Queenes, fourescore Wives, and damosels without number" apparently means "There bee many in the Church of God, and divers orders and degrees within," and in the following verse, "one is my dove" is glossed "Divers particular Churches dispersed, make but one Catholique Church" (Bishops', 6:9). After the religious turmoil of previous decades, the Elizabethan Anglican church was interested in fostering compromise. If radical Protestants demanded faith, and Roman Catholics demanded ritual, Elizabethan Anglicans demanded faith *in* ritual.

Bishops' notes on the Song, while more circumspect than Geneva's, make this paradoxical position clear by emphasizing the role of the Eucharist—a ritual—in Christian redemption—through faith. Bishops' glosses "blacke" simply as "through the spots of sinne and persecution," and "fayre" as "thorowe faith in the blood of Christ"; "fayre, thorowe faith in the blood of Christ," balances the Geneva dependence on Christ's "favour," redemption through election, with the power of doctrinal acts.

Faith in the Eucharist, "the blood of Christ," the ritual, is as important as faith in divine election. Pendergast suggests that the Eucharist functions as a sacrament for Protestants not because the host becomes Jesus's body (as the Catholics believed) but because of "the interaction and participation of the faithful with the symbols" of that faith: "by receiving the symbol in faith the redemptive act is done."[74] Nevertheless, Catholic *and* Protestant acknowledge "the symbolic reality of mediation," without which no sign system can flourish.[75] In other words, even the Protestant interaction between believer and symbol during the Eucharist cannot occur without the presence of another level of meaning. The notes to the Anglican Bishops' Bible attempt to resolve this paradox by emphasizing the believer's need for faith, not just in Christ alone but, as importantly, in the Church's symbolism. Individual Christian faith is necessary for redemption, as the extreme Protestants believed, but acts of worship and liturgy were suitable vehicles for the expression of this faith, as the Catholics believed.

"The British Church"

The battle between works and faith figures as female competition and decorum in George Herbert's "The British Church," which most explicitly associates the Catholic church with "painted" fairness and the Protestant with "undrest" simplicity:

She on the hills, which wantonly
Allureth all in hope to be
    By her preferred,

Hath kissed so long her painted shrines,
That ev'n her face by kissing shines,
    For her reward.

She in the valley is so shy
Of dressing, that her hair doth lie
    About her ears:

While she avoids her neighbour's pride,
She wholly goes on th'other side,
    And nothing wears.[76]

Herbert's strictures against the Roman church, "wantonly" alluring, seem at first to be more forceful than the charges laid against the Genevan, until we learn that the latter "wholly goes on th'other side." His language echoes the parable of the Good Samaritan, who rescued a wounded man abandoned by a priest and a Levite who had "passed by on the other side" without helping him (KJV, Lk. 10:30–37). Extreme

Protestantism denies succor to the spiritually needy because the doctrine of predestination excludes all those who have not been elected to grace, just as the priest and the Levite ignored the man's sufferings because they did not believe he was their "neighbour."

Herbert's "British church" is "Neither too mean, not yet too gay," neither too plain nor too gaudy.[77] Several lines later, he switches from using "mean" as an adjective to employing it as a noun in order to praise the church for a different kind of "mean," Aristotle's golden mean or balance, that renders her unique: "the mean thy praise and glory is."[78] Like a girl on the marriage market, the church should be neither "wantonly" alluring nor "shy" and reserved, but pleasantly inviting. Donne, characteristically, employs the same conceit more outrageously, comparing the Roman church to a proud and "painted" harlot, the Genevan to an unattractive, "rob'd and tore" mourning widow, and the true church to a happy, available housewife, who "is most trew, and pleasing to thee, then / When she'is embrac'd and open to most men."[79] This hierarchy, which places a satisfied (and shared) spouse above either an unmarried woman or a mourning widow, directly contradicts the Roman Catholic value of celibacy over marriage.

Herbert and Donne praise female concern for appearance because, according to Anglican theology, dismissing appearance altogether indicates not a fine disregard for the flesh but a disrespect for the church and for public worship. The Elizabethan Settlement required only outward conformity; one's own beliefs did not matter as long as one attended church along with one's neighbors.[80] Elizabeth's compromise was both practical and compassionate; not faith, but the *appearance* of faith was necessary. Religious leaders justified the settlement on theological grounds. Donne stresses this need for sacramental reverence very logically in his sermons:

He that undervalues outward things, in the religious service of God, though he begin at ceremonial and ritual things, will come quickly to call Sacraments but outward things, and Sermons, and publique prayers, but outward things, in contempt . . . . Beloved, outward things apparell God, and since God was content to take a body, let us not leave him naked.[81]

Geneva's distaste for dressing becomes in Donne's sermon a reproach on behalf of Christ himself, who deigned to wear the very "body" that the extreme Protestants scorn. Donne neatly turns the terms of the settlement from a practical compromise into a precondition for conversion; while the appearance of faith is all that's required, merely the act of appearing faithful and attending church will work a conversion in the churchgoer's heart.

Anglican Reading

Clapham uses his translation of the Song to expound a model of literary criticism that we could call Anglican reading, a middle way between the heresies of the Catholic church and those of the extreme Protestants. His dedicatory epistle to King James balances "glad-sadness and sad-gladness" at the deep "blacke . . . bass" bell tolling for Elizabeth's death and the high-pitched "silverie-one" pealing for James's coronation; like the bride in Bishops' translation, England is both black and fair (A2r). In Clapham's preface the reigns of Elizabeth and James symbolize a return to order, and Clapham offers his translation as a nationalistic project that is inescapably tied up with religion. He connects modes of reading the Scriptures, and in particular, the various interpretations of the bride's blackness, with different kinds of religious heresy. On the one hand, the Origenists, the Evangelical Familists, and the Roman Catholics read everything as a "fanatike forme of Allegorizing" (A6v), treating the Song as though it were only an allegory about the relationship of Christ and the church of the Gentiles (the so-called Origenist fallacy), or only about the individual Christian soul (the Familists), or only about the Virgin Mary (the Roman reading).[82] On the other hand, he argues, by treating the Song as though it applied only to present-day conflicts within the Christian church, radical Protestants ignore the allegorical level and focus only on the literal-historical level. Clapham's definitions of "allegory" and "historie" are different from a modern reader's; he does not consider topical or political readings to be allegorical, but literal. (The idea of reading the Song in a truly "literal" manner, as a sexually explicit love poem, does not occur to him. Here, again, he may be influenced by Luther, who denies the allegorical readings of the Church Fathers in favor of a literal reading that identifies the spouse with the State and her blackness with its discontented citizens.)

Clapham attempts to offer instead a reading that takes account of "Historie and Mysterie, Shadow and Substance, Signe and Thing Signified" (A6v). The Song *is* about the love of Christ and his church, *and* about the individual Christian soul and Christ, but this allegory cannot be understood except through the progress of history, the representation of Christ by Solomon and of the church by Pharaoh's daughter. Like the doctrines and practices of the British church, the practice of Anglican reading requires a combination of faith ("mysterie") and works ("historie"), the spiritual ("shadow") and the practical ("substance"), the symbolic ("signe") and the metonymic ("thing signified"). "[T]hing signified" is metonymic, rather than referential, because, as we have seen, debates within Protestantism justified the use of ornament, allegory, and poetry on the condition that congregations would always recognize ornaments and decorations as referents, not as objects for worship in their own right. Anglican reading requires metonymy alongside metaphor because a truly "literal" interpretation of symbolism is impossible (compare Clapham's definition of topical reading as "historie" rather than allegory).

Anxious to bolster a united English church, Clapham tries to avoid controversy, criticizing other sects for believing they alone are the true church, without confessing their own sins. Clapham makes an implicit comparison between Catholic services and stage plays, arguing that Catholics deny the bride's beauty and fail to confess themselves "black" because they place too much value on outward appearance and on "player-like paintings" (D2r). At the other extreme, the radical Brownists refuse to describe themselves as "black" by believing only in "supposed Saintings," calling all those "black" who are not predestined for election (D2r). In Clapham's model, the Catholic church is superficially beautiful because she is "painted" (as Andrewes, Donne, Herbert, Fenner, and many others insist); in contrast, the extreme Protestants go undressed, undecorated, and plain. But the Anglican church is both black *and* comely—neither light-skinned through cosmetic use, like the Catholic church, nor ugly because of carelessness, like the radical Protestants, but beautiful nonetheless. Her beauty comes not from paint or cosmetics but from decorations and ornaments (as in Fenner's translation).

"beyond the partition wall"

Clapham's bride is black in a sense both literal and allegorical, like his interpretation of the Song as a whole. He argues that she is dark not only because of sin, as in most allegorical readings, but because she is descended from Kedar, Solomon's "Aegyptian" bride (C7v). Fenner, Clapham, John Dove, and Sir Henry Finch follow Origen in explaining the bride's blackness through her foreign origin, whether she be Egyptian, Ethiopian, or Arabian. Maintaining that the bride is black or foreign on the literal level works in two opposing ways. On the one hand, the tracts illustrate a slippage between blackness as a physical attribute and blackness as a moral failing, bolstering the association of blackness with sin, as Kim Hall notes.[83] Clapham himself identifies blackness as "horrour of nature" on the same page that he praises the bride for her foreign origin (C8r).[84]

On the other hand, treating the bride as an Ethiopian or Moor, whose blackness lies in a physically dark skin, allows black-skinned people and strangers to be the equals of white Britons in their access to religious salvation.[85] Contrast the insistence of Theodore Beza, one of the Geneva Bible's most prominent translators, that the bride *cannot* be Egyptian or

Ethiopian. Beza's sermons (translated in 1587) loudly and categorically deny that she is born with dark skin. Beza instead argues that the bride is black because she has been made to "look like a Moore or Arabian" by the Roman Catholics or by the ravaging Muslims when in fact she is "not, for all [her] tanned hew, an Arabian or Aethiopian."[86] He compares the religion of "Mahomet" to "the false painted Church" in Rome and assumes that an "Arabian" or "Aethiopian" bride would necessarily be a Muslim,[87] contradicting the popular Renaissance belief I discussed in my previous chapter, that the mythical Prester John ruled a devout Christian empire in the heart of Ethiopia. Beza's imagined bride is not really black, unlike the Catholics, who are "painted" fair, or the "Arabians," who are dark-skinned.[88] Few of the other English tracts before the 1640s are so emphatic in their equation of Catholicism and Islam and their denial of a foreign origin for the bride. Perhaps a belief in predestination (foretold in the Song and elsewhere in the Bible) prevented Beza from allowing grace to be extended to foreigners in the way that Dove and Clapham suggest and made him restrict it to the elect company of devout European Protestants. Beza certainly implies that Moors, Arabians, Ethiopians, and Egyptians cannot join the elect.[89] Samuel Smith (1633) likewise excludes Turks and Moors from salvation, responding to the contemporary fear of Ottoman expansion by comparing the bride's blackness with the "original sinne" of naturally corrupted human beings that keeps us under "the "extreame slavery and bondage" of the "Turkes."[90] At the same time, he minimizes the consequences of captivity and forced labor by subordinating physical suffering to spiritual anguish: "the Turkes . . . can but hold us in temporall bondage; but by subtle Sathan the Prince of darkeness, where we should have indured, not a temporall, but a spiritual and eternall bondage and slavery."[91]

Clapham, in contrast, makes strangers the conduit for salvation:

had not Salomon gone beyond the partition wall (even unto the Gentiles) for his wife, it could not so aptly have figured the Gentiles people, to whom Messiah was to joyne himselfe, but not till first hee forsooke the Sinagogue of the Jewes. And thus they that are over-precise for admitting Allegories, shall sometimes cast but a censure unworthy their places. (C7r–C7v)

Clapham shoots a barb at the allegorical readers who claim that Solomon's vices, namely his love of foreign women, led to his downfall, and that therefore the Song cannot describe his marriage on the literal or historical level. On the contrary, argues Clapham, exogamy was necessary in order to fulfill the biblical prophecy that Christ would found a church open not just to the Jews but to the Gentiles. Of course, the openness of Christianity to converts corresponds in no way to what we now consider genuine tolerance or cultural openness. Compare James Shapiro's analysis of early modern thinking about Jews, which resists the nineteenth-century classifications of "philo-" and "anti-" Semite because they "were not all that far apart": the former sought to convert or resettle Jews, the latter to exclude them from England altogether.[92] Clapham's conversion narrative opens up a space for imagining the Other and for mutual interdependence at the expense of the differently "Othered" Jews, recalling Origen's ranking of Ethiopia above Judaea because of its willingness to convert. The question of the conversion of the Jews took on a millenarian urgency in the seventeenth century, as conversion narratives proliferated despite a persistent stereotype that such transformations were insincere and indicated only the Jews' supposedly natural tendency towards deception.[93]

Dove's *The Conversion of Salomon* (1613) similarly argues that Solomon's "effeminate" interest in foreign women leads him to mystical revelation, the "conversion" of the title (A1v). The bride's blackness, which is both "natural: she was an Aethiopian" and "accidentall, being tanned with the scorching heate of the sunne," signifies the triumph of Ethiopia over Israel (D2r–D2v):

If she be an Aethiopian, how can she be made faire? to wash a blacke-a-more with us, is to labour in vaine, as much as to plough the rockes, to sowe the sands, to milke the ram-kind goats, to yoake the foxes together in the plough. A black-emore saith Jeremie cannot wash away his blacknesse. S Augustine saith: . . . Aethiopia surpasseth Judaea by putting off the blackenesse of sinne, and putting on the beauty of faith. (E2r–v)

In his keenness to emphasize the miracle of Christ's sacrifice, Dove equates whitewashing with other conversions that seem to contradict fundamental or essential characteristics. It is the nature of rocks to be stony, not friable; of sand to be fruitless, not fertile; of male goats to have dry teats, not lactating ones; of foxes to spoil the crops (as in the Song itself [2:15]), not to plough them. Nonetheless, after conversion, all these miracles can occur.

The characteristics Dove describes are clearly gendered. By associating blackness with hardness, barrenness, dryness, and belligerence, he implies that the converted Christian is white, soft, fertile, lactating, and peaceable; most explicitly, the male "blackemore" in the book of Jeremiah is replaced by the converted female bride in the Song of Songs. Moreover, these converted figures are superior to those who were born white, Jewish, Christian, or beautiful. "Aethiopia" is here a figure for Britain and the bride, once more, for the Anglican church:

As she is . . . blacke through sinne which is inward and dwelleth in her, so shee is . . . beautifull by outward righteousnesse, not of her owne, but of Jesus Christ which is imputed unto her. As Jacob put on Esau his clothes to get his fathers blessing, so wee must put on the righteous garments of Jesus Christ, that wee may appear righteous before God. (E2r–v)

Putting on the garments of righteousness becomes righteousness itself, another example of the Anglican compromise; the congregation must have faith in the sacraments themselves and the trappings of office, so that both election and ritual participation count towards salvation.

Sir Henry Finch's musings (1615) slip between the binaries of sin/ regeneration and black/white most clearly. He reads the Song as in part testifying to "the drawing of others that as yet were strangers and aliens from the common wealth of Israell to the fellowship and participation of Christ," emphasizing the importance of the bride as a redemptive stranger.[94] But she is "cole black, as black as any black-more, or if any thing bee more black then it, through sinne, both originall and actuall, " so that sin is an intensification of blackness.[95] He notes that all those who think themselves "white" contain "no part white but it is blackish also," but in the same breath equates whiteness with "silver" and blackness with "drosse."[96]

The "Tawney" bride in George Sandys's *Paraphrase of the Song of Songs* (1641) is neither Ethiopian nor Aegyptian, although she is a stranger.[97] Sandys identifies this bride with conquest and exploration.[98] A "successful . . . colonizer," Sandys owned shares in the Bermuda Company, served ten years as treasurer for the colony in Virginia, and returned to England in 1631.[99] His Solomon addresses a bride with a body that shines like the gold of Solomon's "burnisht Throne / And ornaments" and whose "Neck the Oceans Treasure weares."[100] He imagines a bride who is not so much African as American, and turns the Song's blazon into a voyage of discovery. To her natural advantages, the king or colonizer will add the benefits of civilization or learning: "I will a golden Zone impart, / Enameled with curious Art."[101]

While Dove and Clapham took the historical level to mean the events of the Old Testament, Nathanael Homes, Arthur Jackson, and Joshua Sprigg interpret the Song as a "Prophetical history, and Historical Prophecie" of the future of the church.[102] During the tumultuous years of the Civil War, radical Protestants ignore the literal explanation for the bride's blackness as dark skin. They also understand Aquinas's literal level of interpretation somewhat differently from earlier scholars. The narrative they read predicts the whole of Christian history, in order; it travels from the days of the Old Testament through the cruelty of the Roman emperors to the early Christians, the burning of Wycliffe, the reign of Queen Elizabeth I, and the ultimate triumph of Protestantism over other world religions—almost as if the Canticles were a version of the Book of Revelation. These exegetes interpret the bride's blackness as mourning, idolatry, recusancy, or the dispersal of the tribes. The bride mourns for the fall of Solomon and his son Rehoboam, a scarcely veiled allusion to Protestant disappointment in King James towards the end of his reign and disenchantment with Charles I. Now Solomon's foreign wives are supposed to have led him not to salvation, but to idolatry, just as Queen Henrietta Maria had allegedly led King Charles I astray into Catholicism. In a drastic reversal of earlier interpretations, the bride is a recusant, in another comment on Charles's supposed crypto-Catholicism, and the dispersal of the tribes prefigures the fierce factionalism of the Civil War.

Under such circumstances, the color of the bride becomes politicized once more. Homes's commentary, published just three years after the execution of Charles I, unabashedly justifies regicide by describing the bride as black through "subjugation, enslaved to a tyrannous king."[103] Perhaps he recalls the pseudo-biblical connection between black skin and enslavement (the curse of Cham) resurrected by seventeenth-century slavers. After an absence of several hundred years, the Jewish interpretation of the bride's blackness as her sufferings in Egyptian slavery resurfaces in the work of John Cotton (1642) to evoke the persecution of Protestant sects in Britain.[104] Like Beza and like Brightman (who predicts the overthrow of Rome and of "all Muhumetans," Homes blames Catholics and Muslims for blackening the bride, who on the literal-historical level again stands for the persecuted Protestant sects.[105] He claims that Catholics and Muslims torture the bride for her religion, smearing her with coal dust and beating her until she is not just "black" but "blue."[106] Of course, some writers retain the earlier literal explanation of blackness as caused by foreign origin or sunburn. As late as 1658 Jackson describes the bride as both tanned like "Country Damsels" and dark like an Egyptian, a telling equation of the exotic and the homespun that I investigate in Chapters Seven and Eight.[107]

Masks of Blackness and Beauty

In two versifications from the 1620s, the bride's foreignness and her negritude disappear. Robert Aylett and Quarles call her not "black" but "brown," perhaps in contrast to the so-called "blackamoors" or real Africans who had begun arriving on Britain's shores. Such translations imply that blackness and comeliness are not merely paradoxical but altogether incompatible. Aylett's translation, from 1621 (the year of the first mention of the sale of dark-skinned slaves in Britain), lightens the bride's blackness into brownness and insists that the bride only *seems* dark to observers, when in reality she is "faire":

Scorne me not (Sions Nymphes) though I seeme browne
For I am faire and comely, as a Rose,
I (till Sunnes scorching beames on me did frowne),
Was like those that in Salomons tents repose.[108]

"Those that in Salomons tents repose" are "faire," not black or even "browne"; the biblical reference to the "tents of Kedar" has disappeared altogether, so that the bride's darkness and the hint of her foreign origin are an illusion. The divine bridegroom equates fairness and sinlessness, making explicit a move that most earlier translations left as a mere hint or suggestion: "Thou art all faire (my love) in thee's no spot."[109]

Quarles treats the bride's blackness as *entirely* an attribute of the onlooker, so that beauty exists only in the eye of the beholder:

But you, my curious (and too nice) Allyes,
That view my fortunes, with two narrow eyes,
You say my face is blacke, and foule; 'tis true;
I'm beauteous, to my Love, though black to you.
My censure stands not upon your esteeme,
He sees me as I am; you, as I seeme;
You see the cloudes, but he discernes the Skie;
Know, 'Tis my Maske that lookes so blacke, not I. (B1v)

The notes to Quarles's translation gloss "blacke" as "through apparant infirmities," "as I am" as "Glorious in him" and "maske" as "Weaknesse of the flesh," so that in this scheme blackness is a mask or cover for white virtue. Spirit or soul is fair, flesh is black, an opposite interpretation from Origen's, where the bride's blackness represents "the Primal . . . image" of God, heavenly spirit rather than tainted white flesh.[110] Quarles's bride is still defiant, but she resists the daughters not because they do not find black beautiful (as in Clapham's or Fenner's translations) but because they see her as black at all. His versification emphasizes the role of comparative, rather than absolute, blackness and fairness; the bride seems black only to the "blinde," with their "two narrow eyes," because "The blinde imagins all things black, by kind; / Thou art as beautifull, as they are blinde" (B2r). Blackness and beauty cannot share the same face.

This bride is so fair that "The maiden blushes of thy cheekes, proclaime / A shame of guilt, but not a guilt of shame" (C4v). Quarles's chiasmus attempts to solve a problem I shall discuss in the next part of this book, "Whiteness Visible," that parallels the seeming conundrum of whether black can be beautiful—how can one tell whether a blush is a sign of innocent shame or furtive guilt? Quarles sets up a distinction between the blushes of "guilt" and those of "shame": the blush of guilt is caused by the bride's personal consciousness of sin, and the blush of shame springs from an external cause (the slurs cast by the daughters of Jerusalem). The bride's blush on this occasion, according to Quarles's own notes, represents "modest graces of the Spirit." Presumably his epigram, "A shame of guilt, but not a guilt of shame," means that the bride is brought to true repentance (guilt) by the Holy Spirit, but that she is not *gilded* with shameful calumnies or cosmetics. The only gilding on her face is the "Maske," beneath which there is "No spot, no veniall blemish" but "Illustrious beames" that burn an onlooker (Dv).

The "Maske" covers the bride's glory but also protects her from the daughters of Jerusalem:

Would beautie fayre be flatter'd with a grace
Shee never had? May shee behold thy face:
Envie would burst, had shee no other taske,
Then to behold this face without a Maske;
No spot, no venial blemish could shee finde,
To feede the famin of her ranc'rous minde:
Thou art the flowre of beauties Crowne, and they're
Much worse then foule, that thinke thee lesse then fayre. (Dv)

Quarles is responding to the current fashion for ladies to wear masks, but he also establishes a structure of "ranc'rous" female competition, where foulness and fairness are comparative terms. As Kim Hall observes about Baldwin's version of Song, in which the groom declares, "Loe thou . . . art fayer: / Myselfe have made thee so," only the bridegroom can confer *absolute* beauty or fairness on the bride.[111]

A tract that takes the bride—including her naturally dark skin—as the type of the perfect female offers a welcome respite from Quarles's denial of her negritude. On the Continent, Ernestus Vaenius, the son of Otho Vaenius (whose engravings I discussed in my previous chapter), composed a medical treatise in Latin detailing the platonic female form, taking as his model the bride in the Song of Songs (1662). Having commented approvingly on the bride's blackness (or, as he also writes, "redness") as a sign of her strength and vigor, he dismisses the current fashion for pallor because "the color white is strongly opposed to virtue . . . White refers to all those who are phlegmatic, cold, and careful, for that color is the element of water, and so Physicians say, corruption."[112] Borrowing both his father's erudition (the Ovidian tag praising the beauty of Andromeda, dark with the color of her native land) and his technique (the unusual use of shading to indicate dark skin [Figure 4]), he appends a poem in praise of black Andromeda and the bride:

Zealous Sirius' furious heat
And Phoebus' coloring flame

Burned black the bride from her head to her feet
And devastated her fame.
She tells us now she lacks ivory, rose,
The gentle curves of so many.
Who'd hurt thee, fair maid? The King himself knows
Thy color's more lovely than any.[113]

Thus despite representing divine femininity, the bride's loveliness requires the presence of a bridegroom for its existence. Vaenius crowns Perseus or "the King" judge of the pageant, the final arbiter of beauty.

From Narrative to Lyric: Thomas Campion

I mentioned earlier that secular poets turned the stable characters and events of the Geneva or KJV narrative into the shape-shifters and ambiguous episodes of lyric. Thomas Campion's lyric, "Followe thy faire sunne, unhappie shaddowe," changes the sex of the black beloved in order to present the sun as both redeemer and captor. Shadowing the fierce gaze of the "sun [that] hath looked upon" the bride, his long Latin poem, "Umbra," offers not just a reversal of the Song but a perversion, in which the sun's power utterly destroys the black beloved. In the biblical analogue, the Shulamite has been blackened by the rays of the darkening sun and will be bleached white by Solomon; in Campion's lyric, the neglected male lover has been "scorched" black by his fair female sun and can only be returned to "brightnes" by her favor:

Followe thy fair sunne vnhappy shaddowe
Though thou be blacke as night
And she made all of light,
Yet follow thy faire sunne vnhappie shaddowe.

Follow her whose light thy light depriueth,
Though here thou liu'st disgrac't,
And she in heauen is plac't,
Yet follow her whose light the world reuiueth.

Follow those pure beames whose beautie burneth,
That so have scorched thee,
As thou still blacke must bee,
Til her kind beames thy black to brightnes turneth.

Follow her while yet her glorie shineth:
There comes a luckles night,
That will dim all her light;
And this the black unhappie shade devineth.

Follow still since so thy fates ordained:
The Sunne must have his shade,

Till both at once doe fade,
The Sun still prou d the shadow stil disdained.[114]

On a physical level, a shadow must follow the sun all day, irresistibly, until the onset of "luckles night," when both shadow and sun disappear into darkness. The poem concedes that the shadow might have some rest when the sun turns it "from black to brightnes," but such a transformation will never happen. As I have discussed at length, the figure of turning black into white is a common Renaissance emblem for impossibility, "washing an Ethiop white," just as, in the physical world, a shadow can never outshine the sun or exist in the sun's absence.

The lover resembles a shadow not only in his compelling attraction to the sun but also in his antithesis to it, his inky darkness next to her "light." Her light, like the sun's, revives the world, which is swallowed

Figure 4. "In truth, the color white is strongly opposed to virtue." Ernestus Vaenius [Ernest Van Veen], *Tractatus Physiologicus de Pulchritudine* (1662). Reproduced by permission of Duke University.

up in shadows at night. Campion uses "word-painting" throughout his music to illustrate his poetry. In this case, the movement of the shadow as it "follows" the sun and the rise of the sun in the sky ascend musically, culminating in "made all of light," which is the highest pitch in the song.[115] I would also suggest that Campion pays attention to the color of his notes, as do Dowland, Gibbons, and other composers of the era. "Shaddowe" and "thou be [blacke]" in stanza one fall on "black notes" or crotchets; in stanza two the crotchets mark "deprive" and "disgrac't," and in three, "burneth" and "scorched."

The poem does not deny, however, the possibility that light can blacken or tarnish as well as make bright. For Campion's forsaken lover, the lady's beams are paradoxically "pure" when they blacken him, "kind" when they brighten, kind in the sense that they are gentle but also in the sense that they are natural to her. The lady's "light" is also her "lightness" or moral ambiguity (a pun we shall encounter with the white-skinned Guendolen of Richard Barnfield's *The Affectionate Shepheard* in Chapter Six). Her light(ness) "thy light depriveth" so that on earth the lover "lives disgrac't." Her scandalous behavior has ruined his name (an alternate meaning might be that she moves in a sphere so far above his that her light "depriveth" or dims his by outshining it). The shadowy speaker unhappily predicts and prefigures the dark night of death that will come. In the final stanza the female sun has died, victim of a "luckles night / That will dim all her light . . . till both at once doe fade," a night that reverses the biblical Song's triumphant statement that "Love is strong as death" (KJV, Song 8:6). Shadowing, like blackness, is both contextual and intrinsic; thus the poem concludes with a triumphant male sun (emphatically not the shadowy narrator) reigning supreme and "proud" while the shadow and his love "do fade." "The Sunne must have *his* shade" (my italics); next to this new and brighter sun, the lady's luminosity disappears in obscurity (just as the moon, ruled by the goddess Phoebe, fades when the sun rises, the sun which is ruled by her brother Phoebus Apollo).

The sun (personified in the god Phoebus) appears as a similar, all-conquering power in Campion's long Latin poem "Umbra," or "Shadow." Campion retains the form of a narrative poem, but writes an Ovidian "metamorphocall toye," as Jud Smith might have said, rather than a biblical paean. Campion published the first half of his Ovidian narrative in 1595, and the completed poem in 1619; from the reference to Elizabeth of Bohemia and her European realm, he must have finished the poem after Princess Elizabeth's marriage in early 1613.[116] In this account of the origin of the shadow, he identifies the sun not with grace or the consciousness of sin but with an amoral, relentless, rapacious masculine force. Phoebus adores the nymph Iole, who rejects him; unable to control his lust, Phoebus drugs and rapes her in the dark, impregnating her with a son, Melampus. The boy is born black, because he was begotten in the dark, all but for a white sun beneath his breast, "candida solis . . . / sub pectore, patris imago" (lines 155–56). "Imago" can mean shape, image, reflection, or even shadow; thus black Melampus bears on his breast the shining shadow of the sun. We may recall Chariclea's black birthmark on her ivory skin; as in Heliodorus's text, the circular mark functions as the impress of paternity.

As he grows up, the lad resembles a black Cupid: "If Love were black, or if somehow the boy were white, you'd swear the god were in both of them" ("Si niger esset Amor, vel si modo candidus ille, / Iurares in utroque deum," lines 207–8). His beauty inflames the desires of Morpheus, god of sleep, dreams, and shape-shifting, who descends to the enchanted garden of Persephone to find a suitable shape in which to seduce the beautiful boy, whose dark face shines with a lightless light ("sine lumine lumen," line 242). Eventually Morpheus decides to mix and match, donning a natty frame composed of Queen Elizabeth, Queen Anne, Elizabeth of Bohemia, and various other royal females. Melampus awakens desperate to find whoever—whatever—has made love to him. Unable to find his lover, he goes completely mad with desire, and through fruitless searching wastes away—to a shadow.

Melampus cannot meet his dream-lover again because he is unable to sleep, in part because of his anxiety, in part because of his father Phoebus's light. Campion's Phoebus controls not only daylight but the nightfall, too, and becomes angered when Melampus seeks the dark. Campion gives us an epigram: "inimica dolori / Lux est, oblectat nox, et loca lumine cassa"; "Light detests sorrow, the night and places devoid of light amuse him" (lines 364–65). He borrows Ovid's descriptions of nymphs turning into echoes, streams or stones to describe Melampus fading into literal obscurity as the red blood drains from his body and his motion stills ("tenui de corpore sanguis / Effluit . . . motusque recedit" [lines 393–95]). The nymphs prepare him for burial, but Phoebus, angered by his son's preference for darkness, prevents them from interring him. Melampus is such a light weight ("non grave pondus" [line 401]) that he floats away into the darkness, a shadowy exile damned forever from the light ("per omne / Tempus perpetuo damnatus luminis exul," lines 403–4).

Like "Followe," "Umbra" ends with a triumphant male sun god, who conquers both sleep and death; Phoebus prevents Melampus's successful burial and renders him uncomfortably immortal, as the shadow. There is no satisfactory explanation for Phoebus's excessive anger in the poem; the sun's power is absolute, his edicts final. The sun destroys consensual sex. Phoebus can rape Iole even in the dark, because he muffles his bright rays in a cloud to prevent them from giving him away. The light further prevents Melampus from going to sleep and encountering his shadowy dream-bride (Morpheus) once more, just as the coy female sun of Campion's lyric is subdued by a stronger, male sun at the end of the poem.

From Narrative to Lyric: Edward Herbert

Edward Herbert's poems on blackness and "Black Beauty" differ radically from the other treatments of the Song we have considered in his insistence that the black beauty is consistently, constantly black. He identifies blackness with poetry and argues that blackness becomes poetic not because it can be washed white but because it can generate multiple interpretations.[117] Herbert concentrates not upon color change but upon stasis and elaboration:

Black beauty, which above that common light,
Whose Power can no colours here renew
But those which darkness can again subdue,
Do'st still remain unvary'd to the sight.
And like an object equal to the view,
And neither chang'd with day nor hid with night,
When all these colours which the world call bright,
And which old Poetry doth so persue,
Are with the night so perished and gone,
That of their being there remains no mark,
Thou still abidest so intirely one,
That we may know thy blackness is a spark
Of light inaccessible, and alone
Our darkness which can make us think it dark.[118]

Lord Herbert emphasizes black beauty's opposition to "common light" in order to rank it above all other colors. Blackness is "a spark / Of light inaccessible," divine illumination rather than earthly brightness, and black beauty radiates a brilliance powerful enough to subsume all other colors. The night, which is stronger than the day, swallows up all the "bright" colors that "old Poetry" sings, red, white, and green, but blackness remains indissoluble, stronger even than the night. Black shines "above that common light," the sun, and its power to dim bright colors in comparison is likewise stronger than the ability of the sun's rays to turn things "black." Old poetry, like the colors it sings, has disappeared without a trace ("no mark").

Herbert borrows the form of old poetry by using an Italian sonnet, but employs the optical and scientific metaphors of the later seventeenth-century poetry. Old poetry took charge of whitening beauty, celebrated the black bride of Solomon who was made fair or white, but new poetry reverses the trope. It is not the bride who must be transformed and whitened, but the observer, the reader, the poet, who must be turned black. This kind of poetic blackness comes not from the sun, as in old poetry, but from blackness itself and the "light inaccessible" that shines from it. In keeping with his model of new poetry, Herbert avoids a word upon which old poetry relies; he rhymes "sight," "night," "bright" and "light," but not "white." New poetry, Herbert implies, will persist because it, too, is black—"entirely one" with the subject that it praises. Old poetry is Petrarchan; new poetry, metaphysical, as Samuel Johnson would say.

Herbert's poem conveys a sense of movement and change, but on the part of the poet, not the unchanging black beauty, who "like an object equal to the view" remains the same from every angle (like a sphere suspended in the physical universe) and at every point in time (like the ageless verse that replaces old poetry). It is "alone / Our darkness" that obscures the inaccessible light of meaning. The Clarendon text emends line six, giving "Art neither chang'd with day, nor hid with night."[119] Keeping the 1665 text, however, allows black beauty's persistence to accumulate through Herbert's layered clauses ("And . . . / And . . . / When . . . / And . . .") and makes its triumph all the more emphatic because the main clause is delayed until line 11, "Thou still abidest so entirely one." After all the bright colors of old poetry have gone through several changes, first in being praised, then in disappearing, black is "still" there.

In praising black light, Herbert addresses the vexed question in Renaissance optics on the status of black as a color, a topic to which I will return in later chapters. His insistence that ordinary light "can no colours here renew" without succumbing to "darkness" appears to prefigure Newtonian optics, which argues that black alone of all the colors does not form part of the spectrum of light, and that darkness and color, black and white, are therefore absolute opposites. Newton did not present his findings to the Royal Society until 1675, nearly thirty years after Herbert's death, but Herbert could have encountered similar theories of blackness and light from a variety of classical and medieval sources, which debated whether black was a color in its own right, or merely the absence of light, whether it was made up of all the colors of the rainbow, or whether it demonstrated the absence of all color. Van Norden usefully summarizes the prevailing beliefs. Aristotle and Democritus call black a primary color, as do most medieval scholars. Scaliger believes that black contains all the other colors, and distinguishes between "black" and "dark" objects, because the former are visible, the latter invisible. Cardano and Anaxagoras characterize blackness as "negation" and black and white as opposites.[120]

Aristotle in fact describes three different ways of perceiving black: first, as the "black light" reflected from "naturally black" objects; second, as "no light," as from "an invisible object surrounded by a visible patch"; third, as the result of seeing objects in "rare and scanty" light.[121] Legh's *Accedence of Armorie* interprets Aristotle's "black light" as "clearnes that is engendred of darkness."[122] Edward Herbert similarly emphasizes Aristotle's first sense and denies the two last, distinguishing between the color "black," which he treats as a positive term, and "dark," which is characterized by negation or absence. While most writers regard them as equivalent, he argues that the negative connotations of "dark" should not apply to blackness. If we see dimly, our own eyes, not blackness, are at fault.

Edward Herbert's "Another Sonnet to Black It Self" alludes paradoxically both to the optical theory that black contains all colors within itself, and to the common association of blackness with night, death, finality, and the absence of light:

Thou Black, wherein all colours are compos'd,
And unto which they all at last return,
Thou colour of the Sun where it doth burn,
And shadow, where it cools; in thee is clos'd
Whatever nature can, or hath dispos'd
In any other here; from thee do rise
Those tempers and complexions, which disclos'd,
As parts of thee, do work as mysteries,
Of that thy hidden power, when thou dost reign
The characters of fate shine in the Skies,
And tell us what the Heavens do ordain,
But when Earth's common light shines to our eyes
Thou so retir'st thy self, that thy disdain
All revelation unto Man denys. (D4r)

In "To Black it self," black is not merely composed of all colors, but creates them and can destroy them again. Black itself can reveal the truth of the universe but chooses to withdraw when "common light" (which Herbert dismissed contemptuously in "Black Beauty") blazes forth. The stars become heaven's messengers, writing "the characters of fate," more powerful than the sun in their ability to confer "tempers and complexions" on mortals.

Galileo's popular *Starry Messenger* (1610) uses the same metaphor of communication to convey the sense that the stars can communicate with earthly scientists just as foreign emissaries greet distant kings. Like Edward Herbert, Galileo finds a lyrical, infinite store of beauty in the heavenly bodies at night, a beauty visible only in darkness, not daylight.[123] Herbert's references to the stars as fate's "characters" seem at first to reinforce the association of physical light and spiritual illumination, but he interprets the stars not as reflecting the sun's glory but as "parts of" "black it self," parts of the "mysteries" of blackness. The stars cannot be interpreted without the black night as their backdrop. Light may write characters, but only blackness can confer meaning, when light sources are "disclos'd, / As parts of" it.

In fact, blackness confers not just a single meaning upon the characters of light but an "infinite" or infinity of possible signification, as Kim Hall points out.[124] In an earlier poem, "To her Hair," Edward Herbert wonders why human sight cannot comprehend blackness:

Is it, because past black, there is not found
A fix'd or horizontal bound?
And so as it doth terminate the white,
It may be said all colours to infold,
And in that kind to hold
Somewhat of infinite? (D3r)

In light of what we now know about Newtonian science, this image of black light separating and enfolding all colors might seem like a poetic reversal of Newton's famous prism experiment separating white light into the colors of the rainbow. But, as I have observed, Newton had not even conducted his experiments when Edward Herbert was writing, although the opposition between black and white light, and between black and the other colors, was widely debated. Herbert's blackness is both made up of different colors and opposed to them, bounding or controlling whiteness but enfolding other colors. Human eyes cannot understand the mystery of blackness because it is too rich, too multifarious, and too poetic; its unchanging qualities (as in "To Black it self") paradoxically enable it to contain every possible meaning and to stay the same. Paradoxically, it holds "somewhat of infinite": infinity cannot be bounded or divided into discrete quantities, so "somewhat" of it is impossible. For Edward Herbert, new poetry should do likewise: it should contain multitudes, and sing a song of itself.

Narrative of the Lyric: Shakespeare

Edward Herbert believes that old, whitening poetry is dead, and will not mourn for it. Shakespeare's sonnets also turn the conflict between the fair youth and the dark lady into the battle of old and new poetry, but unlike Herbert's poems, these sonnets refuse to come down on either side of the debate. Like the Song, the sonnets can be read both as a narrative and as a collection of lyrics; each sonnet, come to that, can be read as an individual narrative. The sonnets both praise and parody old poetry; moreover, they connect old and new poetry not only to historical time but also to modes of writing.

Sonnet 106 is almost anagogical in its expression. It argues that the poem's addressee exemplifies to perfection the "blazon of sweet beauty's best" (line 5) described in "beautiful old rhyme" (line 3), but that "their praises are but prophecies" (line 9) because until now, nobody has lived up to their accolades:

When in the chronicle of wasted time
I see descriptions of the fairest wights
And beauty making beautiful old rhyme
In praise of ladies dead and lovely knights,
Then in the blazon of sweet beauty's best,
Of hand, of foot, of lip, of eye, of brow,
I see their antique pen would have express'd
Even such a beauty as you master now.
So all their praises are but prophecies
Of this our time, all you prefiguring,
And for they look'd but with divining eyes,
They had not still enough your worth to sing;
For we which now behold these present days,
Have eyes to wonder, but lack tongues to praise.[125]

Helen Vendler takes lines 11 and 12 to mean that but for divine inspiration, old poets could not have guessed at the beauty of the young man.[126] But I agree with Stephen Booth that the ironic (and blasphemous) typological reference is more outrageous if the poet is claiming that even religious prophecy could not predict the rareness of his lover.[127] The fact that the line "they had not still enough your worth to sing" can exist as a semantic unit on its own makes it more forceful. Booth emends "still" (line 10) to "skill," objecting that if we read "still," "enough" has no referent. But it does not need one: "divining eyes" are not "enough" to sing the lover's worth. Maintaining "still" emphasizes the contrast between antique and new time. Now beauty has a "master" (line 8), but poetry has none; "these present days," we "Have eyes to wonder, but lack tongues to praise" (lines 13–14). This is the paradox of perfect beauty: it has only become incarnated now, but the beautiful old rhyme that poets would have used in the past to describe it now sounds "barren of new pride," as sonnet 76 complains, "far from variation or quick change" (lines 1–2). Alluding to the "fairest wights" (Sonnet 106, line 2) praised by old poetry employs a deliberate archaism to evoke "old rhyme" and "wasted time," but additionally puns on "fairest *whites*" to establish the opposition between one lover's red and white beauty and the other's blackness.

Sonnet 127 could almost be a response to the claims of "antique rhyme" in sonnet 106:

In the old age black was not counted fair,
Or if it were it bore not beauty's name.
But now is black beauty's successive heir,
And beauty slander'd with a bastard shame;
For since each hand hath put on nature's power,
Fairing the foul with art's false borrow'd face,
Sweet beauty hath no name, no holy bow'r,
But is profan'd, if not lives in disgrace.
Therefore my mistress' eyes are raven black,
Her eyes so suited, and they mourners seem
At such who, not born fair, no beauty lack,
Sland'ring creation with a false esteem.
Yet so they mourn becoming of their woe,
That every tongue says beauty should look so.

Booth notes that the alliteration in line 6 sounds artificial, made-up, like the false beauties the poet denounces. The religious diction of "prophan'd," "holy" and "creation" links the poem to 106 and its religious typology, while "old age" links back to the antique. There is nowhere for beauty to go; traditionally, beauty lives in a mistress's brow, but this lady is black, and all others are falsely fair, so beauty has been exiled from Eden. The lady's eyes are black in mourning for the loss of beauty (like the nymphs in Jonson's *Blackness*), but, as usual, the couplet reverses the sonnet's argument. In mourning for creation's slander, the lady has created a new kind of beauty and a new kind of paradoxical praise poetry: there were no "tongues to praise" the fair youth, but now "every tongue says beauty should look" black.

The "black beauty" sonnets of Edward Herbert and Shakespeare suggest that, far from reinforcing religious values, the poetic form of the Song allows it to effect not a Christian but a poetic conversion—from "old Poetry" or "ancient rhyme" to new. In contrast, the masques of Ben Jonson seem to effect what one critic has called "colonial transformations."[128] My final "Ethiopian history" investigates the early modern relationship between emerging national identities and residual theories of skin color through a comparison of three strange lands imagined as potential colonies by the Jacobean court masque—early modern Ethiopia, Ireland, and Virginia.

Chapter 3

Masquing Race

The question of whether blackness is the most significant mark of "race" in the early modern period continues to inspire critical debate. Most recently, the discussion has coalesced around the early modern Irish, and whether their status as a colonized and subjugated nation in the era affords them an identity as "racial" or "blackened." Erickson argues that it is of limited use to compare, say, the black Africans in Jonson's *Masque of Blackness* (*Blackness*, 1605) to the Irish in Jonson's *Irish Masque at Court* (*Irish*, 1613) because "the concept of blackness stands out as a separate category even at this point in historical time."[1] Moreover, he writes, such a comparison threatens to elide important distinctions and to overplay superficial commonalties. But Arthur Little counters that we can and should call the Irish "black" and describe them as a recognizable racial group, because they participate in an emergent discourse of hybridity and pollution that threatens to taint the English even as it acknowledges their own kinship with them (and here his argument parallels that of Andrew Murphy).[2] Little sees such a discourse at work in, for example, the blackening of Shakespeare's Antony through his association with Egypt.[3]

I am hesitant to concur either with Erickson's restriction of the term "black" to peoples tracing their ancestry to sub-Saharan Africa or with Little's expansion of it to include all those stained by the emergent British discourse of miscegenation. I would like instead to tease out a fuller comparison between the representation of black Africans and that of two groups that are not called "black" but that are nonetheless "othered"—the Irish, and the (Native) Americans—in that most imperial of forms, the court masque. On the one hand, I will argue, *Blackness* does produce an emergent discourse of what the masque itself calls "race" (*Blackness*, line 81), a word that it links overtly to residual mythologies of skin color, hierarchy and lineage. On the other, the English representation of the Irish kern does not conform to modern definitions of racialism, because it lacks the demonology of color.[4] But the accounts of John Derricke, Edmund Spenser, William Camden, and Geoffrey Holinshed as well as, finally, Jonson's *Irish Masque* do participate in a tribal xenophobia that opposes English and Irish, civilized and barbarous, man and beast, open and concealed, divine and devilish. These differences between *Irish* and *Blackness* imply, as we shall see, not a fundamentally barbarous African blackness versus a recuperable Irish whiteness, but the reverse: civilized, wealthy, convertible Africans and barbarous, impoverished, incorrigible Irish.[5]

I conclude with a reading of Chapman's *Memorable Masque* (*Memorable*, 1613), in which Virginian priests and princes lead the English to hidden gold and convert from revering the sun to worshiping King James, the "Briton Phoebus" (line 572).[6] Just as English explorers to Guiana, disappointed in their quest for the Spanish El Dorado or city of gold, substituted reports—what William West calls "verbal promissory notes"—for riches,[7] so Chapman replaces the complex relationships between Europeans and Native Americans in Virginia with emergent hierarchies of "race" imported from Britain. Although no groups in the masque are called "black," the appearance of the "olive" (line 64) Virginian princes each with "two Moors, attired like Indian slaves" (line 72) seems to point to an implicit hierarchy of labor that posits the mental substitution of "Indian slaves" taken in intertribal warfare or pressed by the Spanish for "Moors" captured by Englishmen.

Black Scotland

The central conceit of *Blackness* imagines that the beautiful black princesses of Ethiopia, daughters of the river god Niger, "scorched" (*Blackness*, line 150) by Phaëthon's fall (that is, by the sun's rays), want to turn white. Seeking fair skins, they receive a vision that tells them to travel to Britain, where a "temperate" sun (King James, in a conceit Jonson also uses in his *Gypsies Metamorphosed* [*GM*, 1621]), shines "refine[dly]" enough to bleach their skins and give them perfect beauty (*Blackness*, line 234). Many critics have read *Blackness* and Jonson's *Masque of Beauty* (*Beauty*, 1608) as two halves of a single work, treating *Blackness* as antimasque to *Beauty*.[8] Jonson's description of *Blackness* as the "first" of "The Queen's Masques" (*Blackness*, title), *Beauty*, the "second" (*Beauty*, title), would support this claim. But *Beauty* appears three years after *Blackness*, with different players, different names for the nymphs, and a different plot. Anne Cline Kelly argues that, after such a long gap, the court audience might not have perceived the two masques in relation to one another. She adds that Jonson's yoking of them in the 1608 quarto and then in the 1616 Folio represents his retroactive imposition of masque theory.[9] *Blackness* might have come to us as antimasque, but it first functioned as masque proper.

The queen commissioned the masque and generated its major conceit, and many critics have read the masque as Anna's coded challenge to the King's authority. Leeds Barroll's recent biography of Queen Anna observes that part of what scandalized the masque's first English audience was the fact that noblewomen, not just noblemen, were performing in public. Queen Anna and her ladies performed in the masque before the Spanish ambassador in blackface make-up, with gauzy garments that offended a number of spectators, such as Sir Dudley Carleton, who thought their make-up "lothsome" and their "Apparell rich . . . but too light and Curtizan-like for such great ones."[10] Hardin Aasand, Leeds Barroll, and Marion Wynne-Davies read the masque as a challenge to King James's patriarchal power, while Bernadette Andrea adds that this protofeminist challenge is itself entangled in emergent notions of racial inferiority.[11]

Indeed, I read the queen's recorded desire for herself and her ladies to be "blackamores at first" as a desire for a new coronation, an assertion of her power to surround herself with the kind of court and courtiers she desired in England and to rewrite a long-standing tradition of black faces in Scotland and at the Scottish court. This association is ancient; Fryer describes an African regiment stationed near Hadrian's Wall on the border of Roman Britain, and Paul Edwards speculates that a "blue" man mentioned in early Scottish accounts refers to a dark-skinned African. James IV of Scotland employed several black musicians in his court, including "Pete the Moor," an African musician who received a livery in 1503 and was granted freedom of movement forever.[12] Also at court lived the "More lasses," Ellen and Margaret, who had been rescued from slavery in Portugal to attend the queen and, it seems, were treated (like Peter) as courtiers, not slaves.[13]

King James VI of Scotland seems to have shared his grandfather James IV's interest in Africana.[14] His new bride, Anna of Denmark, was welcomed to Leith in Edinburgh in 1590 by an elaborate entertainment prominently featuring racial masquerade.[15] The Leith entertainment included many standard elements of such processions: the rehearsal of Anna's Danish genealogy, the history of all the queens of Scotland, and King James's lineage; the conferral of the keys to the city by a small boy who descended in a mechanical globe from the heavens; the distribution of sweets, sugar, wine, and wheat; speeches by mythological characters such as the Nine Muses and Virtue and her four daughters, each bearing her own attributes; a play of Solomon and Sheba, commemorating the typological significance of the union of James and Anna; the "weird" or prophecy; the expensive, elaborate "propine," or gift of the city, to Anna—a bejeweled letter "A."

But contemporary accounts are dominated by the whifflers or ushers who seem to have employed various types of the theatrical technology that Ian Smith calls, in a different context, "racial prosthesis" in order to make themselves "seeme Moores" or "lyk Moores."[16] A Danish account written for Christian IV insists that "an absolutely real and native black-amoor" led the whifflers into Leith.[17] We shall probably never know for sure, but it is tempting to imagine that the Danish account is accurate and that the young Afro-Scot who appeared as the chief whiffler at the queen's coronation would play a part in another royal pageant four years later. Ministers had commandeered a lion to pull a banquet table laden with rich and elaborate delicacies, on a huge chariot, to celebrate the birth of Prince Henry in 1594. Suddenly anxious lest the lion affright the ladies, the pageant's designers dismissed the brute and came up with an alternative. Having concealed a platform with wheels beneath the chariot, they employed an African man, dressed in gorgeous robes, to make as if he were pulling the chariot himself along a golden chain.[18]

Whether or not the man who led the whifflers into Leith was an African, contemporary accounts are fascinated by the ways that black-ness was performed during the procession. Two chronicles comment on the whifflers' black visors, and the burgh accounts refer both to black make-up "for painting of the young men," and to masks.[19] The Danish account specifies that the effect of blackness was created by a combina-tion of leathern or metal masks, body and face paint, sleeves, and unpainted skin.[20] The whifflers may have numbered as few as twenty-four, or as many as sixty, clothed in cloth-of-silver and white taffeta, draped with gold chains about their necks, legs, and arms, adorned with diamonds all over their bodies, and bearing white staffs to disperse the crowd.[21] They may also have worn gold tablets upon their foreheads, high headdresses like pyramids, and jewelry in their noses and mouths and around their thighs.[22]

The extent of Anna's collaboration in Jonson's masque remains nec-essarily mysterious, as Lewalski has suggested.[23] But *Blackness* condenses elements of the entire Edinburgh entertainment into a single perfor-mance. Carleton called *Blackness* the queen's "Maske . . . or rather her Pagent," a conflation that indicates the similarities between the two kinds of ceremony, civil procession and courtly performance, and implies that Jonson and Inigo Jones were blurring the lines of the form.[24] Both the Edinburgh entertainment and *Blackness* feature a negritude exaggerated by theatrical technology: make-up, costume, and moving scenery. Carle-ton complained not only about the ladies' costumes and skin color but also about the nature of the ladies' prosthetic color, that is, make-up, rather than vizards or sleeves. Barbour reads his complaint that the ladies presented "a Troop of lean-cheek'd Moors," a reference usually opaque to modern interpreters, as a comment upon the bare faces of Anna and her ladies, who had eschewed the customary theatrical masks.[25]

Symbolic equivalents to the stage manager's problem of physically representing blackness during the performance appear in the poetry of the masque, which offers multiple explanations for skin colors, light and dark. First, it alludes to a standard climatological explanation for dark skin as the effect of the sun's heat and rays, a theory that critics have called heliotropism; think of Shakespeare's Cleopatra, "with Phoebus' amorous pinches black" (*Ant.*, 1.5.28). In *Blackness*, the sun shows "signs of his fervent'st love" (line 118) by offering the daughters of Niger a love token, the gift of a suntan. This explanation is plausible within the diegesis because the ladies are after all daughters of a deity and might reasonably expect to be wooed by the sun god; Lady Mary Wroth uses a similar conceit in her Sonnet 22, "Like to the Indians," a text to which I shall return later.[26] The second explanation is classical. Niger complains that "brain-sicke" (*Blackness*, line 131) poets from England have set up a Western beauty myth, "of one Phaëton, that fired the world" (line 136), the familiar plot of blackness-as-disaster-movie. These mad poets, continues Niger, have made the ladies discontented with their own attractions by praising the "painted beauties other empires sprung" (line 133).

Niger's cutting reference to "painted beauties" is a theatrical in-joke that seems to equate blackness with unpainted or natural beauty, whiteness with artifice (a common tactic of the anticosmetic pamphleteers we shall encounter in the next section of this book, "Whiteness Visible"; they criticize face paint because it hides women's blushes and their natural skin color). It also alludes to the queen's own "painted beauty," her made-up face and body. The third explanation for skin color connects the first two explanations, heliotropic and classical, by linking climate theory with humoral wisdom, and classical catastrophe with mourning. The ladies are now "black with black despair" (*Blackness*, line 139), dark-skinned with an excess of black bile or melancholy; they might also be black from mourning what they now see as the tragic loss of their own beauty.

Like the Edinburgh "Moirs" in white taffeta and cloth-of-silver, the daughters of Niger rely upon contrast and opposition for aesthetic effect. Jonson characterizes his heroines as "Negroes . . . the blackest nation of the world" (*Blackness*, lines 15–16). Their beauty establishes itself as a series of contrasting displays of opulence, between their dark skins and their "orient pearl" (line 60), between the "obscure and cloudy night-piece" (lines 70–71) in the background and the huge mother-of-pearl shell, "glorious[ly]" illuminated (line 49), in which they first appeared. The early use of the word "race" in the masque emphasizes its relationship to skin color, by rhyming "beauteous race" with "black in face" (lines 81–82), a coupling of beauty and negritude undercut by the "but" that qualifies the description. Like the pearl on which they recline, the Daughters of Niger are "bright/ And full of life, and light" (lines 83–84).

The supposed contrast between blackness and beauty praises blackness for its form, an equation that becomes more explicit in the concluding couplet of the first song, which calls "that beauty best, / Which not the color, but the feature / Assures unto the creature" (lines 85–87). The praise of form echoes the paeans to the "black but comely" bride of the biblical Song of Songs. The word "assures" anticipates Jonson's other overarching theme of blackness—fixity, steadfastness, and constancy. Beauty, traditionally transitory and evanescent, can be "assure[d]" and made certain only if the fundamental structure is sound; "color" is superficial. Niger alludes to this association of blackness with permanence or conclusion when he argues "That, in their black, the perfectest beauty grows" (line 119). That is to say, white beauty is something literary, fictional, and contextual; black beauty is literal, true, and complete in itself.

Just as the entry into Edinburgh had concluded with the queen's gift from the city, the propine, incorporating her into its limits, so the masque seems to conclude with a parallel gift from the king, his "sciential" (line 226) conferral of whiteness, "to blanch an Ethiop, and revive a corse" (line 225). Floyd-Wilson brilliantly points out a witty legal pun on *blanch*, "the king's ability [in Scottish law] to transform a subject's material debt to the crown into a merely ceremonial display of allegiance," by excusing the subject from being *blackened* or *black-warded* into military service.[27] Since James insists that his reign is only the renewal of ancient Scottish sovereignty, this blanching/blackwarding pun, she argues, revives "the ancient unity of Scottish and English law" and resuscitates the dead corpse of old Scottish rule.[28]

And yet *Blackness* evokes this royal blanching, the incorporation of the queen's power into the king's, only to delay its enactment. Although the nymphs are commanded to dry their faces in the "sciential" light of the sun, the whitening spell in the text calls for the ladies to wash their faces in "rosmarine" (line 315) or sea foam by moonlight, not sunlight. This adaptation replaces the masculine sun with the feminine moon, just as the male god Oceanus is interrupted by Niger on the entry of moon goddess Aethiopia. The ladies end *Blackness* in the full glory of their make-up, resolutely unbleached by the rays of James's sun.

The person of the queen is thus inseparable from her blackened body as Daughter of Niger, keeping the barrier between black and white in suspension, through technologies of skin color, just as the origins of the Edinburgh whifflers in 1590 remain indistinct. The Danish account posits "a real and native blackamoor" as leader of a troop of blacked-up, vizarded, sleeved, and gowned Scotsmen, but the other accounts of the entertainment do not corroborate his presence, nor do they distinguish between feigned and natural blackness. And just as the whifflers, intended merely to introduce the entertainment proper, diverted the audience's and chroniclers' attention, so *Blackness* exceeds its potential (or intended?) place as antimasque. The queen and her ladies have thus been offered a gift or a blanching, but it is not certain whether, or when, they will choose to accept it.

Black Ireland?

Like *Blackness, Irish* employs the metaphor of *incorporation*, turning desires for the colonial domination of Africa (for Niger, independent god-king, to pay tribute to James's superior power) and for the political subordination of Ireland to England into fantasies of bodily metamorphosis, enforced somatic similitude. *Irish* ostensibly celebrated Frances Howard's second marriage, to the King's favorite, Robert Carr. As David Lindley has convincingly argued, however, the masque also intentionally misrepresents the errand of the Irish lords who were visiting James's court at the time in order to protest the king's interference in Irish politics. Lindley observes that the Irish parliament was in peril, and that the Catholic peers had refused to affirm the King's candidate as Speaker, resisting the religious uniformity that was being imposed upon them. "In subordinating Irish matters to the celebration of a marriage," therefore, "the masque so falsifies them that it is difficult to take the comment on either seriously."[29] More recently, James M. Smith suggests that the masque stages the humiliation of both the native Irish and the Anglo-Normans or "Old English," the twelfth-century English settlers who, to the horror of the Elizabethans, had "gone native" and taken up Irish names, language, customs, and costumes many generations before. Jonson mobilizes "a discourse of cultural degeneration" that conflated Native Irish and Old English societies in favor of James's "New English" colonizers.[30] Rebecca Ann Bach and Andrew Murphy independently read the masque alongside other Jonsonian colonial fantasies, particularly the antimasque *For the Honor of Wales* (1618), which similarly presents serious and pressing political concerns as comedy.

This willful transformation of the solemn into the farcical in the service of conquest and British unity persists throughout all elements of the masque: story, costume, diction, and music. The antimasque begins with four Irish footmen, sent by their masters to explain that the latter might have to dance naked at court because they have lost their rich clothing in the wild Irish seas on the way to the wedding. They wonder aloud which of the finely dressed courtiers can be the king:

Dennis: For chreeshes sake, phair ish te king? Phich ish he, an't be?
                     . . .
Dermock: Phair ish te King?
Donnell: Phich ish te king?
Dennis: Tat ish te king.
Dermock: Ish tat te king? got blesh him. (*Irish*, 4P2v)

Thus the antimasque articulates precisely, humorously, the question whose answer is dramatized in the masque proper; where *is* the king; which one *is* he? The *Irish Masque*, like *GM*, fantasizes a realm readily controlled and contained by James, a realm whose subjects recognize "phich ish te king" and bless him. Dermock's benediction performs a second coronation. The old king of independence is dead; long live the king. The exchange between the supposed footmen turns a genuine Irish disdain to acknowledge James as king—not only of England but of Ireland, not only of the state but also of the church—into a mark of Irish stupidity and intransigence. It is very clear "phich ish te king," given his position in the court, his costume, and his role in the masque (as chief observer). The masque assumes a genuine desire on the part of the visiting Irish lords to acknowledge James's authority, and turns the problem into one of simple identification. They didn't realize which one was the king, because of their slow wits; they had to come over to England and see for themselves which one was he. And this refashioning again replays the subordination of legitimate and serious Irish concerns to a scandalous and frivolous English wedding.

"[W]ee come from Ireland" is arguably the first intelligible line in the masque, rendered closer to standard English than previous lines (*Irish*, 4P3r). It is possibly another joke at the footmen's expense, given that the dialect has made it very clear where they "come from" hitherto. Smith convincingly argues that the footmen represent not autochthonous Irish rebellion but the so-called "Old English." The description of the Irish seas as "vild" enhances this identification; the footmen's association with the "vild" or wild indigenous Irish has degraded them, as it did the Anglo-Normans. The footmen represent Ireland as a whole and in its parts; one of the footmen has even been born "in te English payle," as Smith observes, and although the others come from all corners of Ireland, they nonetheless profess that they are "ty good shubshects" (*Irish*, 4P3r).

Linguistically, Jonson takes over a kind of Irish verbal *copia* that associates the Irish footmen with exaggeration and excess.[31] Falstaff-like, the footmen increase the number of loyal Irish subjects, the depth of that loyalty and its reach: James's "owne shubshects" become "very good shubshects," then, hyperbolically, parodically, "A great good many o' great goot shubshects" (4P3v). These multiple great good subjects begin by loving the king "heartily," but when this proves insufficient, they profess the will to suffer (go through "fire, ant vater") for him and finally even to "fight" for him (4P3v). This belligerent love encompasses not just James but also the members of an extended royal family: Queen Anna ("and for my mistresh tere"), the prince, who will inherit the English pale ("And my little mayshter"), and even the newly married Princess Elizabeth ("And te vfrow, ty daughter, that is in Tuchland" [4P3v]). The repeated "And" heaps up a sense of excess, even of endlessness.

But having established that "tey loue tee in Ireland" excessively (4P3v), the footmen suddenly begin a second round of hyperbole that rhetorically reverses the impression of the first in a kind of chiasmus. Dennis now asserts that James "has not a hundret tousand sush men" as the Irish lords in court that day, and the other footmen continue to assert the lords' uniqueness in a series of diminishing numbers: "nor forty," "not twenty," "not ten in all ti great Britayne" (4P3v). James's most loyal subjects are now exceptional rather than representative, and, what is more, they belong to his most rebellious province. Jonson is joking at James's expense, but the king has the last laugh: even if the footmen utter pure flattery, James remains all-powerful, his grasp on the Irish parliament unshaken.

Just as Jonson enlists Irish *copia* in the service of flattery in the anti-masque, so the masque proper takes over other local powers of resistance. Irish lords, supposedly naked beneath their traditional Irish mantles, dance silently to Irish harps. When the footmen begin to speak once more, they are "interrupted" by a verse-speaking "ciuill gentleman of the nation" (4P4r) who introduces an Irish Bard, also with a harp. When the Bard sings, the lords let fall their mantles, showing that they are not naked underneath but newly clothed, owing to James's beneficent royal gaze. The civil gentleman's speech models a kind of Orwellian double-think where everything means its opposite. James supposedly will free Ireland's "head from seruitude, her feete from fall, / Her fame from barbarisme, her state from want" (4P4v) when, as Bach points out, "it was actually the English wars that brought 'want' to Irish lands."[32]

The Bardic song that follows the Gentleman's verse speech offers not resistance to the English crown but submission. James M. Smith observes that Jonson's masque uses the Bard's charm to convert mantles into robes, bagpipes into "royal orchestration," rudeness into court-liness, "mispronunciation" into impeccable English, and prose into poetry, while James becomes the life-generating sun who makes barren land fertile, tempering "Irish unruliness" with "English husbandry" through "plantation."[33] Smith suggests that Jonson coopts the figure of the Irish poet or bard in order to neutralize the double threat that bards presented. First, bards lived in the courts of Irish lords, in a relationship uncomfortably analogous to that of Jonson with his patrons, and second, bards voiced resistance, and an unhappy awareness of their own planned obsolescence.[34] Jonson's transformation of the Irish bard extends, however, still further, taking over the form of the Irish imagination as well as its subject matter. Even calling the native poet a *bard*, rather than a *fili*, identifies him with an English tradition, rather than with the Irish Celts.[35] Jonson's Bard speaks in rhyming verse, yet his poetry is an alternative not to the footmen's prose but to the irregularly stressed syllabics of the *dán díreach*, a form of Irish poetry that flourished most richly during the seventeenth century, partly in response to the early modern English onslaughts on Ireland. Jonson's Bard maintains the Irish quatrains, but regulates the rhythm, just as he regularizes the footmen's deportment.

The Bard opens his song by prescribing obedience as the cure for all the Irish ailments, obedience in "heads and hearts: Obedience doth not well in parts" (*Irish*, 4P4r). James requires absolute submission, all or nothing, to his person and to his policies: physical obeisance in the "parts" of the body, head and heart, by bowing or kneeling, and political subordination in every "part" of the kingdom, including Ireland and its parliament. The Bard commands the lords, "your slough let fall," to shed their snakeskins, as if the lords have become a strange species in their own land, like the snakes supposedly cast out of Ireland by St. Patrick (4P4v). "[N]ew-borne creatures," the lords don new coats just as the meadows wear fresh "cullord coates" in the spring; their bare heads are covered just as the heads of the "naked trees" in the winter shoot "crisped" curls (4P4v).

Models for Jonson's staged humiliation of the Irish and Anglo-Irish lords appear in many English tracts on Ireland. English and Anglo-Irish tracts present the native Irish, writes Shuger, "as atavists of the northern European barbarians found in Caesar and Tacitus."[36] Travel narratives and ethnographies often compare the Irish with Africans, usually to the Africans' benefit. (Of course, such accounts are only dubiously positive; the praise of African, "heathen" or "Indian" people is usually uttered in a tone of patronizing surprise at finding such familiar behavior in such a distant setting.) Thomas Palmer's *How We May Make Our Trauailes Profitable* (1606) contrasts the table manners of Africans and Irish as part of a critique of the "barbarous" xenophobia of the English. English ethnic snobbery is misplaced, he argues, because all nations begin "barbarous[ly]" and are gradually reformed to "ciuilitie" through God. Although "English, Scottish, French, Italians, & Spanish . . . are the most reformed & courtlike people," and the English "may iustly chalenge preeminence," they are nonetheless "tainted with some blemish of barbarousnesse, the which of other heathen nations they might learne to reforme." In the case of the English, they should learn from "the African heathen Negros" and "the people of the East *India*" to be "charitable to strangers." "Those Dutchmen or our Irish" (you will note the casual possessive), on the other hand, need to learn from "the Turks and Indians, & other Barbarians of Africk" to be "more neat & cleanly."[37]

Jonson's *Irish Masque* shares with other early modern English representations of Ireland motifs of nudity, illiteracy or inarticulacy, dispersal, and reordering in the service of the king. Derricke's *The Image of Irelande: With A Discoverie of Woodkarne* (1581) distinguishes those born in Ireland from the "English race" (Plate II) before calling the Catholic Irish the "deuills sonnes" (Plate IV), "beastly beastes" (Plate IX) who "play . . . the Ape, by counterfetting Paul" (Plate III). If by chance some "ape" should escape from its "hen" and begin to act like a human being, Derricke argues, such a creature is more demonic than its "wildest kern" brethren, because it adds the sin of hypocrisy to its innately evil qualities.[38] These "pernicious members of Satan" engage in "apish toys," such as Papal Pardons, that summon "damned souls from hell."[39] Derricke even generates a separate origin for the Irish kern, with a complicated fable claiming that God (or the gods—he moves between a single, Protestant deity and a pagan pantheon) created the kerns to replace the poisonous vipers and beasts banished by St. Patrick. The Irish mantle is explained as the animal skin that can shelter the kern now that the other wild beasts have been eradicated. Even the "lamentabl[e]" tears of Rory Og, the rebel, become "brinish, salt, wolfish" drops, marks of his savagery and bestiality, rather than his universal, human, grief.[40]

Spenser's treatise in dialogue, *A View of the Present State of Ireland* (*View*, 1596; published 1633) likewise calls the Irish "the moste barbarous nacion in Christendome," "monstrouslye disguis[ed]," the women "Lewed" and the men "thevishe [thievish]."[41] The Irish mantle is a cover not only for immediate nudity but also for all kinds of devilish or lewd concealment: weapons, stolen objects, suckling children and so on, a complaint also made by writers of rogue literature about the capacious mantles of the Gypsies.[42] Many have noted that Spenser derives the Irish from a variety of sources, including the Spanish, the Scots, the Scythians, the Egyptians, and Moors or Africans.[43]

It would be easy to argue that the supposed Moorish or Carthaginian descent of the Irish is used to argue in favor of their subjugation. Spenser singles out the customs of extravagant mourning, or "heathenishe . . . intemperate . . . waylinges of theare dead" (*View*, 105), female unconventionality, or "theire weomens ridinge of the wronge side of the horse" (111), and their pantheism, or "supersticious rites" to the sun (108), as remnants of their African ancestry. Such a reading, however, ignores the context of Spenser's references to Africa, and the significant differences between the twenty or so manuscript copies of the *View* and its first published text, edited by James Ware in 1633.

A manuscript in the Public Record Office (*P*), usually considered to be an early, unrevised draft, contains a long section tracing the descent of the Irish from Moors or Africans, a derivation used to explain not their barbarism but their civility.[44] In fact, barbarism is a charge most often laid to their Scythian heritage, or to their claims of Spanish ancestry; Pliny declares that the "Cannibal Scythians . . . eat human bodies."[45] When Eudoxius, Spenser's naïve questioner, comments that Irish records are untrustworthy, because "havinge bene allwaies without Lettres," the Irish bards "forge and falsefye euerie thinge as they liste," Irenius, Spenser's native informant, retorts that "Irelande hathe had the vse of lettres verie ancientlye, and longe beefore Englande"—not from the Scythians or the Irish Scots, but "from the Africans" (*P*, 84). Indeed, St. Patrick himself, he claims, instructed the Saxons in literacy. The Irish, he continues, learned their letters not from the Scythians or the Irish Scots, "for theye were alwayes barbarous and without lettres," but "from the Africans, whoe were alwayes lettered and much resemblinge the Iryshe" (*P*, 85n.). *P* also includes elaborate etymologies deriving common Irish surnames from Carthaginian ones, "Maccartye" from "a Carthaginian" and "Odriscoll" from "Dursica . . . that valiently served . . . in the first Punicke warres" (*P*, 92n). (Such a connection appears in Irish texts, too. Jeoffry Keating's magisterial *History of Ireland* [1634; trans. 1723], his response to the publication of Spenser's *View*, recounts the conquest of Ireland by "Vagabond Africans, who . . . intirely subdued the old Inhabitants, and made them Tributaries.")[46]

Later redactions of the *View*, however, include few references to the supposed Moorish ancestry of the Irish, emphasizing instead an imagined Irish descent from the Scots, although these, being "barbarous," are not the source of Irish literacy. In Ware's edition, the generous Gauls, not the "foule heathenishe" "mores and Barbarians" who conquer the Spanish, bequeath knowledge of letters to the Irish (*View*, 91). Revised versions of the *View* prefer elaborate etymologies that connect Gallic, not African, names to Irish ones: "theare be of the olde Galles Certaine nacions yeat remayninge in Irelande which Retaine the olde denominacions of the Gaules As the menapij the Cancij the venti and others" (*View*, 93).

Why did the French genealogy supersede the African one? The *Variorum* editors argue that Ware must have had access to *P*, because certain passages are common to both versions and appear nowhere else. Spenser might have changed his mind about the ancestry of the Irish after reading William Camden's *Britannia* (1586), to which he directs us for more detailed Gallic/Irish genealogies, as Roland Smith argues.[47] It is tempting, however, to speculate that the Africans disappeared from the Irish genealogy because conflicting mythologies of color and ethnic prejudices came into collision. In the 1590s it might have seemed acceptable for "foul heathens" to have anticipated literacy in England and for both Scythians and Scots to be "barbarous." But by 1633, more than a generation after Spenser's death, and with an entrenched Scottish ruler, emergent myths of European civility required the removal of Spenser's "heathenish" but educated Africans in order to trace an unbroken lineage linking all the inhabitants of the barely-United Kingdom. (Although "Great Britain" supposedly came into existence with James's accession in 1603—uniting Scotland and England—the Act of Union was not brought into force until 1707.)

Let us now return to Erickson's contention that blackness comprises "a separate category at this point in historical time" from Irishness. One could argue that the fact that Spenser does not call his Irish-Africans "black" supports the belief that black is a radically different classification—that Spenser's Africans are really Carthaginians, somehow "whitened," and that that is why they are associated with letters and knowledge. But the confusion among "African," "Moor," and "Carthaginian" in these Spenserian texts points to fluid distinctions in this period. The absence of markers of skin tone suggests that their skin color is, if not irrelevant, certainly far less important than their religious affiliation ("heathenishe"), their national origin (Moors, Africans, Carthaginians) and their language and culture.

In both *Blackness* and *Irish*, skin figures as the ground of seemingly intractable physical differences that must and can be altered by royal authority. The shed skin in Jonson's masque marks the difference of the Irish lords from the English (or of the Old English from the New English, as Lindley and James M. Smith argue). Gerald of Wales comments that "these Irish people are both of an hoter and moisture [sic] nature than other nations, we may well conjecture. And this we gather by their wonderfull soft skinne."[48] Other writers associate soft skins with "blake More[s] born in Barbary," whose "skine is soft and there is nothing white but their teth and white of the eye."[49] The Queen Mother in *Lusts Dominion* (*LD*, c. 1599), a play I discuss at length in Chapter Five, proclaims her delight in disporting with the "soft skin'd Negro" Eleazar.[50]

Skin marks the natural variation of both the Irish and the Ethiopians, the boundaries between self and world, and between objects in the world. The transformation of the Irish will be worked through the glory of the king's "light" (*Irish*, 4P4v), a metaphor that recalls the earlier *Blackness*, in which the king's "light sciential" wields enough power "[T]o blanch an Ethiop, or revive a corse." One could argue that, in real life, the Ethiopians' black skins might seem to doom them to captivity in a way that the skins of the Irish—however soft, moist, or otherwise classified as different from those of the English—did not. But even the history of slavery and colonialism demonstrates further ambiguities, since (as I discuss in more detail in Chapter Eight) courts did not settle the legal status of African labor in Britain during the seventeenth century. Just as African servants might be snatched up in exchange for English prisoners during the 1590s, so Irish Catholics (especially under Oliver Cromwell) might be seized and taken to Bermuda to work on the new English plantations there.[51] In this period, blackness and slavery are not synonymous.

Native Americans, too, were enslaved in the New World. Their harsh treatment at the hands of the Spanish had been documented by Bartholomé de Las Casas in what would become the "Black Legend" of Spanish cruelty, his *Brevissima Relación de la Destruycion de las Indias* (1552), more familiarly known by the title of John Phillips's 1656 translation, *The Tears of the Indians* (1656).[52] Once rooted in Protestant folklore, the Black Legend instilled an ostensibly pious, if patronizing, desire on the part of the English to convert the Native Americans rather than to put them to labor in the silver mines—a motive used to justify English colonial expansion in Virginia in Chapman's *Memorable Masque*.

"Imitating Indian work"

Memorable Masque formed part of the elaborate celebrations commemorating the marriage of Princess Elizabeth to Frederick, Elector Palatine, and includes several "in-jokes" alluding to earlier entertainments. It combines the Jonsonian conceit of dark-skinned foreign travelers who are converted in some way by James's royal sun (as in *Blackness* and *GM*) with the Christian commercialism of Middleton's *Triumphs of Truth*, in which a Moorish king is likewise converted from sun worship to Christianity by English factors and travelers. Plutus, the god of wealth, complains that the barren rocks he sees have been left over from the previous night's performance (when they metamorphosed into ladies), but they produce instead Capriccio, a half-French, half-Swiss "man of wit" (*Memorable*, line 267) whose shape-shifting comprises only his prior incarnations as "a tailor, a man, a gentleman, a nobleman, a worthy man" (lines 273–74). Capriccio complains that he is forever, vainly, in search of riches, and introduces an antimasque of baboons, dressed as Neapolitans with great ruffs. Although impressed by the performance, Plutus banishes Capriccio, unpaid, and calls to Eunomia, the priestess of Honour, to celebrate the royal wedding.

The masque proper features the Phoebades, or Virginian sun priests, with "strange hoods of feathers" and "turbans, stuck with several coloured feathers" and flies' wings (lines 43–45), and Virginian princes, in "Indian habits" of cloth-of-silver with "a trail of gold, imitating Indian work" (line 48), wearing feathery coronets and "olive" masks (line 64). They are attended by horses and two Moors, "attired like Indian slaves" (line 72) and torch bearers, "likewise of the Indian garb . . . showfully garnished with several-hued feathers," each also with "his Moor" (lines 75–81). The Phoebades sing a hymn that opens a rich mine of gold to reveal the Virginian princes inside; during the next song, Eunomia converts the Virginians to the worship of "him to whom all Phoebus' beams belong" (line 553), "directing [the Phoebades' and princes'] observance to the King" (lines 524–25). After another antimasque, this time of the torch-bearers, the Phoebades sing a hymn to Frederick and Elizabeth (allegorized as Love and Beauty). An invocation to the "Virgin knights" to maintain their new-found "homage . . . To . . . our Briton Sun" concludes the masque (lines 642–43).

D. J. Gordon was the first to point out that, despite its topical conversion narrative, Chapman's masque conspicuously recalls not contemporary plantation pamphlets but Ralegh's *Discoverie of Guiana* (1595) in its focus on gold and its claim that the Virginians, like the Incas, worshiped the sun.[53] Gillies argues that, next to Shakespeare's treatment of the Virginia material in *The Tempest, Memorable* must have seemed quaintly "anachronistic—more Elizabethan than Jacobean,"[54] because it seems to ignore the contemporary eyewitness testimony that specifically debunked the myth of El Dorado. The Council of Virginia's *True Declaration* (1610), for example, blames those who "with dreames of mountaines of gold . . . created the Indians our implacable enemies by some violence they had offered," and piously adjoins: "let no man adore his golde as his God, not his Mammon as his Maker."[55] Lindley, however, reads the masque's belatedness as Chapman's deliberate endeavor, at his late patron Prince Henry's behest, to revive flagging interest in New World travel and to save Ralegh's career. As Mary Fuller observes, "Ralegh wrote the *Discoverie of Guiana* about not discovering Guiana"; the intangibility of his promised gold would eventually contribute to his execution.[56] Lindley suggests that Capriccio, capriciously rewarded by a sovereign and banished summarily for his "wit," is Chapman's figure for Ralegh, whose failure to find the hidden treasures of El Dorado the writer counters by imagining the Virginians willingly guiding the English to the fabled mountains of gold.[57]

I shall return to the questions of labor and gold at greater length in Chapter Eight. For now, let me note that even the princes' costumes, made of "cloth of silver with a trail of gold . . . imitating Indian work," weave a textile allegory of the colonial and economic currents that led Britain to African slavery in the New World. A currency crisis in Jacobean England and a huge trade deficit with the East fueled the hunger for gold and silver, treasures unavailable in Europe in the quantities needed. Bach and Shankar Raman have argued independently that the hunger for silver mined from the Americas by "the labor of enslaved populations" suggested that gold could more profitably be mined from Africa—and that ultimately Africans themselves could be exchanged for riches.[58] The "trail of gold" on a silver background led to Africa, as it were; the quest for a source of gold and labor free from Spanish influence "imitat[ed] Indian work" in the Spanish silver mines.

In addition to its discourses of patronage, wealth, and competition with Spain, *Memorable* outlines complex ethnic hierarchies and slippages, although no groups represented are called "black." Most intriguing for my purposes is the appearance of the "two Moors, attired like Indian slaves" who attend the magnificent horses of the Virginian princes (line 72). The torchbearers, too, "had every man his Moor, attending his horse" (lines 81–82). The princes wear "vizards of olive color, but pleasingly visaged; their hair black and large [long]" (line 64), an opposition between color and feature that recalls both Jonson's *Blackness* and its biblical source, the Song of Songs. The Moors, however, are undescribed except for their function, as grooms. Do they represent Moors, or Indians, within the world of the masque? If they are costumed as "Indian slaves," why specify that "Moors" play the part?

The Moorish grooms might evoke the association between the fine horses we still call "Arabian" and the Barbary coast. The Moroccan ambassador who visited London in 1637 led a retinue including "four horses . . . each . . . led by a black Moor."[59] More importantly, the presence of "Moors" might alert the audience to perceived differences in religious recuperability. Moors by definition are "Moorish" or Islamic, and have a religion of their own. The Virginians in contrast are pagan sun worshippers whose faith simply needs correction, gentle guidance to laud the sun that is James, God's representative on earth and in England, rather than the sun in the sky. Lady Mary Wroth associates sun veneration with both the perceived innocence and the "blackness" of "Indians, scorched with the sunne, / The sunn which they doe as theyr God adore," comparing sun worship to unrequited love. Both expressions of devotion cause pain to the worshiper (emotional injury to the lover, sunburn to the Indians).[60] Like Chapman's, Wroth's Indians are monotheistic, praising the sun alone with a devotion that thus parallels not only the speaker's to love and her lover but also that of Christians to the *son* of God. "To worship the sun was in some sense already to worship God," suggests Gordon, adducing "one of Chapman's favorite authors,"

Marsilio Ficino.[61] *Memorable*'s underlying assumption, like that of most Virginia narratives before the massacre of 1622, might be that, while warlike Mediterranean Moors like those we encountered in Chapter One would not convert peaceably, Virginian Indians would.[62]

But "Moor" and "Indian" are not straightforward oppositions. As we have seen, some early modern accounts (such as Spenser's *View*), associate sun worship, rather than Islam, with the African continent. The plot of Middleton's *Triumphs of Truth* hinges upon the conversion of a pantheistic, nature-worshiping king who identifies himself as "a Moore" (*TT*, 689). Chapman's Virginian sun priests wear the Islamic or Jewish "turban," as do, we may recall, the heliocentric Chariclea and Theagenes in Lisle's *Fair Ethiopian* (*Memorable*, line 44; *FE*, G4r). Chapman's masque thus conflates Moors and Native Americans regardless of their differing religions, colors, and convertibility—and regardless of what was known of both regions.

As I suggested in Chapter One, early modern Europeans perceived the Turks as an immediate threat, rather than as potential slaves. But Matar points out that, although there are no recorded instances of Muslim slavery in Elizabethan and Jacobean England, Drake encountered "Turks and Moors, who do menial service" in Cuba.[63] Matar suggests that a certain amount of wishful thinking infuses a common early modern analogy drawn between North African Moors and American Indians. Alden T. Vaughan has argued that early modern responses to the Native American partake of five principal residual paradigms: the "wild man," the "monster," the early modern Irishman, the ancient Briton, and the lost Jew, each becoming dominant during a different decade in sixteenth- and seventeenth-century Anglo/American relations.[64] Matar adds another paradigm: because they could control neither the religious beliefs nor the colonial expansion of the Turks, "English writers turned to the discourse of superimposition, whereby they yoked the defeated Indian to the undefeated Muslim."[65]

Within the diegesis of Chapman's masque, "Indian slaves" could allude to domestic slaves or prisoners, exchanged in tribal battles, or to Native Americans kidnapped and enslaved by the Spanish to work in the silver mines. Since the Moors serve the Virginian princes, the former seems more likely. At the same time, we are clearly meant to keep the possibility of Indian enslavement by the Spanish in mind. But we are also made aware of the extradiegetic knowledge that Moors were indeed enslaved alongside the Indians in the Spanish silver mines. We do not know whether Chapman's Moors were played by sub-Saharan Africans or other dark-skinned foreigners, in contrast to the chief masquers in their "Indian-like" feathers and masks (line 62). But even if they were played by white actors, the instruction that the Indian slaves be played by Moors points, I think, to an emergent racial logic. The masquers proper can present Indian princes and priests, but the Moors simultaneously figure commodities or tools (African servants or so-called black Moors compelled, like the man who replaced the lion at Prince Henry's coronation, to exhibit themselves), exotic and civilized tradesmen brought low in the New World (so-called white Moors, horsemen, or Turkish citizens), and actors (Africans playing Virginian Indians of a lower class than the supposed Virginian princes). Callaghan has argued influentially that the presence of Moors, Indians, and women in early modern private entertainments, but not upon the public stage, suggests that these groups are thought capable only of "exhibition," display for profit, rather than "mimesis," fictional representation. Deemed unable to appear other than themselves, those selves are then construed solely as objects for profit and exchange. Thus, she argues, the representation of raced and gendered Others upon the Renaissance stage itself produces "gender" and "race."[66]

Chapman's Moors do represent something other than themselves, but they do not, I think, engage in "mimesis," in Callaghan's terms, because their re-presentation as *slaves* is crucial. Early English accounts of the Virginia colony map European social hierarchies on to the Powhatan. A late seventeenth-century Virginia historian adds color consciousness to a discussion of Native American domestic servitude, writing of "People of a Rank inferior to the Commons, a Sort of Servants among them. These are call'd black Boys, and are attendant upon the Gentry, to do their servile Offices."[67] And John Smith famously refuses to allow the newly christened Rebecca Rolfe (formerly Pocahontas) to call him "father" in London although he had addressed her father Powhatan as "father" while in Virginia. Smith explains that Rebecca is a "king's daughter" while he himself is not noble.[68]

The masque therefore enlists what was known of tribal customs (Indian domestic slavery), competition with Spanish military prowess (mighty Turks and Moors reduced to captivity in the New World), and English social mores (rank outweighs pallor as a measure of human worth) in the service of a new model of colonial activity. Chapman's Moors can play Moors who are in turn playing Indian slaves in the masque because they represent themselves in their capacity as slaves; the king and courtiers can fantasize that anywhere in the world, under any regime, Moors both black and white can be enslaved. As part of the supposedly humanitarian English conquest, the Virginian princes' Indian slaves will be converted and liberated, replaced by Moors in a nationalist victory over both Turks and Spaniards.

The hymns and speeches that narrate the Phoebades' conversion maintain both the residual ethnic relativism that calls the Virginians "fair" when they demonstrate their willingness to convert to Christianity and the emergent racial binary that classifies them as "dark" in contrast to the English. Honour calls the Phoebades "the sun's fair priests" (line 502), an adjective echoed by the Phoebades themselves in relation to the "fair sun" (line 507). But this fair Virginia sun is outshone by Britain's "clear Phoebus" (line 522), the "clear sun" (line 555) that turns every other ruler to "clouds and dark effects of night" (line 558). Other suns are "Subject to cloudy darkenings" (line 570), but Honour's priest Eunomia can offer an alternative:

> our Briton Phoebus, whose bright sky
> Enlightened with a Christian piety,
> Is never subject to black Error's night,
> And hath already offered heaven's true light
> To your dark region. (lines 572–76)

Eunomia repeats the conversion already effected by Honour some fifty lines earlier in order to map the language of brightness and darkness on to Virginian territory. She overtly links exploration to religious prose-lytism, suggesting that King James is a sun that will literally "never set" (line 555), eclipsing "all other kings" (line 556).

The song of Love and Beauty, celebrating Frederick and Elizabeth as Eros and Panthaea, argues that the union removes any possible taint from both parties: "Love from Beauty did remove / Lightness, called her stain in love; / Beauty took from Love his blindness" (lines 609–11). The pun on "lightness," meaning both "lightness in color," and "frivolity," em-phasizes Beauty's pure whiteness through a seeming paradox. Light "stains" usually taint objects that are *darker* than themselves. But "light-ness" created a "stain" on Beauty because she is brighter and fairer than lightness itself. Conversely, the proverbial, shadowy blindfold of Love, like the Virginian "clouds" obscuring the "clearest" sun of King James (line 597), is removed by Beauty's white hand.

The hymn additionally picks up the diction of "race," brightness, and purity used earlier of King James, the "flaming day" to "poor dim stars" (line 562) and the "only relic of [his mother's] race" (line 564). In a mythopoeia of his own, Chapman imagines Elizabeth/Panthaea as the daughter not of the Briton Phoebus but of the god Pan upon a woman "Of the noblest race of man" (line 600). The "noblest race of man" could refer to Elizabeth's heritage as James's daughter and granddaughter of Mary, Queen of Scots; it could emphasize the nobility of Christian, moral, civilized humans in opposition to the "race" of pagan, amoral, wild gods such as Pan. But it also predicts what would become the divi-sion of humanity into races or groups corresponding to geographical regions and skin tones. Panthaea/Beauty offers a "white hand" (line

601) to Eros/Love and begets a "fair . . . birth" (line 604) that ushers in a new "golden world" (line 622) in what was formerly the "dark region" of "olive" Indians and "black Error."

Like Shakespeare's *Tempest*, the hymn echoes Montaigne's famous characterization of the "golden age" flourishing in the new world, with "no sort of traffic, no knowledge of letters, no science of numbers," "no care for any but common kinship," and "a great abundance of fish and flesh."[69] Shakespeare's Gonzalo utters hackneyed cliché, ripe for Antonio and Sebastian's mockery and the satire of the play itself (as Gillies has argued).[70] Chapman, instead, creates another fable in the service of empire:

Virtue then commixed her fire,
To which Bounty did aspire,
Innocence a crown conferring;
Mine and thine were then unused,
All things common, nought abused,
Freely earth her fruitage bearing.

Nought then was cared for that could fade,
And thus the golden world was made. (*Memorable*, lines 615–22)

Montaigne's Native Americans already inhabit a golden world; its bliss is in part the result of European absence. Chapman's golden world, in contrast, is licensed and forged by the colonial project, supported by "Virtue," "Bounty," and "Innocence." English and Christian "Virtue" add the fiery heat of conversion to the legendary "Bounty" of the New World; the "Innocence" of its pagan inhabitants "crown[s]" King James and his offspring rulers of a new commonwealth. The freely" fruiting earth offers her gifts as a consequence, not a precondition, of English exploration and conversion. The last song adds biblical precedent to Chapman's Virginian nostalgia. The Phoebades ask sleep to "Bring, in thy oily streams, / The milk and honey age" (lines 637–38), echoing the wanderings of the children of Israel until they find their Canaan, a land flowing with milk and honey (Num. 13:27).[71]

In *Memorable*, categories of labor, ethnicity, and religion serve instead of color as organizing principles; the Indian princes wear "olive" vizards, but the skin color of the Moors who attend their horses is not mentioned. This suggests that skin color in the early modern era is not in itself a fixed category, but one whose boundaries are in the process of solidifying. Early modern Africans are marked not only by differences from but also by important similarities to other "heathenishe" nations, to other "ancient" and "ethnic" civilizations, and even to the English themselves. As we saw in Chapter One, Thomas Lisle's verse translation of

Heliodorus's *Aithiopika* concludes with an implied cultural ranking of Ethiopian, Irish, and British. The Ethiopian festivities conclude with "A curle-head black-boy" singing to the "Irish harp," a skill imported from "th'Isle of Britain" (*FE*, Bbv). Here, the Ethiopians have acquired their skill from the Irish, who are in turn subservient to Great Britain. So while we cannot call the Irish or the Americans "black," neither can we claim that the word or the concept of "black" is somehow distinct or pure in any way in the English Renaissance. The process that should interest us as literary detectives and readers is the gradual disappearance of these residual similarities and the emergence of greater and greater differences. This process gradually made whiteness visible, unique, and contested—most tellingly, on the faces of women "made up" to look white, and in the erotic poetics of Marlowe, Shakespeare, and Barnfield.

II
Whiteness Visible

Chapter 4

Heroic Blushing

Jonson's Niger praises his daughters' beauty for its unchanging, "firm hues" (*Blackness*, line 117); unlike European ladies, his daughters have no need to resort to "paint" (line 133) to conceal their "passion" (line 129), no need to hide a face that grows pale or turns red. Niger reads his daughters' unchanging skins as signs of their constancy and virtue, but his confidence is unusual. More typical are the early modern moralists Thomas Wright and Nicholas Coeffeteau, who in *Passions of the Mind in General* (1601) and *A Table of Humane Passions* (1621) emphasize the importance of blushing and social shaming as a "ground whereupon Virtue may build" because it shows that the blushing subject is capable of experiencing remorse.[1] Wright and Coeffeteau assume a clear correspondence between the bodily language of blushing and an individual's state of mind; those who cannot be seen to blush, cannot experience shame. But while moral philosophy uses the visible blush to reinforce emergent hierarchies of power, gender, and nation, early modern fiction characterizes blushing through residual mythologies of color. Blushing thus marks not a fundamental bodily truth but its literary or hermeneutic breakdown.

In particular, *Hero and Leander* (*HL*) and *Hero and Leander Completed* (*HLC*) figure the fluctuating battle among red, white and black skin tones as the struggle of narrative poetry to give birth to lyric. Renaissance scholars confused the historical Musaeus, a fifth-century grammarian and the author of the Greek poem *Hero and Leander*, with "the Divine Musaeus" (*HL*, 1.52), the mysterious, magical poet-seer to whom Virgil refers as the first poet of all ("Musaeu[s] ante omnes") and who was known variously as Orpheus's tutor, father, or son.[2] Chapman calls the lovers "the first that ever Poet sung" (*HLC*, 6.292). Their "love-deaths" kill the narrative but give birth to poetry. For Marlowe, the price of this new art form is the demise of transparent meaning and the generation of Heroic blushes that create the possibility of literary interpretation. For Chapman, the price of poetry is the birth of Eronusis, or dissimulation. In *Hero and Leander* and *Hero and Leander Completed*, Heroic blushes defy the moral codes of gender and desire that they are supposed to regulate, replacing a narrative of shame with an erotic poetics of the body.

"Betweene Blushing and Shamefastnesse there is a certaine difference"

"Blush" is an Anglo-Saxon word, first defined as a shining forth, or a "glance."[3] The obsolete meaning of "blush" as "look" persists in the expression "at first blush." Today we associate blushes with embarrassment, an acutely personal sense of mental discomfort. But the word "embarrassment" did not enter the English language until 1676, when it means "a perplexing, intangling, hindering," and quickly moves from meaning material encumbrances, like debt, to evoking a state of mental discomfort and shyness.[4] Sixteenth- and seventeenth-century writers usually equate blushing with "shame." John Palsgrave gives us as synonyms "I blusshe, I waxe ashamed," and Wright and Coeffeteau use "blushing" interchangeably with both "shame" and "shamefastnesse." Coeffeteau uses the phrase, "wee blush" to mean "we feel shame" throughout his chapter "On Shamefastnesse."[5]

Can we distinguish between modern embarrassment and early modern shame? Christopher Ricks defines Victorian "embarrassment" as a mixture of bashfulness and modesty, and a blush as the body's embarrassed method of rendering private feelings legible to the outside world.[6] The physical inscription of psychic impressions, the ability to blush supposedly discriminates between the human and the animal, and between human beings of different races. Victorian thinkers were much exercised by the question of whether dark-skinned peoples blushed; Darwin concluded that they did, but invisibly.

Ricks defines what we might call the platonic or imaginary blush, the body's helplessly truthful, or "blushful," response to the world, but the early modern examples he analyzes indicate, at first blush, not bodily truth and poetic composure (what he calls "blushfulness") but textual ambiguity. Ricks suggests that Milton's blushing angel Raphael, who "glow'd / Celestial rosie red, Loves proper hue" (*Paradise Lost*, 8.619), when Adam interrupts him to ask whether spirits in Heaven love, as humans do, by "immediate touch" (8.617), blushes to emphasize the poet's point that physical, sexual activity is not shameful, but an essential part of both earthly and divine love (countering the popular notion that sexual intercourse did not exist before the Fall).[7] Raphael's blush, however, suggests that he is by no means certain of the innocence or chastity of angelic love. A blush is the best answer Raphael can offer; when pressed for specific details, he says, "let it suffice thee that thou know'st / Us happy" (8.620–21), and concludes his tale somewhat abruptly.

The angel blushes not from the happy remembrance of divinely sanctioned, physical love but because he is jolted into a sudden, shameful
awareness of sexual and social difference, just as his steady narrative is
hindered, embarrassed, by Adam's question.

Unlike the acutely individualistic self-consciousness of Victorian embarrassment, Renaissance shame stems from the conflict between a
social and a secret self. In *The Tremulous Private Body*, Francis Barker
defines early modern shame as "subjection," the condition of social differentiation, "a transition, effected over a long period of time, from [the
body as] a socially visible object to one which can no longer be seen."[8]
Early modern selfhood is created not by an internal self-awareness ("subjectivity"), but by "dependent membership" in a rigid, hierarchical order,
"by incorporation in the body politic which is the king's body in its
social form."[9] Shame and concealment usher in a newly internalized system of control; "This state knows no limits because in theory nothing is
outside its domain."[10]

Coeffeteau's account of blushing directly links bodily shame to the
breakdown of rank: "it is a shame to begge for favour or to borrow
money of an inferiour . . . and wee cannot but blush to require money of
him in lone, who hath first demanded it of us."[11] We blush at unexpected
reversals: when something unfortunate happens to us "in the view of" a
patron; when our families catch us in an error that we "had alwaies cun-
ningly concealed," and from nervousness before public speaking.[12] In
another instance,

when as we are to speake before a person of eminent quality, of exquisite knowledge, or of exact judgement, wee blush and are amazed, by reason of the great
respect wee have of him; which makes us feare to fayle before him, and this feare
fills us with Shame, and makes us blush.[13]

In all these examples the blushing individual has experienced or anticipates a loss of face. Asking for money from a social inferior, or from
someone who has previously been in one's debt, transforms one from a
patron into a dependent; blushes maintain a social hierarchy. Being
caught out by one's family threatens one's position in a domestic realm
whose insistence on rank parallels the outside world. The "person of
eminent quality" in the audience reminds us how petty our own achieve-
ments and abilities appear, compared to his "exquisite knowledge." In
this light we can reread and contrast two of Ricks's literary examples
historically: Podsnap's Young Person in Dickens's *Our Mutual Friend*
blushes to herself as she reads a novel, but Marlowe's Hero blushes when
daylight betrays her shining ("blushing") body to Leander's gaze. While
the nineteenth-century reader has completely internalized the sense
of an observer, of being watched, and blushes as if in guilt, the early

modern blush requires the physical presence of another to experience a sense of social shaming.[14]

Thomas Rogers's *The Anatomie of the Minde* (1576) might seem to offer an early modern embarrassment in "Shamefastness," a bashful reluctance about sexual matters. Where shame is "the fear . . . of a guiltye conscience," "Shamefastness" is that "of honest thinges."[15] But shamefastness differs from modern embarrassment in its insistence that blushing is more important as an exemplary sign to observers than as an indication of the inner state of the blushing person. Consider the didactic purpose of Guyon's encounter with Shamefastnesse, who "too oft . . . chaung'd her natiue hew," in the Castle of Alma (*FQ*, 2.9.40–44). Upon asking why she is so "abasht"—whether he has been "too bold," or whether her manners are merely "vncouth," Guyon receives Alma's response:

> Why wonder yee
> Faire Sir at that, which ye so much embrace?
> She is the fountaine of your modestee;
> You shamefast are, but *Shamefastnesse* it selfe is shee.
>
> Thereat the Elfe did blush in priuitee,
> And turnd his face away; but she the same
> Dissembled faire, and faynd to ouersee.

Shamefastness "ouersee[s]" blushing in that she controls and supervises Guyon's embarrassment by pretending to overlook it. Shamefastnessness is publicly "abasht," but Guyon secretly "blush[es]," an implicit distinction defined explicitly by Rogers: "Blushing commonly is judged to be a feare comming of a guiltye conscience: but Shamefastnesse of honest thinges."[16] But the distinction between "the fear . . . of a guiltye conscience" and "Shamefastness of honest thinges" breaks down as soon as Rogers makes it, because both the outward sign, and the *meaning* of the blush (regardless of their origins) remain the same, "a cer[t]aine natural Blushing, by which we are afraid, and ashamed to commit anything which is not honest."[17]

Blushing transforms even bad intentions into goodly acts, individual emotion into social order. Wright asserts that "shame" itself is morally neutral, neither good nor bad. Aristotle numbers shamefastness among the virtues not because it is a "true" virtue (it cannot be a true virtue, says Wright, because it is present in children) "but because it is the seed of virtue, or a spur to virtue, or a bridle from Vice" (82). Blushing, on the other hand, is a force for good, because guilty parties under suspicion, "if they be . . . of an honest behaviour and yet not much grounded in virtue, they blush . . . being afraid lest in the face the fault should be discovered" (82). The offender blushes neither from guilt, nor from remorse, nor from being caught in the act: paradoxically, he blushes

from fear of being seen to blush. Appearance matters more than intention. The fear of public shame, rather than the personal consciousness
of guilt, determines social morality.

Blushes are signs of social and sexual difference, but they are also
signs of national origin. Black Ethiopians and tawny Indians were thought
to be unable to blush and therefore to experience shame. Wright finds a
"natural inclination to virtue and honesty" prevalent in the fair-skinned
inhabitants of Northern climes as opposed to Southerners from hot-
ter lands, claiming that "The very blushing also of our people showeth a
better ground whereupon Virtue may build than certain brazen faces,
who never change themselves although they commit, yea, and be depre-
hended in enormous crimes" (82). Darwin would conclude nearly three
hundred years later that Ethiopians and other dark-skinned races did
indeed blush, but the sixteenth-century moral philosophers make no
such concession: an invisible blush is equivalent to a nonexistent one. In
so doing, they ignore other ways of reading bodies, faces, and emotions
in favor of ethnic prejudice.

By way of comparison, let us turn to Richard Jobson's *Golden Trade*
(1623), a text we shall explore in more detail in Chapter Eight. In the
absence of the blush, Jobson does not conclude that Africans are shame-
less but instead devises alternative methods of diagnosing shame in the
"Tawny Fulbie [Fulani]."[18] In praising the cleanliness of Fulani dairy-
women, he observes that if "by any mischance, there had beene a mote,
or haire [in the milk], which you had shewed vnto her, she would haue
seemed to blush, in defence of her cleanely meaning" (F2v). Furthermore,
"the modesty of a new married woman" prevents a bride from leaving the
house "for certaine Moones." When she finally makes an appearance,

she doth not shew her open face, but with a cloth cast ouer her head, couers
all but one eye, after the maner of the Spanish vaile, obseruing herein a shamefast modestie, not to be looked for, among such a kinde of blacke or barbarous
people. (H4v)

Aware of the convention that "blacke" people are "barbarous" or savage,
because they lack "shamefast modestie," Jobson looks to the women's
clothing and behavior for cues.[19] That Jobson is responding to a common charge against dark-skinned Africans is clear from references in
Shakespeare's *Titus Andronicus* and the other early modern plays that I
discuss in my next chapter. We may also recall the trajectory of somatic
markers for modesty in the versions of Heliodorus's *Aithiopika*. The universal (and universally visible) bodily functions of perspiration and
weeping in the Greek novel and in Underdowne's translation are replaced in Lisle and Gough by a feature thought to be specific to the
light-skinned and characteristic of the English nation—the blush.

Wright asserts that the structure of blushing reinforces social order, but, as we shall see, an Elizabethan blush can mark not a moment of personal truth but a moment of social, sexual, and subjective chaos. Coeffeteau regards shame or blushing as the consequence of "suspence" or "amazement."[20] "Amazement" in the sixteenth century refers to an astonishment that stems from uncertainty and powerlessness in the face of doubt, as if one wanders in "a maze." An amazed blush marks irresolution and delay. The early modern self blushes when faced with the breakdown, or the potential collapse, of social and sexual difference, because personal identity itself then becomes formless and irresolute. As we shall see, the Elizabethan erotic verse of Marlowe and Chapman compares a viewer's inability to explain away the color of skin to the productive logic of poetry. A blush in these texts becomes poetic not because it demonstrates an inescapable bodily honesty but because it is a point at which clarity, morality, and truth collapse.

"Since Heroes time, hath halfe the world beene blacke"

Marlowe's *Hero and Leander,* like Shakespeare's *Venus and Adonis,* became one of the models for Elizabethan erotic narrative poetry. Although it was entered in the Stationers' Register in 1593 and published five years later, it seems likely that the poem had circulated in manuscript before this. It does not, of course, recount the full myth; Marlowe anticipates Leander's final death by drowning with a narrowly escaped erotic death at the hands of the sea god himself, and Hero's only death, likewise, is a sexual one. It was Chapman who took upon himself the arguably much less attractive task of killing off the lovers; he was also the first to divide Marlowe's poem into "Sestiads."[21] In Chapman's continuation, the glassy goddess Ceremonie gently chides Leander for consummating the love affair without the rites of marriage, while a furious Venus refuses Hero's remorseful sacrifice and spitefully creates (for the very first time, according to Chapman's mythopoeia) Eronusis, the spirit of female dissimulation. One of Venus's swans intercedes on Hero's behalf, but the combination of Venus's anger and Neptune's ineptitude (he tries to wound the Fate who is spinning Leander's thread, but succeeds only in cutting the thread itself) drowns Leander in the Hellespont as he tries to swim across to Hero. When Hero discovers his corpse her heart bursts with grief, and Neptune changes them into "thistle-warps" (goldfinches), birds who fly always in couples.

Published in the same year, Marlowe's and Chapman's poems when read alongside each other employ the blush as a metaphor for literary or multiple interpretation. Both Marlowe and Chapman establish the lovers', and in particular, Hero's, red and white beauty in opposition to the mysterious, inchoate darkness of black skin or clothes. But while blushing in Marlowe's text heralds the frank expression of innocence (although there are many hints of the story's tragic outcome), in Chapman's it is the inevitable precursor of a blackness associated with dissembling. Marlowe eroticizes both lovers equally, while Chapman concentrates on Hero, who suffers disproportionately for her offense. Critics have read Chapman's continuation as a moralistic sentence of death upon Marlowe's playful lovers, but Chapman's sympathetic narrator excuses his moralizing, like Venus's and Ceremonie's demands, on the grounds that the exigencies of narrative poetry demand that he adhere to the classical myth. After the lovers' death, narrative poetry gives way to lyric, and the lovers can stay alive forever as singing thistle-warps. If Marlowe depicts the transparent and innocent desire of young lovers, where the blush serves as love's cue, then Chapman paints the blush as a fallen symbol in a guilty world, too easily imitated, no longer clear and limpid as Ceremonie.

Marlowe's lovers are perfect composites of red and white; even Hero's silvery buskins blush (*HL*, 1.32), while Leander combines "the white of Pelops shoulder" (1.65) with "orient cheekes and lippes" (1.73). "Orient" is usually glossed as "ruby-red," but it is also a pun. Leander swims the Hellespont, the conventional division between Asia and Europe. According to early modern biblical exegesis, when the three sons of Noah divided up the world between them, Japhet ruled Europe, Shem governed Asia and Cham colonized Africa. Japhet and Shem were supposed to have parted ways at the Hellespont.[22] This narrow and rockily treacherous strait figures in Elizabethan and Jacobean drama not just as a barrier between lovers but also as a metaphor for the spouse who separates a European lady and a Moor. In *Lusts Dominion*, the Queen Mother tells Eleazar that his wife Maria forms "th' Hellespont [that] divides my love and me" (*LD*, C7r). John Mason's "lascivious queen" Timoclea, believing that she has killed her husband, joyfully tells her Turkish lover Muleassar, "[n]ow ther's no Hellespont betwixt our loves."[23] As Leander lives in Abidus, on the Asian side, he is therefore "orient" in more ways than one. The word itself alludes to both red and white: "orient" pearls are translucent and shimmering, but orient rubies are bright red like the Eastern dawn.[24]

Hero is so fair that even the sun will not "burne or parch" her (*HL*, 1.28), although she walks unbonneted and ungloved; her persistent whiteness marks her out as one who remains honest, untouched by the darkening rays of the sun of unchastity. Moreover, the "solemne feast" (1.93) held on the night she meets Leander turns into an inversion of the myth of Phaëthon. The revelers shine like burning stars, as though "another Phaëthon had got / The guidance of the sun's rich chariot"

(1.101–2), but instead of shriveling in the fiery heat of the sun's rays, which also burn black the Ethiopians, the earth turns into a heaven. This inverted myth raises the lovers above the gods themselves, just as Hero and Leander walk upon "Venus glasse" (1.142), the pavement decorated, like Arachne's web, with the amorous escapades of the gods; they are physically, as well as figuratively, above divine love. Later Chapman will use a similar mythopoeia to invert the positions of the supposedly mortal Hero and her supposedly divine mistress.[25] The celestial allusions play upon Hero's name: in Greek mythology, the "heroes," who ruled the earth during the Fourth Age, were a race between angels ("daimones") and men ("anthropoi").[26]

Hero's status as girl-angel gives her fair beauty the power to control even the onset of darkness:

So lovely faire was Hero, Venus Nun,
As nature wept, thinking she was undone;
Because she tooke more from her then she left,
And of such wondrous beautie her bereft:
Therefore in signe her treasure suffred wracke,
Since Heroes time, hath halfe the world beene blacke. (*HL*, 1.45–50)

Half the world enjoys daylight while the other half is shrouded in darkness, mourning both for Hero's existence, which used up Nature's store of beauty, and for her death, which then "bereft" Nature of Hero herself. L. C. Martin compares the lines to Ovid's account of Phaëthon's disastrous, blackening chariot ride;[27] half the world's population, below the equator, is dark-skinned. We can add this Marlovian myth to our collection of fables on the origins of black skin, fables that variously attribute negritude to the heat of the sun, to Phaëthon's fall, to the excessive use of cosmetics, to a hereditary taint from the mark of Cain. ("Blacke" can, of course, refer to dark hair during the period, but in the context of the geographical imagery throughout Marlowe's poem it seems more likely that he is referring to skin color and to a catastrophe with global consequences rather than to an abundance of brunettes in Britain.) Half the world is black "in signe" of Nature's loss; just as mourners wear dark clothing as a token of their bereavement, so the inhabitants of the torrid zone fix their mourning in their faces and their hair. This ostensible meaning is the familiar conceit of fundamentally white human faces masked or covered by blackness. But the lines also imply the opposite, that the primary condition of human beings is "blacke," not white, because Nature now lacks the white "treasure" necessary to finish the task of bleaching the world.

Whiteness becomes "Nature's treasure," gilding initially dark skin or hair, like the white pancake make-up that Elizabethan beauties wore upon their faces, bosoms, and hands. Certainly this is the opinion put forward by poets who praise women for retaining an unmade-up, "black" or natural face rather than "fairing the foul with art's false borrowed face," donning a falsely painted white and red one.[28] Elizabethan cosmetics were often literally "treasure," containing valuable Eastern minerals such as ivory, vermilion, or henna. Female beauty is compared to "treasure" throughout Marlowe's poem. The milkmaid whom Mercury woos bears a rich "silver" face (*HL*, 1.396). Hero's red and white beauty shines like diamonds over glass (1.214), like a gold mine (1.232), like golden strings that must be tuned lest they jar (1.229–30), like a magnificent brass vessel (1.231), like gold that is for use (1.233–34). In hoarding her virginity, says Leander, she becomes like "the poore rich man that starves himselfe, / In heaping up a masse of drossie pelfe" (1.243–44). When Leander arrives exhausted at Hero's turret, he finds his way by the light of her white limbs gleaming through the dim night: "rich jewels in the darke are soonest spide" (2.240). Leander's topographical discoveries on Hero's body continue the metaphor of darkness into light: her "silver body" (2.263) lights the dark sea between them and her breast becomes an "yv'rie mount" (2.273) or a "globe" (2.275) to be mapped and charted by the keen surveyor.

Marlowe returns again and again to the paradoxical relationship of fair beauty and black darkness: beauty illuminates the night, but its wealth can only be enjoyed after sunset, when "night . . . / Heav'd up her head, and halfe the world upon, / Breath'd darkenesse forth (darke night is Cupids day)" (*HL*, 1.189–91). The lines echo the earlier "Since Heroes time, hath halfe the world beene blacke," giving Hero's shining face the power to turn day into night, and vice versa. The inverted conceit of night as Cupid's day is a familiar feature of minor epic.[29] The image of half the world in darkness that appears immediately before it also indirectly alludes to the account of the creation in Genesis and the separation of light from darkness. The lovers illuminate their dark half of the world with their blushes, "sparkes of living fire" (1.188) in the air, "Loves holy fire" itself (1.193). Blushing, like light, and like sexual union, inspires creation. Leander's blushes are usually fiery and encourage the more bashful Hero to express her own sentiments: Hero sees the "fire that from [Leander's] count'nance blazed" (1.164) and is "strooke, / Such force and vertue hath an amorous looke" (1.165–66). Instead of being cooled by Hero's blushes, Leander begins to argue in favor of consummating their love, insisting that virginity has no real existence:

This idoll which you terme Virginitie,
Is neither essence, subject to the eie,
No, nor to any one exterior sence,
Nor hath it any place of residence,

Nor is't of earth or mold celestiall,
Or capable of any forme at all. (*HL*, 1.269–74)

Virginity is formless, empty, and absent, unlike sexual union, which confers shape and presence. Women, like wax, "receave perfection" (1.268)
through "mens impression" (1.266), rather than through the preservation of virginity; Leander's ideal, his "mold celestiall," as Myron Turner
suggests, is the perfect Platonic hermaphrodite, both sexes united in
one to make up the sum of the other's imperfections.[30] Hero's blushes
mark a virgin state of irresolution or suspense, the deferral of perfect
unity.

Leander's sexual politics, however, are not his narrator's: in fact
Marlowe characterizes Leander rather than Hero as apt to "receave perfection" through "mens impression." It is Leander whose delicate verte-
brae recall the fingerprints of some strange god, Leander whose "white
. . . bellie" (*HL*, 1.66) the narrator himself can recall, and Leander who
becomes subject to the erotic gaze of Neptune and the "barbarous
Thratian[s]" (1.81) who "swore he was a maid in man's attire" (1.83).
Leander's body is organic, ready for consumption, "even as delicious
meat is to the tast" (1.63).[31] In contrast, Hero's body is artificial and
inaccessible. The long parallel descriptions of the lovers at the beginning of the poem contrast Hero's clothing and Leander's skin. Critical
opinion finds the description of Hero to be "a parody of art," "a travesty
on the whole tradition."[32] Such moments of ekphrasis delay narrative
and sexual progress, so that, as Braden writes, "Hero's very impressive-
ness as a sexual object is part of what limits her functioning as a sexual
agent."[33] Hero remains untouched, as in a glass case, unpenetrated by
the rays of the sun, by the stings of bees, or by the gods themselves. She
represents the final triumph of art over Nature, form over matter; in this
way the poet reverses the expected association of femininity with matter
and impressionability and masculinity with the imposition of firm form.
The embedded episode of Mercury and the milkmaid seems to displace
the divine erotic encounter Hero has not had and to render women's
bodies penetrable again. Like Hero, however, the nubile milkmaid is a
creature whose "faire vermilion . . . and silver tincture" (*HL*, 1.395–96)
suggests she is an artifact rather than part of the natural world. Only
Leander is soft, consumable, and seemingly available sexually.

These reversals highlight the erotic comedy of hermeneutics: "even as
an Index to a booke, / So to his mind was yoong Leanders looke," comments the narrator (2.129–30). But if Leander's face is like a book, it is
written in a language that not everyone can understand. Neptune, for
one, cannot read Leander's face or body: "The god seeing [Leander]
with pittie to be moved, / Thereon concluded that he was beloved"

(2.219–20). Leander's "colour went and came" (2.214) with a natural, helpless response, like the "fresh bleeding wound" (2.213) of Neptune to which it is implicitly compared, but it is nonetheless unfavorable to Neptune's cause. Both Hero and Leander become the subject of intense sexual scrutiny and neither can resist blushing beneath it; Leander, albeit unwittingly, deceives Neptune.

Leander's encounter with Neptune is one of several moments that prevent Hero's association with the world of artifice from becoming a conventional dismissal of women as cunning and hypocritical, as in the anticosmetic tracts discussed in my next chapter. The workmanship of Hero's clothing deceives "both man and beast" (1.20), but neither is any the worse for the experience; in fact, this tempering of art with nature replaces the sexual perfection or impression that Leander craves. Braden again suggests that "the sexual impulse threatens to end, not in orgiastic release, but merely in its own elaboration."[34] If narrative ekphrasis delays erotic activity, it also turns sex into art. Ultimately the only escape from ekphrastic elaboration to erotic energy comes through the language of the body, which interrupts the measured line of Marlowe's verse and Hero's speeches. The narrator seems to criticize Hero for her calculated coyness (she drops her "painted fanne" [HL, 2.11] only to find that Leander, "being a novice" [2.13] does not understand what he is supposed to do and sends her a letter instead) but then reveals that the language of passion is uncalculated and corporeal. Despite Hero's attempts at reserve, the words "come thither"

> unawares . . . from her slipt,
> And sodainly her former colour chang'd,
> And here and there her eies through anger rang'd.
> And like a planet, mooving severall waies,
> At one selfe instant, she poore soule assaies,
> Loving, not to love at all, and everie part
> Strove to resist the motions of her hart. (HL, 1.358–64)

Hero's own body belies her would-be archness; "come thither" falls from her lips involuntarily, just as her face flushes. Her utterance falls "at one selfe instant," a narrative and spoken moment at which her true "selfe" shines through—but only for an "instant." She is "mooving severall waies," but the blush is a reliable indicator of what she really wants to do. Blushes form the language of Marlowe's lovers, and only they two can interpret each other's. Those who try to translate them, like Neptune, run the risk of misunderstanding, but the fault lies in the viewer's gaze rather than the lovers' blush.

Hero's climactic blush at the end of Marlowe's poem combines a sense of radiant glory, like the "twilight breake . . . from an orient cloud"

(2.319–320), with disturbing hints of the tragedy that is to follow; the luminous dawn that Hero creates proves to be but a "false morne" (2.321). Chapman picks up these hints from Marlowe's text. In a sense his whole poem explicates Marlowe's line, "Heroes ruddie cheeke, Hero betrayd" (*HL*, 2.323), offering us a paradoxical blush that is simultaneously the incarnation of love itself and a treacherous sign that leads lovers into untimely dalliance in order to reveal them to the avenging gods.[35]

"red and black ensignes of death and ruth"

Marlowe suggests that both men and women become subject to the erotic comedy of misreading and that this involuntary deception is an essential aspect of learning the language of love. *Hero and Leander Completed* asserts similar loving paradoxes of love through neoplatonic theories of color and light. Although Chapman's literal translation of Musaeus, *The Divine Poem of Musaeus* (*DP*), was not published until 1616, "it seems likely from the subject and from the use of couplets that he had translated it before completing *Hero and Leander*."[36] Chapman attempts a rendering that is both literal and literary, yet there is one point at which the talented translator appears to be stymied, in an early description of Hero:

All over her she blush't; which (putting on
Her white Robe, reaching to her Ankles) shone,
(While she in passing, did her feete dispose)
As she had wholly bene a mooving Rose. (*DP*, lines 88–91)

Chapman provides us with a long, extenuating footnote, giving us both his Greek and Latin sources, the Latin text reading: "Euntis vero / Etiam Rosae candidam (indutae) tunicam sub talis splendebant puellae," literally, "And indeed even the very roses underneath the girl's white robe would shine out below her ankles." A modern translator gives, "as she moved roses / Flashed also from round the ankles of the white-robed girl."[37] Chapman defends his freer rendition on the grounds that the literal sense is ridiculous:

To understand which, that her white weede was al underlin'd with Roses, & that they shin'd out of it as shee went, is passing poore and absurd: and as grosse to have her stuck all over with Roses. And therefore . . . she seem'd (blushing all over her White Robe, even below her Ankles, as she went) a moving Rose. (*DP*, Note g)

Chapman's translation is more polished than a doggedly literal one could be, but, as he acknowledges, something is lost, some "elegancie, . . .

strange and hard to conceive" (*DP*, Note g). Chapman's lines render the fact of Hero's luminous blush, but he has lost the original's sense of the transparency of Hero's skin, the legibility of her body, and the power of her blushes to make themselves visible not just underneath but *through* her clothing.

Human beings in Chapman's continuation of Marlowe's poem are opaque or impenetrable, but the narrator envisions the goddess Ceremonie as "Cleere and transparent as the purest glasse" (*HLC*, 3.118). Her diaphanous body emphasizes her argument that private words and public deed, soulful vow and bodily action, should be simultaneous, immediate, and publicly displayed. "Glasse" of course refers both to a window and to a mirror; glassy Ceremonie provides us with a mirror of our own actions and also offers a window to observers. She is an antidote to "Venus' glasse" in Marlowe's poem; instead of the heady riots of the lustful gods, she reflects tempered, moderate, and above all highly social ritual. She is "all presented to the sence" (*HLC*, 3.119): what you see is what you get. Moreover, she remarks, "substance without rites" (3.147) (a phrase reminiscent of the Anglican compromise I discussed in Chapter Two) is like unseasoned meat or matter without form; without the benefit of formalized ritual, lovers' vows become opaque and murky, and "darknes decks the Bride" (3.154). Later the narrator reminds us of limpid Ceremonie and the conversion of mental matter into physical form when he suggests that the human eye is as "an animate glasse that showes / In-formes without us" (3.237–38). Chapman coins the term "In-formes" to make a neoplatonic pun; just as Phoebus's rays shine through the clouds when he is hidden, so the body's sun, the soul, our inner form, must be filtered through our "cloudie" (3.248) eyes and faces to *inform* observers of our emotions (*HLC*, 3.239–49). This is a careful modification of Marlowe's conceit of Hero's blushing "like a planet, mooving severall waies" through the sky (*HL*, 1.361). "Inform" means in Elizabethan English not just an inner form but also something unformed, inchoate, shapeless, so that our faces, according to Chapman, reveal an inner soul that is in a state of formless confusion. For Marlowe, the blush is heavenly, illuminating; for Chapman, it is cloudy and obscure.

The long "Tale of Teras" in Sestiad Five mingles cloudiness and brightness. "Admired Teras with the Ebon thye" (*HLC*, 5.62) sings to lovelorn Hero the lay of Hymen and Eucharis to celebrate a wedding that Hero has performed. Teras is an eccentric creature, an infallible prophet "term'd [Apollo's] Dwarfe" (5.70) for her small stature and much loved "though oft times she forewent Tragedies" (5.79), as indeed she does in Hero's case. Her black thighs seem at first a mystery. It is possible that Chapman confused "ebony" for "ivory" because he was thinking of the Latin word for "ivory," *eboreus*.[38] But Chapman employs both "ivory" and "ebony" correctly elsewhere: his first extant published work, "The Shadow of Night" (1594), contains a description of black Night's "pitchie vapours, and . . . ebone bowes" and concludes with the pale moon's shimmering "Iuorie chariot."[39] In addition, just a few lines prior to Teras's entrance, we learn that she bears an "Ivory" (*HLC*, "Argument" to Five, line 13) or "silver" (5.67) lute, given to her by Apollo.

Teras's ebony blackness forms a *deliberate* contrast to her ivory lute: her name means "omen," or "portent," and her thigh is "Ebon," just as her body is wreathed in "black and purple skarfs" (5.68), because she foretells doom to Hero. She is a "Comet-like" star (5.483), a "shooting exhalation" (5.488), but

> the turning of her back
> Made them all shrieke, it lookt so ghastly black.
> O haples Hero, that most haples clowde
> Thy soone-succeeding Tragedie foreshowde. (5.489–92)

Teras owns the shining, star-like gift of prophecy, but signals Hero's future darkness, as if the illuminating rays of Apollo, whose "beames enclosde / His vertues in her" (5.72–73), gave her the gift of prophecy but burnt her black at the same time. Teras's blackness also explains her "strangenes" and her "smalnes"; classically inspired early modern theories of skin color blamed the power of the sun's rays not only for dark skin but also for "strange and monstrous" bodies of varying proportions, including "those little dwarfes called Pygmei."[40]

On a purely formal level, the Tale of Teras delays the catastrophe and mimics the activities of Aurora, Neptune, and Leucothoe in postponing the lovers' tragic end; thematically, it repeats the story of Hero and Leander's enforced separation and jeopardy, but with a happy ending. Gerald Snare suggests that Teras's lay highlights Leander's failure to wait for wedded love and its ritual sanctification. If Hymen, the god of marriage himself, must wait for due ceremony before gaining his desire, he argues, then "why not Leander?"[41] But Teras's very "strangenes" makes it hard to read her tale as predominantly didactic, despite her black portentousness; she retains Chapman's aphoristic style, tempered with irony, to warn us that Hymen's love prospers despite, rather than because of, his blushing reticence: "Preferment seldome graceth bashfulnesse" (*HLC*, 5.144). Indeed, Chapman's aphorisms frequently function as distractions rather than as signposts to the poem's moral trajectory. John Huntington notes astutely that even if we can work out what one of these aphorisms means, we can't necessarily figure out its application, and adds that the narrator's sympathies are clearly *with* Hero and *against* Venus and Ceremonie.[42]

Chapman's text is concerned with forms and origins, neoplatonic but not moralistic. Although blushes in Chapman's poem are invariably followed by blackness, as windowless grief succeeds the transparent blazon of emotion, at the same time Chapman's account of color and form makes it clear why, in this imaginative universe, mimetic, reciprocal blushing should act as such an effective aphrodisiac. In a passage reminiscent of *Venus and Adonis*, Cupid becomes embodied in the white light beaming from the hands of Hymen and Eucharis, mingling the pallor of the lily and the faint flush of warm skin:

As two cleere Tapers mixe in one their light,
So did the Lillie and the hand their white:
She viewd it, and her view the forme bestowes
Amongst her spirits: for as colour flowes
From superficies of each thing we see,
Even so with colours formes emitted bee:
And where Loves forme is, love is, love is forme;
He entred at the eye, his sacred storme
Rose from the hand, loves sweetest instrument:
And beate in bashfull waves gainst the white shore
Of her divided cheekes; . . .
        . . .
So ebd and flowde the blood in Eucharis face. (*HLC*, 5.221–31, 5.241)

It is difficult to avoid reading this as a gloss on Marlowe's simple sally, "Who ever loved, that loved not at first sight?" (*HL*, 1.176), or on Leander's own words to Hero about the formlessness of virginity and its invisibility to "exterior sence" (1.271). If the hallmark of Marlowe's narrator is an easy, humorous cynicism, the tone of Chapman's is an aphoristic, complicated mysticism. This is why the poem is not, as so many critics have argued, merely a punitive coda to Marlowe's erotic impromptu. While Ceremonie puts forward her plea for clarity and transparency, the narrator emphasizes the futility of her quest, the impossibility of unmediated, luminous, and synchronous emotion. Ceremonie wishes above all for bounds to be set and maintained, but, as the poem makes clear, love itself cannot exist until those boundaries are broken. Color marks the outward surfaces or forms ("superficies") of emotion in human beings, and emits the quiddity or quintessence of inanimate objects. Color defines what an object is, but refuses to remain within that form, exceeding the boundaries of physical surface in order to penetrate the eye of an observer ("as colour flowes / From superficies of each thing we see, / Even so with colours formes emitted bee"). "[W]here Loves forme is, love is, love is forme": Color is Love made flesh. Ultimately, Love or Cupid animates, takes for his form, the colors that exude from lovers' cheeks, which are already themselves a sign or form of love. Color is both the outer manifestation of feeling ("superficie") and the feeling itself, the "in-forme," to use Chapman's term (*HLC*, 3.238). Ceremonie herself might argue that the proper "form" of love is pellucid ceremony or ritual, but there is no suggestion of this in the passage.

Given that color embodies emotion, it is unsurprising that, despite Chapman's sympathies with Hero, her blushes are darkening and predict her fate as surely as did Teras's "ghastly black." Her hot flush the morning after her first night with Leander "purple[s] round about" (*HLC*, 3.176) her chamber, creating a red morning that ushers in a "black day" (3.177). Chapman's poem offers a deliberate contrast to the rosy daybreak, the "false morne" that Hero illuminates in Marlowe's text (*HL*, 2.321); her blush still lights up the world, but it is a world of shame rather than joy. Marlowe's poem includes suggestions of this dimness, too: the dawn is "red for anger" (*HL*, 2.89) after Leander's first night with Hero, and the poem itself ends strangely with the dawn mocking "ougly night, / Till she o'recome with anguish, shame, and rage, / Dang'd downe to hell her loathsome carriage" (2.332–34). I call this conclusion strange (Braden calls it "strangely brutal") because in the minor epic, as Donno observes, "darke night is Cupids day" and the night is usually a friend to lovers (*HL*, 1.191).[43] Moreover, although the rosy dawn has overcome darkness, the poem itself ends on "loathsome" night and a descent into hell. Death and consummation are equivalent in narrative terms, since they foreclose meaning; thus Hero's blush the morning after her first night with Leander illuminates not only dawn but also the prospect of death. The ambiguous blushes that initiated their courtship have given way to the flush of shame and danger. Chapman picks up these hints: Hero's "naked" body (*HL*, 2.324) is glowingly and innocently displayed to Leander by her bright complexion in Marlowe's poem, but when she is alone in her chamber she generates a dawn that is sister to dusk. Hero fulfills Ceremonie's prophecy and decks herself in darkness when she hides her painful blushes in "black Cypres" (*HLC*, 3.293) and returns to obscure and formless chaos:

No forme was seene, where forme held all her sight:
But like an Embrion that saw ne'er light:
Or like a scorched statue made a cole
With three-wingd lightning: or a wretched soule
Muffled with endles darknes, she did sit. (*HLC*, 3.301–5)

Hero's inchoate, light-absorbing blackness seems to set her up as the diametrical opposite of the transparent goddess Ceremonie, who imposes order upon word and world and presents all that she is directly to observation or "sence." Along these lines, Hero resembles "an Embrion," or fetus, not just because she lurks in the dark but because she is unfinished and premature; she has returned to a state of chaos that mimics the moral anarchy that the lovers' untimely and unsanctified coupling has brought to pass. Her "in-forme," her state of mind, has become "inform" and shapeless. Ceremonie had warned that "darknes decks the bride," and Hero now sits "Muffled with endles darknes," unable to take on or attribute form, unable to confer meaning or narrative upon the events of her life. The girl whom the sun refused to "burne or parche" (*HL*, 1.28) and whose tears like "liquid pearle . . . / Made milk-white paths" (*HL*, 1.297–98) down her face has been "scorched" like an ember and sheds tears now black and opaque, "Mourning to be her teares" (*HLC*, 3.310). Shakespeare's Venus expresses a similar sentiment in her lament for Adonis:

Bonnet nor veil henceforth no creature wear:
Nor sun nor wind will ever strive to kiss you;
Having no fair to lose you need not fear—
The sun doth scorn you, and the wind doth hiss you.
But when Adonis lived, sun and sharp air
Lurked like two thieves, to rob him of his fair. (*Ven.*, lines 1081–86)

Just as Marlowe's world has been "blacke" since Hero's demise, and Chapman's Hero sheds black tears since the death of her virginity, so since Adonis's doom fair beauty has passed away.

Paradoxically, if Hero could remain in a state of black obscurity she would escape Venus's wrath. Hero becomes an unwilling dissembler because the brilliant blush that blazes in her cheeks is indistinguishable from the shamefast flush of maidenhead, the situation endured by her namesake in Shakespeare's play (*Ado*, 4.1) that I discuss in my next chapter. "[C]ustome" (*HLC*, 4.265) has not yet "brazde [her] brow with impudence" (3.268); she cannot stop herself from blushing. Nor will she disguise herself as other women do, like the "painted Moones" (3.259) who camouflage their true natures with the use of cosmetics, habit, and wantonness, or like the "Lapwing faces" (3.261) who distract an observer from the nest they have fouled. Chapman's Hero has no need of paint, since she still blushes of her own accord. Yet despite her good intentions and her exceptional purity, her "sharpe wit, her love, her secrecie" (3.397), force her to "dissemble" (3.400), to remove the black robe that befits her state of mind and to return to the temple as minister. Hero's illuminating blushes finally mislead even Leander: when all the stars of the sky are shrouded in "clowdes, as if they mournd" (6.167), Hero alone "shines" (6.165), outburning heaven itself and encouraging Leander to begin his ill-fated final journey across the stormy Hellespont with her warning torch. Hero's body no longer illustrates a natural truth to observers; in order to reveal her shame, she must turn to exterior, artificial signs like the black robe she dons or the scarf that she weaves to propitiate Venus.

The scarf, which Venus rejects, figures Hero's emotions in all their doubleness and doubtfulness. Hero blushes as furiously as the virgin depicted on her scarf, with "the division of her minde" (4.42), "And stood not resolute to wed Leander" (4.44). The text deliberately mingles the blushes of Hero and her creation, just as in the Tale of Teras, the ebb and flow of Eucharis's Hellespontine blushes evoke the sufferings of Hero herself, who is acting as minister while Teras sings her lay.[44] Hero has the full sympathy of the narrator, who muses, "nothing is thy sin, / Wayd with those foule faults other Priests are in" (4.210–11), but Venus refuses her offering. Since Hero still *looks* like a maid, although she is "counterfeit" (4.251), the goddess decrees, "Be never virgins vow worth trusting more" (4.259).

Venus points exactly to the problem of Heroic blushing: it is Hero's readiness to blush, the fact that she is *not* brazen, that challenges the word of every maid. Were she *truly* pale or swarthy, marked like Cain by her fault, Venus would rest satisfied. Vengeful Venus creates the monstrous Eronusis, the "Architect / Of all dissimulation" (4.312–13):

> the bright flame became a mayd most faire.
> For her aspect: her tresses were of wire
> Knit like a net, where harts all set on fire
> Strugled in pants and could not get releast:
> . . .
> Her doune parts in a Scorpions taile combinde,
> Freckled with twentie colours; pyed wings shinde
> Out of her shoulders; Cloth had never die,
> Nor sweeter colours never viewed eie,
> In scorching Turkie, Cares, Tartarie,
> Than shinde about this spirit notorious;
> Nor was Arachnes web so glorious. (*HLC*, 4.289–302)

Like Spenser's snowy Florimell with "burning lampes" for eyes and "golden wyre" for hair (*FQ*, 3.7.1), Eronusis is created in and of flame and has wires on her head; she is also the first woman to use false colors or cosmetic artifice to entrap too-credulous men. The "sweeter colours [that] never viewed eie," even in far-off, exotic lands suggest shades surpassing vermilion or coral, exotic beauty aids from the East. The comparison of a made-up woman to a multicolored fabric or a rainbow occurs frequently in the anticosmetic tracts; Thomas Tuke (1616) compares a "painted wench" to "a rainebow, colours altogether," and Richard Braithwait (1631) complains of "Pye-coloured fopperies."[45] Even more humiliatingly, Eronusis acts as Hero's monstrous double: "freckled with twentie colours," her shoulders bearing "pyed wings," she parodies Hero's face, which mirrors her changing emotions like Phoebus's prismatic "twentie-coloured eie" in the clouds (*HLC*, 3.243). Eronusis, Venus's artificial creature, shimmers more gloriously than "Arachnes web" while Hero's own dexterously woven web, with its many earthly colors, is ignominiously rejected. The "nets" and traps in Eronusis's hair correspond to the "trifling snares" (4.103) of the lazy shepherdess and the exhausted fisherman depicted in Hero's tapestry, while the "Serpent" (4.90) that Hero weaves stinging the fisherman to death corresponds to Eronusis's "Scorpions taile." Chapman's reading of Marlowe is so careful that he offers us here a barbed commentary on Marlowe's initial description of Hero's clothing, "Whose workmanship both man and beast deceaves" (*HL*, 1.20). Hero's tapestry for Venus illustrates "snares" and traps for both men and beasts, but Eronusis is the embodiment of deception itself.

The final, ironic parallel of Eronusis with Hero is only apparent at the end of the poem. Venus sets the winged Eronusis free at a "steepe . . . height / That all the world she might command with sleight/ Of her gay wings" (*HLC*, 4.307–9). When Hero falls to her death from her high turret she acquires a pair of wings of her own. They are not, however, dappled and iridescent, impossible to classify, but solid-colored, black, yellow, blue, and red, "Colours, that . . . paint / [The lovers'] states to life" (6.288–89): "the yellow shewes their saint, / The devill Venus, left them; blew their truth, / The red and black ensignes of death and ruth" (*HLC*, 6.289–91). These colors have fixed and firm meanings, unlike the colors of the misleading blushes that have angered Venus, or the shimmering shades that Eronusis wears to counterfeit honesty. Black is more frequently associated with mourning and death than red, which usually suggests passion, but since red passion is inevitably the precursor of black death in this poem, the inversion is appropriate. The metamorphosis of the lovers into goldfinches is, in addition, a sadly ironic reworking of Marlowe's description of Hero on her first night with Leander, when "as a bird, which in our hands we wring / Foorth plungeth, and flutters with her wing / She trembling strove" (*HL*, 2.289–91). Hero's bird-like struggles culminate in a luminous blush, which shines like the sun in "an orient cloud" (*HL*, 2.320); in Chapman's text, however, Hero's bright "[b]lushes that ble[e]d out of her cheeks" (*HLC*, 6.263) glow like torchlight on Leander but only enlighten her to the fact of his death. As the spirit of female dissimulation, Eronusis is identified with the use of cosmetics, and exotic cosmetics at that. Such dissimulation is a necessary part of lyric or fictionality, Marlowe and Chapman seem to say. Chapman picks up Marlowe's identification with Musaeus, the first poet, to impose a narrative conclusion and morality upon Marlowe's defiantly, amorally, erotically, lyrical fragment.

Chapter 5
Blackface and Blushface

Anticosmetic writers Tuke, in *A Treatise Against Painting and Tincturing* (1616), and Barnfield, in "The Complaint of Matilda Fitzwater" (1594), blame women's use of fucus, or make-up, for masking or falsifying the blush, thereby rendering pink cheeks unreadable as signs of innocence or guilt, prurience or purity, Englishness or strangeness.[1] But early modern stage plays turn the invisible, intangible emotion of a blush into dramatic action, its existence into metatheatrical self-consciousness, and its absence into a trope of the viewer's powerlessness to distinguish between what seem like self-evident categories. Shakespeare's *Much Ado About Nothing* (*Ado*, c. 1598), the anonymous *Lusts Dominion* (*LD*, c. 1599), and John Webster's *The White Devil* (*WD*, 1612) link make-up used to simulate a blush (what I shall call blushface) and make-up used to simulate black skin (blackface), in order to foreground the tactics and purposes of theater.[2] *Much Ado About Nothing* demonstrates that the platonic or ideal blush makes for easy reading, but a fallen, earthly flush is a free-floating sign detached not only from personal but from public meaning as well. *Lusts Dominion* and *The White Devil* turn the notion of a readable blush or legible skin into a metaphor for dramatic illusion.

These connections between blushing and blackening reveal an early modern "beauty myth" that offered women a dubious privilege: they could express themselves through paint, but at the same time they would be reinforcing the associations of red and white with chaste elegance, as well as applying mortal poisons. Fair, painted ladies have in effect rendered themselves "black," their faces unreadable, through their fixed cosmetic pallor. Such a substitution is crucial to the very nature of early modern drama, in which male actors represent femininity, and white ones personate black.

Much Ado About Blushing

Shakespeare dramatizes the blush as a measure of sexual chastity in the church scene, in which Claudio disowns Hero in public:

Behold how like a maid she blushes here!
O, what authority and show of truth
Can cunning sin cover itself withal!
Comes not that blood as modest evidence
To witness simple virtue? Would you not swear,
All you that see her, that she were a maid,
By these exterior shows? But she is none.
She knows the heat of a luxurious bed.
Her blush is guiltiness, not modesty. (*Ado,* 4.1.34–42)

Coeffeteau and Wright interpret even guilty blushes as good signs, because they indicate the capacity for remorse, but Hero's blushes convince Claudio that she is "but the sign and semblance of her honour," the painted façade of modesty without a foundation of virtue beneath (*Ado,* 4.1.33). As Anthony Dawson argues, she is a "sign disconnected from its proper referent."[3] Like an actor, Hero puts on an "exterior show" to camouflage her true nature; like a woman who wears cosmetics, she has "covered" herself with false evidence, tricks to deceive the eye. She is "like a maid," but is a mere simulacrum. Her blush intends the opposite, argues Claudio, of what its spectators believe; her blush publishes her infamy rather than her innocence, and her "authority" is false.

Claudio's disavowal also traces an inexorable association among women, dissimulation, and decay. In Claudio's mind his falsely painted Hero becomes a death's head under his gaze, tainted meat, a "rotten orange" (4.1.32)[4]:

For thee I'll lock up all the gates of love,
And on my eyelids shall conjecture hang
To turn all beauty into thoughts of harm,
And never shall it more be gracious. (4.1.105–8)

The eyes, the "gates of love," no longer offer beauty and grace but lie closed to all but "harm" and decay, so that sight itself is corrupt because what it sees is no longer the truth. Even Hero's own father, Leonato, takes her fainting ruddiness as ocular proof: "Could she here deny / The story that is printed in her blood?" (4.1.121–22) Hero's disgrace can "blot out" (4.1.82) her virtue, like a "pit of ink" that stains her indelibly (4.1.140). A smudged and dirty text has replaced a familiar and legible one; Leonato's metaphor is even more explicit in the Folio, which describes Hero as "smeared" where the Quarto reads "smirched" (4.1.133).[5]

The Friar who officiates at this abortive union, however, appears as a witness for the defense. "By noting of the lady" he has observed

A thousand blushing apparitions
To start into her face, a thousand innocent shames

In angel whiteness beat away those blushes,
And in her eye there hath appeared a fire
To burn the errors that these princes hold
Against her maiden truth. Call me a fool,
Trust not my reading, nor my observations,
Which with experimental seal doth warrant
The tenure of my book . . .
If this sweet lady lie not guiltless here
Under some biting error. (*Ado*, 4.1.159–70)

At first glance it might seem that the Friar redeems the bashful blush, that for him, Hero's rosy face reverses Claudio's aphorism, and says, "Her blush is modesty, not guiltiness." The Friar, too, however, mistrusts the blush: Hero's pink cheeks, according to him, are not the body's inadvertent blazon of corporeal truth (in this case, also of her virginity, her bodily integrity) but chimeras, false fiends, to be "beat[en] away" by "angel whiteness." According to him, Hero takes no active part in her blushes; they are "apparitions" that mimic the ghost of an accusation and play across her face rather than concrete embodiments of her own shame. Whiteness is an "angel" because now Hero is Claudio's blank book once more, holy and original, the only red fire in her face being that which flames in her eye, "maiden truth" to "burn" the heretical "errors" into which the princes have fallen. The friar's rhetoric associates Hero's face with the true and unvarnished word of God in the Bible, which he must expound for the laity in a "book" of his own. Hero is restored to her prior state of canvas-like pallor, the white page upon which "innocence" and "shame" battle for supremacy. She even bears the Friar's "seal" or stamp of approval, which belies Claudio's assertion that her "authority" (4.1.35) is false. Hero's vindication in the eyes of Messina is effected by another text, "an epitaph upon her tomb" (5.1.284) relating her innocence, and Claudio atones for his hasty and erroneous judgment by marrying a "copy" (5.1.289) that is "fair" (5.4.69).

Dawson astutely notes that Claudio cannot interpret sign systems (Claudio misreads Hero's blushes just as he misinterprets Benedick's pallor), but then asserts that the Friar reads Hero's blushes correctly, "in context."[6] In fact both Claudio *and* the Friar are mistaken in their diagnoses of Hero's blushes, if indeed she is blushing at all. The debate about Hero's blushes is a tale told between men, as Carol Cook suggests.[7] "Noting of the lady" means both "taking note" of her and "making notes" on her body. Hero "is the 'nothing' that generates so much ado."[8] Claudio claims that her ruddy cheeks are a sign of shame at her guilty fornication; the Friar avers that the changing color of her face mirrors the stain on her name (the deep flush of illicit passion) which must be cleansed by her supposed demise (the deathly pallor that follows). But

Claudio and the Friar create the symptoms they interpret and describe simultaneously. They can have no direct access to her thoughts and feelings; any claims based on an interpretation of her face are unavoidably misleading, because it seems to offer a window to her heart but in fact can grant observers no such thing. Claudio, the Friar and Leonato have constructed an elaborate drama among themselves. Beatrice, in contrast, remains silent until Hero faints under the cruel comments of Claudio. As Cook remarks, the subsequent events of the play cast more doubt on the validity of blushes as empirical proof of a straightforward innocence or guilt. Contrary to the Friar's surmise that once Hero is thought to be dead, Claudio will cherish her memory more highly and the stain on her name will naturally fade with time (failing which, the Friar helpfully suggests, Leonato can always shut her away in a convent), the news of Hero's supposed death makes no difference to Claudio's state of mind. He does not regret his repudiation until after hearing Borachio's confession and the mechanics of the plot to discredit Hero. In contrast to Leonato's grief, Claudio shrugs off the news of Hero's death, joking tediously with Don Pedro at the expense of Hero's grieving father and uncle, and initially mocking Benedick's challenge. The Friar's failure to anticipate Claudio's indifference to the death of Hero suggests that the former's skills at "noting" are not as assured as he would have us believe.

Cook calls Hero's epitaph the "petrified monument to her virginity" in contrast to "the fluid, vital, ambiguous text of her face"; the Friar's rhetoric implies that the perfect maiden is bloodless, pale, cold, and dead. He has "cleansed [Hero] of carnality, of the blood that has been read as the sign of sexuality and guilt."[9] The Friar's insistence on her "angel whiteness" and upon Hero's face as dead and bloodless, like the cold gravestone that redeems her, draws attention to the paradox of marble or alabaster pallor as a sign of female beauty and innocence. According to the false but widely believed Renaissance etymology, the Latin word for woman, *mulier*, derived from *mollis aer*, soft air, making the air impressionable matter and associating women with it. But whiteness also signifies chastity, a lady's icy firmness against her burning, melting lover. Paradoxically, women can only live up to expected standards of sexual chastity if they exhibit an unfeminine, marmoreal hardness and rigidity.

Hero's blush, as the helpless, immediate surge of blood to the skin, is a sign of incontinent, porous, femininity. Gail Kern Paster connects the gendering of early modern shame to a conflict between premodern theories of the body and scientific taxonomies of bodily functions. She argues that the premodern, humoral body is permeable, porous, open, like the "grotesque body" that Bakhtin describes, and that it requires periodic "evacuations" of effluvia into the outside world to maintain good health. During the early modern period, however, she suggests, bodily fluids, such as blood, sweat, tears, semen, and milk, became classified, discrete, unmentionable, and the body becomes separate, finite, bounded. Women were associated with incontinence, flux, and leakiness, men with control, stability, and impermeability. Paster argues that early modern "embarrassment" is "bodily shame," displaced onto women's bodies and female fluids. She suggests that there is an important distinction to be made between virile, voluntary, and extraordinary bloodshed (the gory injuries of war and the wounds of Christ) and feminine, involuntary, and regular bleeding (menstruation and childbirth).[10] Certainly Shakespeare's Cleopatra suggests that blushes indicate a feminine helplessness when she taunts Antony, "Thou blushest, Antony, and that blood of thine / Is Caesar's homager; else so thy cheek pays shame / When shrill-tongued Fulvia scolds" (*Ant.*, 1.1.30–32). By reddening at Cleopatra's teasing, Cleopatra suggests, Antony confirms that he is not only Caesar's humble vassal but also a henpecked husband who meekly obeys his domineering wife. Cleopatra even manages to imply that Antony's bleeding battle wounds in the past were not marks of self-conscious manhood but emblems of his powerlessness before Caesar. Ricks writes, "We have no way of telling whether Antony has indeed blushed or whether [Cleopatra] is dextrously making it up," but in either case Antony has been feminized by Cleopatra's assertion, as Little suggests.[11] Claudio's exposition renders Hero helpless, her blush a betrayal of both her femininity and her alleged incontinence.

We never find out why—or *whether*—Hero was really blushing. Her face does not reveal her inner moral state to the outside world, nor does it solely highlight a deeply personal sense of conflict and betrayal. Ricks wonders whether Shakespeare drew attention to his actors' blushes in order to emphasize their skill in summoning one or in order to conceal their inability to change color.[12] Surely the latter surmise is correct: even if Elizabethan actors could flush at will, their blushes would have been invisible under the chalk-white fucus that probably "makes up" whiteness on the Renaissance stage. As Callaghan has argued, both whiteness and blackness on the early modern stage are impersonations, created through cosmetic prosthesis, and femininity itself is associated with whiteness.[13] The truly legible blush can belong only to the realm of the imaginary. Whether Hero or the young actor who plays her genuinely changes color is less relevant than the idea that her affianced husband and the Friar believe that they can read her and the irony that the audience knows they cannot. Hero's blushes mark an ideological conflict; they prove that in this situation any response she makes—speech or silence, blushing or pallor—will be construed by men. If she blushes at all it might be taken as proof that she has more sexual knowledge and awareness than a decent girl ought to have, but if she remains pale she might be considered brazen or unrepentant in her sin. The ambiguity of a blush mimics the contradictory demands of marriageability: a nubile girl must be sexually available and attractive, but only to her future husband.

Many feminist critics of *Much Ado About Nothing* read its conclusion as a more sophisticated version of *The Taming of the Shrew* (1593). While Katharina is "tamed" by rough treatment, starvation, and humiliation, Beatrice's mouth is gently "stopped" with a kiss, after which she is silent for the remainder of the play, and Hero's marriage is conditional upon her restored and monumental virginity.[14] Cook argues that the play ultimately reinforces women's status as "ciphers until named by men," and that it perpetuates the "masculine ethos" that the church scene challenges so effectively.[15] Hero's resurrection and her insistence that she is not "Hero that is dead!"—the Hero who "died defiled" (5.4.63)—but a new Hero, who is "a maid" (5.4.64), seem to reinscribe the play's demand for female chastity: even the mere imputation of unchastity taints Hero so irrevocably that the old Hero must die. Lewalski tries to redeem Claudio by reading his love as neoplatonic allegory; having learned to value inner beauty over the evidence of his senses, he agrees to take his bride "wholly on faith."[16] Yet such a recuperation seems worthless, since he places this "faith" in Leonato: the final wedding seems ultimately to teach us not trust in women's fidelity but—as Jean Howard observes—"a lesson in having faith in the authority of social superiors."[17]

The final wedding might seem to reinscribe what Howard calls "the politics of rank and gender" by asserting the correctness of Leonato's judgment, but it shakes them up by introducing a final ambiguity. The plot demands that Hero's uncle, Antonio, give Hero away, since Leonato has forfeited his authority by his mistrust; Claire McEachern concludes that the play exposes the limitations of the patriarchal structures it establishes.[18] Cook finds that the entrance of the four veiled or masked women in the final scene "effaces" their identity, giving the power of naming to their husbands.[19] A veil or a vizard, however, like cosmetics, can deceive men's eyes and return a degree of control to women over the image they present to others. Critics have read Claudio's vow to go through with this blind marriage, arranged by Leonato, "I'll hold my mind, were she an Ethiope," as submission to Leonato's rank, or to a residual neoplatonic ideal of love (*Ado*, 5.4.38).[20] Little argues that this episode can only work because "Hero is supposedly quite the antithesis of an Ethiope . . . sacrificed . . . and . . . reborn as the white heroine."[21] But it seems to me that Hero is reborn not as the white heroine but as the Ethiope, as Claudio acknowledges that men can neither read or control blushes and that women are ultimately, perpetually, illegible.

Moors and Ethiopians, as we have seen, are notorious in early modern literature for their supposed inability to blush and experience shame. Eleazar gives "[t]hanks that [he has] not wit to blush" (*LD*, C4v) and Moorish Zanche crows that she "may boldly [speak] without a blush" (*WD*, 5.1.214). Shakespeare's Aaron turns the accusation of brazen fixedness into a virtue, mocking his pale interlocutors with the charge that white skin, unlike black, can be painted over like a canvas:

What, what, ye sanguine, shallow-hearted boys,
Ye white-limed walls, ye alehouse painted signs!
Coal-black is better than another hue
In that it scorns to bear another hue. (*Tit.*, 4.2.97–100)

The adjective "sanguine" reveals the "hue" Aaron is imagining: blood-red paint upon a white tavern sign. Aaron's unchangeability is reiterated in the blank verse echo of "another hue." Pallor, in contrast to negritude, is, as I have quoted before, a "treacherous hue, that will betray with blushing / The close enacts and counsels of thy heart" (*Tit.*, 4.2.117–18).[22]

In vowing to marry an Ethiope, then, Claudio is agreeing to marry a woman whose blushes he could not even see, let alone "note"—a woman, moreover, whom Renaissance culture associated with shamelessness and sexual incontinence.[23] Hero is not "an Ethiope," but she might as well be—Claudio can never know what is going on behind the mask that is her face. We may recall that unruly Beatrice cannily describes herself as "sunburnt" (*Ado*, 2.1.319); ostensibly she is lamenting that she is too brown to be beautiful, but her tawniness also means that she is too dark for her blushes to betray her to critical observers. In the same scene, Benedick has just associated Beatrice with dark-skinned foreigners, claiming he would rather

fetch you a tooth-picker from the furthest inch of Asia, bring you the length of Prester John's foot, fetch you a hair off the Great Cham's beard, do you any embassage to the Pigmies, rather than hold three words' conference with this harpy [Beatrice]. (*Ado*, 2.1.266–70)

Beatrice's suntanned exuberance links her to these exotic and physically distinct peoples, the Ethiopians ruled by Prester John, the Great Khan of Mongolia (who is connected by the usual spelling of his title as "Cham" to the black descendants of Noah's son who colonized Africa), and the pygmies. The "harpy" was thought to be part woman, part animal, further characterizing Beatrice as wild or dangerous. Now, it seems Hero has learned from Beatrice to cover her face, to veil her blushes.

We can read Benedick's advice to Don Pedro and his jokes about the "staff . . . tipped with horn" of the married man in the same light

(5.4.123–24): far from attempting to control female sexuality, Benedick and Claudio have concluded that men must resign themselves to women's liberty. The jokes, of course, reinforce the misogynist stereotype of the unreliable woman, the leaky vessel; Carol Thomas Neely argues that they support masculine moral authority to keep unruly women in check.[24] Linda Woodbridge warns us of "jest's insidious power" to support misogyny.[25] At the same time, however, the jokes compensate for the unwelcome recognition that masculine mind control is only a conventional, convenient fiction.

Claudio's masked bride is therefore a figure for poetic faith and female freedom. Faces, words, and bodies cannot be deciphered in an orderly manner, and any hermeneutic will break down. The play remains morally ambiguous, and theatrical or literary systems of interpretation and plotting are similarly vague. Don John attempts to make Claudio and Don Pedro enemies by encouraging Claudio to eavesdrop upon a "private" conversation, but the same eavesdropping strategy turns Beatrice and Benedick into lovers.[26] Blushes prove nothing except their own ambiguity. The marriages at the end of the play are poetic fictions (in Beatrice and Benedick's case, literally so, as they are condemned to wed by their own sonneteering hands).

The Friar counters Claudio's claims with an elaborate fantasy of battling blushes on Hero's face, concluding with the triumph of "angel whiteness." In this he reinforces traditional ideals of feminine beauty as the combination of red and white skin together. There is a material reason for the Renaissance anxiety about reading women's faces, and it is part of an early modern beauty myth.[27] The increasing availability of a greater variety of cosmetics than ever before, and women's interest in using these products, partly in imitation of Queen Elizabeth, who made up elaborately all her life, led to a burgeoning antifeminist literature denouncing women for using deceptive arts to lure men into matrimony at best, into hellish sin at worst. If Hero's complexion were fixed and unchanging, it would suggest that her red cheeks were cosmetic and artificial in origin, rather than the involuntary, momentary response of her body.

Paint, Pencil, and Poison

The early modern debate about face painting corresponds to cultural anxieties about female autonomy.[28] Tuke's *Treatise*, Braithwait's *English Gentleman* (1630), *English Gentlewoman* (1631), and *The Good Wife* (1618), and Paolo Lomazzo's *Tracte Containing the Artes of Curious Painting* (1598) inveigh against cosmetics that camouflage female faces; the poet Richard Barnfield rewrites a complaint poem by Michael Drayton to incorporate an apostrophe against "the Divells dye."[29] Although men as well as women wore make-up, especially at court (when the lovestruck Benedick starts to "paint himself," he complies with Elizabethan custom [*Ado*, 3.2.57]), and Tuke's, Lomazzo's, and Braithwait's treatises are addressed ostensibly to both sexes, they direct the main force of their invective against women. Jacobean drama, as both Shirley Nelson Garner and Annette Drew-Bear have demonstrated, associates women who paint with both physical and moral corruption; Garner remarks that poets and playwrights treat the "painted lady" as a *memento mori* all of whose artifices cannot delay the inevitable onset of decay. This association of cosmetic camouflage with feminine disease is hardly surprising, given that the "ceruse" or white lead that formed a base for rouge and the "Soliman" or mercury sublimate used as a chalky foundation corroded skin, hair and teeth and eventually poisoned the wearer.[30] Homemade recipes for fucus often included hazardous compounds. Sir Hugh Platt, for example, who in 1602 offers ladies recipes "to adorne their Persons, Tables, closets and distillatories," suggests that the young housewife compound "with great labour foure ounces of [mercury] sublimate, and one ounce of crude Mercurie . . . with the oyle of white poppey."[31] In Drew-Bear's witty sentence, "What helped to make [the poisoner] Frances Howard's face white helped to kill her victim, Sir Thomas Overbury."[32]

As Dolan notes, however, the anticosmetic writers are concerned not primarily with the physical depredations of painting, but with its moral consequences. Dolan describes early modern female face painting as "cosmesis" or cosmetic poesis: she argues that treatises written against the use of make-up criticize women for rewriting the face God had given them, usurping a masculine, creative power. When Tuke writes, "[a painted woman's] own sweet face is the booke she most lookes upon; this she reads over duly every morning . . . as her eie or chambermaid teaches her, somtimes she blots out pale, and writes red," he contrasts the lady's "eie or chambermaid," a faulty, earthly teacher, with the "book" she *ought* to be contemplating, that is, the Bible, and the jealous God she *ought* to propitiate: "A good face is her god: and her cheeke well died, is the idoll, she doth so much adore."[33] The description of a woman who uses cosmetics is "the picture of a picture";[34] a made-up woman has, according to Tuke, turned herself into art, "competing with and opposing her Maker,"[35] as Dolan observes. The verb "to make up" appears for the first time in the context of cosmetic enhancement in the latter half of the sixteenth century, carrying connotations of "making up" a measure that is lacking (like a grocer adulterating his goods) and fabricating a lie (like an old wife recounting a fireside tale). There is a language in women's faces, and painted ladies have blotted their copies.

Kim Hall finds that "the language of painting and cosmetics is the most widespread component of the rhetoric of women's fairness and value"; in painting, women are casting themselves as rare and valuable items for exchange.[36] In fact, Hall suggests, what she calls "the traffic in beauty" contributes to an emerging discourse about sex, skin color, and subjectivity: "the whitening of the dark lady becomes crucial for the exercise of male poetic power."[37] Red and white are signs of chaste femininity, but are only valuable when they are conferred by the praise of a man. Nancy Vickers has identified a similar semiotics in *The Rape of Lucrece* (1594), where Lucrece's blushing beauty becomes the shield and the arms of her husband, a blazon of his wealth as well as her chastity. Lucrece's face blazes her shame and sorrow and, crucially, enkindles a corresponding shame in the viewer or reader. Her face is her fortune; after the rape her familiar roses fade to "sorrow's livery," and the red and white of chastity become the stain of blood and the pallor of death.[38] The value of Lucrece's beauty comes to lie in its evanescence and its predictive abilities.

Color that comes and goes fleetingly provides a moment-to-moment update on the state of the subject's soul. The optimistic Platt lists several concoctions not only to whiten a dark or spotted face but also to cure one that flames persistently red—as a result, one wonders, of wearing the potions he earlier prescribed? One of these compounds, he boasts, "helped M. Foster an Essex man . . . whose face was . . . of an exceeding high and firy colour . . . and had spent much money in physicke without any successe at all."[39] Color that changes from red to white and back again proves that a blush is "native [rather] than artificiall," and inspired by shame.[40]

Anticosmetic pamphleteers fear face paint because it conceals women's blushes and threatens to destroy the hermeneutics of early modern shame. Tuke, Braithwait, and Barnfield fear that if women create artificial, fixed complexions for themselves, those masks will become an integral part of them and they will genuinely lose the ability to experience shame because they cannot blush. "How can [women] begge pardon," asks Braithwait, "when their sinne cleaves unto their faces, and when they are not able for to blush?"[41] Barnfield bewails the maids whose virtue fails, since their "lovely Cheeks (with rare vermilion tainted) / Can never blush because their faire is painted."[42] The capacity for change and the ability to feel shame allow the possibility of spiritual redemption and of remorse for sin; moreover, the faulty grammar of white pancake will prevent the blush from speaking comprehensibly to observers:

It is not enough to be good, but she that is good, must seeme good: she that is chast, must seeme chast: shee that is humble, must seeme humble: shee that is modest, must seeme to bee so, and not plaister her face, that she cannot blush upon any occasion (tho she would) so as to be discerned of another.[43]

Just as Wright and Coeffeteau analyze the blush as a sign to outsiders that tells the world one is capable of shame, and as a ground or basis for imitative virtue, so Tuke here fears that a blushless woman sets a pernicious example. The fact that she might *want* to blush ("tho she would") is irrelevant, if her blushes are invisible, since she has a responsibility towards all those who pause to read her. Tuke implies that blushing is a voluntary act, like experiencing shame, with which he equates blushing. Women are seen as cultural signposts, which is why their own cosmetic urges lead to moral anarchy, and why their self-absorption or vanity (another frequent charge of the treatises) inexorably leads to chaotic confusion. If women are too occupied in rewriting their own faces, what do men have left to guide them?

Shame reinforces sexual difference; in the absence of shame, sexual difference breaks down. If a sudden, helpless rush of blood is quintessentially feminine, as Paster suggests, then women who paint are not merely tinkering with God's handiwork but also going against their essential, feminine, bodily nature in creating deliberate rather than involuntary blushes when they apply rouge. Braithwait advises a prospective husband: "I'de have her face and blush to be her owne, / For th'Blush which Art makes is adulterate."[44] "Adulterate" in the Renaissance carries both the sense of "adulterous" and "adulterated"; just as men could be rendered "effeminate" by too much sexual interest in women, so women could be not only "adulterated" by affairs with men but even virilized. Tuke expounds this sexual paradox with a grammatical metaphor: "a plaine woman is but halfe a painted woman, who is both a substantive and an adjective, and yet not of the neuter gender: but a feminine as well consorting with a masculine."[45] Like the antifeminist pamphlet *Hic Mulier* (1620), which complains that made-up women are "monsters" and hermaphrodites, Tuke couples a feminine "substantive" noun with a masculine "adjective" to ridicule such women.[46] His discussion of cosmetics asseverates that women who follow fashion (in this case, by using make-up), ostensibly in order to *enhance* their femininity, are finally neither male nor female, but a strange combination of both. Thus a "plaine," unmade-up woman is "halfe" a painted woman because she is all female, in contrast to the painted women who are "adulterate," impure mixtures, both male and female in one body, hermaphroditic horrors who employ the grammar of an incomprehensible tongue.

Many anticosmetic writers fearfully associate painted women with the foreign, possibly because of the Eastern origin of cochineal, ivory, henna, and other ingredients used in make-up.[47] In addition, travel narratives

emphasize female adornment as part of the exoticism they describe. Leo
Africanus already makes the connection between nation and female decoration, blaming the Arabians for introducing "counterfeit colour" to
African women, who "before then . . . neuer used any false or glozing
colours" (*HDA*, C1r). He adds that the women of Barbary,

contenting themselues onely with their naturall hiew . . . regarde not such fained
ornaments: howbeit sometimes they will temper a certaine colour with hens-
dung and safron, wherewithall they paint a little round spot on the bals of their
cheeks, about the bredth of a French crowne. Likewise betweene their eie-browes
they make a triangle; and paint vpon their chinnes a patch like vnto an oliue
leafe. Some of them also doe paint their eie-browes: and this custome is very
highly esteemed of by the Arabian poets and by the gentlemen of that countrie.
(*HDA*, C1r)

Although it has claimed that the Barbary women do not paint, and consider themselves distinct from the Arabian women, Leo's account collapses both distinctions, painted/natural, Arabian/African.

John Bulwer's *Anthropometamorphosis* (1653) provides a cosmetic ethnography. Surveying the globe, he notes "The American Women with a
certain Fucus paint their Eye-brows, which they lay on with a pencill,"
"The Guineans use to paint one Eye red many times, the other white or
yellow," and "The people of Molalia in the East-Indies . . . colour their
Teeth red with Beetle [betel leaves]."[48] He ends several chapters by iden-
tifying the limits of permissible cosmetic use—at what point feminine
body modification moves from elegance, cleanliness, or utility to what
Dolan calls "cosmesis," "taking the pencil out of God's hand." For example, he concludes his chapter on eyebrows with a justification of depila-
tion but a condemnation of the use of black paint or powder to make
them darker. In a seeming aboutface, he adds that Turks demonstrate
good taste in drawing their eyebrows into arches, because that is an "imitation of Nature," and in making them meet, which overgoes Nature, but
that to paint them triangular, like the Arabian women, "we cannot allow"
(O3v). Similarly, the Turks use a black powder called "Alchole [kohl]"
to paint the area beneath their eyelids and lashes. On the one hand, such
an innovation is wrong, Bulwer maintains, because it attempts to improve nature. On the other hand, Turks could be excused for painting
if they did it to improve their vision, since, he observes, it is known that
black lashes help protect the eyes in bright sunlight by "cast[ing] a
shadow upon the Eye" and increasing the blackness of "the thin mem-
brane Chorion, the first that covereth the Optique sinew, and prohibits
the diffusion of the splendor of the Christalline" (P3v).

Bulwer's text includes an appendix that mocks European fashions by
comparing them to the exotic practices of cosmesis that he has described

throughout the volume. And, as Kim Hall points out, he responds to Browne's comments on cultural relativism and beauty with an "idiosyn- cratic theory" that "from this Artifice the Moores might possibly become Negroes, receiving atramentitious [blackish] impression, by the power and efficacy of imagination" (3P4r).[49] Thus a third reason for the pam- phleteers' xenophobia is surely the fear that, because of paint, white women may turn into black ones, or at least, that it is impossible to use the blush to distinguish between black and white skin or chaste and faithless women. Stephen Gosson's *A Glasse, to View the Pride of Vaine- glorious Women* (1595) complains that "fashions fonde of country strange" turn women into "Turkes" and "Amazones" whose faces cannot be seen underneath their masks,

the tallow-pale[,] the browning-bay,
The swarthy-blacke, the grassie-greene,
the pudding-red, the dapple-graie,
　　　So might we judge them toyes aright,
　　　To keepe sweet beautie still in plight.[50]

The author worries that English ladies have exceeded even the Turks in their use of veils and masks; instead of hiding from "wantons bolde," these women will use their masks to "sport . . . sometime by night, some- time by day."[51] A "natural" blush even becomes a patriotic duty.

Singled out for such opprobrium, poisoned at their toilet tables, why did women continue to paint, and in increasing numbers? It is tempting to agree with the anticosmetic writers and blame the increase in foreign trade for the availability of fucus, and the use of make-up for the difficulties in reading the blush. Demand as well as supply, however, fuels consumption. Neville Williams suggests that "one factor" in the surge in cosmetic consumption "was the increasing wealth of the coun- try," and increased trade with Eastern nations who provided new dyes. He concludes, however, that the burgeoning use of make-up reflects a Renaissance concern with "life . . . beauty, form, and colour which . . . did not begin to blossom in England until the reign of Elizabeth I."[52] Carroll Camden attributes the popularity of cosmetics during the six- teenth and seventeenth centuries partly to Queen Elizabeth, a pale red- head who made fairness fashionable.[53] But, as Dolan and Kim Hall point out, the use of cosmetics offered women the chance for poetic, as well as economic, display. Women painted precisely *in order* to hide their blushes. Wearing make-up allows women to rewrite the texts that men attempt to read on their faces; cosmetics create a private mask behind which the tender subject can retreat. Consider Beatrice's self-deprecating description of herself as "sunburnt"; "sunburn" gives her a modicum of control over the face she presents to the outside world. And if we return to Leo's account of North African cosmetics, we learn that the Barbary women, too, make up not for the sake of the Arabian male poets who laud them but for their families' and their own pleasure:

> they will not vse these fantasticall ornaments aboue two or three daies together: all which time they will not be seene to any of their friends, except it be to their husbands and children: for these paintings seeme to bee great allurements vnto lust, whereby the said women thinke themselues more trim and beautifull. (*HDA*, C1r)

The cross-cultural example above suggests that make-up also, conversely, enables women to *conform* to expected standards of behavior and appearance; after all, cosmetics are supposed to enhance rather than damage one's looks.[54] Women (and men) painted to follow fashions at court; to exert some control over their appearance; to maintain the appearance of youth; to appear sexually attractive and available. And we also cannot assume that men did invariably find painted women attractive—Pepys, famously, hated painting, but Donne wrote a defense of make-up that is only partly tongue-in-cheek.[55] We might call such painting "blushface" make-up, or gender masquerade, by analogy with blackface make-up, or racial masquerade. Blushface and blackface could work together on the Renaissance stage to create and ironize fictions of sexuality and power.

Blacking, Blanching, and Blushing: *Lusts Dominion* and *The White Devil*

Lusts Dominion and *The White Devil* illustrate the breakdown of blacking, blanching, and blushing as signs of moral conduct, poetic power, and national origin. Both plays ally deceitful, painted women with black Moors (Eleazar and Aaron respectively), and both plays use the theatrical devices of paint and playwriting to trick both Moors and women. We have seen that Shakespeare's Aaron assumes that black skin is unpaintable, uncrafted, but Eleazar sees his blackness as the work of an artistic hand:

Ha, ha, I thank thee provident creation,
That seeing in moulding me thou did'st intend,
I should prove villain, thanks to thee and nature
That skilful workman; thanks for my face,
Thanks that I have not wit to blush. (*LD*, C4v)

Elliot Tokson argues that in this play the "black face of sin contrasts definitively with the whiteness of virtue" and that Eleazar has "quite accepted the moral significance of blackness," but he misses the play's theatrical and literary ironies.[56] Far from accepting the belief of his

Spanish enemies, that black and white always stand for evil and good respectively, Eleazar mocks the Spaniards' assumptions by using their gullible faith in legible faces and truthful whiteness to his own advantage. When Eleazar describes his face as "in nights colour dy'd" (G8r) he seems to reassert an ingrained, unchangeable blackness, but he breaks down his binary opposition as soon as he has uttered it: "The whitest faces have the blackest souls" (G8r). Phillippo grumbles, "Thou true stamp'd son of hell, / Thy pedigree is written in thy face" (E5r). Eleazar's pedigree is *not* written in his face, however; he wants to be more than a blackamoor, to be King of Spain, and he is writing his own pedigree, as well as his own play.

The common people of Spain complain that Eleazar spends the king's money "on smooth boies, on Masks and Revellings" (B3r). Evidently the common people believed, like Elizabethan antitheatrical writers, that theatergoing would lead naturally to unnatural desires and that the "smooth boies" who acted on stage would inspire lust in both older men and women of all ages. Eleazar tells his mistress, the Queen Mother, to "paint out" her face in blushface, the rosy colors of "penitence" (C4r), to convince the friars that her son Phillippo, the heir to the throne, is illegitimate and therefore cannot become king. The Queen obligingly blushes on cue:

Would I were covered with the vail of night,
You might not see red shame sit on my cheecke;
But being Spains common safety stands for truth,
Hiding my weeping eyes, I blush, and say;
"Phillippo's father sits here." (F8r)

The Queen Mother's painted blushes convince the court. Blackness and whiteness are not ineradicably "stamp'd," as Phillippo suggests, but "paint" (C4r) or "ink" (B11r), rhetorical or literary colors. Until the Spaniards realize that Eleazar is scripting a play, they cannot conquer him; he is invincible. King Fernando attempts to seduce Eleazar's wife, Maria, to write his own play, a "Tragedy I'le write with my own hand," in which "A King shall act it, and a King shall dye" (D4r), punning on the sexual "act" that he would like to enjoy. He fails to realize, however, that Eleazar and the Queen Mother have already seen the script—and arranged to frame him for the murder of Maria.

Eleazar utters a hymn of praise to "Tragedy, thou Minion of the night," arguing that tragedy is black, as he is, because "Thou . . . never blushest, though thy cheeks are full of blood" (G9r). To turn Eleazar's "Tragedy" into the "Comick joy" (G11v) that the Spaniards desire, Isabella realizes that the only way to match Eleazar is to write a different play, but one that uses the same theatrical devices of paint and deception that Eleazar and the Queen Mother employed before. Isabella imagines herself as a female playwright, asking her slow-witted colleagues, "cannot you see / your play?" (G7v), and the Spanish revengers disguise themselves as Moors in blackface make-up, called "the oil of hell" (G7v). These "false" Moors are then indistinguishable from the characters that are supposed to be "real" Moors, equally indistinguishable to Eleazar and to the audience. The device asserts that black skin and black make-up are the same when represented on stage; neither darkness *nor* whiteness is a fundamental condition of human faces, but a mask or cover for truth. The process of blackening, masking, or covering can assert a masculine, creative control parallel to the movement Kim Hall finds in "making fair." Think of Iago turning Desdemona's "virtue into pitch" (*Othello*, 2.3.360)—again by creating a fable, a story which additionally undoes the bleaching that Othello's tale of his sufferings has established (and after recounting which the Duke calls him "more fair than black" [1.3.290]).

In *The White Devil* these sequences of female blanching, blacking, and blushing are theatrically linked to paint; the play presents men using paint and metaphors of cosmetic deception to reassert their authority over women and their complexions. The men who wish to control her sexuality paint Vittoria's blushes out of existence. At the start of the play, blushing represents Vittoria's natural desires; when Brachiano entices Vittoria into adultery, Flamineo muffles her objections with the curt command, "Come sister, darkness hides your blush" (1.2.196). The harsh Cardinal Monticelso, who is, as Vittoria acidly observes, judge, jury, and executioner, responds to Vittoria's spirited verbal defense at her arraignment by attempting to control her cosmetic self-expression: "I shall . . . paint out / Your follies in more natural red and white / Than that upon your cheek" (3.2.51–53). The accusation of blushface denies any value to the complexion Vittoria presents and insists that only Monticelso's painting hand can make her beautiful or, in this case, foul; Monticelso turns her blush into paint. Isabella, Brachiano's last duchess, is poisoned by the picture of her husband that she kisses every night; she is literally poisoned by paint. The same lead- and mercury-based paints were used on both faces and paintings (as the artist Paolo Lomazzo observes in his own anticosmetic treatise).

We saw earlier that Moorish Zanche delights in her dark complexion because she "may boldly say without a blush / I love you" (*WD*, 5.1.214–15) to the man she assumes is the warlike Moor Mulinassar. Zanche believes her blushlessness allows her to escape not only the confines of gender (permitting her to be an aggressive wooer) but also of race, the conjunction of skin color and rank: she asserts that she will be "washed white" with the wealth that she can bring her lover. She is, of course, mistaken; the supposed Mulinassar is Francisco, Duke of Florence, painted black in order to deceive Brachiano and achieve his revenge.

One could argue that the very title of *The White Devil* highlights the conceit of the fair lady, the devil in "good shape" (*WD*, 3.2.217), whose heart is corrupt and whose red and white is the artificial product of cosmetic deception. Painted pallor cannot "betray with blushing / The close enacts" of the heart. Wright's "brazen faces" may belong to dark-skinned Southerners, but they may also belong to faces too hardened in sin to change from white to red. Drew-Bear has briefly outlined some of the play's references to cosmetics, and suggests that these images prove Flamineo's point that "As in this world there are degrees of evils: / So in this world there are degrees of devils" (*WD*, 4.2.56–57). She adds that these images distinguish between degrees of white and black devils, confirming the proverb from which the play takes its name, "the white devil is worse than the black."[57] I would suggest, however, that the imagery of cosmetic deception in the play voices a very different fear: that the white devil is *indistinguishable* from the black.[58] Even if there are "degrees of devils," we cannot tell them apart: "the term 'black' is obsessively used to describe all of them."[59] And, of course, *all* the actors are painted: when Zanche complains to her old and now reluctant lover, Flamineo, "A little painting and gay clothes / Make you loathe me"—an instance of painting that Drew-Bear misses—her sentiment is richly ironic (*WD*, 5.1.169–70). The actor playing Zanche is painted too—but in blackface rather than the customary whiteface make-up. The play establishes, through theatrical devices such as eavesdropping, spectatorship, and report, that truth is indistinguishable from fiction, painted color from permanent complexion.[60]

Such ambiguities color not only the racialized meanings of skin tone but also the methods and mechanics of theatrical representation and the boundaries between art and life. The substitution of boys for women on the Renaissance stage implies that femininity is a free-floating signifier, as many have argued. Femininity is also allied with theatricality through fucus; painted women smear the distinctions between chaste and unchaste, real and imaginary, and black and white. And just as the taxonomies of black and white collapse on stage, so whiteness in Shakespeare's *Venus and Adonis* and Richard Barnfield's *Affectionate Shepheard* comes to figure the breakdown of not only desire but also of fundamental sexual difference itself.

Chapter 6

Whiteness as Sexual Difference

Much Ado About Nothing blackens both Beatrice and Hero. Benedick associates the "sunburnt" Beatrice with "Prester John" and the "Pigmies," and Hero hides behind her "Ethiop[ian]" veil. Here I shall argue that Shakespeare's *Venus and Adonis* (*Ven.*) and Barnfield's *The Affectionate Shepheard* (*AS*) interrogate these expected associations of color and chastity, but neither in praise of women nor in the service of an originary heterosexuality. Both provide, problematically, examples of mixed kind or genre—*Venus and Adonis* an abortive epyllion, *The Affectionate Shepheard* a failed pastoral eclogue. Both poems seem to shift into complaint mode, but they change mode yet again before concluding, Shakespeare's poem into the comic, and Barnfield's into the pious. This generic or formal mixing corresponds, I shall argue, to each poem's negotiations of early modern sexual difference and skin color. *Venus and Adonis* exercised what I shall call a hermaphroditic attraction for readers of both sexes during the period for two reasons. First, it foregrounds the act or the art of reading poetry and its similarity to interpreting gender difference; second, it emphasizes the shifting sexual ambiguity of both Venus and Adonis. Venus's desires at once reinforce the parallel drawn by the one-sex model between women and young boys (as both characters are rendered indistinguishable by their green or lovesick pallor, and written into a satire), and challenge it through the goddess's unruly attempts to take charge of the poem as writer and reader, and to turn it into epyllion. *The Affectionate Shepheard* ironizes the Petrarchan convention of fair female beauty by shunning whiteness, because it is the "ensign of every common woman" (*AS*, 2.307) and of opposite-sex love, and by praising blackness and color as the hues of a male homoerotic paradise and a relationship characterized by equality rather than domination and submission. Barnfield's equation of sexual difference with black and white corresponds to the color scheme of what is, as Joseph Pequigney and Duncan-Jones observe independently, the only other Elizabethan poem sequence directly addressed to a young man—Shakespeare's first 126 sonnets.[1] But where Barnfield dismisses whiteness altogether, whether in men or in women, Shakespeare's sonnets re-turn the trope to conclude that only *female* fairness is flawed. The sonnet tradition can evoke the transcendent beauty of fair masculinity, but female beauty now needs a counter-Petrarchan impulse in order to survive.

Reading for Pleasure

The tale of Venus and Adonis was well known during the sixteenth century; a search on Chadwyck-Healey's *English Poetry* database reveals, for example, 147 references to "Adonis" as Venus's lover between 1500 and 1603.[2] Shakespeare's poem on the subject was extraordinarily popular, going through nine editions during Shakespeare's lifetime (six before the turn of the century) and almost as many more between his death and the Civil War.[3] The *Shakspere Allusion-book* finds 61 direct allusions to Shakespeare's poem between its publication in 1594 and 1700. Why should the poem have sparked so much interest? And who was reading it? Duncan-Jones suggests that the poem became something of an Elizabethan sex manual, and that young Elizabethan men found Venus, a powerful older woman, "irresistible" because of her sexual assertiveness. Citing the examples of other sexually predatory women in erotic poetry, like Thomas Heywood's Oenone, or Francis Beaumont's Salmacis, Duncan-Jones marshals an impressive overview of allusions to the poem to prove its ubiquity in Elizabethan culture and concludes that sixteenth-century readers regarded strong women in a more positive light than did their Victorian or twentieth-century counterparts.[4] Her analysis ignores, however, the Elizabethan pamphlet wars about unruly women and the strictures of Swetnam, Gosson, Stubbes, and others against the female whom "no bridle will hold . . . back" and who "too much . . . coveteth of chamber play."[5]

"The fact that Venus's advances to Adonis are unsuccessful seems to have been scarcely heeded," asserts Duncan-Jones, but, on the contrary, the notion of an unwilling Adonis seems to have been the most piquant aspect of the poem to later writers.[6] Douglas Bush argues that there existed both a classical and a sixteenth-century tradition of a reluctant Adonis and a hungry Venus, and quotes Spenser's treatment of the tale to demonstrate a "faint hint of initial coyness" (*FQ*, 3.1.34–38).[7] The very three lines that Bush quotes as proof, however, emphasize the crucial difference between Spenser's and Shakespeare's treatments of the myth: "she / Entyst the Boy, as well that art she knew, / And wooed him her Paramoure to be" (*FQ*, 3.1.35). Spenser's Venus *succeeds*: Adonis becomes "her Paramoure," and she "joyd his love in secret unespyde" (*FQ*, 3.1.37). In addition, of the 147 references to "Adonis" in nondramatic verse before 1603, only one reference to Adonis as "proud" or "coy" possibly antedates Shakespeare's poem—Marlowe's "proud Adonis" (*HL*, 1.14).

Abraham Fraunce includes a lengthy treatment of the story in *The Third Part of the Countess of Pembroke's Ivychurch* (1592), but his Adonis expresses no concern when Venus caresses him:

Sometimes downe by a well with Adonis sweetly she sitteth,
And on Adonis face in well-spring lovely she looketh,
And then Adonis lipps with her owne lipps kindely she kisseth,
Rolling tongue, moyst mouth with her owne mouth all to be sucking,
Mouth and tong and lipps, with Joves drinck Nectar abounding.[8]

Fraunce's rhetoric conveys an idea of Venerian self-absorption (through the repetition of "owne" and the suggestiveness of "kindely," as if Venus is kissing *only* her "owne lipps"), but there is no sense that Adonis is actively resisting her.

There is, however, a cluster of references to a coy or arrogant Adonis *after* the publication of *Venus and Adonis*, including Thomas Edwards's "Faire Adonis in pride that shewes so hot" (1595), Bartholomew Griffin's "wayward" Adonis (1596), and Nicolas de Montreux's "coy" Adonis, who is compared to "peevish" Narcissus (1607, pub. 1610).[9] Perhaps the poem went through so many editions and was passed from hand to hand precisely *because* Venus was unsuccessful and Adonis unmoved, as Heather Dubrow suggests. The poem might present a fantasy of controlling powerful women by proving their ultimate dependence upon male favor. Dubrow argues that Shakespeare's poem might not be so much a celebration of strong, mature femininity as an attempt to parody the threat posed by a powerful female monarch upon the throne, comparing this poetic urge to the "shaping" impulse Louis Montrose finds in *MND.*[10]

Bruce Smith finds that Elizabethan erotic poems featuring androgynous young men appeal to another early modern male fantasy, this time a "bisexual" one. The youthful figures of Adonis and Leander, he argues, appealed because of their sexual indeterminacy to a Renaissance male sexuality that was "inclusive" rather than "exclusive" in its desires and that eroticized the "incorporation" of a young man into the powerful homoerotic bonds between men.[11] Smith's characterization of these poems as men's "bisexual fantasies" is appealing, and in fact supports Dubrow's suggestion that *Venus and Adonis* attempts to control the figure of the powerful woman by making the goddess finally unsuccessful in her love for a mortal. But I want to query his use of the word "bisexual" to describe the poem. The kind of masculine (and homosocial, to borrow Eve Sedgwick's term) consolidation he describes binds men together through the subordination or outright exclusion of women who are exchanged "between men," just as his reading of the poem excludes Venus as a female character. Might women have identified with both male and female characters, and have been attracted to the androgynous

Adonis or the panting Venus? Might *Venus and Adonis* be a "hermaphroditic" narrative, as well as a "bisexual" one, and have attracted a female audience, too?

Richard Halpern lists references to courtesans, lusty widows, and dreaming young girls as eager readers of the poem, suggesting that women, too, found Adonis's androgyny and youthfulness attractive, despite the fact that, according to him, the poem is designed specifically to frustrate female satisfaction with "misogynist humor . . . center[ed] on Shakespeare's debasing and slightly grotesque portrayal of female sexual desire."[12] Venus finds Adonis unable to penetrate her, even in "the very lists of love" (*Ven.*, line 595) because "all is imaginary she doth prove" (line 597), a comedy that, Halpern argues, depends upon the absent (or at least flaccid) phallus.[13] Female readers, according to this interpretation, are like the frustrated birds pecking Zeuxis's painted grapes, doomed to perpetual dissatisfaction, except in the realm of the aesthetic (*Ven.*, lines 601–02).[14] All the early modern authors Halpern mentions, however, are male; the purported female readership of *Venus and Adonis* might reflect an early modern male fantasy, rather than actual reading practices. We cannot presume that, because Middleton, Peele, and others imagine *fictional* women sneaking away copies of *Venus and Adonis* to read for titillation, real women actually did so. More useful is Sasha Roberts's discussion of historical female readers such as Frances Wolfreston (1607–77), who lived in Staffordshire, or the printer Elizabeth Hodgkinson. Wolfreston's first quarto contains a highly variant text of *Venus and Adonis*, one that "allow[s] for different readings of specific lines," including some that exaggerate and others that downplay the poem's misogyny.[15]

Halpern's interpretation privileges the poem's ending—and Adonis's negative responses—over the process of Venerian persuasion and the possibility of success to which it dedicates so much time, and it also fails to take into account the selective reading practices that early commentators (including the ones Halpern cites) described. Early modern men worried that Shakespeare's female readers might, like Venus, read for pleasure, rather than moral enlightenment. Unlike Venus, real women might not learn to heed the true meaning of "signs and prodigies" (*Ven.*, line 926) by the end of the poem, because they could choose to rewrite the narrative in their imaginations. Venus reads solipsistically, for her own pleasure, ignoring Adonis's reluctance and willfully misunderstanding his entreaties. Urging Adonis to "mark" (*Ven.*, line 643) her face and the sufferings of poor Wat, the hare, she herself only hearkens to "signs and prodigies" at the end of the poem, when they indicate Adonis's death.

Pamphleteers and playwrights accused the poem of engendering lascivious feelings in womankind because women could choose to read only the salacious bits. Consider a famous allusion in Thomas Middleton's *A Mad World My Masters* (1608), in which the jealous Harebrain prevents his lady from perusing "all her wanton pamphlets, as *Hero and Leander*, *Venus and Adonis*, oh, two luscious mary-bone pies for a young married wife!"[16] "[M]ary-" or "marrow-bones" are early modern aphrodisiacs, the source of animal spirits and vigor, but one sucks the "luscious" marrow and leaves the dry bone, just as one extracts the pith or "marrow" from a book.[17] Harebrain fails in his attempt to expurgate his wife's reading, even encouraging a courtesan, whom he believes to be a "pure virgin," to visit her (1.2.59). The courtesan offers Mistress Harebrain some sage advice, but not of the kind her harebrained husband would like:

If he chance steal upon you, let him find
Some book lie open 'gainst an unchaste mind
And coted scriptures, though for your own pleasure
You read some stirring pamphlet, and convey it
Under your skirt, the fittest place to lay it. (1.2.87–91)

The courtesan's image turns a mental tool for masturbation into a manual one; "under your skirt," the pamphlet lies in direct proximity to the organs it supposedly inflames. The play ends by restoring Mistress Harebrain to her husband, literally chaste-ned, when her adulterous lover undergoes a religious conversion effected through both literary means and a visit from a succubus. "[R]ead that place again!" he admonishes himself, perusing a tract (4.1.1). The she-devil in the next scene woos him in the guise of Mistress Harebrain and the tone of Shakespeare's Venus: "Had women such loves, would't not mad 'em? / Art a man? or dost abuse one?" (4.2.50–51). Saucy literature can inflame lust, but religious tracts can calm it. And in both instances, Mistress Harebrain and her penitent lover are reading snippets, draining the marrow.

Heywood's *The Fair Maide of the Exchange* (1607) mocks the thoughtless filleting and literal application of literary texts, but recommends sage and judicious editing. The besotted gallant Bowdler tries to woo the witty Mall Berry by quoting *Venus and Adonis*, but fails to emend (we might say, anachronistically, *to Bowdlerize*) his text.[18] Adopting Venus's lines wholesale, Bowdler urges Mall, "Vouchsafe thou wonder to alight thy steed," only to be cautioned by the canny Cripple, "Take heed, shees not on horseback."[19] As Duncan-Jones observes, Heywood is ridiculing those who read *Venus and Adonis* literally, as an instructional manual, rather than literarily.[20]

Venus and Adonis appealed to a variety of early modern readers because it dramatized the role of interpretive reading in perceiving sex and gender difference. Early modern readers employed their skills not just on books but on bodies, because sex and gender difference were ambiguous enough that such interpretation might be necessary. Laqueur suggests that there existed during the early modern period a "one-sex" model that regarded men and women as points along a continuum of sexual difference rather than as polar opposites, as earlier scholars such as Ian Maclean had suggested.[21] Aristotelian medicine regarded women as imperfect men, because of their perceived coldness and wetness; Galenic medicine extended Aristotle's theories by supposing women to be inverted men, whose sex organs remained inside the body because of their lack of heat. While women were associated with chill, moistness, softness, and matter, and men with warmth, dryness, hardness, and form, Laqueur argues that "hot" women and "cold" men could meet in the middle. A man with too much sexual interest in women could become "effeminate," woman-like, through prolonged association with them; a woman who demonstrated too much desire for men, a woman who generated too much heat, could become a virago or mannish woman. Given sufficient heat or cold, Laqueur observes, both men and women were thought able to perform what we now consider sex-specific functions like ejaculation or lactation. Some scholars (in particular, Paster, and Katharine Park) have argued that Laqueur's argument oversimplifies the conflicts between biological "sex" and socially determined "gender" by declaring them the same thing.[22] But his version of sex/gender as a process of differentiation, something that would require reading or interpretation, rather than the existence of physically determined, absolute physical opposites, clearly exists during the period, *alongside* more familiar (to us), emergent beliefs in biological, determinable, binary sex.

The tensions between these two versions of sexual difference turn *Venus and Adonis* into a hermaphroditic narrative. The poem is polymorphously perverse. Shakespeare's Venus is an unruly female reader, like Middleton's Mistress Harebrain, determined to wrest Adonis's sexual acquiescence from him despite his protestations, to read only the "marrow" of her text, and to write an epyllion. She is also, however, the victim of a narrative that subjects her to sexual humiliation and bereavement and writes her into a satire. The poem offers men the fantastic opportunity to triumph over a goddess (and by extension, their queen) and attempts to wrest rhetorical and sexual control away from women. At the same time, it allows the free play of cultural anxieties about female sexual satisfaction and men's inability to arouse, gratify, and fertilize their wives. Moreover, the poem's systematic interrogation of sex difference allows the possibility of a female reader with a space for desirous fantasies of her own, a space in which to appreciate the satire not merely of female desire, as Halpern suggests, but also of male patterns of courtship and seduction.

"more lovely than a man"

I shall discuss the connections of color, sex determination and reading shortly, but first I wish to establish the early modern association between language and femininity. For the mode of Venus's wooing couples female loquacity with masculine sexual assertiveness. As Dubrow and others have observed, Venus out-talks Adonis on every occasion, muffling his lines with five times as many.[23] "Where many geese be, are many turds, / And where be women, are many words," grumbles the author of the anonymous *Schoolhouse of Women* (1541). This text also complains that one devil can make a woman begin to talk, but all the demons in hell cannot silence her: "A devil a woman to speak may constrain, / But all that in hell be cannot let it again."[24] A popular fable told an alternative story of woman's creation: the first woman was born tongueless and speechless, until the Devil offered her dozens of aspen leaves for tongues, so light and mobile that they were never thereafter still. Since then, women have employed their "boister babble" to wear down their husbands.[25] Gosynhill's *Mulierum Paean* (1542) turns this association with words and eloquence to women's defense, giving Venus herself the task of defending women. Gosynhill's Venus praises women for their labor in rearing and bearing children, cataloguing the heroic women of the Bible and dismissing as "a lye" the popular fable of women born tongueless, because "god made all thynge parfetlye." More important than sex is "complexion":

All maner cloth is nat lyke fyne,
Nor yet all men complexyoned lyke
Some more of colour [choler], some more sanguyne
Some malancoly, some fleamatyke [phlegmatic]
Some longe and small, some shorte and thycke
Nat every man of one compleccyon,
Nor every woman of one condycyon.[26]

Venus's pun on "colour" and "choler" emphasizes the double meaning of "complexion," as both humoral personality traits and the skin colors associated with those tendencies. According to humoral theories of skin color, choler and blood turned people red; melancholy and phlegm made them pale; an excess of any one of these humors would turn the sufferer black. Venus connects temperament to skin color through the term "complexion" in order to play down temperament's association with gender difference, responding to antifeminist tracts, such as the *Schoolhouse of Women*, that characterized all women as lewd, talkative, and faithless. Finally, Gosynhill's Venus argues that "mother wit" is so called because it derives from the mother.[27]

Shakespeare's Venus seems to bolster the complaints of the antifeminist literature by her excessive talk. But her chatter is employed in the service not of scolding or moral elevation but of seduction. Venus's alluring speeches to Adonis mimic the advice given in gynecological manuals to husbands whose wives were unwilling to have sexual intercourse with them. Laqueur notes that female desire was considered essential to conception, and that "talk and teasing were regarded as a good beginning."[28] Ambroise Paré suggests a combination of words and deeds:

When the husband commeth into his wives chamber hee must entertaine her with all kinde of dalliance, wanton behaviour, and allurements to venery: but if he perceive her to be slow, and more cold, he must cherish, embrace and tickle her . . . intermixing more wanton kisses with wanton words and speeches.[29]

This mingling of kissing with speech is thought to be irresistible, and Venus offers both: 547 lines of verse interspersed with twenty-nine requests for (and successfully stolen) kisses. Venus usurps masculine behavior in order to seduce her lover, but men also use kisses to silence recalcitrant women. Shakespeare's Benedick complains, "I cannot endure my Lady Tongue" (*Ado*, 2.1.274–75) and "stops [Beatrice's] mouth" with a single kiss (5.4.97). Venus kisses to quiet Adonis, too; she "kissing speaks, with lustful language broken, / 'If thou wilt chide, thy lips shall never open'" (*Ven.*, lines 47–48), and overwhelms Adonis with multiple embraces and utterances not so much to enkindle desire but rather to suppress his responses.

At one point Adonis seems to refer to the myth of the aspen leaves:

If love have lent you twenty thousand tongues,
And every tongue more moving than your own,
Bewitching like the wanton mermaid's songs,
Yet from mine ear the tempting tune is blown;
For know, my heart stands armèd in mine ear,
And will not let a false sound enter there. (*Ven.*, lines 775–80)

Venus's eloquence seems to Adonis a sign of her hyperfemininity, and he identifies the love of women with "Lust" rather than "Love" because women "do it for increase" (*Ven.*, line 791), making love in order to reproduce sexually, rather than enjoying a heavenly or spiritual love. That such a distinction is bound to break down is clear even to the narrator, who identifies Venus with "Love" (*Ven.*, line 814) once more just twenty-two lines later.

Venus's wordiness is feminine, her words and actions masculine; her attacks on Adonis disturbingly imitate the assaults of Jupiter on human women like Europa and Io, even down to her metamorphosis into a beast through an Ovidian epic simile:

Even as an empty eagle, sharp by fast,
Tires with her beak on feathers, flesh and bone,
Shaking her wings, devouring all in haste,
Till either gorge be stuffed or prey be gone—
Even so she kissed his brow, his cheek, his chin,
And where she ends she doth anew begin. (*Ven.*, lines 55–60)

The cruelty of Venus's hunger makes visible the violence behind other mythological tales of erotic surrender, complicating a reader's pleasure with the awareness of the virgin's coercion.[30] The fact that Venus lacks the phallic "sharp . . . beak" makes the critique of divine male courtship more pronounced. Compare Marlowe's description of Hero, courted roughly by Leander, when "as a bird, which in our hands we wring, / Foorth plungeth, and flutters with her wing, / She trembling strove" (*HL*, 2.289–91). Both Shakespeare and Marlowe turn the love object into prey, to be pecked or strangled to death.

As if to heighten this sense of violent, male heterosexual identification, Venus relates to Adonis her own fantasy of female seduction:

Who sees his true-love in her naked bed,
Teaching the sheets a whiter hue than white,
But when his glutton eye so full hath fed,
His other agents aim at like delight? (*Ven.*, lines 397–400)

Venus is excusing Adonis's rampaging courser, but the obsession with whiteness, with surfeit, and with the beloved's passivity, supine in bed, is all her own. Venus reads whiteness as availability. Just as she concentrates on the "glutton" satisfaction of the viewer, rather than the "true-love," so Adonis's responses, whether reluctant, eager, indifferent, or angry, do not matter to her: "Being red, she loves him best, and being white, / Her best is bettered with more delight" (*Ven.*, lines 77–78). Pallor usually indicates cold disdain or angry withdrawal rather than eagerness; just like Follywit in *A Mad World*, who unwittingly marries the courtesan because he is smitten by her (feigned) reluctance to be wooed, Venus finds "more delight" in Adonis's passivity than in his active blushes. Venus's ambiguous sensations are mirrored by the narrator's grammatical uncertainty; both Venus and Adonis are alternately "red" and "white," and the present participle ("Being") refers not only to Adonis's fluctuating color (as most commentators read) but also to Venus's own changing emotions.

Whiteness elsewhere in the poem evokes a sexual exchange, what Woodbridge calls "sexual chiasmus . . . the crossing over of qualities between the sexes."[31] In a poem that, like *Hero and Leander*, uses color and color change to fill in the progress of love and attraction, Venus and Adonis become indistinguishable in a famous stanza that compares degrees of whiteness only to conclude that male and female, like "two silver doves," cannot be told apart:

Full gently now she takes him by the hand,
A lily prisoned in a gaol of snow,
Or ivory in an alablaster band:
So white a friend engirts so white a foe.
   This beauteous combat, wilful and unwilling,
   Showed liked two silver doves that sit a-billing. (*Ven.*, lines 362–67)

Who is "friend" and who is "foe"? Venus takes Adonis's hand, but her grasp is simultaneously evanescent, like "snow," and monumental "alablaster." Venus's pallor encompasses both feminine melting and masculine memorializing; whiteness is not just sexual difference but its collapse. Two lines later, Venus even calls aloud for transgendering and wishes that Adonis "wert as I am, and I a man" (*Ven.*, line 369). Here, however, Venus's ostensible wish for sex change does not enable heterosexual passion. "[A]s I am" turns out to mean "My heart as whole as thine, thy heart my wound," so that Venus here wishes that *both* she and Adonis were male, she heart-whole, and her only sexual "wound" (with the obvious pun on female genitals) hidden in Adonis's heart (*Ven.*, line 370). One of the anonymous contributors to *The Passionate Pilgrim* (1599) evidently took Shakespeare's Venereal "wound" in precisely this sense:

Fair was the morn when the fair queen of love,
. . .
Paler for sorrow than her milk-white dove,
For Adon's sake, a youngster proud and wild,
Her stand she takes upon a steep-up hill.
Anon Adonis comes with horn and hounds:
She, silly queen, with more than love's good will,
Forbade the boy he should not pass those grounds.
"Once," quoth she, "did I see a fair sweet youth
Here in these brakes deep-wounded with a boar.
Deep in the thigh, a spectacle of ruth!
See, in my thigh," quoth she, "here was the sore."
She showed hers, he saw more wounds than one,
And blushing fled, and left her all alone.[32]

As in Shakespeare's poem, Adonis's blush demonstrates not sexual desire but sexual revulsion.

   Even Adonis's "trampling courser" (*Ven.*, line 261), that epitome of uncontrollable male lust, turns out to have undergone a sex change. Adonis's stallion was "like a jade" (*Ven.*, line 391), before he broke free for love, like an exhausted nag but also like a woman worn out from sex work. Sexual desire renders him masculine once more; "his ears up-pricked . . . now stand on end" (lines 271–72) as he threatens to rape or impregnate the earth's "hollow womb" (line 268), but in throwing off his reins he resembles a shrew flinging off the scold's bridle:

> When he saw his love, his youth's fair fee,
> He held such petty bondage in disdain,
>> Throwing the base thong from his bending crest,
>> Enfranchising his mouth, his back, his breast. (*Ven.*, lines 393–96)

Using the terms "mouth," "back" and "breast" (all of which feature prominently in *Venus and Adonis* and *Hero and Leander*) to describe the animal's body anthropomorphizes the horse, focusing only on those parts that are "enfranchised" rather than using the more technical terms in the itemized description that introduced him:

> Round-hoofed, short-jointed, fetlocks shag and long,
> Broad breast, full eye, small head, and nostril wide,
>> High crest, short ears, straight legs and passing strong,
>> Thin mane, thick tail, broad buttock, tender hide. (*Ven.*, lines 295–98)

Yet even this clinical description carries a humorously erotic charge, recalling as it does Venus's own catalogue of her charms to Adonis:

> Thou canst not see one wrinkle in my brow,
> Mine eyes are grey and bright and quick in turning,
> My beauty as the spring doth yearly grow,
> My flesh is soft and plump, my marrow burning.
>> My smooth moist hand, were it with thy hand felt,
>> Would in thy palm dissolve, or seem to melt. (*Ven.*, lines 139–44)

Venus turns female dampness and liquescence into an image of spiritual union, as if her skin were as ephemeral as the "snow" (*Ven.*, line 362) it resembles. C. S. Lewis believed that a "flushed, panting, perspiring" Venus would "arouse disgust."[33] For Donne, however, the "fast balme" that "cimented" lovers' sticky hands together was a sign of "extasie" and the perfect communion of souls, while, for Marvell, his "Coy Mistress"'s "morning glew" was, if not a spiritual conjoining, at least a sexual en-counter with cosmic significance: "though we cannot make our sun / Stand still, yet we will make him run."[34] "Glew" combines a sense of "glowing" health and erotic deliquescence.[35] Melting moistness was a frank Elizabethan expression of sexual desire.

Venus dissolves, but the images of Adonis's pallor render him, too, in Venus's wishful gaze malleable, feminine, and apt to impression: "His tend'rer cheek receives her soft hand's print, / As apt as new fall'n snow takes any dint" (*Ven.*, lines 353–54). (We may recall Leander's back,

"That heavenly path, with many a curious dint" [*HL*, 1.68] and his "white . . . bellie" [1.66] in Marlowe's poem.) Venus has praised Adonis for being the "Stain to all nymphs, more lovely than a man" (*Ven.*, line 9), as if masculinity is less attractive to her than womanhood, as if Adonis is competing for her attentions against her own nymphs rather than against the hypermasculine Mars or the impotent Vulcan. When, however, she begs him later in the poem, "Set thy seal manual on my wax-red lips" (line 516) she returns to conventional notions of female impressionability.

Like the anticosmetic treatises in my previous chapter, Venus praises femininity and whiteness that is soft and that changes color, above the fixed or "painted" (line 212) alabaster whiteness of Pygmalion's statue, an emblem of "senseless" (line 211) femininity:

Fie, liveless picture, cold and senseless stone,
Well-painted idol, image dull and dead,
Statue contenting but the eye alone,
Thing like a man, but of no woman bred!
    Thou art no man, though of a man's complexion,
    For men will kiss even by their own direction. (*Ven.*, lines 211–16)

If Adonis fails to relent, he will become neither man nor woman, but neuter, like a doll. Men take what they desire ("kiss even by their own direction") and women softly succumb to a wooer's charms, but idols and statues remain sexually indeterminate because they are not activated by desire.

Both soft and hard whiteness are conventional attributes of female beauty, but Venus manages to eroticize even ugly pallor. Such a rhetorical move would not become popular until fifty years later in the poems to "Aethiopian," "yellow" and "greensickness" beauties by John Collop and Lord Herbert of Cherbury, as Dubrow observes.[36] Adonis calls himself "green" (*Ven.*, line 527), referring to his extreme youth, but Venus willfully misunderstands him. She diagnoses him with greensickness, and offers him the conventional cure for the "virgin's disease"—sexual intercourse.

Greensickness and "growth's abuse"

Johannes Lange described the symptoms and causes of greensickness in 1554:

Nor has this disease a proper name, as much as it is peculiar to virgins, might indeed be called "virgineus," which it is the custom of the matrons of Brabant to call white fever, of pale face & the fever of love: since every lover becomes pale, & this colour is proper for a lover. But this disease frequently attacks [female] virgins, when now mature they pass from youth to virility ["quum viro iam maturae ex ephebis excesserint"]. For at this time, by nature, the menstrual blood flows from the liver to the small spaces & veins of the womb: which are not yet distended, also obstructed by thick & crude humours, and finally from the thickness of the blood, cannot escape.[37]

This account combines two Hippocratic sources, the *Prorrhetic,* which describes "a greenish complexion" and an abnormal appetite for "stones and earth," and *The Diseases of Girls,* which observes the "delirium," "violent emotions," and "terrible" utterances of virgins who, although mature, are not yet sexually active and are therefore stifled by the rapid flow of blood to their unopened wombs.[38] In 1615 Johannes Varandaeus coined the term "chlorosis" to describe the fever, pale complexion, and wasting disease of "nobly-born and beautiful young girls who have abstained from all sexual intercourse."[39] The medical treatises avoid the popular term "greensickness," preferring "chlorosis" or "Pale face." Nicholas Culpeper comments on the disease's names in the *Compleat Practice of Physick*: "This Disease by Hippocrates, is called Chlorosis; by the Modern Physitians, the white Feaver, the Virgins Disease, the Pale Colour of Virgins, the white Jaundice, but vulgarly the Green-sickness."[40] Hippocrates's cure is to "marry as soon as possible," a solution with which Lange agrees: "I instruct virgins afflicted with this disease, that as soon as possible they live with men and copulate . . . In the treatment of this disease of virgins I have never been deceived or my hopes frustrated."[41]

The medical cure for greensickness coincided with what Culpeper might call "vulgar" belief. Capulet contemptuously dismisses Juliet's distaste for Paris as the fancies of a "green-sickness carrion" (*Rom.,* 3.5.156) a "tallow-face" (3.5.157) who will be cured by enforced marriage to parallel her enforced chastity. The Bawd who attempts to "cry up" (*Per.,* 4.2.93–94) Marina's beauty in the marketplace is driven to cry, "A pox upon her green-sickness!" (4.6.13) when Marina's chastity freezes the ardor of her best clients, and to suggest that only by contracting the "pox" through sexual intercourse can she "be rid on't" (4.6.15). Even fifty years after Varandaeus, and a century after Lange, Culpeper recommended "Copulation, if it may be legally done," as well as "the use of opening Medicines" to widen the passageway out of the womb and encourage women to expel their seed.[42]

Paré justifies medical intervention and marriage by arguing that female sexual desire in fact makes the illness worse. The English translators abridge and modify his account of greensickness, for reasons I shall discuss shortly, so I quote here the 1579 French edition, which gives a sustained account of the disease. Greensickness gives young women palpitations ("battement et deffaillance de cœur"), asthma ("elles gemissent et souspirent"), a pathological appetite ("l'appetite depravé"), and a "pale, yellowish color" ("la couleur pale et jaunastre") that makes them look "more dead than alive" ("plustot mortes que vives"):

> when they fall in love, [they] feel a heat in their genital parts, which disturbs, titillates and warms them, which makes them expel their seed by themselves: which remaining in the spermatic vessels, or in the womb, corrupts, and turns to venom . . . which sends putrid vapours to the higher regions.[43]

Hippocrates and Lange had blamed an excessive flow of blood to the womb, blood that was then trapped there, for the symptoms of chlorosis. Paré argues instead that, even if women try to force their own "seed" to descend from their "stones" or ovaries, once it is descended they cannot expel it from the womb because the opening is too small. Greensickness is caused by the presence of the female seed itself, unnaturally descended, putrefying and corrupting *in utero* in the place where a child should be.

Venus mounts a similar argument against autoeroticism when she recounts the tale of Narcissus: "Things growing to themselves are growth's abuse. / Seeds spring from seeds, and beauty breedeth beauty; / Thou wast begot, to get it is thy duty" (*Ven.*, lines 166–68). She later justifies Adonis's desire "To grow unto himself" (line 1180), however, and even fashions a reproductive method by which seeds will not spring from seeds. Beauty will breed beauty by transforming him into "A purple flow'r" (line 1168), traditionally identified with the anemone. This flower grows not from seeds but from bulbs that "grow unto" themselves underground, reproducing apparently by parthenogenesis, unpollinated by bees.

Paré's seventeenth-century English translators abbreviated the account of the physical symptoms in order to make the role of the imagination and of the suffering, greensick virgin's desires more explicit:

> the genitall parts burning and itching, *they imagine the act of generation*, whereby it commeth to passe that the seminall matter, either remaining in the testicles in great abundance, or else powred into the hollownesse of the womb, *by the tickling of the genitalls*, is corrupted, and acquireth a venomous quality, and causeth such like accidents as happens in the suffocation of the mother.[44]

The translator blames the woman's visions of sexual intercourse for the expulsion of her seed, and "the tickling of the genitalls" for the seed's corruption. "Burning and itching" are clearly unpleasant, but "tickling" suggests not only the possibility of pleasure but the application of an external stimulus, something that is doing the "tickling" (like Mistress Harebrain's "wanton pamphlets"). Marie H. Loughlin points out that most early descriptions of greensickness support the construction of virginal desire as naturally-directed toward and only towards marital intercourse, since a woman is immediately diagnosed as mentally unbalanced if her desires stray from these bounds, or if they are corrupted by her lack of marital opportunity.[45]

The sexual cure for greensickness also deflects the possibility that suffering virgins will try to relieve their discomfort by masturbating, Loughlin argues—as Paré fears.[46]

The sexual cure for greensickness is not always, however, directed towards lawful matrimony but, more importantly, toward the diversion of the virgin's desires to correspond to the demands of those who have power over her. The Bawd urges a sexual cure for Marina's greensickness not to marry her off legitimately but to debauch her, just as Polonius calls his daughter a "green girl" when he wishes to circumvent her love for Hamlet (*Ham.*, 1.3.101). In its power relations, greensickness differs crucially from medieval lovesickness. Mary Wack observes that, while medieval physicians had diagnosed "lovesickness" primarily as a male wasting disease or "cachexia," from the fifteenth century onwards it became more and more associated with young women and the "virgin's disease" or greensickness. (When Falstaff wishes to impugn the manhood of "demure boys" [*2H4*, 4.3.90] who sup "thin drink" [4.3.91], he argues that "they fall into a kind of male greensickness, and then when they marry, they get wenches" [4.3.93–94]. "Getting wenches" would be a sign that a man had become too cold to create boys, and thus that he had slid farther along towards damp, cool femininity.) Wack argues that, in the medieval period, the symptoms of lovesickness feminized male sufferers, and were therefore undiagnosed in women, but that the rediscovery during the Renaissance of classical texts relating cases of female lovesickness made the disease visible in women once more. She speculates that female lovesickness enabled women to choose a mate, purportedly for therapeutic reasons, at a time when women outnumbered men, chastity was strictly enforced, and marriage was by no means inevitable.[47]

Wack's hypothesis seems plausible: Moll Yellowhammer, Middleton's *Chaste Maid in Cheapside* (*CMC*, 1611, pub. 1630), manages to turn her diagnosis to her advantage. Her parents complain that she is suffering from "green-sickness" (*CMC*, 1.1.4) which makes her a "dull maid" (1.1.3) and try to marry her against her will to Sir Walter Whorehound. Later in the play, however, Moll uses her deathly lovesick pallor to feign her own demise and marry her true love, Touchwood Junior ("Gold into white money was never so chang'd / As is my sister's colour into paleness" [5.2.20–21], remarks her brother). The fact that spiritual lovesickness is almost completely replaced by pathological greensickness in the early modern period makes me wonder, however, whether male lovesickness becomes female greensickness in the Renaissance not because women were actively choosing partners but because early modern culture wished to pathologize and control women's desires. Lovesickness stems from one's own desires for a particular object; greensickness is conveniently non specific and can be cured by anyone of the opposite sex, anyone who can fertilize one's seed. A lovesick medieval man was sickened by the desire to win a particular woman, and cured by intercourse with her alone, but a Renaissance diagnosis of female greensickness could compel a woman to take a husband she did not desire (like Shakespeare's Juliet) or engage in sexual intercourse against her will (like Shakespeare's Marina), again, ostensibly, for therapeutic reasons. Lovesickness, in contrast, manifests itself aggressively, regardless of the suitability of the love object in terms of rank, physical appearance, national origin, and parental fiat. The Jailer's Daughter in *The Two Noble Kinsmen* falls madly, we might say, in love with Palamon despite the disparity in rank; Desdemona elopes with Othello, fitted to her by neither clime, complexion, or degree; Juliet's lovesick desire for Romeo becomes in her parents' eyes nonspecific greensickness, curable not by marriage to her beloved but by intercourse with the man of their choice. Lovesickness can even be non-gender-specific in its direction, as Neely argues with regard to *As You Like It* and *Twelfth Night*.[48]

With the possibility of coercion in mind, we can now return to Chapter One and to Chariclea's otherwise unaccountable reluctance to confess her lovesickness for Theagenes. Sandford's *Amorous Tales*, as we saw, translates only Chariclea's lovesickness, including her swollen eyes, her "looke set awry," her "pale" face, and her silence as symptoms. He includes, however, the cure along with the ailment: "Thou muste seeke some man Charicles," admonishes Chariclea's physician.[49] Charicles conveniently assumes that Chariclea is greensick and may be cured by marriage to "some man," any man, preferably the nephew to whom he has already promised her. Calasiris, a better father and a better physician, realizes that she is lovesick and requires one particular man, namely Theagenes: a love match instead of an arranged marriage.

Venus and Adonis inverts the gendered associations of greensickness with women in order to emphasize the power dynamics of the diagnosis. The first description we have of Venus is "Sick-thoughted" (line 5); "love-sick" (line 175), "like a bold-fac'd suitor" (line 6), she demands a specific object to sate her love. Calling Adonis greensick allows her to ignore his protest in the name of therapy. The pale, unwilling virgin is Adonis, who calls himself a "green" plum (line 527), "sour to taste" (line 528), "unripe" fruit (line 524), "ungrown fry" (line 526). "Green" refers to Adonis's youth and immaturity, but to his complexion too; his appetite is "leaden" (line 34) like his pale "frosty" face (line 36). Culpeper describes chlorotic virgins with faces "of a Lead colour."[50] Adonis resents having to fend off Venus's advances once more; his "text is old, the orator too green" (*Ven.*, line 806). (And here his sexual reluctance and his rhetorical weakness become equivalent). Even after his death, transformed into a flower, Adonis produces "green-dropping sap" (line 1176). Venus quibbles even on the meaning of "unripe," interpreting Adonis's adjective as "not rotten" rather than "not ready": "the tender spring upon thy tempting lip / Shows thee unripe; yet mayst thou well be tasted" (lines 127–28). Greensickness was a disease of female adolescence, an ailment associated with sexual maturity and, in women, the beginning of menses; the text satirizes the pathological explanations for greensickness by correlating its supposed appearance to Adonis's *male* symptoms of the onset of puberty, his faint mustache ("the tender spring"). A secondary sex characteristic becomes a sign not of ultimate, biological sex difference but of a virginal likeness between adolescent girls and boys—their vulnerability to sexual coercion.

The text articulates cultural anxieties about the role and function of sexual difference and heterosexual intercourse most strongly in the narrator's description of Venus and her desires. Venus's virilization—through "wanton words," her violent assaults on Adonis, her emphasis on kissing and fondling and on sexual reversal—disturbs the narrator sufficiently that he has to reassert the ultimate importance of penetration and the phallus, the sign of absolute sexual difference:

Now is she in the very lists of love,
Her champion mounted for the hot encounter.
All is imaginary she doth prove;
He will not manage her, although he mount her:
    That worse than Tantalus' is her annoy,
    To clip Elysium and to lack her joy. (*Ven.*, lines 595–600)

This is the narrator's account of Venus's desires and his explanation of her "continual kissing" (line 606); it also finds the narrator's most determined and personal interjection: "But all in vain, good queen, it will not be" (line 607). The narrator mentions Venus's power (she is a "queen") only to emphasize its seeming limits, vehemently: "it will not be." But Venus "sinketh down" (line 593) not with lust but with the "sudden pale" (line 589) fear that "usurps" it (line 591). The anxieties Venus voices immediately after her long clinch with Adonis pertain to the boar, and *its* penetrative abilities, rather than her own "annoy":

O be advised, thou know'st not what it is
With javelin's point a churlish swine to gore,

> Whose tushes never sheathed he whetteth still,
> Like to a mortal butcher bent to kill.
>
> On his bow-back he hath a battle set
> Of bristly pikes that ever threat his foes. (*Ven.*, lines 615–20)

Adonis cannot "gore" the beast, who, it seems, will wield the "javelin's point" and "bristly pikes" himself against his hunter. The boy's ostensible sexual function is displaced onto his attacker:

> Being mov'd, he strikes whate'er is in his way,
> And whom he strikes his crooked tushes slay.
>
> His brawny sides, with hairy bristles armed,
> Are better proof than thy spear's point can enter. (*Ven.*, lines 623–26)

Penetrative heterosexual intercourse becomes identified with the pikes," "bristles," and sharp "tushes" of the boar, the "javelin's point" or "spear's point" that cannot "enter" him. In her lament on Adonis's demise, Venus turns the boy's wound into an explicitly sexual one, comparing intercourse with a sexually assertive woman to violent death:

> nousling in his flank, the loving swine
> Sheath'd unaware the tusk in his soft groin.
>
> "Had I been tooth'd like him, I must confess,
> With kissing him I should have kill'd him first. (*Ven.*, lines 1115–18)

Venus repeatedly voices her fear of penetration, ostensibly for Adonis, but also for herself; she demands from Adonis only "kisses," which she successfully obtains. Venus's own plants offer a demonstration of sexual desire that contrasts with the boar's assault and Venus's fantasies: the plants do not scratch or enter her flesh but "kiss her face" (line 872) and "twin[e] about her thigh" (line 873) as she had kissed and entwined Adonis.

Venus and Adonis both reinforces and challenges early modern notions of what constitutes a sexual act: the narrator stridently emphasizes that Venus's satisfaction is imaginary, because of Adonis's impotence, but ultimately it is the boar's sharp tusks, not Adonis's refusal, that end the love affair. Valerie Traub observes that most religious and legal accounts of early modern erotic encounters assume that sexual acts are impossible without penetration and that, therefore, two women together can only enjoy a sexual encounter if one of them either becomes a man or uses a prosthesis to simulate the male organ. The most famous classical myth of female homosexual desire, the story of Iphis and Ianthe, concludes with the metamorphosis of Iphis into a man; legal cases limit themselves to prosecuting women who act as "tribades," who allegedly use dildoes or monstrously enlarged clitorises to penetrate their lady-loves. Traub, however, finds in gynecological tracts and in the theater a space for female same-sex desire, arguing (much as Bruce Smith does for male homosexual desire) that women's sexual feelings in the period might belong on a continuum of loving attraction where "the direction of object choice hardly figured at all" rather than in opposition towards or transgression against heterosexual marriage.[51] Women's homoerotic desires only become threatening to early modern culture when they threaten sexual reproduction by preventing women from mating with men.[52] The words of Venus and the narrator offer a reader two different versions of female desire: frustrated by the presence of the phallus (the marauding boar) or frustrated by its absence (Adonis's missing erection). One version emphasizes difference and reassures Harebrained husbands (women with other women, or alone, can never be satisfied with only kisses and words), the other worries them (women can satisfy themselves alone or through other women, with amorous kisses and wanton words).

Venus and Adonis uses whiteness or greensickness to collapse the division of the sexes: the poem suggests that sexual difference and erotic desire, far from being self-evident bodily truths, are filtered through power and fantasy. Social signs of gender, like loquacity or assertiveness, silence or passivity, are clearly labile. Neither can biological signs like blushes, greensickness, or even the sex act itself, be taken as ultimate signs of gender or sex difference. Whiteness provides only the background upon which a reader or viewer can inscribe masculinity or femininity. In contrast, Barnfield's *Affectionate Shepheard* employs pallor as a sign of absolute sexual difference, criticizing women for false fairness and praising men for honest blackness. The praise of blackness, as part of a larger strategy of ironic reversal, allows Daphnis, the "affectionate shepheard," to outline a strategy of seduction that is uniquely masculine and a marital model based on equal partnership rather than on submission and domination.

"be my Boy, or else my Bride"

The full title of Richard Barnfield's 1594 volume is *The Affectionate Shepheard. Containing the Complaint of Daphnis for the love of Ganymede.* The first two poems in the volume, *The Teares of an Affectionate Shepheard sicke for Love, or The Complaint of Daphnis for the Love of Ganimede,* and *The Second Dayes Lamentation of the Affectionate Shepheard* form two halves of a complete narrative of Daphnis's unrequited love for Ganymede, his jealousy of Ganymede's fair female love, Guendolen, and his ultimate

rejection of earthly love altogether. Bruce Smith calls the two parts
"eclogues," comparable to Spenser's divisions in *The Shepherd's Calendar*; Harry Morris describes them as "lamentations" or "querelae," written in imitation of Spenser's style and Abraham Fraunce's form in his
Latin poem *Amyntas*.[53] The title poems present us with a shepherd,
Daphnis, who loves the young shepherd boy Ganymede passionately and
unrequitedly:

O would to God (so I might have my fee)
My lips were honey, and thy mouth a Bee.

Then shouldst thou sucke my sweete and my faire flower
That now is ripe, and full of honey-berries:
Then would I leade thee to my pleasant Bower
Fild full of Grapes, of Mulberries and Cherries;
Then shouldst thou be my Waspe or else my Bee,
I would thy hive, and thou my honey bee. (*AS*, 1.95–102)

Perhaps the most provocative aspect of Daphnis's plea is his continued
role play within the context of a clearly homoerotic (possibly pederastic)
love. Bruce Smith reads the image of honey and bee as a reversal of "the
usual Petrarchan conceit" where "the lady's lips are the honey," but
the image also interrogates conventional Elizabethan wisdom about the
position of a "Boy"-lover with an older man.[54] "Ganymede" or its corruption, "catamite," referred in Elizabethan English to the passive partner in a male homosexual encounter. Daphnis reverses the convention
by turning himself into the hive or home and Ganymede into the searching bee. Julie W. Yen takes the lines' ambiguity still farther, arguing that
the lines indicate a deep sexual ambivalence: "[Daphnis] remains am-
bivalent about the role change, reluctant to let the beloved actually take
over the more powerful male position."[55]

Evidently Barnfield's frankness (and perhaps his playful inversion of
Ganymede's role) proved slightly too much for his first readers; he pref-
aced his next volume of verse, *Cynthia*, with an apology for any offense
his last book might have given:

Some there were, that did interpret *The affectionate Shepheard*, otherwise then (in
truth) I meant, touching the subiect thereof, to wit, the love of a Shepheard to a
boy; a fault, the which I will not excuse, because I never made. Onely this, I will
unshaddow my conceit: being nothing else, but an imitation of *Virgill*, in the second Eglogue of *Alexis*.[56]

Virgil's "second Eglogue of *Alexis*" recounts the love of the shepherd
Corydon for "lovely Alexis," "his master's joy" ("Formosum . . . Alexin, /

delicias domini").[57] Alexis, like Ganymede, scorns Corydon's rustic gifts, but unlike Ganymede, prefers a male rival, "Daphnis," not a female, above the poet. Barnfield takes from Virgil not only the situation but many of Corydon's arguments, most importantly, the praise of black over white. Corydon urges Alexis not to heed color too much, when white flowers fall unnoticed to the ground and black berries are eagerly gathered ("nimium crede colori: / alba ligustra cadunt, uaccinia nigra leguntur").[58] As Virgilian imitation, Barnfield's poem is highly successful, providing lush English counterparts for Corydon's rustic catalogue of treats. Renaissance readers would have picked up Barnfield's Virgilian echoes immediately, both through the situation portrayed in the poem and through the name "Daphnis."

Why, then, did Barnfield need to reiterate his debt to Virgil? His emphatic defense is somewhat disingenuous. Corydon's and Daphnis's accounts differ significantly in the depth and seriousness of the shepherd's affection. Virgil's Corydon laments for Alexis, but at the same time acknowledges that he, too, has spurned eager suitors and that, should Alexis continue to refuse him, he can choose from both men and women lovers (black ["niger"] Menalcas and arrogant ["superba"] Amaryllis).[59] In the lament of Barnfield's Daphnis, these suitors have become mere shadows or hints; he asks why Ganymede should "disdaine to kisse, / And sucke that Sweete, which manie have desired" (AS, 2.103–4). In Barnfield's poem, these "manie" are unnamed; the spotlight shines more narrowly upon the dramatic trio of Daphnis, Ganymede, and Guendolen. When Ganymede persists in disdaining Daphnis, the latter forswears love altogether (and urges Ganymede to do likewise). Virgil's Corydon, on the other hand, concludes his lament with the half-sarcastic, half-practical comment that if this Alexis continues to be too proud to love him, he can always find another one ("inuenies alium, si te hic fastidit, Alexin").[60] Corydon's litany of lovers, past and present, conjures up a world of interchangeable partners, but Daphnis pleads for monogamy. His invitation to Ganymede to "be my Boy, or else my Bride" (AS, 2.78) has no equivalent in Barnfield's immediate Latin source. Insisting that his love is essentially literary allows Barnfield to escape the implications of the differences between Virgil's second eclogue and The Affectionate Shepheard, including Daphnis's praise of same-sex union over opposite-sex marriage.

Barnfield's most recent editor, George Klawitter, explains the objections towards The Affectionate Shepheard as anger at Barnfield's portrayal of Guendolen, her dead lover, her elderly husband, and Ganymede, whom he takes to be Lady Penelope Rich (Sir Philip Sidney's "Stella," Barnfield's patron and the dedicatee of The Affectionate Shepheard), Sidney, Lord Rich, and Charles Blount (Penelope Rich's long-standing lover) respectively. Klawitter is not the first to make such claims. In 1935, H. H. Hudson offered a topical interpretation of *The Affectionate Shepheard* and in particular of the account of Guendolen's dead lover, who is mistakenly struck by Death's ebony arrow instead of Cupid's golden one, which strikes a "doting foole" instead (*AS*, 1.55).[61] As Morris observes, however, *The Affectionate Shepheard* is dedicated to Lady Rich, and it is unlikely that Barnfield would have accused her of moral laxity, or described her husband as an elderly buffoon who "wipes the drivel from his filthy chin" (*AS*, 1.62), if he wished to attract her patronage.[62] In addition, Charles Blount, the supposed Ganymede in Klawitter's scheme, was hardly a "sweet fac'd boy," being eleven years older than Barnfield himself and approximately the same age as Lord and Lady Rich.[63] On the contrary, Blount and Penelope Rich may have consummated their affair as early as 1583, before Sidney's death, when Barnfield himself would have been indeed a "sweet fac'd boy"—less than ten years old.[64]

Klawitter also insists that Barnfield's open homoeroticism "fit into the mainstream of Elizabethan life.[65] Such an understanding of Elizabethan sexual mores seems at best naïve, at worst misleading. Active same-sex passion did *not* fit easily into "the mainstream of Elizabethan life." Alan Bray points out that, although the modern category of "homosexual," as a person whose identity is defined by a fixed or firm sexual orientation, was not available to the early moderns, *sodomy* was a punishable crime.[66] The legal situation is complex; as Jonathan Goldberg and Bray both observe, in the Renaissance sodomy is a vaguely defined offense. Although Pulton's collection of statutes includes "to commit Buggery with mankinde or beast" under the heading of "Felonie," even men caught in the act of having sex with other men are rarely called "sodomite," unless they commit crimes against the state, such as atheism or treason, too.[67] Nonetheless, many early modern writers carefully attempt to distinguish between same-sex love in the abstract and the act of love itself. Spenser's E. K. notes (on Hobbinoll's love for Colin in *The Shepheard's Calendar*):

pederastice [the love of boys] is much to be praeferred before gynerastice, that is the love whiche enflameth men with lust toward woman kind . . . let no man thinke, that herein I stand . . . in defence of execrable and horrible sinnes of forbidden and unlawful fleshlinesse. Whose abominable errour is fully confuted.[68]

"Pederastice" is to be praised insofar as it excludes "fleshlinesse," physical love, which is identified only with men's love for women. E. K. assumes that the love of men for boys is by definition spiritual, not carnal.

Barnfield's poem opens with the assumption that his love is both physical and, therefore, sinful:[69]

I began to rue th'unhappy sight
Of that faire Boy that had my hart intangled;
    Cursing the Time, the Place, the sense, the sin;
    I came, I saw, I viewd, I slipped in. (*AS*, 1.3–6)

The rhyme of "sin" and "slipped in" makes Daphnis's dilemma clear: the "sin" is the "sense," the sensual, physical aspect of his love, "slipping in." Later in the poem Daphnis claims that his love for Ganymede is purely spiritual, but at this point, trapped by his own admission of physical desire, he cannot demand that Ganymede give up his female lover on the grounds that heterosexual love is "fleshlinesse," as Spenser suggests, and homosexual love, idealism. Instead, Daphnis urges Ganymede to forget Guendolen, the beautiful but hardhearted woman who stands at the third point of this love triangle, because she is a hypocrite:

Leave Guendolen (sweet hart) though she be faire
Yet is she light; not light in vertue shinning:
But light in her behaviour, to impaire
Her honour in her Chastities declining;
    Trust not her tears, for they can wantonnize,
    When teares in pearle are trickling from her eyes. (*AS*, 1.157–62)

Dismissing Guendolen's beauty here sets the scene for Daphnis's later encomium to blackness, and the equation of women with falseness and promiscuity, through the pun on "light" as both fair-skinned or whitish in hue and as lewd or frivolous. Guendolen may be physically beautiful or fair, but her lovely pallor is not a sign of shining, brilliant virtue but of moral laxity or unchastity. Like a fallen star, her "Chastities declining." Even her pearly tears are crocodiles'; as they flow down her cheeks, they "wantonnize," tease and inspire wanton lust, rather than tender pity, in observers.

Daphnis spreads his own "teares" or "lamentations" over two days. The first day praises Ganymede in conventional Petrarchan and pastoral terms, delighting in his "Ivory-white and Alablaster skin . . . / . . . staind throughout with rare Vermillion red" (1.13–14), offering the boy a catalogue of rural delights such as "Apples, Cherries, Medlars, Peares or Plumbs" (1.146), "yong Rabbets" (1.190) and fresh "hearbs" (1.170). But on the second day Daphnis tries a different strategy. Ganymede has evinced no inclination to sit in a bower, so Daphnis offers him the chance to "goe shoote at little Birds / With bow and boult (the Thrustlecocke and Sparrow) / . . . A fine bowe, and an yvorie arrow, / . . . [to] catch the long-billd Woodcocke and the Snype" (*AS*, 2.43–50). As Bruce Smith observes, the bow and ivory arrow, the thrustlecock and woodcock, are explicit images of male same-sex desire.[70] Ganymede can use the arrow to catch a woodcock or a snipe with a long bill or beak; hunter and hunted share sexual characteristics. The hunting imagery is also a masculine version of the sonnet mistress as huntress with nets and traps in her hair, eyes and brow to snare the enchanted lover—compare the eyes of Spenser's lady, shooting "legions of loves with little wings . . . darting their deadly arrowes" and her "golden tresses" that form a "golden snare."[71]

Daphnis offers Ganymede an increasing catalogue of delights, culminating in marriage: "[My nightingale] shalt thou have, and all I have beside: If thou wilt be my Boy, or else my Bride" (*AS*, 2.77–78). It seems plausible that Barnfield and his comrades at Brasenose would be familiar with the numerous Latin accounts of male marriages that Martial, Juvenal, Cicero, and the biographer of the Emperor Nero observed and that John Boswell describes in *Same-Sex Unions in Pre-Modern Europe*. Boswell finds the accounts predominantly sarcastic: Martial mocks the wedding of "the bearded Callistratus" and "the rugged Afer"; Juvenal censoriously notes "a friend is marrying another man"; Cicero acidly observes that Curio the Younger is "united in a stable and permanent marriage" with a male friend whose debts he has agreed to honor. But what horrifies these writers is not the extraordinary nature of these formal ties but the widespread acceptance of such unions by Roman society.[72] The third century saw a moral and legal backlash against same-sex unions, but

it is obvious from the wording of the law that gender roles and expectations are as much at issue as same-gender sexuality. The word employed for "marry" is *nubere*, the Latin term for the bride's part, the word used in derision by Martial, Juvenal, and the biographers of Nero . . . to describe a male's playing what was seen as an archetypally female social role: being given away in marriage, surrendered into the power and control of the husband.[73]

Cicero, likewise, compares young Curio's lover to a "matron," as if the mere idea of formalizing the same-sex relations that existed between men in the Roman world necessarily turns one of them female.[74]

Daphnis's distinction between "Boy" and "Bride" does not, however, offer Ganymede a blunt choice between male and female roles, but a combination of equal rights and feminine housekeeping. As a "Bride," Ganymede will be entitled to "all I have beside," the sharing of property, but he will also move from the green world outdoors to the domestic world within. A "Boy" hunts, but a "Bride" keeps the "Lardarie" (*AS*, 2.79), raises "pretie Cubs" (2.88) and "Whelps" (2.89), wears "A silken Girdle, and a drawn-worke Band" (2.92), and protects his fair complexion: "With Phoenix feathers shall thy Face be fand / Cooling those Cheeks, that being cool'd wexe red, / Like Lillyes in a bed of Roses shed" (*AS*, 2.100–102). The phoenix reproduces asexually, parthenogenetically,

laying an egg and then immolating itself in its own flame. Fanning Ganymede's face with "Phoenix feathers" would not cool him but fire a new
love from the ashes of the old, so that his cheeks turn "red" with heat.
"Lillyes in a bed of Roses shed" inverts Spenser's "roses in a bed of lillies
shed" (*FQ*, 2.3.22), and I find in line 101 an allusion to *Venus and Adonis*,
"Claps her pale cheek, till clapping makes it red" (*Ven.*, line 468).

Just as this bridal, feminizing imagery reaches its height, the poem begins to change tone, accusing Ganymede of being "cold yce" (*AS*, 2.108),
too proud of his complexion. Such female flintiness, implies Daphnis, is
unworthy of his Ganymede; Daphnis demands ironically that Ganymede
cut his brown hair to display his white face, before coming out with his
true aim—"To prove th'indecencie of mens long haire" (*AS*, 2.134). Perhaps through an association with false hair (an Elizabethan cosmetic sta-
ple), inappropriately long hair takes Daphnis into an exordium on vanity:

Oh lend thine yvorie fore-head for Loves Booke,
Thine eyes for candles to behold the same;
That when dim-sighted ones therein shall looke
They may discerne that proud disdainefull Dame. (*AS*, 2.145–48)

Who is the "proud disdainefull Dame" who personifies Love? Is she
Guendolen, appearing in Ganymede's eyes because he thinks about
her? Klawitter suggests that she is an abstraction, the personification
of "unrequited love."[75] Bruce Smith finds in the image an originary
moment of "disgust" for "texts of heterosexual experience."[76] The next
stanza makes Daphnis's meaning clear, however; the "proud disdainefull
Dame" is a figure for Ganymede himself, if he follows Daphnis's mocking advice to

Learne of the Gentlewomen of This Age,
That set their Beuties to the open view,
Making Disdaine their Lord, true Love their Page;

   Learne to look red, anon waxe pale and wan,
   Making a mocke of Love, a scorne of man. (*AS*, 2.157–61)

Daphnis is contrasting a female path familiar to us from my previous
chapter (pride, "yvorie" disdain, flirtation, and false blushes) with what
he is going to set up as a male model of seduceable sincerity. What Bruce
Smith calls "texts of heterosexual experience" (even simply the *desire* for
heterosexual experience) threaten to feminize Ganymede. If Ganymede
wants to charm the woman he loves, he will have to act like a woman and
follow a pattern of coy and meaningless blushing, to stain himself with
the "vilde spot" (*AS*, 2.175) of pride, "A blemish that doth every beauty
blot" (2.177).

Proud, deceptive female fairness concerns Barnfield elsewhere; "The Complaint of Matilda Fitzwater," printed in the same volume as *AS*, identifies female face painting as the "faire-foule Tincture" that is the "Divells dye."[77] Cosmetics corrupt femininity, giving white fairness an "impure complection."[78] "Complection," as we have seen, puns both on the color of women's faces and on the humoral composition or compounding of women. Female essence has been adulterated and turned into a "Monster of Art, Bastard of bad Desier."[79] "Monster" alludes to its Latin etymology, from *monstrare*, to show, whereby display itself makes women horrific, and "bastard" parallels the anticosmetic rhetoric of female adulteration that we encountered in my previous chapter. Before make-up, complains the poet, "Then women were the same that men did deeme, / But now they are the same they doo not seeme."[80] In the old days, women were as men believed them to be, but now they are the same as something—something unspecified—that they do not resemble.

Daphnis's encomium to blackness in *AS*, which lasts for some sixteen stanzas, reinforces these concerns with false female fairness. He inverts conventional images of purity and whiteness such as the lily or the dove, arguing that black sage is more fragrant than putrefying white lilies (*AS*, 2.229–32) and that blackbirds (harbingers of doom since classical times) are better than doves because they are tastier (2.233–34).[81] Just as black sturgeon is "a daintier dish" (2.226) than the white whale, so "ripe red Cherries" (2.250) or black damson plums have "the sweet smacke" (2.250), black rabbits have softer skins (2.239), and black or colored fish are more nourishing than their paler brethren:

Salmon and Trout are of a ruddie colour,
Whiting and Dare is of a milk-white hiew:
Nature by them (perhaps) is made the fuller,
Little they nourish, be they old or new:
    Carp, Loach, Tench, Eeles (though black and bred in mud)
    Delight the tooth with taste, and breed good blud. (*AS*, 2.283–88)

Daphnis evidently believes that the way to a man's heart is through his stomach. Losing or failing to produce "good blud" was thought to cause greensickness; thus eating dark foods, he claims, prevents excessive, unhealthy pallor. The shepherd here veers away from standard humoral medical guidelines, however, in his diet-plan of mud-bred fish for Ganymede; *The Castel of Helthe* (1539) in fact singles out "the fyshe . . . which are in muddy waters" as "the warse [worse]" because they produce "moche fleume and ordure."[82]

The "ruddie" and "milk-white" shades that Daphnis praised in Ganymede before now are worth less than blackness. "The blacker still the brighter dims" (*AS*, 2.274), he insists, reversing the religious trajectory of black turning to brightness through Christ's suffering and the associations of black with obscurity. "Sable excels milk-white in more or lesse" (2.276); "Sable" is a term from heraldry, the armorial black that signifies constancy, sacred lore, and mourning.[83] Heraldic white or "Argent" would normally signify chastity, virginity, freedom from sin, and charity,[84] but in Daphnis's blazon "White is the Ensigne of each common Woman" (*AS*, 2.308), the arms of pride, moral corruption and promiscuity. Exceptional women *do* exist: "The learned sisters sute themselves in blacke" (2.301), and "Vertue and Gravity are sisters growne" (2.305). But these exceptional women in black are pointedly abstractions.

"Thy black is fairest in my judgement's place"

Barnfield shares with Shakespeare the distinction of producing Elizabethan love poetry addressed directly to a young man, poetry that employs the contrast of black and white to distinguish between men and women and between male and female desire. Both Barnfield and Shakespeare employ the ironic praise of blackness (including its associations with the exotic, as we shall see) in order to establish the superiority of same- to opposite-sex love and lovers, but Shakespeare argues that whiteness can be rescued—when it is personified not in a woman but in a man. In its masculine incarnation, a lover's whiteness transcends the abilities of poetry to portray it, as in Sonnet 82:

I grant thou wert not married to my muse,
And therefore mayst without attaint o'erlook
The dedicated words which writers use
Of their fair subject, blessing every book. (Sonnet 82, lines 1–4)

Sonneteers, like women who paint themselves, color or decorate faces that require it in their ugliness; but "their gross painting might be better us'd / Where cheeks need blood; in thee it is abus'd" (lines 13–14). Sonnet 83 repeats the praise of whiteness and the dispraise of poetry by insisting, "I never saw that you did painting need, / And therefore to your fair no painting set" (lines 1–2); in fact, the young man is so perfect that not only is the poet unable to "paint" or embellish, he cannot even describe him accurately, because "a modern quill doth come too short" (line 7). Compare the Shakespearean battle I discussed in Chapter Two, between "beautifull old rime" (Sonnet 106, line 3) that praises the "fairest wights" (line 2) of the first 126 sonnets, and the modern quills of sonnets 127–154 that praise "black" beauty, which "in the old age . . . was not counted fair" (Sonnet 127, line 1). Joel Fineman argues that the "dark lady" sonnets establish a new kind of subjectivity in lyric poetry, a subjectivity based upon verbal paradox rather than visual correspondence, in contrast not only to previous sonnet sequences but also to the Shakespearean sonnets earlier in the 1609 sequence (as we have it) addressed to the fair young man. If we accept this reading, then the dark lady sonnets supersede the ones addressed to the fair youth; a new age praises black over white, new poetry over old rhyme, ironic or startling conceit over elegant and mellifluous blazon.

Duncan-Jones argues for the opposite position in her edition of the sonnets, claiming that the earlier sonnets work more effectively and originally as poetry. She finds in the sonnets to the dark lady (as does Katherine Wilson) empty parodies of conventional love lyric that misogynistically mock the female sex.[85] Any praise, Duncan-Jones suggests, derives from the fact of possession; she hears Touchstone's barbed characterization of his Audrey as "a poor virgin . . . an ill-favoured thing, sir, but mine own" echoing throughout the dark lady sonnets (*AYL*, 5.4.58).[86] Sonnet 131 might seem to prove her point. It puns on every sense of the word "black" to conclude that the lady is beautiful, but black-hearted:

Thou art as tyrannous, so as thou art,
As those whose beauties proudly make them cruel,
For well thou know'st to my dear doting heart
Thou art the fairest and most precious jewel.
Yet in good faith some say that thee behold
Thy face hath not the power to make love groan;
To say they err I dare not be so bold,
Although I swear it to myself alone.
And to be sure that is not false I swear
A thousand groans but thinking on thy face
One on another's neck do witness bear
Thy black is fairest in my judgment's place.
In nothing art thou black save in thy deeds,
And thence this slander as I think proceeds. (Sonnet 131)

Her "black" is her complexion, the calumnies of others against her, her sinfulness, her beauty, and the ugliness attributed to her by others. The complicated syntax of the third quatrain mitigates what seems at first like a straightforward claim "Thy black is fairest in my judgement's place." But the witnesses to this claim are the "thousand groans" that the poet utters in order to test both whether the observers err and whether or not his own private swearing is "not false." Consider what happens if we give a different emphasis to lines 5 and 6: "Yet (in good faith) some say that thee behold / Thy face hath not the pow'r to make love groan." "In good faith" between parentheses becomes over-emphatic, an interjection that casts doubt on the veracity of the poet's own report or "good faith": the poet turns from being the lady's champion into her detractor.

Not only the measure of her beauty but the measure of truth itself is sub-jective, hidden in his "dear doting heart." The "slander" is other people's strictures upon her beauty, but also the poet's praise of it: in praising her, he slanders beauty, and in slandering her beauty, "some" slander morality by believing that her lack of beauty, rather than her lack of truthfulness, is what makes her "black." To read the sonnet as univocally woman-hating, however, misses yet another level of irony. The poet's caustic admission that his judgment is flawed (something stands "in . . . place" of his judgment, after all [line 12]) makes us wonder whether the lady's deeds are indeed "black" or whether this conclusion is another lapse in his judgment: if the lady is untrustworthy, so is her lover (com-pare also Sonnet 138, in which the lovers "lie" together in every sense).

Sonnet 144 presents similar ambiguities of color and conscience, iden-tifying the bad angel with "a woman color'd ill," the good one with "a man right fair" (lines 3–4), and concluding that the poet shall "live in doubt, / Till my bad angel fire my good one out" (lines 13–14). The good angel is supposed to chase away the bad, but the next sonnet in the sequence presents the opposite scenario: the woman, the supposed *bad* angel, rather than the good, chases away "a fiend / From heaven to hell" (Sonnet 145, lines 11–12) and transforms "hate" to love (line 13). The triumphant couplet of 130, "And yet, by heaven, I think my love as rare / As any she belied by false compare" (lines 13–14) raises the female sonnet mistress to the level of the "master-mistress" of Sonnet 20 (line 2) by claiming that poetry misrepresents her with "false compare" just as it fails to represent the "man right fair" (Sonnet 144, line 3). And Sonnet 132 argues that, since female whiteness is irredeemably cruel, the dark lady alone possesses compassion or "pretty ruth" (line 4). Shakespeare's sonnets argue that fair women are corrupt, but assert (unlike Barnfield's sonnets or the poems in *The Affectionate Shepheard*) that neither whiteness nor femininity is consequently worthless. Pallor *can* survive (but only in men), and women *can* remain beautiful (but only in blackness).

Barnfield's erotics of irony is less nuanced and consequently more extreme. In *AS*, he questions not merely the moral and gendered values of whiteness but also its nationalistic associations by praising colored objects from foreign lands over white ones from Britain. Black pepper, a precious commodity from the Spice Islands, is more valuable than white snow, black jet rare next to plain white pebbles, "yellow burnisht gold, that comes from th'East" (*AS*, 2.219–20) more desirable than "The whitest silver . . . / Lead, Tynne and Pewter" (2.241–43). Britain had sil-ver, tin, and lead mines, and used pewter to make eating utensils, but gold was imported from India and the New World.

Daphnis's examples of desirable foreign objects contradict Barnfield's assertions in "The Complaint" that homegrown customs and products are better than imported ones like make-up. Barnfield grumbles that face painting is "Staining our Clymate more than anie Nation."[87] The use of cosmetics is especially unseemly in a country where maidens blush easily and can easily be seen to blush. But Daphnis, like *Lusts Dominion*'s Eleazar, praises black for its immunity from blushing and pallor:

And last of all, in black there doth appeare
Such qualities, as not in yvorie:
Black cannot blush for shame, looke pale for fear,
Scorning to wear another livorie.
Blacke is the badge of sober Modestie,
The wonted weare of ancient Gravetie. (*AS*, 2.295–300)

In praising black skin for its unvarying color, the narrator here reverses the common belief that we encountered in my previous chapters—that dark-skinned peoples were incapable of shame because they did not blush visibly.

Daphnis inverts the associations of whiteness with courtliness and rank, too, by arguing that the "paltry miller" is white, presumably because he is covered in flour (*AS*, 2.307). The miller's pallor is the result of an occupational hazard, a sign of his labor. While the chapters in this section, "Whiteness Visible," have considered the ways that the language of skin color is mobilized in the service of early modern anxieties about sexual difference, desire, and female self-fashioning, the next section, "Travail Narratives," looks at the ways that ethnic and bodily discourses engage with changing seventeenth-century taxonomies of labor to produce an emergent complex of race.

III
Travail Narratives

Chapter 7
Artificial Negroes

In the Renaissance, the so-called Gypsies were thought to come from Egypt, although Sir Thomas Browne includes this belief as one of the "Vulgar and Common Errors" that his *Pseudodoxia Epidemica* attempts to correct. Browne calls the Gypsies "Artificial Negroes" or "counterfeit Moors" who darken their skins cosmetically: "Artificial Negroes, or Gypsies acquire their complexion by anointing their bodies with Bacon and fat substances, and so exposing them to the Sun" (*PE*, 3:255). But, as is now well known, the Gypsies call themselves "the Romany people" or "Roma," and their language, "Rom." Linguists note that the Romany language resembles Punjabi and that the words "Rom" and "Dom," the name for a North Indian caste of nomadic dancers and musicians, are probably cognates. Most scholars agree that the Gypsies came from India, gradually making their way across Europe as dancers, tinkers, and fortune-tellers.[1] Among Romanies, the story of their Egyptian origin is supposedly known as "the Great Trick."[2] Upon their landing in France in 1427, the Gypsies told King Charles VII that they belonged to a tribe of "Little Egypt" that, having refused to shelter Mary and Joseph after the slaughter of the innocents, was doomed to wander the world doing penance for its sin by visiting all the Christian shrines in Europe. Such claims of religious penance earned them special privileges in medieval Scotland and Tudor England. James V, James VI's grandfather, paid them lavishly for dances in court and even drew up a (short-lived) treaty with John Faw, self-proclaimed "Lord and Earl of Little Egypt," agreeing that the constables and officers of Scotland would help Faw regain his throne from a Gypsy usurper and return to his mythical kingdom of "Little Egypt." In England, Gypsies had the right to be tried by a jury half of whose members were also Gypsies, and they were permitted to hunt; moreover, as pilgrims they were entitled to receive alms when churchmen and aldermen distributed them.[3]

But successive monarchs removed the Gypsies' rights and imposed harsh legislation forcing them to settle in one area, doff their "outlandish" clothing, and take up a trade, accusing them of being "counterfeit Egyptians." Rogue literature similarly accuses Gypsies of counterfeiting, of using costume to hide their bodies and make-up (ochre, walnut juice, or pig fat) to hide their faces. This willful use of costume and make-up links the Gypsies to actors, and indeed Thomas Dekker structures his *Lanthorn and Candlelight* (*Lanthorn*, 1608) like an antitheatrical tract. He complains first that the Gypsies are "counterfet," an old platonic objection to actors of all kinds, and devalue the original, the ideal.[4] Second, they are lewd and cozening. Third, they entice observers into sin both by setting a precedent themselves and by collaborating in sinful activities with spectators. Fourth, they wander about, and since they play so many parts and live in so many regions, their loyalty is under suspicion. The Gypsies owe no fealty to the monarch, as they are "Land-pyrates" who have their own king and queen and flout the authority of the throne by establishing their own, semiparodic system of government (E4r).[5]

Legally, of course, wandering Gypsies were subject to the same laws as wandering players and minstrels. Those actors who could not demonstrate that they were "Players of Enterludes belonginge to any Baron of this Realme, or any other honourable P[er]sonage . . . authorized to play" were deemed "rogues, vagabonds and sturdy beggars," and compelled to give up their travels.[6] Dekker wrote many plays and masques; he objects not to the fact that the Gypsies are actors, but to the manner in which they conduct their business, performing under their own auspices rather than under the benevolent patronage of a nobleman. Gypsies, like traveling players, conducted performances under nobody's arms but their own illicit ones.

Concerned that these Gypsies, like actors, play multiple parts before outsiders while concealing their true nature, Dekker (characteristically) literalizes the metaphor: "The women . . . (like one that plays the Rogue on a stage)" steal householders' livestock in order to kill and consume it in the open air, telling curious passersby that the dying squeals of the animals are merely the screams of a Gypsy woman in childbirth (*Lanthorn*, E4r). Dekker describes this "massacre" of "Innocent Lambs, Sheep, Calves, Pigges" as though it were the dénouement of a particularly gory Jacobean tragedy:

So cruell they are in these murders, that nothing can satisfie them, but the very heart bloud of those whom they kill . . . A Goose comming amongst them learnes to be wise, that he never will be Goose any more. The bloody Tragedies of all these [animals] are onely acted by the women, who, carrying long knives or Skeanes under their mantles, doe thus play their parts: The Stage is some large Heath, or a Firre-bush Common, far from any houses: Upon which casting themselves into a Ring, they inclose the Murdered, till the Massacre be finished. (*Lanthorn*, E4r)

While actors on the Jacobean public stage were all men, in the drama Dekker imagines the players are women. On a literal level the all-female cast gives credence to the excuse that the Gypsies make to onlookers for the rumpus, that the women are assisting at a childbed, and on a figurative level, it allows Dekker to transform the traditionally feminine activity of preparing dinner into a witches' Sabbath. The plucked geese bleed upon a "stage" of suffering within a "conjuring circle" (E4r) while Dekker's female Gypsies, like the witches in *Macbeth*, add purloined and secret ingredients to their broth. The activity is thus quintessentially feminine, but its transformation into "tragedy" is a sign of the female Gypsies' unruly, transgressive virility; the "long knives or Skeanes" concealed under their clothing become a phallic symbol. Antitheatrical writers such as Philip Stubbes or William Prynne complained that men in women's clothing on the stage were effeminized by their role. As far as the playwright Dekker is concerned, however, the converse is true: the stage is so clearly a masculine preserve that an all-female cast can only be a company of witches.

The "massacre" heightens another of Dekker's fears: if the Gypsies were merely pretending, like actors, they would not be half so dangerous. As in Hamlet's device to extract a startled confession from Claudius, the Gypsies perform one tragedy only in order to enact another of their own. Dekker sees the Gypsies as rogue actors who use their theatrical skills to commit larceny. Referring directly to the murder of Polonius, he imagines that the only person who can catch the Gypsies *in flagrante* is some "mad *Hamlet*, [who] hearing this, smel[ls] villainy, and rush[es] in by violence to see what the tawny Divels are doing" (*Lanthorn*, E4r).

But where Elizabethan and Jacobean legislators and the writers of rogue literature castigate Gypsies as illicit or unlicensed laborers (arguing that they are in effect unemployed and unemployable), Middleton and Rowley's *Spanish Gypsy* (*SG*, 1623, pub. 1653) characterizes wandering Gypsies as unauthorized actors or performers.[7] Jonson's *Gypsies Metamorphosed* impudently asserts that "the power of poetry" and theatrical costume can not only destroy Gypsy nationhood but also create courtly convention. Finally, Shakespeare's *Antony and Cleopatra* pushes the relationship between Gypsy actors and the Renaissance stage still further through its "right Gypsy" of a heroine, foregrounding an underlying metaphor that unites the suspiciously playful work of the wandering Gypsy, the histrionic toil of the actor, and the invisible labor of the artist.[8]

Gypsies, Rogues, and Peasant Slaves

Henry VIII's act against vagabonds in 1530 was unremittingly severe, forbidding "outlandishe people callynge them selves Egiptians" to enter England and compelling those already there to leave within sixteen days, or risk forfeiture of their worldly goods (22 Hen. VIII c. 10). The penalties for remaining in England grew increasingly harsh: by 1535, a Gypsy caught in England could be "whipped" the first time he was caught in England, mutilated the second, and declared a felon, subject to death, the third (27 Hen. VIII c. 25).[9] Edward VI retained his father's statutes, adding the proviso in 1547 that *anyone* caught wandering was to be considered a vagabond, branded with the letter V, and enslaved for two years to the first man who offered him or her employment. These slaves were to be soundly whipped and chained and fed upon bread and water. If they ran away from their masters, they were branded with the letter *S* to signify eternal slavery (1 Edw. VI c. 3). The act was repealed two years later, presumably because of its cruelty and the difficulty of enforcing it.[10]

Queen Elizabeth broadened existing Poor Laws in 1562 to include "counterfeit" Egyptians as well (5 Eliz. c. 20). Elizabeth's act expresses concern that there is some "scruple or doubt arysen" as to whether British-born subjects who dressed and spoke in a Gypsyish manner should be punished in the same manner as those who were "straungers borne." These "scruples" were easily laid to rest, as the act concluded that "counterfeit" Gypsies were just as liable to punishment and to being declared felons, even if they could not be deported.[11] This severe sentencing does not suggest that vast numbers of Englishmen were running off with the Gypsies, but rather reflects a new problem, one concerning the definition of national identity, as both John Timpane and Mark Netzloff discuss. By this time a significant number of Gypsies had been born in England and were thus Englishmen, who could not be deported. Gypsies entering England from Scotland presented the authorities with a particularly murky dilemma. They were not liable to deportation, as they were considered to be Scottish, rather than Egyptian, immigrants; yet at the same time their very Scottish provenance raised for the Elizabethans the specter of espionage and popish plots, as Gypsies reportedly smuggled Catholics into the country.[12] After all, contemporary accounts accused the Babington conspirators of dyeing their faces with walnut juice and disguising themselves as Gypsies in their flight from the law, when their plot to replace Queen Elizabeth with Mary, Queen of Scots was discovered.[13]

The anti-Gypsy statutes of Elizabeth I had been severe, but their implementation contrastingly lenient: wandering Gypsies had rarely been executed, as the law demanded. A 1596 statute reiterated that all "p[er]sons not being Fellons wandering and p[re]tending themselves to be Egipcyans, or wandering in the Habite Forme or Attyre of counterfayte Egipcians" were rogues and vagabonds (39 Eliz. c. 4). Previous statutes had assumed that *all* Gypsies were "Fellons," but this act "did not so readily equate Gypsies with felons."[14] It limited the death penalty to dangerous criminals who flouted their sentence of banishment and reentered the country. The 1596 statute also broke down the categories of "real" and "counterfeit" Gypsies: only "counterfayte Egipcians" appeared in the legislation, because the idea of the genuine Egyptian had disappeared altogether.

The laws of King James I similarly assumed that all remaining Gypsies must be counterfeit. As king of Scotland James had ordained in 1579 that "strang and idill beggars" (including Gypsies) could be nailed by their ears to a tree and mutilated before they were banished on pain of death.[15] In 1592 he ordered "feinzied [feigned] fooles and counterfaict Ægyptians" to settle down in one place, on pain of banishment, and again ratified the 1579 act.[16] A 1609 act made it illegal for anyone to shelter a Gypsy from the reach of the law.[17] By 1612, Scottish Gypsies no longer held the right of self-government; as the oath for ministers asserts, "no foreine Prince, State or Potentat, hes or ought to have any jurisdiction, power, superiority, pre-eminence, or authority."[18]

In England too, James began immediately to strengthen the laws against vagrants of all kinds. In 1603 he toughened Elizabeth's 1596 statute by requiring that captured rogues, including the Gypsies, be branded "with a greate Romane R," for "Rogue" (1 Jac. I c. 7). In 1621, the year of Jonson's masque of *The Gypsies Metamorphosed* (so beloved by King James that he requested it three times), a bill urging "the continuance of a number of old statues . . . on rogues and vagabonds" narrowly missed being upheld, as an urgent matter of Monopolies attracted Parliament's notice instead.[19]

Why were these punishments so cruel? The ostensible reason for the continuing crackdowns on vagrancy during the early modern era was the claim that masterless men posed a menace to the commonwealth on the large scale and a thieving threat to individual gulls on the small. But, as Woodbridge points out in her exhaustive and principled *Vagrancy, Homelessness, and English Renaissance Literature*, there is little or no historical evidence that these so-called "rogues" deserved such vituperation or engaged in any of the organized criminal activities of which statutes and cony-catching tracts accused them. Marx, most famously, objects to the breakdown of the connection between the land and the serf who farmed it for his own subsistence, suggesting that economic forces freed the serfs only to render them subject to the vagaries of employers and landlords, who in turn suffered from fluctuations in wealth. Woodbridge adds to Marx's economic analysis sociocultural reasons for the harshness of the laws against vagrants. Rescuing the early modern wandering poor from their misrepresentation in rogue literature and jest books, she suggests that the Poor Laws speak in part to England's desire to develop a sense of national identity through the exclusion of the poor and the homeless.[20]

This process of national development involved dismantling the remnants of the feudal system—including residual categories of labor. England did not use the term *serf* during Elizabeth's or James's reigns, but there were still villeins, who were also called "bondmen" or "bondwomen" and who did not have the right to leave the land where they were born, or to sell their own labor.[21] Villeinage was technically never outlawed in Britain, although individual owners could and did free their bondslaves.[22] In 1574 Queen Elizabeth gave to William Cecil and Walter Mildmay "full Power and Aucthoritie . . . to accepte admitte and Receive to be Manumysed Enfranchesed and made Free, such and so many of our Bondmen and Bondwomen in Blood," and all their descendants, in several counties in southwestern England. Elizabeth saw the connection between freeing her villeins and generating a labor market. Practicality, not sentimentality, dominates her response to her bondslaves' "humble Suyte": she concludes that, once freed, "they theire Children and Sequells may become more apte and fitte Members for the Service of Us and of our Common Wealthe."[23]

Elizabeth's act was limited in region and in scope, liberating only those who were bondslaves to the crown, not villeins in general. "Villenage may be pleaded," specified Pulton's collection of "all the penal Statutes which be general, in force and vse" thirteen years later.[24] Pulton quotes laws from the reign of Richard II to the effect that even if the villein had a writ of manumission pending, his lord could request the local Justices of the Peace to "enquire of Villaines which do vse them selues rebelliously" and return him to bondage.[25] Leaving the land for "any citie, towne or place infranchised" would do such a bondslave no good: "ye Lord shal not be barred of his villaine, because of his aunswere in law."[26] This era uses the terms "bondslave" and "villein" indiscriminately; later law cases distinguish between slavery and villeinage on the grounds that an owner may inherit, but may not sell or kill, a villein. This is what Chief Justice Holt meant when he held, controversially, in 1701 that "One may be a Villein in England, but not a Slave."[27]

A villein who ran away to London and went into service might not improve his or her standard of living. "If slavery is defined as labor without material recompense," writes Maurice Hunt, "then many English servants were basically enslaved," theoretically entitled to wages in addition to room and board but often denied them—often, too, beaten cruelly.[28] The freedom to sell one's labor was further restricted by means tests and by the apprentice system. Those with an income of less than forty shillings per year could not choose where to work; "Craft masters might ask for and compel the labor of persons under . . . thirty who had completed apprenticeship in a trade"; ablebodied adults who "were neither bound apprentices nor practitioners of a craft could be forced to work as farm laborers."[29] The law recognized several kinds of worker—small-holding peasant, servant, craftsman, farmworker, and apprentice—and forced Elizabethan laborers into each category. Slave, villein, peasant, rogue, and vagabond were thus recognizable castes in early modern England. The first three were born into their rank and the first two could be inherited by landowners, while rogue literature imagines that vagrants form a family or guild of related persons passing on a tradition of organized crime. The very title of John Awdeley's tract is *The Fraternity of Vagabonds* (1561).

But where did the Gypsies fit in? Neither lords, nor bondslaves, nor peasants, nor wageworkers, nor merchants, they lacked the villeins' and lords' ancient connection to the country and the merchants' burgeoning connection to the city. They were not common rogues such as beggars or thieves (although the rogue literature tries hard to put them into these categories), because they did work when they felt like it, dancing, mending pans, and telling fortunes up and down the country. The objects and services they sold, however, were neither necessary (like food) nor valuable (like gold), so they could not be called merchants or craftsmen. They sold not products but play; their labor resembled leisure.

The Gypsies' defiance of existing divisions of labor inspires British anthropologist Judith Okely to argue that Gypsies have never fit into England's rigid class structure. Okely's *The Traveler-Gypsies* has become the standard textbook on Gypsies in Britain, popularizing the term "traveler" in law and the press.[30] She contends that English Gypsies were not "exotic" strangers but a group of indigenous Britons who, like wandering actors, "chose to reject wage-labour rather than be proletarianised."[31] Her study is synchronic; she is more interested in analyzing English Gypsies as a tribe or ethnicity than in tracking down their origins. In fact, she rejects outright the evidence of earlier Gypsiologists identifying English Gypsies with the Roma and with North India. I find her suggestion that the Gypsies challenged the institution of wage labor compelling, but would like to modify her ascription of individual, politicized resistance to the Gypsies and her insistence that they were autochthonic, by historicizing it. As Netzloff argues, the Jacobean era lays the psychic groundwork for the blossoming of nationalism that Benedict Anderson and others locate in the eighteenth century. Jacobean Gypsies comprise a group that claims to be another nation; Netzloff adds that this Gypsy nation is sufficient unto itself and in effect *performs* its nationality. In the past, the Gypsies had had different legal rights based upon their supposed distinct foreign origin, but as more Gypsies were born in England and as England itself developed a stronger sense of nationhood, this nuanced coexistence seemed impossible.[32] English Gypsy bands in the late sixteenth and early seventeenth centuries probably incorporated not only native runaways but also wanderers who traced at least part of their ancestry back to the Roma. The Gypsies therefore threatened residual feudal structures of villeinage, dominant structures of apprenticeship (in which the village or the county was responsible for the welfare of its citizens) and ethnic prejudice, and emergent capitalist norms of wage labor, nationalism, and racialism.

In any case, from a legal standpoint, such debates about Gypsy origin did not matter. If the overt virulence of the laws against Gypsies, rogues and vagabonds stemmed from the belief that they committed crimes, then the covert outrage of these statutes derived from the perception that such nomads had deliberately decided to be outcasts. Elizabeth's and James's statutes imply that those who settled in one parish, took up a steady trade, and refrained from calling themselves Gypsies would be entirely excused. Even the early statutes of Philip and Mary had conceded this; wandering Egyptians, they claimed, had only to wander no more in order to remain unmolested. Being a member of the Gypsy people during the Jacobean period was imagined (like unemployment or vagrancy) as entirely voluntary, and therefore completely reversible.[33]

At the same time, the rogue literature points to the impossibility of such seamless integration between English and Gypsy, counterfeit and real. The early modern discourse of Gypsydom reveals the ambiguous and uneven process by which several modes of difference become racialized: clothing (in contrast to the fetish of nudity in the travel narratives that I discuss in my next chapter), resistance to labor (another classification that appears in travelers' tales), unsanctioned geographical mobility, a supposed autonomous governing structure (as Netzloff discusses at length), theatricality, and dark skin. Defined by unauthorized play (theatrical performance and wanton idleness), the Gypsies not only exposed the workings and constraints of an emergent wage economy but also contaminated the shaky categories of Gypsy and Englishman, Jew and Christian, strange and homegrown, counterfeit and real. Such national, religious, and corporeal categories (English, British, Jewish, white, tawny) were of course tenuous in the period, as Floyd-Wilson, Murphy, and others have shown. As we saw in Chapter Three, however, their flexible boundaries made it all the more crucial to maintain and manage such distinctions as they gradually emerged.

"Tawny Moores Bastards"

Andrew Boorde's description of "Egiptians" (1542) highlights the Gypsies' strangeness but cannot explain what it is:

The people of [Egipt] be swarte and doth go disgisyd in theyr apparel contrary to other nacyons they be lyght fyngerd and use pyking [pilfering] they have litle maner [ill manners] and evyl loggyng [poor lodging] & yet they be pleasunt daunsers.[34]

It is unclear whether the Egyptians are "contrary to other nations" in their clothing or in their digital dexterity. According to Boorde, an "Egyptian" is defined by disguise, yet we have no indication of what one might look like *un*disguised. Boorde differs from later commentators in his ready acceptance that the so-called "Egyptians" do in fact derive from Egypt and that the Christian Gypsies were fleeing the "infydele alyons" who had overtaken their native land, which he locates "ioyned to Jury [Jewry]."[35] Later writers occasionally pick up this association between Jews and Gypsies, as we shall see.

Samuel Rid's *Art of Jugling* (1614), however, insists that "the name of Egiptians" belongs only to rogues and counterfeiters. These supposed Egyptians imitate the long-lost foreign original by wandering, by "coulouring their their faces," and by adopting similar garments, "yet if you aske what they are," he continues, "they dare no other wise then say, they are Englishmen, and of such a shire, and so are forced to say contrary to that they pretend."[36] Given the compelling legal reasons that would make it highly expedient to claim to be an Englishman with a home "shire," it is unsurprising that so many of Rid's informants did so. Dekker, and Samuel Rowlands in *Martin Marke-All, Beadle of Bridewell* (1610), likewise assert emphatically that even though the wandering bands of Gypsies are called "Egyptians," they are not from Egypt. Those who "[call] themselves by the name of Egyptians" are "rogues . . . [who] live by cousening and deceit," "delighting . . . [the common people] . . . with the strangenesse of the attire of their heads . . . and practising palmistry."[37] Note that now only the Gypsies' "attire" is "strange," not they themselves. Again, they challenge acceptable patterns of work and leisure. They offer "toys," childish pastimes, and "new fangles," invention in the service of spurious entertainment.[38] Even the "fortunes" they tell are written on the palm rather than earned through the sweat of one's brow. "[F]ayning themselves to have knowledge" in palm-reading or other estoteric craft, or "p[re]tendinge" that they could foresee the future connected the Gypsies to witchcraft, as James I's 1603 act proclaims.[39]

Dekker compares these fortunetellers and cheiromancers to the Egyptian conjurers whom Moses and Aaron defeated. A modern plague of Egypt, they descend like "those Egyptian Grasshoppers that eate up the fruits of the Earth, and destroy the poor corne fields" (*Lanthorn*, E4v), infesting the country like "Egyptian lice" (E3v). In a parody of biblical history, they reverse the course of scripture: in the Old Testament, the Jews wander through the desert after their liberation from Egypt, yet these Egyptians are "a people more scattered then Jewes, and more hated" (E3r). As in Dove's commentary on the Song of Songs, here prejudices against one group (in this case, the Jews) are mobilized in the service of those against another (the Gypsies). Dekker similarly evokes the Irish when discussing the Gypsies' lack of fealty to the crown, comparing them to the "Irish kern" (*Lanthorn*, E3v). This association reappears in his comments upon their "patched filthy mantles uppermost, when the under garments are handsome and in fashion" (E4r), a description that recalls the conceit of Jonson's *Irish Masque*, in which the dancing Irish lords are supposedly naked beneath their mantles.

Fears of adulteration and indeterminacy fuel Dekker's outrage at the Gypsies' dark skin:

a man that sees them would sweare they had all the yellow Jawndis, or that they were Tawny Moores bastards, for no Red-Oaker man carries a face of a more filthy complexion, yet are they not borne so, neither has the Sunne burnt them so, but they are painted so. (*Lanthorn*, E3r–v)

Dekker suggests that the Gypsies, like their skins, belong to no recognizable category. A medico-humoral explanation would suggest that they suffered from the "yellow Jawndis," an excess of black bile or melancholy, but such is not the case. A vocational explanation would claim that their skins were stained by some occupational hazard, like the face of the "Red-Oaker man." But the Gypsies follow no such profession. Their complexion's "filth" does not come from dirt, nor is it inherited (they are not "borne so"). The heliotropic explanation for blackness is likewise untrue. Unlike all the previous examples, their skin tone comes from an artifice that, he claims, they have chosen, rather than from nature or from society at large. Such face painting is even worse than the sort in which women indulge when they "make [them]selves another" (*Ham.*, 3.2.143–44), because "they are not good painters either: they doe not make faces, but marre faces" (*Lanthorn*, E3v).

A glancing reference to Gypsies in Jonson's *Volpone* (1606) likewise associates Gypsies with religious and sexual commixture.[40] Dekker's "Tawny Moores bastards" may remind us of the lineage of Volpone's "[b]astard" servants, sired "on beggars, / Gypsies, and Jews, and black-moors, when he was drunk" (*Volpone*, 1.5.43–45). This time three different racial groups are evoked towards the othering of the poor. Androgyno, Castrone, and Nano are adulterate or miscegenated in national origin and in their own characters or bodies. Androgyno, a hermaphrodite, can enjoy "the delight of each sex" (1.2.54); Castrone, a eunuch, is excluded from the sexual economy but partakes of both genders; Nano, the dwarf, belongs to the "nation" of fools (1.2.66). They embody the theme of adulteration that pervades the play in Volpone's diluted medicines and debased gold. Volpone's bastard servants are only three of his "dozen, or more" illegitimate, beggar children (1.5.44). Rowlands likewise connects Gypsy bastardy with excessive fecundity, poverty, and dark skin, claiming that they travel "with . . . bastards and baggage" "never under an hundred men or women, causing their faces to be made blacke, as if they were Egyptians."[41] The groups form a fraternity related not just by association but also by blood. Like Perdita's gillyflowers (*WT*, 4.4.79–103), they are a strange and illegitimate hybrid, neither Egyptian nor English, neither black nor white.

Gypsy face painting is thus more than cosmetic, although cosmetics effect it, as a ballad called "The Brave English Jipsie" boasts:

With Painters we can paint;
Our dye is not in vaine,
For we doe dye in graine:
The Walnut tree supplies our lacke,
What was made faire, we can make black.[42]

That their visible difference is assumed like a disguise makes it nonetheless real. They "doe dye in graine": the walnut juice that colors their faces does not merely stain the surface but penetrates deep inside. The ballad identifies the Gypsies with the natural, as if their bodies become part of the "graine" of the "Walnut tree," and with the artificial "dye" of "Painters."

"be thou thy selfe, / And not a changeling"

Dekker characterizes Gypsies as rogue actors, but Middleton and Rowley's *The Spanish Gypsy* suggests that Gypsy actors can be agents for moral reform. The situation of the heroine, Pretiosa, and her name, come from "The Little Gypsy Girl" ["La Gitanilla"], one of Cervantes's *Exemplary Stories* (1613).[43] The adapters, however, transform Cervantes's romance into a play that celebrates the power of drama to uncover the truth. They use the association of Gypsies with acting to create a world in which several separate Gypsy bands all turn out to consist of nobles in disguise and in which a young man's conscience is caught by a Gypsy play. The first group of disguised Gypsies consists of the old Spanish gentleman Alvarez, his wife, and their supposed daughter, beautiful and witty Pretiosa (who eventually turns out to be the long-lost daughter of Fernando, ruler or "Coregidor" of Madrid). They pretend to be Gypsies in order to avoid the vengeance of rampaging Lewys, who wishes to avenge his father, slain by Alvarez in battle. Alvarez warns his followers, however, that they are to be Spanish—not English—Gypsies: "Gipsies, but no tann'd ones, no Red-oker rascalls umberd with soot and bacon as the English Gipsies are . . . Spanish Gipsies, noble Gipsies" (*SG*, C2r).

Alvarez repeats the accusations common in anti-Gypsy literature. English Gypsies smear their faces with soot, pig fat, and ochre in addition to being darkened by the sun; they march out to steal chickens and ambush housewives for as mean a prize as a rope of onions, as if they were Welsh pirates. He mocks both the Gypsies and the poverty-stricken Welsh captains they ape. His Gypsies, in contrast, will be honorable: "Be not English Gipsies . . . there is no Iron so foule but may be guilded, and our Gipsie profession, how base soever in shew, may acquire commendations" (C2v). The anti-Gypsy pamphlets complain that Gypsies cover themselves with false colors, both in their faces and in their hearts, but Alvarez argues that his band can turn these accusations to their advantage. They will disguise themselves as Gypsies, and color their faces, but their darkened skins will not demean them but instead raise the entire level of the "profession."

Noble Don John joins the Gypsies when he falls in love with Pretiosa, "the prettiest toy / That ever Sung or Danc'd," "the wittiest rogue," "a Gipsie . . . / In her condition, not in her complexion" (Cv). He offers to undergo all kinds of penalties and to brave foreign potentates to win her: "Any thing; kill the great Turke, pluck out the Magul's Eye-teeth; in earnest Pretiosa, any thing!" (Dr). Such allusions link the Gypsies to exotic Moorish civilizations that the Spanish had deposed. We may also recall Benedick's plea that he would "fetch you a tooth-picker from the furthest inch of Asia, bring you the length of Prester John's foot, fetch you a hair off the Great Cham's beard, do you any embassage to the pigmies" rather than talk to Beatrice (Ado., 2.1.262–68). Don John's speech echoes Benedick's words but reverses the sentiment. Although Benedick calls for outlandish errands in order to escape Beatrice, while Don John calls for them in order to woo Pretiosa, both young men are forced by their ladies to renounce their desire for foreign, romantic adventure. Instead, they must show their allegiance at home in more prosaic but more difficult tasks.

Like Beatrice, Pretiosa is witty, independent, and demanding. Beatrice demands that Benedick "[k]ill Claudio" (Ado, 4.1.289); Pretiosa commands Don John to "turne Gipsie for two years" (SG, Dr). Don John can countenance a visit to the "great Turk" more easily than a sojourn with these strangers at home:

Turn Gipsie! for two years! a capering Trade,
And I in th'end may keepe a dancing Schoole,
Having serv'd for't, Gipsie! I must turne;
Oh beauty! the Suns fires cannot so burne. (SG, Dr)

Don John's last line suggests that turning Gypsy is worse than being burned by the sun, that is, it is worse than being born a suntanned

"Turk" or a Moor. Joining a group of outsiders at home is more difficult than plundering exotic monarchs abroad.

The last two groups of feigned Gypsies have baser motives than Alvarez or Don John. The foolish ward Sancho and his merry man, Soto, turn Gypsy in order to escape their gambling debts and the wrath of Sancho's guardian. They do not strive to be "noble" Gypsies like Alvarez's company but call themselves "Egyptian Spaniards; . . . we are . . . Juglers, tumblers, any thing, any where, every where" (D4r). Jugglers are both magicians and tricksters; tumblers are both entertainers and sexual adventurers. In masquerading as Gypsies, Sancho and Soto continue much as they did before; their disguise as tricksters reveals who they really are. The final character to turn Gypsy is the impulsive and somewhat cruel Rodrigo, who disguises himself first as an Italian, then as a Gypsy, in order to gull his strict father and to seek out Clara, the lady whom Rodrigo debauched and abandoned in Act 1, but now cannot forget (although he refuses to marry her).

The play's attitude towards disguise and theatricality is highly nuanced, ironizing both the strictures of antitheatrical writers, who call all actors and players immoral, and the conventions of the stage itself. Alvarez and his wife worry that Pretiosa's disguise is too charming and will inspire "amany Dons /. . . [to] . . . throw down Gold in Musses" to discover whether she is "a Boy / In Womens Cloaths" (C3r). Alvarez repeats the concerns of Stubbes and other antitheatrical writers that men in women's clothing prove more attractive to observers than real women: the measure of Pretiosa's sexual attractiveness is her gender ambiguity. He imagines that men will want to undress her not because she is a beautiful girl but because she might be a beautiful boy. Tempted by gold, argues Alvarez, Pretiosa may become "a changeling," inconstant and flirtatious (C3r).

Pretiosa reassures him by punning on "changeling" in a different sense and by defending her ability to act a part and yet remain herself:

How! not a Changeling!
Yes, Father, I will play the changeling;
I'le change my selfe into a thousand shapes
To court our brave Spectators; I'le change my postures
Into a thousand different variations
To draw even Ladies eyes to follow mine;
I'le change my voyce into a thousand tones
To chaine attention; not a changeling Father,
None but my selfe shall play the changeling. (*SG*, C3r–C3v)

Pretiosa will exploit her capacity to be a "changeling" in the sense of one who changes not her heart but her shape. She will remain herself throughout ("none but myself") and her popular disguises and tricks will be "play" or pretense. She will "court" the nobles who come to woo her, but will win their hearts as an actress, not as a mistress. Pretiosa disarms her foster father's criticism, but at the same time, her speech acknowledges the dangers of masquerade. In playing the changeling, she runs the risk of becoming a changeling indeed, of lacking a coherent, constant self and producing a "thousand different" selves instead. But Middleton and Rowley provide us with a final layer of irony: Pretiosa turns out to be a changeling in its final sense, a baby stolen at birth from her true parents, and in playing a changeling, Pretiosa is indeed playing "none but my selfe." Acting and disguise can reveal the truth, even while they seem to conceal it.

The Pretiosa plot dismisses antitheatrical anxieties that acting and Gypsydom conceal villainy; the plot concerning Rodrigo concedes that wrongdoers may turn to Gypsydom and acting to protect themselves, but suggests that, when correctly employed, theatricality can be used to reform prodigal children. While, according to standard comic convention, nobody recognizes Alvarez and his family, or Don John, until they unmask themselves, Rodrigo's astute father Fernando sees through his son's disguise instantly. He casts his son in the role of "rake-hell, a debosh'd [debauched] fellow" (G3v), in the play he has written for the Gypsies, overriding Rodrigo's assertion that he is "no Player" (G3v) and implying that his son will not be playing but acting his true self. Rodrigo wonders whether his father "spies . . . me through my vizard?" (G4r), but is confident that his acting skills can outmaneuver his father's newfound talent for literary invention: "No matter in what straine your Play must run, / But I shall fit you for a roaring Son" (G4r).

The plot of the play-within-the-play centers on an old gentleman's attempts to marry off his "rake-hell" son to a rich but ugly heiress, a marriage that Rodrigo vehemently refuses both in character (in Fernando's play) and as himself (when the play is interrupted). Rodrigo believes that he is gulling his father, but Fernando is employing reverse psychology: having threatened Rodrigo with an arranged marriage, he pretends to acquiesce reluctantly to Rodrigo's wish to wed a beautiful stranger who is attending the play. Only after the ceremony does Rodrigo discover that the woman he has just married is Clara, the virgin he deflowered in Act 1, and Fernando's choice for his son's bride after all.

In both *Hamlet* and *The Spanish Gypsy*, wandering players receive a commission from a nobleman to inspire remorse in an erring family member. In these instances, the device confers a double legitimacy upon the theater: first, it gives theater a moral purpose in which to clothe the spectators' naked pleasure in watching, and second, it gives these masterless players a noble patron, and inserts them into a wage economy. Like Gypsies, stage actors, too, demanded payment for their performances,

but they performed in established companies and under the pleasant
fiction of tempering instruction with delight. Furthermore, stage actors
and playwrights had no interest in contaminating the categories of the
fictitious and the real. They defended themselves against the hysteria of
the antitheatrical tracts by pointing out that they were, after all, only creating representations, not reality itself (a defense made wittily by Jonson
in the puppet show in *Bartholomew Fair* [5.4]). But the Gypsies did not
respect this distinction. In playing the counterfeit, they threatened to
alter the nature of the original.

The Gypsies Metamorphosed

The mythologies that the Gypsies wove about their lives, histories, and
intentions make them the perfect subject for a masque by Jonson. Orgel
has established that in the Jonsonian masque the character one plays
represents an important or essential facet of the masquer's personality,
"a representation of the courtier beneath . . . [who] retains . . . his position in the social hierarchy," a position confirmed when the audience
members acknowledge his parity by joining in the dance. "[A] professional dancer," in contrast, "is like an actor; he plays any part; he can
assume all personalities because he has none of his own," except the
mask that

> is not a *representation* of the reality beneath, but the reality itself . . . . Whereas the
> courtier's unmasking is the point of the mask, through which its significance is
> extended out beyond the boundary of the stage into the real world, the actor's
> unmasking is the destruction of the dramatic illusion, through which we see that
> what we have been watching is nothing, a mere trick, a lie—a "pageant."[44]

The Gypsies' constant self-fashioning connects them to the courtiers
who play them: as Randall has argued, the Buckingham clan was noto-
riously Gypsyish in its meteoric rise to power. Randall finds in *GM*
Jonson's dangerously clever jab at the Buckingham cabal. It is important,
however, neither to overread Jonson's irony nor to see his Gypsies as a
swashbuckling threat to empire; on the contrary, the masque cannot have
been *too* cutting, since James demanded to see it three times and since it
was written to order for Buckingham. Jonson's masque was resoundingly
successful because it enacted a kingly fantasy of ordering the realm and
metamorphosing all wandering rogues and Gypsies into loving, loyal, sta-
tionary subjects through authorized theatrical representation.

   In *GM*, Jonson reasserts the power of poetic and royal authority, allowing the king to control and define the pleasures of Gypsydom without
countenancing the existence of the Gypsies themselves. Jonson's masque
casts King James's minion, the Duke of Buckingham, and his entourage

as a group of "tawny" Gypsies who are transformed into "white" courtiers.[45] Buckingham plays the Gypsy Captain, flanked by a singing Patrico (an unofficial priest) and a Jackman (a professional forger). Reputedly James's favorite masque, *GM* was performed three times, more than any other: at Burleigh, the seat of Buckingham; at Belvoir, the home of Buckingham's father-in-law, the Earl of Rutland; and at James's own Windsor Castle, before the king and his councilors.

The centerpiece of the masque is the scatological Ballad of Cock Lorel, which mocks all the petty bourgeois who engage in wage labor, in contrast to the freewheeling Gypsies. The ballad describes Cock Lorel as the first Gypsy king, although, according to Jonson's sources, Cock Lorel was no Gypsy but a trueborn English rogue.[46] Cock Lorel wished to sup with the devil, feasting him upon members of various professions, including "Six pickled tailors sliced and cut" (*GM*, line 991), a "rich fat usurer stewed in his marrow" (line 995), and "a lawyer's head and green sauce" (line 996). The devil enjoyed his gourmet spread so well, according to the Patrico, that he let fly a monstrous fart, creating the underground cavern, since known as the Devil's Arse, where the Gypsies hold their annual meetings. John Timpane suggests that the ballad of Cock Lorel provides a way of reinforcing an aristocratic solidarity against the new middle classes, a kind of Gypsy alliance with the court. But even if this is a function of Cock Lorel's song, this union of Gypsy and courtier is short-lived. Although the Gypsies seem to have been objects of delight during the masque, the Patrico's concluding benison to the King in the Windsor version of the masque is to protect James "From a gypsy in the morning" (line 1237), a pun that emphasizes the reputation of Gypsy women for lustfulness. Other stanzas implore his rescue "From a strolling tinker's sheet" (line 1264) and add to the list of unwelcome visitors foul-breathed ladies, students, fishmongers, "loud pure wives," (line 1258) and prostitutes. By this point, any affinity between the court and the Gypsies has clearly been removed along with the Gypsies' transformation into courtiers; now the "strolling tinker," the wandering Gypsy, the "lawyer, three parts noise" (line 1250), and the Puritan wife are all equally royal curses.

The Gypsies Metamorphosed shores up masculine and royal pride at the expense of several sets of noncourtly outsiders: the Gypsies, the bourgeoisie, rustics, and all classes of women. As one of the country clowns remarks, these are "Male gypsies all, not a mort [woman] among them" (line 708), in notable contrast to the all-female company described by Dekker. Those who take the place of the female "Gypsies," as far as the masque is concerned, are the "room-morts" (line 152) or fine ladies who watch the performance, as well as the country wenches within the story whose clothes are disarrayed when the Gypsies return their stolen belongings. At Burleigh and Belvoir, the Patrico threatens to "make [the watching ladies] turn Gypsies" (line 205a) and the Gypsies entertain them with double-edged prophecies that promise fair fortunes while casting a shadow over each lady's reputation:

But lady, either I am tipsy,
Or you are to fall in love with a gypsy;
. . .
Yet he's not to wed ye:
He's enjoyed you already,
And I hope he has sped ye. (*GM*, lines 408–19)

In all three versions of the masque, the country wenches come in for more explicit sexual teasing. "The virginity o' the parish" (lines 780–81) turns out to have had "five scapes" (line 783), and "straight-laced Christian" (line 789) learns she shall need "a loose-bodied gown" to hide her illegitimate pregnancy (line 800). At Windsor, with an audience free from feminine influence, the Patrico's blessing smuttily saves the King from the sight of "a smock rampant, and the itches / To be putting on the britches" (lines 1244–45) and the touch of a "doxy, and her itch" (line 1286), conflating a female "itch" for power with the scabs of venereal disease. There are also many joking references to James's lack of interest in women. The Jackman teases the Lord Chamberlain with the accusation, "You never yet helped your Master to a wench" (line 548), and the King's palm proclaims, according to the Captain, "You are no great wencher, I see by your table, / Although your *mons Veneris* ["mount of Venus," on the palm] says you are able" (lines 279–80).

The masque's Epilogue, which was pronounced by Buckingham, links the Gypsies' conversion to Jonson's earlier *Blackness*. Remember that the Daughters of the river Niger, played by Queen Anne and her ladies, are driven to distress by their dark complexions and seek the magical monarch of a far-off land who wields the power "To blanch an Ethiop, or revive a corse" (*Blackness*, line 225), as I discussed in Chapter Three. This monarch, of course, is King James, a royal sun whose rays, perversely, render skin pallid rather than tawny. The religious overtones to the conversion in *Blackness* are clear, as we saw in that chapter: James is figured as King Solomon in Canticles, with his bride who is "black but comely," and is made "fair" by the grace of God (1:5, 15–16).

In *GM*, however, any elements of a religious or mythological conversion are deliberately, even systematically, debunked. I commented in Chapter Three that *Blackness* avoids showing the blanching of the Daughters of Niger, despite the presence within the diegesis of several mythological explanations for this blanching. In *GM*, in contrast, we see the whitened Gypsies, but the masque and its plot offer us no explanation.

Buckingham's Epilogue facetiously blames the poet for this absence, claiming, "Good Ben slept there, or else forgot to show it" (*GM*, line 1384), a nod to Horace's *dormitat Homerus*. Buckingham alludes to *Blackness* only to insist that the Gypsies' metamorphosis is no miraculous "wonder," like the earlier masque, but a purely cosmetic conversion, effected by the skill of Johann Wolfgang Rumler, nicknamed "Master Wolf," the King's apothecary:

> . . . lest it prove like wonder to the sight,
> To see a gypsy, as an Ethiop, white,
> Know, that what dyed our faces was an ointment
> Made, and layd on by Master Wolf's appointment,
> The court *lycanthropos*, yet without spells,
> By a mere barber, and no magic else.
> It was fetched off with water and a ball [of soap]. (*GM*, 1385–91)

The make-up artist is jokingly called a "lycanthropos," a werewolf, but there is nothing supernatural in his skill; he is a "mere barber." Bach observes that the Windsor masque earlier even specifies the nature of the "ointment" he concocts, when the Patrico teases Clod and the other bumpkins with the promise that they, too, can learn to be Gypsies, with the aid of "the noble confection / Of walnuts and hog's grease" (*GM*, lines 1121–22).[47] Timpane argues that the frequent references to the courtiers' made-up faces render any Gypsyish threat, any nationalistic fear, toothless: the "Gypsies" are always "really courtiers."[48] Randall, too, remarks upon Jonson's emphasis on the Englishness and elaborate disguise of his Gypsies, and takes this as evidence that Jonson's Gypsies are too "gentleman-like" (*GM*, line 706), as the country folk say, to be considered "real" Egyptians. And Bach similarly concludes that Jonson transforms the Gypsy nation into a purely theatrical "wildness . . . made completely English," since "By the time of the masque, the gypsies were already legislated out of England."[49]

But by calculatingly omitting a mythological explanation for the whitening like the one in *Blackness* and by rewriting Gypsy history, Jonson implies that Gypsydom has *no* original or prior existence and that it is purely, essentially, literary. When the courtier-Gypsies reappear whitened, a portion of the Gypsy nation has been successfully (*artfully*, we might say) incorporated into James's realm. Moreover, Jonson asserts creative control over the Gypsies' history. The first Gypsy king was "one Giles Hather: he carried about with him his whore called Kyt Calot which was termed the Queene of Egipties."[50] Jonson substitutes an English rogue leader for a Gypsy one, blurring the distinction between Gypsy and Englishman (as was already beginning to happen in the numerous "guides to the canting language," like Taylor's or Harman's, available to Jonson) in order to suggest that the Gypsies are already assimilated.[51] Buckingham himself plays the Captain of the Gypsies, who is clearly analogous to Cock Lorel, king of the Gypsies in Jonson's mythology and the hero of the scatological ballad at the heart of the masque.

Bach suggests that Jonson's masque *contains* the meretricious appeal of Gypsy life by a transformation of Gypsies into courtiers that privileges the world of the court, providing a simulacrum for the benefit of a king who legislates strenuously against its original. But, as we have seen, Dekker, Rid, and even Elizabeth's 1562 act maintain that one's Englishness, one's courtliness, and one's whiteness are not incompatible with simultaneously inhabiting the Gypsy realm. It seems to me that Jonson also challenges the status of the courtly. The most daring aspect of *GM* is that Jonson, typically, has reserved the final plaudits for himself. The knotty Epilogue, which I quote from the 1640 Folio, includes a confusing switch of subjects and pronouns:

For to Gipsies Metamorphosis;
Who doth disguise his habit, and his face,
And takes on a false person by his place:
The power of Poetrie can never faile her,
Assisted by a Barber, and a Taylor. (*GM*, K4v)

Some readers of the masque take the pronoun "her" to refer to the metamorphosed Gypsy. This would add perhaps an allusion to the transvestite theater, where boys disguise their habits and faces to take on a false person before employing the power of poetry. Such a reading is plausible, but I believe the meaning of the passage is more straightforward. It is "The power of Poetrie . . . Assisted by a Barber, and a Taylor," rather than the king's grace and favor, that has changed Buckingham and his Gypsyish clan into true courtiers. Randall finds the "power of poetry" to be an "unconvincing" explanation in a masque that makes no overt allusions to poetry.[52] Dismissing "the power of poetry," however, overlooks a central tenet of Jonson's masque theory: costume, make-up, and movement transform the Gypsies, but the soul of the masque (and therefore the strong magic of the metamorphosis) is Jonson's poetry. Those who disguise their habits and faces, and "take on a false person" by standing in another person's "place," perform only half a miracle. The full transformation can occur only temporarily, within the masque itself, during the artistic union of paint, apparel and poetry. Jonson slyly implies that Buckingham is only a "true" courtier when he is playing one in the masque. Both courtliness and Gypsydom turn out to be literary fictions.

"after the high Roma(n) fashion"

I have hitherto discussed Gypsy lore in light of Gypsy labor, but I take to heart Adorno's warning that narrowly Marxist analysis is of limited use in reading Shakespeare:

> the reduction of Shakespeare's plays to the idea of class struggle . . . goes too far and misses what is essential, except in those dramas where class struggle is clearly a theme [for example, in *Coriolanus*] . . . What is social in Shakespeare is categories such as those of the individual and passion: traits such as . . . the complete disgust for power in *Antony and Cleopatra.*[53]

While the plays have an explicit social content, argues Adorno, this content (what he elsewhere calls truth-content) will not become manifest until after the disappearance of the circumstances that produced it. Until this truth-content becomes clear, it behooves us, he continues, to remember that Shakespeare's plays dramatize the struggles not of groups but of individuals, and that it is on the level of personality or character that social conflicts are written. The "disgust for power" that he finds in *Antony and Cleopatra* includes the titular characters' interrogation of Roman hierarchies and pieties.

Adorno's caveat is particularly well taken when it comes to the figure of Cleopatra, who performs such a richly complex and shifting identity. Critical interpretations have located the play and its heroine within the early modern discourses of national origin and blackness, sexual difference and desire, classicism and innovation, and identity and the theatrical. Adelman tentatively comments on Cleopatra's blackness that "all we can conclude is that Cleopatra's tawniness contributes to the sense of her ancient and mysterious sexuality."[54] Linda Charnes argues that Cleopatra embodies "what is necessarily theatrical in all successful forms of subjectivity," and Singh reads the heroine's histrionics alongside early modern strictures against the transvestite theater.[55] Loomba sees the heroine as artifice personified, a composite of sexual and racial differences that mutually and theatrically construct one another, while Little maintains that, just as Antony becomes an Egypto-Roman hybrid, so Cleopatra's ambiguous blackness exists as a space for the performance of whiteness.[56] Floyd-Wilson and Little both read Antony's shame in humoral and racial terms, arguing that Egypt's climate or complexion affects him (although their approaches are very different).[57] Archer concludes that Cleopatra's negotiation of sex and race, and in particular, her Roman suicide, challenge gender stereotypes of passive heterosexual femininity, while consolidating new myths of African cultural inferiority.[58] Adelman has recently revisited the play to argue that it speaks to the debates between the one-sex and two-sex models.[59] Whitney and De Sousa read Cleopatra as Gypsy; the former points out the strong connections between Gypsy fortunetelling and witchcraft, and their appearance within *Antony and Cleopatra*, while the latter discusses Gypsy vagrancy and wandering, taking Cleopatra's self-ascription of beggary as a comment on the loss of her kingdom.[60] He singles out her call to death as a "puzzling . . . almost . . . metadramatic awareness of her status as queen of the gypsies" who commands troops of "babes and beggars" (*Ant.*, 5.2.47), describing her Egyptian idleness as something feminine, sexual, and poisonous, in contrast to the masculine, Roman vigor of martial Fulvia.[61]

To talk about Cleopatra as a Gypsy might seem to erase the serious play at work in her continuous and continuing engagement with identity. Cleopatra, after all, disrupts the early modern oppositions of dark/fair, Egyptian/Roman, Gypsy/English, male/female, strange/native, real/counterfeit, queen/beggar, Isis/Venus, bride/whore, subject/object. But it is my contention that what Adorno would call the truth-content of the play is its complex negotiation not only of sex, skin color, and rank but also of artistry and labor, and that these negotiations (like the Egyptian labor that looks like idleness to Rome) are inseparable from each other. Without negating Sousa's useful observations, therefore, I want to tease out not the *metonymies* of Gypsy idleness and beggary, but the underlying structural *metaphor* that unites queens, Gypsies, babes, beggars, and artists.

As we have seen, English Gypsies are characterized in legal statutes by their resistance to wage labor. This is not, however, the only trait that links the artist to the Gypsy. Neither Gypsy nor artist works for an employer; neither produces material goods as a result of labor. Neither do actors, of course, and Loomba, Jankowski, Charnes, and many others comment on Cleopatra's consummate acting ability. But a Gypsy Cleopatra, as we shall see, is not only actor but also artist. Like the women whom Thomas Tuke accuses of "taking the pencil out of God's hand," or like Dekker's Gypsies who "doe not make faces, but marre faces," character and actor engage in what Dolan calls "cosmesis" to turn impersonation into an artwork.

Despite the skepticism of Dekker or, later, of Browne, Renaissance lawmakers and writers use the terms "Egyptian" and "Gypsy" synonymously. Rowlands refers to the Gypsy queen "Kit Callot" as the "Queene of Egipties," a name that conveniently conflates her geographical terrain (the two supposed Egypts or "Egipties": "Great" Egypt, the land of Cleopatra and Ptolemy, and "Little" Egypt, from whence the Gypsies were supposed to spring) and the individual Gypsies or "Egipties" over whom she rules.[62] Jonson and Shakespeare further identify Cleopatra not just as an Egyptian queen, but as queen of the Gypsies. Jonson calls her "the gypsies grand-matra" (*GM*, line 160), and Shakespeare's Cleopatra is explicitly called a "Gypsy" at two key moments within the text, in Philo's denunciation before we even meet her and in Antony's grief when he believes that she has abandoned him. Both instances engage Gypsydom with mythologies of color and racialized discourses of difference: hypersexual blackness (the "tawny front" [*Ant.*, 1.1.6] associated with her "gipsy's lust" [1.1.10]) and the "triple-turn'd whore" [4.12.13]); deception ("like a right gipsy, hath at fast and loose / Beguil'd [Antony] to the very heart of loss" [4.12.28–29]); dirt and corruption ("foul Egyptian" [4.12.10]).[63]

Tudor and Stuart monarchs regarded the king and queen of the Gypsies and their tribe as a threat because they established a parallel system of government, choosing to remain outside the legal economy rather than join the servant or mercantile classes. Jonson even makes a joke of these fears of class mobility by having his Gypsies become courtiers with the aid of nothing more than "water and a ball." Antony and Cleopatra flout Caesar's sense of decorum; not the least of Caesar's objections is their easy familiarity with their servants (he complains that Cleopatra's women manage the war) and Antony's refusal to behave as a coruler should. Caesar is offended not only by Antony and Cleopatra's illicit romance but also by their impropriety. His anger when Octavia comes "A market maid to Rome" (*Ant.*, 3.6.51) suggests that appropriate ceremony stands for more than mere appearances; she has "prevented / The ostentation of our love which, left unshown, / Is often left unlov'd" (3.6.51–53). The general public needs to see ostentation in order to consider her "loved" by Caesar, and the ceremony *creates* the affectionate feelings it is supposed to be displaying; authority depends upon the display of authority. As if to emphasize his disjuncture with Caesar, when Antony does perform elaborate rituals they are not in honor of Rome or of his legal wife but in order to crown himself and Cleopatra co-rulers of Egypt and name their illegitimate children their heirs.[64]

Cleopatra responds to Caesar's threat to "hoist [her] up / And show [her] to the shouting varletry of censuring Rome" (5.2.55–56) by organizing a show of her own, the news of her faked suicide. She has specialized in presenting shows throughout the play, as Jankowski argues. Cleopatra expresses the feelings that finally drive her to real suicide in perhaps the most famous metatheatrical reference in the Shakespearean canon:

> Now Iras, what think'st thou?
> Thou an Egyptian puppet shall be shown
> In Rome as well as I. Mechanic slaves
> With greasy aprons, rules and hammers shall

Uplift us to the view. In their thick breaths,
Rank of gross diet, shall we be enclouded
And forc'd to drink their vapor. (*Ant.*, 5.2.207–13)

Here Cleopatra asserts a commonalty between the queen and the beggar, the aristocrat and the Gypsy, against the "mechanic slaves" who carry the tools of their trade. Aristocracy, beggary, and Gypsydom all become ways of avoiding the supposedly stultifying logic of emergent wage labor by turning modes of social identity into theater. Compare Middleton and Rowley's counterfeit Gypsy nobles, and contrast them again to Cleopatra's earlier challenge to Caesarian decorum in spending time with "slaves" and "knaves," chambermaids and grooms (*Ant.*, 1.4.19, 21). She even evokes the "smell[y]" (1.4.21) perspiration of these knaves in her complaint that what seems like idleness is really "sweating labor" (*Ant.*, 1.3.93).

Before the crisis, Thidias has urged Cleopatra to shroud herself under the greatness of Caesar, "the universal landlord" (3.13.72). Shakespeare uses the word "landlord" only three times in the canon. *A Lover's Complaint* compares unrequited lovers who worship a cold-hearted beloved to renters who foolishly imagine disposing of the "goodly objects" owned by their "gouty landlord," a comment on his greed (presumably his gout is the result of high living) and the poverty that they deny (*LC*, stanza 20). John of Gaunt blames Richard II for his weakness in making himself "Landlord of England," "bondslave to the law" (*R2*, 2.1.113), putting profit above power and encouraging lordly squatters. The "gouty landlord" in "A Lover's Complaint" is more powerful than his renters; the "landlord of England" in *Richard II* is less potent than the lords on whose goodwill he depends. In *Antony and Cleopatra* Caesar and his messenger allow both meanings, the hidden threat and the hidden promise, to appear. Thidias (who has probably been trained) says of Caesar "he partly begs / To be desired to give" (*Ant.*, 3.13.66–67), casting Cleopatra as royal tenant in a grace-and-favor apartment. That "partly," like the "universal" in landlord, belies Caesar's modesty. The speech's awkwardness comes in part from the grotesque conjunction of the grandiose "universal," which is allied with the cosmological, colossal images the lovers use throughout the play, with the sudden and petty London resonance of "landlord." It is the perfect term for Caesar.

But having implied these commonalties between the royal Egyptians and impoverished Gypsies, against the bourgeois landlord Caesar and his rude mechanical wage slaves, the second half of Cleopatra's speech seems to uncouple the traditional association of Gypsies with actors, performers, and prostitutes:

> . . . Saucy lictors
> Will catch at us like strumpets, and scald rhymers
> Ballad us out o'tune. The quick comedians
> Extemporally will stage us and present
> Our Alexandrian revels; Antony
> Shall be brought drunken forth; and I shall see
> Some squeaking Cleopatra boy my greatness
> I'th' posture of a whore. (*Ant.*, 5.2.214–21)

Cleopatra's resounding metatheatrics set up an echo chamber for the material practices of the Renaissance stage, as Callaghan, Rackin, and others have remarked—its use of boy actors, racial and gender prosthetics, and the spaces and machines of the early modern theater, such as the balcony or the gods.[65] Little boldly asserts not only that Shakespeare imagined a black Cleopatra, but that such a character must have been played in blackface make-up. Such an appearance would heighten an audience's awareness of Cleopatra as paradoxically both a royal queen and a Gypsy.

Some might counter that a blackface Cleopatra would surely have inspired at least some commentary from Shakespeare's contemporaries, comparable to Sir Dudley Carleton's famous strictures on Queen Anne's black paint in Jonson's *Blackness*. But Carleton's comments were triggered by his shock at seeing those red and white beauties, the queen and her ladies, incongruously transformed. Cleopatra, in contrast, is an Egyptian—not an English or Scottish—queen, and her blackface make-up would seem unremarkable, like blackface make-up on Othello or Aaron. Cleopatra's "squeaking" speech and her suicide therefore expose the theatrical and material practices that sex and race the heroine as a

white boy actor [who] challenges his audience to see him as cross-gendered and cross-racialized, exposing the underpinnings of a theater that traffics not only in women's bodies but in black bodies as well . . . a theater that traffics, too, in the bodies, the tenderly eroticized bodies, of white boys.[66]

Charnes and Little independently comment upon the "pornographic" subtexts of Cleopatra's presentation, in what Little calls the "pornographic ethnography" of Enobarbus's Cydnus speech and the imagined sexual "squeaking" of the whore. [67]

More to my purposes, Cleopatra's speech differentiates between *being* herself the performance or artwork upon which the crowds gaze and *watching* a representation of herself performed by other actors. Judith Butler distinguishes "performance" as a "bounded 'act,'" in contrast to "performativity," which "consists in a reiteration of norms which precede, constrain, and exceed the performer and in that sense cannot be taken as the fabrication of the performer's 'will' or choice."[68] Performativity is a process of "iteration," the repetition of "compulsory . . . social imperatives" and the constraints of the law. In "performing" identity, we are repeating a set of citations that we have learned. But individual acts of "performance," taking up a social imperative or voluntarily adopting a name for a finite period of time, can turn the "iteration" of those norms into an interrogation and explosion of the very category that the term has created. "[T]his kind of citation will emerge as *theatrical* to the extent that it *mimes and renders hyperbolic* the discursive convention that it also *reverses*."[69] Butler calls this theatrical inversion "queering" and discusses the political power of theater with regard to drag.

Cleopatra distinguishes between her own willed performance, in Butler's sense, and the mise-en-abyme of endless Roman iteration that reduces it to the merely performative. She first imagines herself and her maids as "Egyptian puppets," dolls moved by another's strings. In this vision she and her maids hold the stage, however unwillingly, and are themselves the objects of the general view. The audience moves closer and closer until Cleopatra and her women can smell the foul breath of the mechanicals who mock them, hear the scurrilous ditties at their expense, and feel the lewd grasp of fumbling hands. They are now part of the audience as well as of the show. Finally, however, Cleopatra is pushed completely to the sidelines, a reluctant spectator. The crowd's eyes linger not on her but on the parodic representations of their "Alexandrian revels," upon a "drunken" actor-Antony and a "boy" Cleopatra "i'th' posture of a whore." In a reversal of antitheatrical logic, Cleopatra critiques not the wandering performances of Gypsies but the promenade performance that will be sanctioned under Caesar's authority. Remember that rogue literature characterizes Gypsies by their counterfeiting, in particular by their racialized use of make-up and costume. The resemblance between the self-consciously blackened Gypsy actor and the actor who plays Cleopatra is thus crucial to the character's dynamic of disruption. S/he defies categorization not merely by shifting from one binary to the other but by creating and occupying spaces of performance in between that theatricalize all of them: as Charnes succinctly puts it, "Cleopatra may be predictably histrionic, but she is never 'identical' with any one performance of herself."[70]

Enobarbus's description of Cleopatra as a "wonderful piece of *work*" seems to go to the heart of the problem (*Ant.*, 1.2.153–54, emphasis mine). Elaine Scarry writes that a work of art is always a work of pain, because of the hidden labor that imagines the object soliciting another's comfort or pleasure, while itself being the product of labor or controlled discomfort.[71] But the hidden labor that goes into artistic production is always invisible to Rome, or visible only as "idleness" or the "vacancy" that leaves a great gap in nature. Clusters of words related to work and effort appear in the scenes of Antony's botched suicide and of Cleopatra's successful one (*Ant.*, 4.14 and 5.2 respectively). Labor's respite has been Gypsy performance; now the only escape from toil must come through death—or art. Once Antony's "long day's task is done" (4.14.35), "all labor / Mars what it does" (4.14.47–48) unless it is directed towards the final rest. Unsuccessful and in pain, Antony cries for help to finish his deathly task: "I have done my work ill, friends: O make an end / Of what I have begun" (4.14.105–6). Cleopatra realizes too late "how it might work" (4.14.125), that Antony can see no escape from work except through pain and death. Nor can the guard who asks, upon first seeing Cleopatra dead in her trimmed royal robes, "What work is here? Charmian, is this well done?" (5.2.325).

It *is* work well done, as Charmian retorts, the only labor fitting for one descended of so many kings. That word itself, *work*, additionally displays the labor of actor, author, and artist. Shakespeare is very close to North's Plutarch here, which reads "Is that well done Charmion?"[72] The play keeps this vivid moment of dialogue, but adds the *work* that Cleopatra transforms into play once more, serious play. Her "strong toil" turns death into sleep, says Caesar, punning on the imaginary net or "toil" (*Ant.*, 5.2.348) that snared Antony even before the play began; the toil of the actor turns death into art.

I would like to stop here and to say that the Gypsiness of Cleopatra and of the actor who plays her defies the limit of Roman "demuring" and turns her into an autonomous artwork; I would like to agree with the many critics who attribute to her even a qualified resistance or escape. But for me, Cleopatra's death points to the limits of both performance and performativity as modes of engagement with the social (even though such a reading is at odds with my own emotional response to the play). Neither her performance nor her performativity can save Egypt from Rome, as Little points out. Is this collapse a sign of the play's failure, its unactability on the Renaissance stage? Because we have no quarto or commentary from Shakespeare's lifetime (with the exception of Blount's copyright for a book called "Anthony and Cleopatra" in 1608, and the possible evidence of Samuel Daniels's revisions to his *Cleopatra*), some critics aver that there might have been no contemporary performance of this play. But the Lord Chamberlain's records from 1669 refer to the play as having been acted at the Blackfriars, which was open from 1609 until 1642, and there is no reason to disbelieve this.[73]

What we *can* perhaps infer from the absence of contemporary commentary and from the fact that the play was apparently never published, even in a pirated edition, is that Renaissance audiences did not find the play as remarkable as modern critics do. Adorno would find such a conclusion unsurprising. For him, the autonomy of the art object depends upon its imbrication in the social, that which is excluded from the art-work but that which alone inspires it. Art defines itself by its distance from "the merely empirical," yet "Art acquires its specificity by separating itself from what it developed out of," that is, from the historical and material circumstances that enabled its first production.[74] The meaning or truth-content of a work of art may become—*can only become*—apparent at the moment that it seems most distant from these material practices. Perhaps then if Cleopatra engenders resistance, it appears not on the Renaissance stage but within our own critical and iterative performances around her, as we untie the strong toils that bind even a fictional world.

Chapter 8

Suntanned Slaves

This chapter contrasts the associations between black skin and wealth in the city pageant and in the ethnographic accounts of dark-skinned Africans produced by England's first slave traders. I begin with a short history of England's involvement in the African slave trade before moving to the Jacobean interest in exotic, dark-skinned foreigners and to city pageants that feature sun-worshiping Moors "hurling . . . gold and silver."[1] The connection of blackness with wealth elides the forced labor employed in the American mines, as I pointed out in Chapter Three. I maintain that, in addition, it conceals England's renewed involvement in a commerce that linked blackness with wealth not merely through metonymy or association but through metaphor or substitution, the conversion of black bodies themselves into currency. The final sections of this chapter uncover this hidden history by turning to geography, contrasting the triumphalism of the city pageants in England's famous metropole to the tentative and ominous commerce of John Hawkins's second and third slaving voyages and Richard Jobson's *Golden Trade* in a distant land, one hitherto mysterious to England's travailers. The accounts of Hawkins and his crew mobilize emergent racial discourses of bestiality, blackness, miscegenation, hypersexuality, wealth, and labor. These narratives render directly visible the emotional and material stakes of travel/travail. The first English slavers to return from the Senegambia produce tribal ethnography that rapidly mutates into what I argue is already a version of racialism—a hierarchical ordering of human beings that depends upon skin color and labor, especially slavery. But I conclude with a reading of the unexpectedly humane warmth that exists in Jobson's *Golden Trade—alongside* these new ethnographic and racial taxonomies.

"too pure an Air for Slaves to breathe in"

John Hawkins has the disgrace of being the first British trader in African slaves, having "got into his possession, partly by the sworde, and partly by other meanes, to the number of 300.[sic] Negros at the least" along the coast of Guinea in 1562 (*PN*, 10:8).[2] An eighteenth-century commentator alleges that Queen Elizabeth called for "the Vengeance of Heaven" to chastise slave traders, but since the same writer also asserts that Hawkins intended to transport Africans *with their consent* (a claim belied by Hawkins's own narrative), his account of Elizabeth's scruples is of doubtful veracity.[3] Elizabeth lent Hawkins money and a ship in which to continue his depredations, promoted him to treasurer of the navy, and allowed him a hideous new addition to his coat-of-arms—the figure of a shackled black man.[4] Hawkins made two more voyages, in 1564 ("going every day on shore to take the Inhabitants, with burning and spoiling their townes") and—with spectacular failure—in 1567 (*PN*, 10:17).[5] "The Portuguese who were to have directed them in their enterprize . . . fled."[6] The Jalofs of Senegal ambushed his crew with "envenomed arrowes" (*PN*, 10:64). A herd of hippopotami sank a fully laden pinnace. Kings Sheri and Yhoma of Castros and Sierra Leone promised to provide him with slaves in exchange for his help in battle against the chieftains of Conga, only to deliver to him a few dozen prisoners instead of the hundreds he expected. Hunger compelled Hawkins's crew to eat their nonhuman merchandise, so that "rats, cats, mice and dogs . . . parrats and monkeyes that were had in great price, were thought there very profitable if they served the turne one dinner" (*PN*, 10:73). "Oppressed with famine," many sailors died or were so weakened "that [they] were scantly able to manage [the] shippe" (*PN*, 10:74). Finally, the Spanish took over four of Hawkins's ships, to his outrage and ignominy. The disasters of this voyage, retold in the only one of the accounts to be authored by Hawkins himself and the only one to be published (in 1569) before Richard Hakluyt's ambitious collection of the *Principal Navigations*, discouraged would-be traders until the 'teens and 'twenties of the next century.[7]

I have throughout this book followed established practice in calling Africans in Britain at this time "slaves," but their precise legal status is impossible to ascertain. A famous decision in 1569 (the same year that Hawkins published the account of his third slaving voyage) freed "a Slave from Russia" because "England was too pure an Air for Slaves to breath[e] in."[8] The first decades of King James's English reign seem to have ushered in the widespread acquisition of Africans not as paid servants, entertainers, or sex workers but as unpaid slaves. Founded in 1618, the Guinea Company was trading in slaves by 1651. The first reference to the sale of dark-skinned workers in England is recorded in the letter of a merchant who objects strenuously to the trade and refuses to accept payment for human beings. William Bragge writes to Thomas Smith and the "East India and Sommers Island [Bermuda] Company" in 1621 requesting reimbursement for various items that his deceased brother, who had accompanied Sir Henry Middleton on voyages to the East and West Indies, had brought back to England, including hogs, plantains, potatoes, sugar cane, brass vessels, and twenty dogs and "a greate many" cats (he requests £5 apiece for the dogs, but agrees to "let the Catts goe").[9] His claim from the Sommers Islands company lists "Item more for Thirteen Negroes or Indian people Six women Seauen men and boyes, the price of them also not to bee vallewed."[10] A modern eye notes first of all the casual confusion between "negroes or Indian people"; Fryer assumes these people were "Asian," but I do not think we can make any assumptions about their ethnic provenance, given that "M[aste]r Powell brought them into" Bermuda.[11] Thomas Smith, the letter's addressee, was at one time chairman of the Bermuda Company, and may have been involved in setting up the first English plantations there. These plantations were staffed by African slaves (whose status *as* slaves was legally more evident in the tropics than back in England), Irish indentured servants (some of whom were indentured for life and had been kidnapped from their homes, just as the "Negroes" had), and "Indian" (both East- and West-) laborers. Bragge's "poore Soules" could have been "black" Africans, "red" East Indians, or "tawnie" Native Americans.

Bragge offers two reasons for his inability to price these people. First, the tobacco they helped to grow in Bermuda has increased in price fivefold. Second, "theis poore soules . . . are not to bee vallewed at any price . . . because the Lord Jesus hath suffered death aswell for them as for all you, and therfore will I not reckon for in time the Lord may call them to be true Christians."[12] Bragge digresses (as he frequently does) into a paean to the Lord "our sweete Sauior" before concluding emphatically:

And now for the Thirteene heathens . . . God forbidd with the saying of Dauid in [2 Sam. 23 and 17] . . . ô Lord bee it farre from mee that I should doe this . . . So farre now wo[rshi]p[fu]ll M[aste]rs, I most humbly beseech my heauenly god, I may not receiue rewards either of gold or siluer for such as are created after ye image similitude and likenes of god.[13]

Few shared Bragge's scruples. In 1662 a company—the Royal Adventurers—was established whose charter explicitly required English plantations in America to be supplied with African labor. From 1672–98 the Royal African Company replaced the Royal Adventurers, importing "an annual average of 5000 slaves" between 1680 and 1686.[14] A 1677 court found "by special Verdict" that "Negroes being usually bought and sold among merchants, so Merchandise, and also being Infidels, there might be a Property in them sufficient to maintain Trover [recoverable property]."[15] But in 1701 Chief Justice Holt challenged this decision when he determined that Africans could not be considered trover in England (although in Virginia, "negroes . . . are saleable as chattels"), because "the Laws of England take no notice of a Negroe." Moreover, he opined, "as soon as a Negro comes into England, he becomes free . . . one may be a villein in England but not a slave."[16] Similarly, in the same year, the King's Bench found that "a Negro cannot be demanded as a Chattel; for he is no other than a slavish Servant." That is, his master could be recompensed for the "Loss of his Service, and not for the Value, or for any Damages done to the Servant." The jury was also confused as to "Whether the [Negro's] Baptism was a Manumission," but "the Court gave not Opinion."[17] Fraser concludes that "[t]he economic relations between West Africa and England . . . had more to do with gold and ivory than slaves until the end of the 17th century."[18]

A few cases demonstrate the ambiguous nature of seventeenth-century slavery in Britain. An African or Asian slave in Britain in 1600 would almost certainly have spent a lifetime as an expensive, liveried status symbol in an aristocratic household, and (always excepting the horror of capture) might not have been treated very differently from the other servants. But as the century goes on, this unspoken understanding comes into dispute. In 1687 the Christian convert Dinah Black appealed to the Bristol courts for protection from her mistress, Dorothy Smith, who had attempted to sell her for field work in America (she was rescued from the very boards of the ship by white sympathizers). Dinah's legal situation was unclear, but unfortunately we do not know the outcome of the case.[19] Shyllon and Fraser record the complicated case of Katherine Auker, from 1690. Brought to England from Barbados by a plantation owner, Katherine had converted to Christianity and subsequently been "turned . . . out," "tortured," "caused . . . to be arrested and imprisoned," and prevented from serving any other employer by her master and mistress. She asked the court to release her from her master, who was visiting Barbados. The court gave her the right to hire out her own labor while her master was away. Shyllon reads this decision as evidence of the court's inability to come to a definite decision; Fraser concludes that Katherine retained dual status, as slave (unable to hire herself out) in Barbados and servant (able to "serve any person") in England, at least during her master's absence.[20] The infamous Talbot and Hardwicke decisions (1729 and 1749) finally pronounced that an enslaved African did not become free either upon arrival in England or upon conversion to Christianity.

"hurling ingots of gold and silver"

Alongside the renewed seventeenth-century involvement in slaving flourished an interest in Africana, including entertainments presenting "Moors" and strangers of all hues, such as Jonson's *Blackness*, the masque of *Solomon and Sheba*, and "A Mask of the Knights of India and China."[21] Masques not only featured exotic strangers but also entertained visiting dignitaries, such as the Spanish ambassador who attended *Blackness* and gallantly kissed the queen's hand, or "the Virginian woman Pocahuntas" who, famously, attended the king and was "well placed at the mask" a week before she died at Gravesend.[22] The Jacobean love of the exotic was not limited to courtly audiences; both Middleton's civic pageant for the grocers, *The Triumphs of Truth* (*TT*), and Anthony Munday's for the fishmongers, *Chrysanaleia* (1616), intended for Londoners of all classes, include Moorish kings, and of course Shakespeare's *Othello* (1608) takes a Moorish general for its hero.

Civic pageants associate sun-worshiping blackness with fabulous, hyperbolic wealth. *TT* stars a Moorish king whose transformation from moral blackness to saintly whiteness is effected by his conversion from sun worship to Christianity. His conversion provides the central victory for Truth over Error. Middleton's king begins by insisting that, contrary to popular prejudice, he is the representative not of dark falsehood but of bright Truth herself:

I being a Moore, then in opinion's lightnesse
As far from sanctity as my face from whitenesse,
But I forgive the judgings of th'unwise,
Whose censures ever quicken in their eyes,
Onely begot of outward forme and show,
And I thinke meete to let such censurers know,
However darknesse dwels upon my face,
Truth, in my soule sets up the light of grace. (689)

Those who equate "sanctity" with whiteness alone are demonstrating their own "lightnesse," in the now familiar Renaissance pun that compares lightness in color to lightness of conduct or constancy. Whiteness and honesty are not necessarily equivalent, because inward morality and outward appearance have no correlation.

The pageant conflates abstract Truth with Christian religious faith and Error with paganism:

And though in daies of error I did runne
To give all adoration to the sunne,
The moone, and stars—nay, creatures base and poor,
Now onely this Creator I adore. (689)

In these passages, Middleton opposes voluntary and involuntary sunburn. The king has renounced voluntary sunburn by turning away from nature worship to Christianity; his involuntary sunburn, his naturally dark skin, he cannot help. Unlike, say, the monotheistic Indians of Mary

Wroth or George Chapman, whom I discussed in Chapter Three, this pantheist presents a more difficult case for conversion. With a flattering nod to his sponsors, Middleton makes his Moorish king suggest that the upstanding company of grocers effected his transformation: "by the religious conversation / Of English merchants, factors, travailers, / . . . / Wee all were brought to the true Christian faith" (*TT*, 689). As Bach observes, "in the King's discourse, 'commerce' becomes a highly valued transformative force, its enlightening benefits automatically accompanying business with English merchants."[23] "Conversation" plays on three meanings of the word: the travelers' talk (perhaps they recount tall tales about England to the Moors that are as fabulous as the stories they spread in England about the Moors), their frequent presence in the Moorish kingdom, and their spiritual beings.[24]

The sun is a sign of the king's "error" when he worships it, but of his salvation once he has accepted Christianity. During the first half of the pageant, Error tries to rule London and to claim "light," "fire," and "joy" (*TT*, 685). Error rejoices to see the Moorish king, believing that he is one of her elect because of his black skin (we may also recall the description of "black Error" in Chapman's *Memorable Masque*, another drama of conversion and gold [*MM*, line 574]). Once converted, however, the Moorish king is subject no longer to the erroneous association of blackness with devilry:

Error smiling betwixt scorne and anger to see such a devout humility take hold of that complexion, breakes into these:
"What have my sweet-fac'd devils forsook me too,
Nay then my charmes will have enough to doo!" (690)

After Truth triumphs over Error a second time, sunlight and brightness return to her control and illuminate the city. The metaphorical "scales of darkenesse" that shrouded London's eyes fall away (692). Middleton's pageant insists that spectators distinguish the king's sun-blackened skin from his inherent nobility, as if these two characteristics are at first glance incompatible.

Munday's *Chrysanaleia* displays "the King of Moores, gallantly mounted on a golden Leopard, he hurling gold and silver every way about him," surrounded by Moorish attendants who hurl "ingots of golde and silver" likewise.[25] Unlike the Moorish king in *TT*, Munday's king has no lines to speak; merely his presence and his gold are enough to honor the fishmongers' colleagues, "the worthy Company of Golde-Smythes."[26] The new trade with and in Africans, and the religious tradition that identified King Solomon's bride with the Queen of Sheba and her opulence, reinforced each other to create an association that went without saying (literally so, in Munday's pageant). But the association of blackened figures with conspicuously displayed wealth elides the conditions under which such goods were unearthed, as Bach argues: "the display of Moors and riches represents not Indian miners, the actual laborers who produced treasure, but the English traders' and craftsmen's (desired) control over Indian resources."[27]

As I hinted in my earlier discussion of Chapman's *Memorable Masque,* such an elision conceals the underlying connections between riches and slavery, Old World and New. Raman provides a useful summary of the "structural demand for a sudden and massive increase in the quantity of money in circulation":

Throughout the sixteenth and seventeenth centuries the European colonial powers ran a deficit trade with the East. In order to buy eastern commodities they had to enter into already well-developed local trading structures and to pay for goods in gold and silver. But there were no reliable sources within Europe that could sustain a deficit trade over the long term. Thus, the bullion had to come from elsewhere. And it did: from the silver mines in the Americas. The commodities that flowed in from the near and far East needed this colonial treasure and the labor of enslaved populations in order to be . . . bought and sold.[28]

Just as silver came from the Americas, so gold came from Africa, in particular from the Guinea coast. Spanish silver was mined by Native American slaves, and even a few Moors captured in battle—a sharp contrast to the European slavery under the Ottomans documented by Francis Knight and others. But the late sixteenth and early seventeenth centuries saw the convergence of European conspicuous consumption, American forced mining labor, Asian trafficking, and African enslavement.[29] In addition, the English desired a "golden trade" of their own in order to compete with the Portuguese and the Moors, those convenient and ever-changing Islamic bogey-monsters. Later, of course, sugar would replace bullion as the desired treasure and African slavery would all but supplant Native American.[30]

The trade in objects, argues Bartels, is privileged over the trade of bodies in travel narratives (such as Jobson's *Golden Trade,* a recurring text in my analysis). She adds, "Before Jobson, and for some time after, Africa showed no signs of becoming a colony, or Africans of becoming the hottest commodity on the market."[31] But Jobson's very interest in taking over the "golden trade of the Moors" reflects the urgent need in Britain for bullion, gold and silver, as Europe moved towards a monetary economy. Bartels also uses the ethnographic detailing of early travel narratives to critique the postcolonial model when applied to early modern literature, arguing that the accounts of difference in these texts are not reducible to modern categories of "racism" (her term) or objectification. While Bartels is correct to insist upon the differences between particular accounts, it is more productive to avoid instituting ethnography/racism as a new binary, when in early travel writing they mutually constitute and challenge each other.

Let us return, for example, to John Bulwer's ethnography of human decoration, *Anthropometamorphosis*, which I first discussed in Chapter Five. Bulwer directly contradicts the (albeit limited) religious tolerance extended by the writers of city pageants; the (again limited) praise of black beauty extended in Jonson's *Blackness*, or early seventeenth-century exegeses of the Song of Songs; and the cultural relativism of the mid-seventeenth-century Sir Thomas Browne. Browne, we may recall, points out that all human beings belong to the same stock and that standards of beauty are comparative and culturally derived, spending several pages dismissing the argument that particular skin colors (such as blackness) or facial features (such as noses) are in themselves unattractive. But Bulwer describes the preference of the "Bashaw of Cairo" to enslave "Negro Girles . . . for their uglines," "to send them for a present to the grand Signior, who bestowes them upon his women . . . to serve as a foile to set off the splendour of [the Sultana's] beauties." Such women are, he continues, the "most ill-favoured, cole black, flat nosed girles" (S3v).

Bulwer insists that a "flat" nose can never be beautiful:

this Nose being gentilitious and native to an Ape, can never become a mans face: the Native beauty of the Nose consisting rather in the elevation, then depression of it; . . . A flat Nose being therefore excepted against in the Leviticall law, and excluded any priestly approach unto the Altor, as accounted an unnaturall blemish and deformity. (Tv–T2r)

Here we see the coming together of various mythologies of color and myths of race: the demonology of color ("ill-favoured, cole black"); the literal denigration of physical features ("flat nosed"); the classification of a group of people as a separate race ("Negro") and the identification of them predominantly as slaves or as aesthetic objects ("a foile"); the purported religious justification for their subjugation. In his "Appendix," Bulwer introduces another emergent myth of race, that of excessive black African virility. He ascribes the erstwhile popularity of the codpiece, "the vaine and unprofitable modell of a member, which we may not so much as name with modesty," and of "filthy and Apish Breeches," to Englishmen's desire to match the "reall bulke" of the men of Guinea, or the penis sheath of "the Indians of . . . La Trinidad" (4A3r). Such garments are, he continues, as immodest as the "Irish Trowses [that] too manifestly discover the dimensions of every part" (4A3r). The word "Apish" here primarily evokes the idea of mimicry, but with a twist: the "ape" derives its name from its imitation of human beings, but here, Bulwer implies, humans of various origins are imitating the genital displays of apes.

In this emergent mythology, libidinous apes or monkeys (early modern writers do not usually maintain the distinction) were endowed with enlarged sexual organs. The "babion" or baboon who dances in Shakespeare and Fletcher's *Two Noble Kinsmen* (1613) flaunts his "long tail and eke long tool [penis]," and Edward Topsell's *Historie of Foure-Footed Beastes* (1607) recounts an anecdote of a baboon at the French Court who "above all loved the companie of women, and young maidens," and whose "genitall member was greater then might match the quantity of his other parts."[32] Herod in Elizabeth Cary's *Tragedy of Mariam* (1613) mobilizes an ugly association of apes, Africans, and sexuality that became increasingly popular during the seventeenth century. In comparison to Mariam, Salome is black, bestial, and burned, "an ape . . . a sun-burnt blackamoor."[33]

Bulwer treats the "Negro girles" as merely signs of the great Bashaw's riches, as economic tokens to be traded between Signior and Bashaw and sexual favors to be exchanged between the Signior and his harem. The women's black bodies themselves become wealth, a cruel currency the conditions for which were established earlier in the century when England suffered a shortage of gold and silver coin. Where the civic pageant associates blackened skin with wealth produced or generated, the cosmetic ethnography regards the enslaved women's dark flesh as currency in itself. The disheartening narratives of John Hawkins's second and third slave voyages, written respectively by John Sparke (a member of Hawkins's crew) and Hawkins himself, foreground the shadowy overlap between the ethnographic cataloguing of perceived bodily variations and the establishment of hierarchies of skin color, labor, and race.

"white teeth as we have"

Both Sparke and Hawkins actively committed the crimes of kidnapping, torture, enslavement, plunder, and, from what we know about the conditions on slave ships, possibly rape as well (although Sparke speaks disapprovingly of one his mates who, more "licorous then circumspect," tries to reserve "a few [female slaves] for him selfe" and has his throat cut by their defenders) (*PN*, 10:21). And yet their representation of the people they meet differs widely. Recall that Hawkins collapses all black Africans into "Negros"; he also characterizes the "Negro" as a "nation," one "in which . . . is seldome or never found truth," adding a political boundary to this imaginary kingdom (*PN*, 10:65).[34] Hakluyt's marginal gloss backs him up: "No trueth in Negros" (10:65). Later in his triangular journey, Hawkins dismisses all Native Americans as "Infidels" (10:73). In contrast, crewman John Sparke's relation of Hawkins's second voyage begins by distinguishing among the cultural practices, physical appearances, and languages of various coastal tribes in Africa and America. As his account continues, however, the literal commodification of human beings in his text seems to engender a corresponding linguistic collapse. More specifically, his account reifies all these hitherto individuated peoples into the loose category "Negro" once they become part of the racialized economy of slavery.

Initial corporeal classifications in Sparke's account include skin tone, scarification, tattooing, face paint, costume, and nudity. In Guinea, he details the "tawnie," "long-haire[d]" people of Cape Blanco, "without any apparell"; the "blacke . . . Negros . . . without any apparell, sauing before their priuities," and the Leophares, "the goodliest men of all," both from Cape Verde (*PN*, 10:14–15). The Kongo of the Cape of Good Hope are "next" goodliest (10:15) after the Leophares in his list. On the island of Sambula he sees the Sapies with "filed" teeth and the Samboses with decorative scarification (10:17). In the Americas, he comments on the "Indians" who are "tawny like an Olive" with "haire all blacke . . . and without beards, neither men nor women" (10:27). They go "naked" but for the men's "yard, upon which they weare a gourd" or for the women's "hand-breadth" of cloth over their "privities" (10:22). Sparke is shocked by what he sees as a step below nudity in the Indians' appearance—the deliberate drawing of attention to the "privities" with the men's penis sheath or the women's length of cloth. The Floridians, in contrast, wear "Deere skinnes" painted with "red, blacke, yellow, & russet, very perfect, wherewith they [also] so paint their bodies . . . that with water it neither fadeth away, nor altereth colour" (10:57). In addition, they tattoo themselves "with curious knots, or antike worke, as every man in his owne fancy deviseth, which painting, to make it continue the better, they use with a thorne to pricke their flesh, and dent in the same, whereby the painting may have better hold" (10:52).

Sparke further subdivides the Guineans into "sundry sortes" according to their weaponry, belligerence, and diplomatic relationships with other tribes (10:15). The Leophares use "bowes and arrowes, targets, and short daggers" that differ from those of other tribes because they carry "five or sixe small [spears] a peece" instead of one long one in their war with the Jalofs (10:15). Despite their weapons, "These men also are more civill then any other, because of their dayly trafficke with the Frenchmen, and are of nature very gentle and loving" (10:15). The Sapies and Samboses, though enemies from different nations, share military technology and an ability to wage psychological warfare, using two-headed iron darts and spears tipped with poison from "the juyce of a cucumber" and uttering terrifying battle cries that "may bee heard two miles off" (10:20). Many of these intertribal wars were the direct result of the transatlantic slave trade itself. The trade converted an existing pattern of small-scale domestic slavery into mass economic exploitation, with wide-ranging social effects including the destruction of large kingdoms in favor of small states and the advent of drastic gender imbalances.[35]

Sparke's most sustained comparison of the Sapies and the Samboses is worth quoting at length for its employment of ethnographic detail implicitly to justify slave holding:

These inhabitants [Samboses] have diuerse of the Sapies, which they tooke in the warres as their slaues, whome onely they kept to till the ground, in that they neither haue the knowledge thereof, nor yet will worke themselves, of whome we tooke many in that place, but of the Samboses none at all, for they fled into the maine. All the Samboses have white teeth as we haue, farre vnlike to the Sapies which doe inhabite about Rio grande, for their teeth are all filed, which they doe for a brauerie, to set out themselves, and doe jagge their flesh, both legges, armes, and bodies, as workemanlike, as a Jerkin-maker with vs pinketh a ierkin. These Sapies be more ciuill then the Samboses: for whereas the Samboses liue most by the spoile of their enemies, both in taking their victuals, and eating them also, The Sapies doe not eate mans flesh, vnlesse in the warre they be dri-uen by necessitie thereunto, which they haue not vsed but by the example of the Samboses, but liue onely with fruites, and cattell, whereof they haue great store. This plentie is the occasion that the Sapies desire not warre, except they be thervnto prouoked by the inuasions of the Samboses, whereas the Samboses for want of foode are inforced therunto, and therefore are not woont onely to take them that they kill, but also keepe those that they take, untill such time as they want meate, and then they kill them. There is also another occasion that pro-voketh the Samboses to warre against the Sapies which is for couetousnes of their riches . . . for the Samboses have not the like store of golde, that the Sapies have. (*PN*, 10:17–18)

Sparke expresses what seems at first like a surprising cultural relativism, comparing the Samboses' teeth to those "as we have" and the Sapies' rit-ually scarred skins to the elaborately worked leather jerkins fashionable in Elizabethan England. But the overt comparison of both groups to the English works not in the service of compassion, understanding, or even of wonder, but ultimately towards the justification of slavery. For the covert parallel between the Samboses and the English sailors is their mutual reliance upon forced labor to perform agricultural work, the for-mer in Guinea, the latter in Barbados or Bermuda, and their shared hunger for gold. Unlike the humanizing reference to the Samboses' white teeth "as we have," the implicit comparison of the Sapies' scars to the "pink[in]g" of the "workemanlike" Jerkin-maker tans the skins of the Sapies, turning their human skins into leather hides and establishing the Sapies "slaves" as natural toilers. In the claim that the Samboses "eate mans flesh," including that of their slaves, the account figures bondage as cannibalism, strangely testifying to its atrocity and explaining it away by the slave owners' "want of foode," lack of knowledge, and lack of the will to work. And the final sentence of the quotation implicitly equates

"English" with "Samboses," and—say—the Spanish, Portuguese, or Guinean, with "Sapies": the other "occasion that provoketh" the English to war "is for covetousness of . . . golde," of which the English "have not the like store."

That the ethnographic catalog serves as an implicit justification for slavery is further supported by Sparke's detailed account of the Samboses' justice system. He describes the convening of the elders, and their power to mete out punishment, decide when crops should be gathered, and distribute palm wine. Admiring their equitable system for sharing palm wine ("this surely I judge to be a very good order" [10:20]), he claims that the Samboses treat slavery lightly, that "if a man be taken with . . . but a Portugal cloth from another, hee is sold to the Portugals for a slave" (10:19). After Hawkins's crew capture "certaine Negros," however, Sparke identifies the people of the Guinea region not by ethnicity ("Samboses and Sapies") but by race ("Negros")—by their skin color and status, not by their cultural practices or by what they call themselves (10:20). From this point onwards in his narrative, the only Africans to retain their own nomenclature are the Tangomango, who, as we shall see, do not form part of the racial economy of slavery and who threaten to disrupt or reverse its hierarchies by their plan to enslave the slavers.

Such attempted reversals dominate the remaining African portion of Sparke's narrative. On December 27, Hawkins's crew went to the town of Bymba, having heard that there were only forty able-bodied men to a hundred women and children, and lots of gold. They separated in order to "ransack" the huts for gold, but "in the meane time the Negros came upon them," followed them down to the boats, and attacked them vigorously until Hawkins shot at them (10:22). Having "returned backe some what discomforted," Hawkins's "heart inwardly broken in pieces for it" (10:22), they found that they had captured ten prisoners, but only with the loss of "seven of [their] best men" and "27 of [their] men hurt" (10:23). The Englishmen expected their prisoners to be cowed by their guns and powder (Figure 5). But less than a week later, while the sailors were replenishing their fresh water supplies, "the Negros set upon them in the boates, and hurt divers of them," also sabotaging the water butts and delaying their departure by several days (10:23).

Three weeks later, Sparke and his mates tried to make a final foray, but decided against it upon seeing "an Negro in a white coate, standing upon a rocke, being ready to have received them when they came on shore" (10:24). The man in the white coat served as the sentry for the king of Sierra Leone and the Tangomango, who had formed a plan to capture some of Hawkins's crew. Had the English sailors gone ashore, they would have found themselves captive in the king's court, satisfying

Figure 5. European with gun. Benin, sixteenth-seventeenth century. 1898. 1–15 no. 11. Reproduced by permission of the British Museum.

his curiosity about "what kinde of people . . . had spoiled his people at the Idols" (10:24). Sparke thanks "the Almightie God, who never suffereth his elect to perish," but adds a secular reason for their escape. When they saw a "monstrous fire" on the shore, they realized it must have been lit by the Tangomango army, who, Sparke writes, are the only battalion who generally signal to each other in this way (10:24).

An awareness of tribal differences saved the slavers on that occasion, just as knowledge of various types of weaponry and social structures allowed them to attack vulnerable towns or buildings. Slave traders routinely tried to kidnap Africans from different tribes, with different languages, to make it difficult for them to communicate with each other and to rebel. In this way Sparke's ethnic catalog served his racial objective; once he had kidnapped his cargo, Samboses, Sapies, "goodly" Leophare and Kongo all became "Negros." The kidnapped men and women on board Hawkins's ships might have had nothing in common with each other except their common tragedy and their raced objectification by the white men around them. And when these disparate, desperate black people fought for their freedom, defended themselves from rape, and sabotaged their captors' pinnaces, they perforce shared what Lani Guinier and Gerald Torres call "political race": an oppositional identity based on their common racialization.[36]

"a race and kind of people, who . . . will not bee brought to worke"

Sparke and Hawkins employ a term, "Negro," that fetishizes skin color as a mark of one's potential to be enslaved. Trafficker Richard Jobson, in contrast, is best known for his expression of natural horror at slavery and of fellow feeling with the captive African women he encounters. On his 1620–21 quest for gold, he meets the "greate blacke Merchant, called *Buckor Sano*" (*Golden Trade*, subtitle), who offers to sell him young women:

I made answer, We were a people, who did not deale in any such commodities, neither did wee buy or sell one another, or any that had our owne shapes; [Buckor Sano] seemed to maruell much at it, and told vs, it was the only marchandize, they carried downe into the countrey . . . and that they were solde there to white men, who earnestly desired them, especially such young women, as hee had brought for vs: we answered, They were another kinde of people different from vs, but for our part, if they had no other commodities, we would returne againe. (M4v–Nr)

Note that Jobson subdivides the "white . . . kinde of people" into the English, who, he claims, will not trade human flesh, and the Spanish or Portuguese, who "earnestly desire" it. Earlier in his account, he outlines the mechanics of the trade. The "Portingales" living in North Africa (whom Jobson classifies as renegade Portuguese and their "Molato" or mixed-race descendants) kidnap or buy "the country people, who are sold vnto them, when they commit offences" (E2v) and sell them in turn to the Spanish, who take them to the West Indies to labor in the mines or elsewhere. Perhaps Jobson was engaging in wishful thinking; perhaps he was unaware of Hawkins's rapacious voyages forty years earlier.

Jobson's account of Portuguese/Pulbe/Mandinka relations in the Senegambia region subordinates skin color to tribal or national affiliation and the division of labor. *The Golden Trade* identifies the three main groups of Africans there as the "Portingales" (Portuguese), the "Fulbies" (Fulani or Pulbe, plural Fulbie), and the "Maudingos" (Mandinka). Banished men "from forth either of Portingall, or the Iles belonging vnto the gouernement" (E2v), or the "poor distressed children . . . naturalized" of such exiles (E3v), the people who call themselves "Portingales" fall into three groups. These groups vary in skin color between the pale few who "seeme the same" (that is, who resemble the Portuguese); "Molatoes, betweene blacke and white"; and those who are "as blacke, as the naturall inhabitants" (E2v). Although they "reseru[e] . . . the name of Christians, these tricolored "naturalized" Portuguese "haue amongst them, neither Church, nor Frier, nor any other religious order" (E2v). They can thus be distinguished from the other inhabitants of the country neither by skin color nor by religious practice (unless its absence itself constitutes a distinctive feature), but by language ("the vse of the Portingall tongue") and by their self-appellation (E3v). They willfully perform an identity constituted through exclusion, expressing "great disdaine, be they neuer so black, to be called a Negro" (E3v). Note Jobson's easy assumption that "black" and "Negro" should be synonymous, even as he documents distinctions of rank, religion, and labor among what he has called a "nation" of "blacke people"; thus nuanced ethnography and reductive racial classification inhabit the same text (E3r).

These Portingales live by "vent[ing]" "the country people," who have been sold into slavery "when they commit offences" (E2v). At one point in Jobson's narrative, it is unclear who is doing this vending:

the blacke people are bought away by their owne nation, and by them either carried, or solde vnto the Spaniard, for him to carry into the West Indies, to remain as slaues, either in their Mines, or in any other seruile vses, they in those countries put them to. (E3r)

"[T]hem" in the phrase "by them . . . carried" seems at first ambiguously to refer either to the "blacke . . . nation" who have "bought away" their own compatriots, or to the "vent[ing]" Portingales. But I paraphrase the passage thus: "the black people are bought away by their own nation, and either carried by the Portuguese, or sold to be carried by the Spanish, to the West Indies." The confusion stems in part from the shifting associations of the Portuguese, who are both black and white, African and European, godless and Christian. I commented on Jobson's naïveté with regard to slave trading; here he shows a similar ignorance. The silver mines in Spanish America fed the hunger for specie in Jacobean England, which greedily sought Eastern goods it would otherwise lack the coin to buy.

Different associations of skin color and labor appear in Jobson's account of Mandinka/Fulani relations. He compares the "Tawny" Fulani to Egyptians, praising, as I have quoted in earlier chapters, the beauty, modesty, and cleanliness of their womenfolk (albeit expressing surprise thereto and taking the chance to complain about Irish women in contrast) (F3r). He characterizes the Fulani life as one full of hard toil and vagrancy, as they follow their cattle across the country. "This is the poor Fulbies life, whereunto he is so enured, that in a manner he is become bestiall," continues Jobson, the evidence for which he finds in their tolerance of insects who land upon their bodies. Their hands and faces, he writes,

would stand so thicke of flyes, as they vse to sit in the hot Summer time vpon our horses, and teemes here in England, and they were the same manner of flye wee haue, which the Fulbie would let alone, not offring to put vp his hand, to driue them away, therein seeming more senslesse, then our Country beasts, who will wiske with their tayles, and seeke any other defence, to auoyde or be rid of them, but of our owne parts we were faine, during our parley with them, to hold a greene bow, to beate of the flie, finding his stay neuer so little, very offensiue. (F2r)

Despite his affection for them, Jobson here ranks the humanity of the Fulani below that of the "Country beasts" who pull the plough in England and flick flies away with their tails. The Englishmen, in contrast, cannot bear even the slightest touch of a fly, be "his stay neuer so little," and wave green branches before themselves to fan away the flies. It is as if the flies pollute or contaminate the human beings on whom they land, dehumanizing them. This degradation, Jobson argues, is not innate but the result of the Fulani's "great subiection to the Mandinka," who take the greater part of any meat they kill and compel them to serve them.

In Jobson's account, the black Mandinka enslave the lighter-skinned Fulani; in turn the Portuguese and mulattoes capture and enslave the Mandinka. He sees a definite racial or tribal hierarchy, but it does not correspond conveniently to degrees of pigmentation. One could argue that Jobson's evident sympathies for the "poor Fulbies" and his repeated equation of "blacke and barbarous" (his surprise at their good behavior) proves that he maintains his own mental hierarchy, ranking people according to the shades of their skin tones, white/tawny/black. But at the same time, he characterizes the tawny Fulani as more bestial than the black Mandinka, because of poverty, and is keen to distinguish the English from those other "white men" who buy and sell those of their own shape.[37]

Thomas Palmer makes a similar argument for the dehumanizing effects of hard labor in *How to Make Our Travailes Profitable*, where he distinguishes between "seruile" and "free" peoples of the world.[38] Having conceded that all people are naturally "seruile to sinne and vnrighteousnesse," he goes on to classify people who are "politicall[y] . . . seruile to slauery, miserie, and subiection" (K3r). England, France, and Germany are "by prescription enfranchised," he claims, citing laws of France and Kent that immediately free bondsmen who land there (K3r). Denmark is almost too free, "licentiously" free "by arrogation," holding an elective monarchy, like the Venetians (K3v). The "Switzers" are free "by policie . . . as euer striving against seruitude," just like the Hungarians against the Great Turk (K3v). "Such are the people of Ireland, who not being accustomed to ciuility and obeisance, spure so much against the same," he adds, identifying "the markes of liberty and freedome of people [as] riches & ease" (K3v).

Servile peoples, on the other hand, are enslaved either by tyranny or by poverty ("oppression" or "depression," in Palmer's terms [K4r]). The first kind of servile person includes Muscovites, who are "so seruile . . . that they call themselues the slaues of the Duke" and who cannot own property (K4r). Other slaves are "those people, whose ouer-rulers are Tyrants, and the Turke generally thorow his Dominions, the Pope ouer the Cleargie, and many temporall States" (K4r). The second kind are rendered servile by a poverty imposed on them by their superiors in rank, like "the husbandmen and tenants of Italie" (K4r–K4v) and the German "Boores" under the nobility (K4v). "[S]o finally are al those commons whose Nobility like Solons great flies breake thorow the net of the Lawe, and where the Prince is remisse in gouernment" (K4v), he concludes, thereby undercutting his own neat binary by linking oppression/tyranny with depression/poverty. He summarizes his findings: "Now the markes of seruile people are hereby gathered, namely, Pouertie and Want, and excessiue paines-taking and moyling to gaine their liuing. Such were the Irish: such are the Moores" (K4v). Presumably the Irish were "servile" until the English began their project of colonizing them. But what Palmer means by "the Moores" is impossible to tell. Is he referring to the subjects of the Turk whom he has mentioned above as examples of oppressed people? Or is he alluding to Africans, and sowing the seed for the (to us, unconscionably stupid) notion that the Guineans Hawkins kidnapped "would be glad to change [their country], and whose Condition of Life [was] so bad, that they could not fear any other being worse"?[39]

Whatever Palmer intends to say, the link among enslavement, poverty, and "moyling" seems to resonate with Jobson, too, not only in his description of the Fulani but also in his discussions of first, the "Marybuckes" (Marabout priests) and second, the sociable baboons that he observes. "[S]eperated . . . both in their habitations & course of liues," writes Jobson, the Marabout priests follow "leuiticall law" and keep to their own townships and houses, away from "the common people,"

except such as are their slaues, that worke and labour for them, which slaues they suffer to marry and cherish the race that comes of them, which race remaines to them, and their heires or posterity as perpetuall bondmen; they marry likewise in their owne tribe or kindred, taking no wiues, but the daughters of Marybuckes, and all the children they haue, are nourished and bred vp, vnto the ceremonies of their fathers. (I3v)

"Race" here encompasses bondage on the one hand and parentage (one's own and one's offspring's) on the other; the Marabouts might also embody a race, "seperated from the common people" by geography and what can only be called caste, an inherited vocation. "Slaues" are defined by their "worke and labour," as in Palmer's analysis.

Jobson later uses labor as the most important criterion in classifying human beings. In some ways his distinctions recall the early modern strictures against Gypsies, vagabonds, and actors, who will not settle down in one place and work for an employer. In a strange digression, Jobson calls baboons "absolutely a race and kind of people, who in regard they will not bee brought to worke, and liue vnder subiection, refuse to speake" (Vr). Here Jobson almost prefigures Engels's claim that the division of labor, and humans' sophisticated use of their hands, minds, and larynxes, enabled the evolution of humans from apes.[40]

But Jobson does not even seem to make Engels's distinction between "ape" and "man." Citing a Spanish source and his own observations, he comments on how human the baboons seem, with their establishment of a "kind of common-wealth" that takes care of their old, their sick, and their young (Vr). Not only do these baboons follow a certain rule of law, he claims, they also engage in cultural production and the arts of architecture and dance, fabricating sunshades and elaborate arbors where they engage in primate ballets.[41] Impressed by their "tree-top gouernement," he swears that he will never eat them, although the people of the country do (Vr). And here Jobson seems to engage in both an idealism bordering on the absurd (even the animal-rights activist and philosopher Peter Singer would grant legal rights only to the Great Apes, not to lesser ones like baboons) and a desperate cynicism.[42] He suggests that not only are the baboons able to speak, but that they willfully refuse to converse with human beings because the inevitable outcome is "worke," "subiection," and the eradication of their leisurely and artful way of life (Vr). Once more, Jobson's voice echoes uncertainly across the centuries. Does his engagement with baboons conform to the nasty bestializing of Africans in, say, Elizabeth Cary's closet drama?

I do not read Jobson as a dehumanizing writer, despite his evocation of the baboons here and of the "country beasts" earlier. Instead, in contrast to the coarseness of Hawkins's text or the gradual hardening of Sparke's, Jobson's account is characterized by compassion. In addition to the charismatic but unscrupulous merchant Buckor Sano, Jobson is befriended by the seventeen-year-old Samgulley. The latter, Jobson writes, "withall had taken such an affection towards vs; that he did seeme euen hartely to neglect father and mother, and his owne home, in his desires to follow vs" (P2v). Jobson calls him "our blacke boie" and "our Samgulley" throughout his narrative, a possessive that to me indicates not financial but emotional investment, since Jobson both dissociates himself from the Portuguese slave buyers and clearly affirms the free status of his interpreters: "I did hire Blacke-men, as I had occasion to vse them, to serue as Interpreters, likewise to send abroade, and to helpe to row, and get vp the boate" (Dr–Dv). Having missed his ritual circumcision because he was traveling with the Englishmen, Samgulley refuses to return for the ceremony, even when his embarrassed mother threatens to drown herself alongside the English ship unless he comes home. He relents, however, when he recalls "it was the time of the cutting of Prickes; for so hee cald it, and that hee was come time enough" (P3v). That "so hee cald it" is intriguing; is this one of those all too rare moments in early travel writing where the subaltern almost seems to speak? Samgulley "spake pretty English," so it might well be (P2v).

Jobson's account of the ritual circumcision he eventually witnesses displays, as one might expect from such a narrative, a disdainful horror at the custom. Yet his description of Samgulley's teenage independence and wanderlust rings true. Perhaps I am essentializing, mapping modern American conceptions of adolescent rebellion onto an early modern African setting. We do not know anything about Samgulley's tribal affiliation and cultural expectations, after all. But I think that to assume that only Englishmen desired to see the world and to observe the lives of strangers denies agency to the traders and travelers who met, took advantage of, and befriended Jobson and his crew.

We cannot take either Jobson's idealism or his companionate interest in strangers as axiomatic during the period, given Hawkins's resolute and repeated reference to "Negroes," and Sparke's gradual dehumanizing of the people he captures. The ethnographic impulse participated in the creation of race just as race colors the development of ethnography. But what we *can* find in Jobson's text are moments of recognition and compassion on his side, of wit and initiative on the part of the men and women who were his guides, and of mythologies of color and labor that both support and challenge those that are more familiar to us today. Similar shades of difference color the science and fiction of Margaret Cavendish, Duchess of Newcastle, who on the one hand insists that black and white people belong to separate species and on the other provides nuanced and rarefied classifications that recognize all shapes, all skin tones, all castes, and all religions as variations on the human.

Chapter 9

Experiments of Colors

I end, as I promised, where I began—with an investigation of romance and the marvelous. Where versions of Heliodorus, however, relied upon pseudoscientific evidence from the classical world and upon anecdote, the work of Margaret Cavendish, Duchess of Newcastle, engages with seventeenth-century empiricism. When Cavendish published *Observations on Experimental Philosophy* (*Observations*) in 1666, she became the first British woman to write and publish scientific work.[1] Perhaps eager to demonstrate her knowledge of the newest scientific theories, Cavendish added a new section to the second edition of *Observations* in 1668, a section that responded, as Rosemary Kegl remarks, to current debates about racial origin, and in particular to the question of whether white and black men were descended from the same human ancestor—Adam. In the 1668 text, Cavendish argues that black men are *not* descended from Adam: "Blackmoors [are] a kind or race of men different from the White . . . For, if there were no differences in their productions, then would not onely all men be exactly like, but all Beasts also; that is, there would be no difference between a Horse and a Cow, a Cow and a Lyon, a Snake and an Oyster."[2] The differences between white and black men are as pronounced as those between "a Cow and a Lyon, a Snake and an Oyster." The comparison is also gendered, contrasting the lactating cow with the fierce lion, the vigorous snake with the flaccid oyster. Kegl suggests that this statement collapses two different senses of the word "race": species difference and color difference; Cavendish concludes that the "Blackmoors" are as different from "White" people as cows are from lions. But Kegl brilliantly observes that Cavendish's romantic utopia, *The Description of a New World, Called the Blazing World* [*BW*], which was bound and published together with *Observations*, carefully *distinguishes* between "race," meaning species difference, and "race," meaning variants of skin tone:

the ordinary sort of men [in the Blazing World] . . . were of several complexions: not white, black, tawny, olive or ash-coloured; but some appeared of an azure, some of a deep purple, some of a grass-green, some of a scarlet, some of an orange-colour, etc. . . . The rest of the inhabitants of that world, were men of several different sorts, shapes, figures, disposition, and humours . . . some were bear-men, some worm-men, some fish- or mear-men [mer-men], . . . some bird-men, some fly-men, some ant-men, some geese-men, some spider-men, some lice-men, some fox-men, some ape-men, some jackdaw-men, some magpie-men, some parrot-men, some satyrs, some giants, and many more, which I cannot all remember. (*BW*, 133)

The subjects of the Blazing World comprise people who are racially diverse in two different senses: they have skins of varying colors, and they belong to diverse species. Cavendish's romance thus "draws a distinction between difference based on species or complexion, understood as 'humours,' on the one hand, and difference based on complexion, understood as 'colour,' on the other."[3] Kegl suggests that this apparent inconsistency on the subject of racial difference between *Observations* and *Blazing World* reflects seventeenth-century confusion about the meanings of both race and color, citing Samuel Pepys's appreciative description of Cavendish's "black" Italian waiting woman, Ferrabosco, and of a little "black boy" who ran up and down the chamber when Cavendish visited the Royal Society. Pepys's editors gloss "black" as "brunette," but Samuel Mintz imagines the child to have been an "exotic graft in an English garden"; we have no way of knowing whether he was the black-haired son of a lady-in-waiting, or an African page.[4]

This cultural confusion about the meaning of skin tone and its relationship to racial or species difference might contribute to Cavendish's fantastic Blazing World of colors, as Kegl proposes, but I will argue that Cavendish's riot of color is not a response to late seventeenth-century confusion about color as much as a romantic reply to the emerging pseudoscientific discourse that *did* connect color with race—and the residual humoral discourse that, contra Kegl, interpreted skin color/complexion not as different from humor/complexion but as an erratically visible expression of it. Throughout her romances, Cavendish imagines herself and her heroines in positions of absolute royal power. She also briefly envisions situations in which the hierarchies of race and species difference that were emerging in the seventeenth century do not exist. Both Cavendish and her husband, William, Duke of Newcastle, were ardent Royalists who lost their estate and fortune during the Interregnum and were forced into exile in Antwerp.[5] (Since "The Duchess of Newcastle" and "The Duke of Newcastle" both appear as characters in *Blazing World*, I shall henceforth refer to the author as "Cavendish," her husband as "William," and their literary incarnations as "The Duke" and "The Duchess.") Cavendish's fictional worlds were a Royalist riposte to the Interregnum, a rejoinder that affirmed the supremacy of distinctions of rank above all other categories—race, gender, or religion.

This is only possible, I will argue, in her blazing worlds of fiction. As a scientist, Cavendish affirmed the inferiority both of women to men and of black men to white. As a royalist and a romancist, however, Cavendish's belief in the primacy of rank as a way of distinguishing between classes of people leads her in her monarchical romances to contradict various theories of sexual and racial inferiority which were current in Restoration England and which she herself espoused in her scientific writings. Fiction allowed her both the freedom to imagine such a world, and the security of knowing that such a world could never come to pass.

Polygenesis and Scientific Racism

When Cavendish adds a commentary to *Observations* describing "Blackmoors" as a separate "race" from white men, she is responding to the newest pseudoscientific theories connecting race, skin color, and species origin, theories that contradicted earlier beliefs that accounted blackness a mystery but did not consider black skin to be a sign of species difference. As we saw earlier, although George Best had connected skin color with biological inheritance as early as 1578, even in the mid-seventeenth century Thomas Browne explicitly states that "Negroes" descend from "the seed of Adam" (*PE*, 3:240). Nonetheless, Browne offered a "quasi-genetic explanation" for blackness that asserted its essential nature.[6] Like Browne, most early mythologies of skin color assume that all men and women, regardless of skin tone, are descended from Adam, a theory of creation called monogenesis. Even Best, who assumed that "blacke Moores" were "cursed" by God (*PN*, 7:264), never doubted their kinship to Englishmen. While Jonson carefully annotates *Blackness* to take account of the classical theories of blackness that suggest that the Ethiopians and Egyptians were created not by God but by the heat of the sun upon the soil, few writers take seriously the notion that black Africans, white Europeans, and tawny Moors descended from different species, or through polygenesis. To do so would be to doubt the word of the Bible.

But in the 1650s, Isaac La Peyrère and François Bernier insisted that there were several different species of human beings, descended polygenetically, and that "black people were in some way intermediate between white people and apes."[7] La Peyrère speculated that there were *Men Before Adam* and propounded a theological system that denied that human beings were all descended from the same race or root. According to La Peyrère, Adam was not the first man; the Jews were descended from Adam, but the Gentiles sprang from the very first men, who lived on Earth *before* the creation of Adam. He argues that those Gentiles who converted to Christianity became a newer (and superior) race of Jews through a "mystical adoption," which changed "both their kind and their lin[e]age," both their race and their rank.[8] La Peyrère's argument has clear implications for the status of African slaves in early modern Britain and America. His treatise offers a theological basis for polygenesis, and for the belief that certain races or species of human were created superior to others. One part of his argument has a particularly pointed resonance for the slave trade: he implies that the unconverted Gentiles are "servants," while Christians become "free-men."[9] According to this belief, unconverted Africans had not undergone a "mystical adoption" into the race of the Jews and were therefore slaves, not free men. This religious excuse was so powerful that, as Jordan and others observe, during the 1660s New England slave-owners grew anxious lest their slaves' conversion force their masters to set them free and hastily enacted a law in 1664 that "provided that This Law shall not extend to sett at Liberty Any Negroe or Indian Servant who shall turne Christian after he shall have been bought by Any Person."[10] The wording of the law is exemplary of its kind: the future perfect tense ("shall have been bought") suggests that there is no destiny, apart from slavery, open to Native American or African slaves, while they are carefully denied humanity, in contrast to the "Person" who might buy them.

Polygenetic theories, and the notion of an inherited slave caste, were more common in New England and the West Indies than in Britain. Richard Ligon divides the inhabitants of Barbados into three groups, "Masters, Servants and slaves," concluding that "the slaves and their posterity" are "subject to their Masters for ever." Henry Whistler lists in 1655 "all sortes: English, french, Duch, Scotes, Irish, Spaniards thay being Jues [Jews]" and finally "Ingones [Indians] and miserabell Negors borne to perpetuall slavery thay and thayer seed."[11] A tract in defense of the tobacco colonies which circulated in 1656 maintained that, while white women could do domestic work, black women should be sent to work in the tobacco fields because they were "nasty, and beastly."[12] Theories of polygenesis did not become widely popular in Britain until the eighteenth century, but their first appearance marks a radical change from the mythologies of color that predominated during the Elizabethan and Jacobean periods. The notion of species difference was not a cause but a symptom of Britain's increasing involvement in the slave trade, and polygenesis provided a convenient explanation of racial difference that conflated variation with inferiority. Cavendish's own addition to *Observations* in 1668 is one of the earliest British statements of polygenesis. But, as we have seen, in *Blazing World* she distinguishes between species difference and skin color as signs of race, in a fictional challenge to her own polygenetic beliefs. This romantic challenge to the analysis of skin encompassed not only pseudoscientific pamphlets from the New World but also the emerging empirical discourse investigating the origins of color itself, a discourse that Cavendish interrogated in both "philosophical" and fictional terms.

Observations of Color

Robert Hooke explains blackness as absence or "privation of Light." The first person to observe cell structures through a microscope (and to use the word "cell" to describe them), he usually calls these plant and animal cells "pores" and believes that the depth, frequency and dryness of these pores in charcoal, coals, and burnt objects explains their blackness:

certainly, a body that has so many pores in it. . .from each of which no light is reflected, must necessarily look black, . . . black being nothing else but a privation of Light, or a want of reflection; and wheresover this reflecting quality is deficient, there does that part look black . . . from a porousness of the body.[13]

Hooke defines the color black as an absence not only of light but of matter and movement, suggesting that burnt objects have lost the water that filled their cells and reflected the light back to the eye of the viewer. Black objects enjoy a strange "universal kind of transparency . . . that light onely is reflected back which falls upon the very outward edges of the pores, all they that enter into the pores of the body, never returning, but being lost in it."[14] Thus we can see the shape of a black object, but its center is like a black hole, to use an anachronistic comparison: once light or energy goes into it, it cannot come out again. Hooke and his Royal Society colleague Robert Boyle discovered independently that light was a wave (or, as Hooke put it, that "there is no luminous body but has the parts of it in motion more or less").[15] They also argued that the phenomenon of color was dependent upon this motion of light (we would now say, upon its wavelength) and upon its refraction and reflection in various media, such as air, water, or "Muscovy glass" (mica).[16]

Cavendish knew and responded to the work of Hooke and Boyle. She was an interested, indeed, keen observer of the new science; when she visited the Royal Society in 1667 she was reported to be "full of admiration, all admiration" for its "Fine experiments of Colours, Loadstones, Microscope, and of liquors."[17] Mintz conjectures that the "experiments of Colours" that Pepys and Cavendish observed were probably those described by Boyle in *Experiments and Considerations Touching Colours* (1664), in which he produced "a red colour out of two transparent liquors" and turned red Rhenish wine "a lovely green."[18] On her visit to the society, Cavendish professed her admiration for their experiments, but both *Observations* and *Blazing World* regard empirical science with a quizzical, sometimes satirical, eye. She expresses her critique partly through what seems like the incongruous yoking of a scientific treatise and a romance in a single volume. Cavendish links the two works expressly in her "Epilogue to the Reader," calling the one her "Philosophical World," the other her "Blazing" one, and claiming that they both come from "the most pure, that is, the most rational parts of . . . my mind," a "pure" rationality that she contrasts to the "conquests of *Alexander* and *Caesar*" (*BW*, 224). In her praise of the "rational," Cavendish is extolling a Cartesian model of abstract thought over experimental science. She argues that her imaginary, female worlds are superior to the masculine model of colonial domination exemplified by Alexander because she has not "caused so many . . . deaths as they did," "esteeming peace before war" (*BW*, 224). In the same way, Cartesian rationalism provides Cavendish with her response to the Baconian empiricism of the Royal Society, whose experiments attempted a kind of experimental "conquest" over the natural world.

Cavendish challenged the new science in specific instances as well as in her general approach to natural philosophy. As Anna Battigelli points out, Cavendish's *Observations* and *Blazing World* both include direct responses to Hooke's *Micrographia*. Battigelli argues that Cavendish mounts a threefold attack on lenses, both microscopic and telescopic: first, far from demonstrating an objective truth, as their adherents claim, they distort the true nature of things (for example, by showing a louse to be as big as an lobster); second, they cannot alter the characteristics of the creatures they show (they cannot prevent the louse from biting its host); third, and most important, they refuse "to acknowledge the inevitable interference of their own subjectivity."[19] Cavendish thus attacks both the physical means (lenses) and the philosophical methods (observation and experiment) of the new science.

She continues to criticize Hooke's discoveries in a section of *Observations* that pointedly parallels his discussion of charcoal. First, Cavendish insists, colors cannot be caused only by the presence of light, because refraction or reflection (she does not distinguish between the two) alters continually, and "if [the reflections] were the true cause of Colours, no Colour would appear constantly the same, but change variously . . . . whereas on the contrary, we see that natural and inherent Colours continue always the same" (*Observations*, 51). Cavendish argues here that color remains constant despite the fluctuations of light, which is constantly changing.

Second, she argues that blackness cannot be caused by the absence of light and the presence of "pores," for if the blackness of a Charcoal, did proceed from the absence of light in its pores, then a black Horse would have more or deeper pores then a white one . . . also a black Moor would have larger Pores then a man of a white complexion; and black Sattin, or any black Stuff, would have deeper pores then white Stuff: But if a fair white Lady should bruise her arm, so as it did appear black, can any one believe that light would be more absent from that bruised part then from any other part of her arm that is white, or that light should reflect otherwise upon that bruised part, then on any other? (*Observations*, 52)

It is unclear whether Cavendish is using "pores" in the sense that Hooke intends; she mocks a science that is based on observation, but here she uses her own observations to challenge its results. Her examples reflect her gender and rank: Hooke observed charcoal, cork, and "Muscovy glass," but Cavendish observes horses, the African slaves of her noble acquaintances, satin, and her own skin, and finds no difference in their apparent porosity. Reducing colors to pores, she feels, is ridiculous, and her examples get progressively more farfetched (she argues that, if the porous theory of color is true, then, because the eye has a vast number of pores, light entering the eye ought to make it perceive all objects as if they have as many colors as a rainbow). Moreover, darkness cannot be merely the absence of light, she avers, because if we can only perceive sensations or objects through light, we would be unable to recognize the dark and distinguish night from day, which is "contrary to common experience, nay, to sense and reason" (*Observations*, 54). Cavendish's appeal to "common experience" and "sense" contrasts the kind of observation that she prizes (like the appearance of black versus white satin) with the microscopic observation of Hooke, which she finds so misleading.

Eyes are misleading, reason tells the truth; thus colors are by no means "lost or lessened in the dark, but . . . onely concealed from the ordinary perception of humane sight" (*Observations*, 55). Just because you can't see them doesn't mean they aren't there. If we cannot see colors at night, it is our sight that is imperfect; Cavendish interprets night vision as a sign of the inferiority of the physical senses next to the superior sense of reason. She insists that colors do not change or disappear, thereby combining a belief in both the similarity and the difference of the "black Moor" and the man of a "white complexion"; they have similar pores or cell structures, but their skin colors are "fixt and inherent" (*Observations*, 56). Cavendish's chapter on blackness concludes with a vehement belief in the fixedness of colors.

She modifies her theory of colors, however, in her next chapter, "Of Colours," in which she concedes that there may be two sorts of colors, "Homogeneous" and "Heterogeneous," that is, colors that are fixed, innate, and unified and colors that are changeable, external, and varied respectively. Superficial colors, like those caused by "the Yellow or black

Jaundies," by blushes (and, presumably, by the black bruises on the arm of a "fair white Lady") are heterogeneous, but underlying colors are homogeneous or unchanging (*Observations*, 59, 61). Where a residual geohumoral discourse might have explained all skin colors in environmental terms, Cavendish offers an emergent racial logic to distinguish between the skin color with which one is born and the tones that external events and influences may cause. She provides a characteristically personal example to illustrate heterogeneous color change: she compares color change to the unchanging appearance of a "Traytor" in "the Politick body of a Commonwealth," who encourages "all the Kingdom to take armes," even if those members "know not particularly of the Traytor, and of the circumstances of his crime" (*Observations*, 61). The initial crime is the stimulus that prompts the whole body politic to blush or grow pale; color change is a sign of "Civil War" (*Observations*, 62).

Arguing both for and against the possibility of color change is typical of Cavendish. In *Blazing World*, she mocks both the experimental scientists of the Royal Society for their need to find a logical explanation for everything, and her own desire to avoid a single, unified conclusion. But whereas in *Observations*, she comes up with an answer to the conundrum of color, however concessionary, in *Blazing World* she refuses outright to explain why her Blazing Worlders have complexions of such astonishing shades as "azure," "deep purple," "grass-green," "scarlet," or "orange-colour":

Which colours and complexions, whether they were made by the bare reflection of light, without the assistance of small particles, or by the help of well-ranged and ordered atoms; or by a continual agitation of little globules; or by some pressing and reacting motion, I am not able to determine. (*BW*, 133)

This tongue-in-cheek parenthesis alludes to several different competing theories of light, color, and matter.[20] In 1637 Descartes argued that light was made up of particles or atoms, that light was stable, unified, and homogeneous, and that color was the result of refraction or modification to a beam of white light. In 1665, while the plague ravaged Cambridge, Newton was writing a treatise "On Colours" that subscribed to the particle theory, but he suggested that light was unstable, various, and heterogeneous, and that color was not a modification of white light but the result of separating white light into its constituent colors. The same year, Boyle and Hooke were arguing that light was not a particle but a wave that pushed forward ("made by . . . a pressing and reacting motion"). Hooke and Newton would in fact fight so bitterly on the subject of waves versus particles that Newton would retire to Cambridge in disgust, to study alchemy. In her lighthearted summary of competing theories of color, and in refusing to cite any one of them to explain the skin colors of the Blazing Worlders, Cavendish steps whimsically over the whole dispute.

Cavendish complained in the preface to *Observations* that she was insufficiently educated to understand the new science, but she clearly knew the terms of the debate—she just couldn't or wouldn't accept them. In particular, she saw no place for a unified theory of color in a *romance*, any more than she saw the need for a notion of identity that cohered around any characteristics other than nobility. Her understanding of identity in the romances veers between essential characteristics that cannot be changed (this is the case with rank and, in *Blazing World*, with gender) and fluid attributes that change constantly within the narrative (such as color, race, nationality, or the direction of sexual desire).

Assaulted and Pursued Chastity

Cavendish first addressed the connections among fiction, skin color, rank and gender in her romantic fable *Assaulted and Pursued Chastity* (*APC*, 1656). *APC* plays in a controlled manner with the limits of identity—royal, racial, and gendered—by erasing these limits briefly during the narrative only to redraw them at its conclusion. Cavendish's heroine changes her name and her gender according to her circumstances. She goes by the name "Miseria," which refers to her first state of "assaulted and pursued chastity," when she is pursued by a rapacious Prince; "Affectionata," when she shoots and wounds this Prince to preserve her chastity and escapes on board a ship; and "Travellia" when, dressed as a boy, she is adopted by a Captain and travels the world. Cavendish, somewhat confusingly, often uses the male personal pronoun to refer to the cross-dressed Travellia, as if the heroine (like Woolf's Orlando) does indeed change sex for the duration of "his" adventure (until the Prince discovers "him," when "she" becomes female once more). Marina Leslie argues that the pronominal confusion, like the unorthodox methods by which Travellia preserves her chastity, thwarts a reader's expectations of the narrative; as Orgel observes, however, such pronominal ambiguity is typical both of early modern romances and of Elizabethan and Jacobean accounts of the transvestite theater.[21] On their voyage, Travellia and the Captain encounter and civilize a land of royal cannibals before being sold into the service of the Queen of Amity. It turns out that the Prince has likewise been sold into servitude—to the King of Amour, who is waging war on the Queen of Amity. Travellia, who becomes captain of the Queen's army, escapes the Prince's military assaults and his recognition until, in a parody of the masculine exchange of women in marriage contracts, the Queen of Amity, who has fallen in and out of love with Travellia, hands him/her over to the Prince as part of a peace treaty with the King—on condition that Travellia become "Viceregency" of the Kingdom of Amity, and that the Queen shall marry the King of Amour (*APC*, 116). Travellia is perfectly willing to marry her Prince at this point, having defeated him in battle and won the hearts of the people.

Disembarking in a strange land with the Captain, the cross-dressed Travellia encounters "such complexioned men" as she

> never saw . . . for they were not black like Negroes, nor tawny, nor olive, nor ash-coloured, as many are, but of a deep purple, their hair as white as milk, and like wool; their lips thin, their ears long, their noses flat, yet sharp, their teeth and nails as black as jet, and as shining; their stature tall, and their proportion big; their bodies were all naked, only from the waist down to their twist [crotch] was there brought through their legs up to the waist again, and tied with a knot, a thin kind of stuff, which was made of the barks of trees, yet looked as fine as silk, and as soft; the men carried long darts in their hands, spear-fashion, so hard and smooth, as it seemed like metal, but made of whales' bones. (*APC*, 63)

At first it seems that these natives contradict all a seventeenth-century reader's expectations and assumptions about foreign climes, with their brilliant, nonnatural skin tones that Cavendish carefully contrasts to the inhabitants of the world we know. Cavendish explicitly distances her natives from "Negroes" and their skin tones from the "many" that are familiar to Earth-dwellers. But on closer inspection, her description repeats the orientalist tropes of the travel narratives we considered in Chapter Eight. Her natives are "naked" but for a loincloth, like the savages that Leo Africanus describes; they carry spear-like implements, again like wild men or savages; although their clothing looks like silk and their darts like metal spears, in fact they use "the barks of trees" and "whales' bones," products of the natural world, rather than artifacts of artisanship or civilization. Despite the fact that they are "not black like Negroes," their noses are "flat" and their hair curls "like wool," a combination that evokes common stereotypes about African features. Later in the novella, Cavendish directly compares their hair to "wool, and very short as Nigers have" (*APC*, 71). This "wool" in fact saves Travellia from human sacrifice: when "he" lets down "his" long hair, the priest is "amazed at the sight," because he has never seen such long locks before, and lays down the knife before worshipping "him" as a god. Travellia's long hair is a sign of her female gender, but it saves her life despite—or even because of—the fact that her captors cannot interpret it as a sign of femininity. For the natives, Travellia's hair signifies not sex but rank and power; this is part of a larger pattern in the novella that inverts feminine disadvantage and turns it to account.

While Travellia can transcend gender because of her rank and superior knowledge, none of the people she encounters can transcend their rank, here explicitly connected to skin color. As Kate Lilley remarks, in this world skin color illustrates "a profound physical difference between subjects of different rank."[22] While the common folk are purple, "all those of the royal blood, were of a different colour from the rest of the people, they were of a perfect orange colour, their hair coal black, their teeth and nails as white as milk, of a very great height, yet well shaped" (*APC*, 68). In addition, while the commoners have teeth "black as jet," the royals have teeth and nails "white as milk"; while the commoners have hair "white as snow," the royals have hair that is "coal black" (*APC*, 68). The royal family and their subjects belong to tribes who are physical opposites.

Just as the inhabitants of this new world recall distant African tribes, so the landscape is rich in exotic and marketable commodities such as nutmeg, mace, cinnamon, ginger, oranges, and lemons. One of the "governors" that Travellia meets lives in a house

built with spices; the roof and beams . . . made of cinnamon, and the walls . . . plastered with the flakes of mace . . . the planches . . . out of nutmegs; the long planches out of ginger . . . ; the house was covered on the top, some with pomegranates' rinds, others of oranges and citrons but the pomegranates last the longer, but the other smelled the sweeter, and looked the more pleasant to the eye. (*APC*, 65)

The house is like an oriental version of the witch's gingerbread cottage in Hansel and Gretel, edible from roof to floor. Another palace is inlaid with "Turkey stone," as if to heighten the Eastern opulence in Cavendish's mind (*APC*, 67).

Such opulence can be a sign of barbarous excess or of absolute royal power, both of which are characteristic of this savage monarchy. It turns out that not only is the governor's house consumable, but so are his people:

they had a custom in that country, to keep great store of slaves, both males and females, to breed on, as we do breed flocks of sheep . . . The children were eaten as we do lambs or veal, for young and tender meat; the elder for beef and mutton, as stronger meats. (*APC*, 69)

Cavendish's tone is deliberately sardonic; from her enforced exile in Antwerp, the duchess can contrast the "tyrannical" monarchy of her fictional world with the comparatively gentle regime that her real compatriots had overthrown (*APC*, 69). At the same time, the fact that the cannibals are *royal* connects them viscerally to the ancient sovereigns of England: "these of the royal blood all their skins were wrought, like the Britons" (*APC*, 69). "Wrought" means decorated, perhaps with blue woad, which the ancient Britons were known to use, or perhaps with tattoos or scars, like the Sapies described by John Sparke in my previous chapter. Compare Dionise Settle's description of the Inuit. The natural skin color of the Eskimos makes them resemble the "Sunne burnt countrey man" in England, but they scar themselves with indigo ink, for beauty: "some of their women race [scar] their faces proportionally, as chinne, cheekes, and forehead, and the wrists of their hands, whereupon they lay a colour which continueth darke azurine [blue]" (*PN*, 7:224). The blue color of their markings links the Inuit to the woaded ancient Britons. In *APC*, the image of the ancient Britons evokes both difference and kinship; the cannibals are primitive, like the ancient Britons, or like distant tribes who scar themselves, but they are also potentially civilized relatives to the English. Part of what makes Cavendish's vision utopian (for her) is the fact that the cannibals have power that is so extreme that they can eat their subjects; she expresses a slight wistfulness that civilization entails a necessary sacrifice of royal authority.

The cannibals' royalty and their respect for social hierarchies render them morally recuperable in Cavendish's worldview; it also makes it possible for Travellia to reinscribe the colonial and masculine power structures of Cavendish's own world, as Leslie observes.[23] Cavendish does not provide a "popular or populist feminist vision"; women can become powerful rulers, but only through marriage.[24] Having married her Prince, Travellia responds to his submission by giving him back his authority:

all the soldiers . . . cried out, Travellia shall be Viceregency.
   But the Prince told his mistress, she should also govern him.
She answered, that he should govern her, and she would govern the kingdom. (*APC*, 116)

This formulation contrasts female political power with domestic order; while Travellia will continue to rule the people, she will give up her personal authority to her husband.

Travellia's sacrifice of domestic power for political control corresponds to the strain of "Tory feminism" that Catherine Gallagher identifies in Cavendish's writing. Gallagher observes that Cavendish imagines herself as absolute and omnipotent; she even sets herself up as a monarch in her own right. Consider her well-known defense of *Blazing World*:

though I cannot be *Henry* the Fifth, or *Charles* the Second, yet I endeavour to be *Margaret* the *First*; and although I have neither power, time nor occasion to conquer the world as *Alexander* and *Caesar* did, yet rather than not to be mistress of one, since Fortune and the Fates would give me none, I have made a world of my own: for which no body, I hope, will blame me, since it is in every one's power to do the like. (*BW*, 124)

Gallagher observes that such a "self-sufficient" sense of self might seem to contradict a belief in the supremacy of the real monarch, but that, for Cavendish, "the monarch becomes a figure for the self-enclosed, autonomous nature of any person."[25] Gallagher's influential article argues that Cavendish's blind faith in the monarchy might have been what enabled her to question the subordination of women and that "the ideology of absolute monarchy provides, in particular historical situations, a transition to an ideology of the absolute self."[26] She maintains that Cavendish sees only two possible ways of conceiving the self, as monarch and as subject; however, since women are excluded from citizenship and full subjecthood, the only available position for them is absolute monarchy. In exile from England, kingless, William loses his sense of self because he is no longer a subject (he becomes *abject*, lost, incomplete), but his wife becomes an absolute monarch, one whose feminine, imaginary realm poses no threat either to the exiled English sovereign whom they both support or to her husband's domestic authority.[27]

Exchanging power in the home for power in the province enacts precisely the gendered Royalist paradox that Gallagher identifies: a man can achieve autonomous subjectivity through service to a monarch, but a woman can become an autonomous subject only by being a monarch herself, which in *APC* immunizes her from gender. When their leader announces that she is a woman, "although . . . habited like a man," the faithful soldiers of Amity exclaim, "Heaven bless you, of what sex soever you be" (*APC*, 115). Travellia's sex makes a vast difference to her love life, but none "what . . . soever" to her subjects. Her compromise allows both herself and her Prince to be complete subjects, at least in Cavendish's Tory utopia. We need to extend Gallagher's model, however, to take full account of Cavendish's utopianism. What gives Travellia her authority to civilize the cannibals (who are, after all, royal by birth, as she will become by marriage) but her own sense of superiority to beings different from her in color, shape, and culture? In *APC*, rank can outweigh differences of gender and color, and women can appropriate the power of rank, but only through marriage; likewise, "moral" or rational knowledge can replace all these categories as a ground for authority. Ten years later, Cavendish undertakes another literary experiment with race, romance, and royal power. In *Blazing World*, however, rank is displayed not through but in spite of variations in skin color and species, perhaps in response to the observations of the new science.

Blazing World

The fantastic plot of *Blazing World* recalls *APC* in several ways, beginning with an attempted rape, featuring multicolored natives, and concluding with a successful female monarchy. A young Lady, kidnapped by a rapacious merchant, finds herself adrift at sea, progressing through the Arctic; while the sailors on board the ship die of cold, her chastity preserves her and she crosses the North Pole to the adjoining pole of the Blazing World, of which she eventually becomes Empress. Like Cavendish herself, or like Travellia in *APC*, the Empress takes the rank of her husband, the Emperor, whose narrative function is to forward the romance plot by ennobling the Lady (the only instance of class mobility that Cavendish countenances). Deciding to write a Cabbala, the Empress summons the Duchess of Newcastle from Earth to be her scribe. Having left their bodies behind in the Blazing World, the Duchess and the Empress travel to our world as souls in order to investigate alternative systems of government. When the Duchess of Newcastle becomes discontented because she wishes to rule a world, like her friend the Empress, the Empress counsels her to make a world of her own in her imagination, where she too can enjoy absolute power.

The people of the Blazing World exist in a variety of colors and humors (as in the quotation with which I began this chapter), but these physical variations replace cultural or religious ones:

the men were of several complexions, but none like any of our world . . . there was but one language in all that world, nor no more but one Emperor, to whom they all submitted with the greatest duty and obedience, which made them live in a continued peace and happiness, not acquainted with other foreign wars, or home-bred insurrections. (*BW*, 130)

Enjoying absolute power over her subjects, scientists and soldiers, and their absolute devotion, the Empress rules by controlling knowledge and its production; the narrator implies that if subjects can be kept ignorant of foreign uprisings or domestic troubles, they will remain at peace. Carrie Hintz suggests that female autonomy in *Blazing World* exists only under conditions of political control and censorship; there is one language, one ruler, and one religion.[28] Within that religion, there is "no diversity of opinions in that same religion" (*BW*, 135), and only one form of worship. In this sense it is Restoration England's opposite: in England there are fewer variations in human color, and none in shape, but multiple religions, varying opinions within single religions, and even more forms of worship.

In the Blazing World, the most important cultural or social distinctions are those between "the imperial race," who are princes "made eunuchs for that purpose"; "the ordinary sort of men," who are multicolored; and the "rest of the inhabitants," who are animal-men scientists (*BW*, 133). These distinctions seem to replicate some of the divisions of Restoration England, but with important differences. Rank is not inherited in the usual sense, since the princes are "eunuchs," nor is it visible through bodily variation (in contrast to *APC*), but has to be enforced through what Kegl rightly identifies as "sumptuary laws":[29]

None was allowed to use or wear gold but those of the imperial race, which were the only nobles of the state; nor durst anyone wear jewels but the Emperor, the Empress, and their eldest son, notwithstanding that they had an infinite quantity both of gold and precious stones in that world. (*BW*, 133)

As in *APC*, the "imperial race" of the utopian world is verbally linked to "the King, the Queen, and all the royal race" of England (*BW*, 192); England serves as both tacit parallel and counterexample, where royalty is likewise established through custom and taboo rather than through explicit bodily differences, but where reproduction is of paramount importance.

The three distinct classes of people in the Blazing World cannot be identified as separate "races" by many of the usual criteria of Restoration England (sex, skin color, religion, species difference). The "imperial race" lacks the physical signs of gender difference; the "ordinary . . . men" lack a recognizable taxonomy of skin color, since the paratactic parade of colors in the Blazing World contrasts knowingly with the hierarchies of color in Cavendish's real world (they are "*not* white, black, tawny, olive or ash-coloured"); the variously shaped "inhabitants" are both "men" and animals, rational scientists and irrational beasts (*BW*, 133). Occupation or caste seems to figure as the main distinction among the three groups, although even this system breaks down; we don't really know how the "ordinary," multicolored men spend their time (perhaps this reflects Cavendish's own ignorance of middle-class life).

The Empress reinforces the loose connection between vocation and species difference by setting the various fish-, bear-, bird-, ape- and fox-men to various types of scientific experimentation "proper to their species." For example, bird-men investigate the nature of the wind, fish-men enquire why the sea is salty, worm-men look for the sources of minerals, and lice-men—in a somewhat churlish swipe at Robert Boyle— attempt to weigh air. The tasks assigned to the scientists connect physical shape and species to intellectual function, creating a scheme of classification that repeats the real-world associations of various races (in Cavendish's pseudoscientific thinking, different species) with particular qualities. Just as species difference in Cavendish's seventeenth-century world is used to assign "beastly" work to black women and domestic work to white ones, just as gender difference is used to assign domestic work to white women and intellectual work to upper-class white men, so species difference among the "ordinary sort of men" in *Blazing World* alters the kind of scientific work that they can do. Unlike the real world, however, species difference does not bar them from participating in intellectual work altogether, but it does limit them to engaging in empirical science, in observations of *physical* objects in the material world.

The Empress, on the other hand, can enjoy pure Cartesian logic, with no material or tangible basis. She convinces the scientists that, for example, black cannot be caused by the absence of light, because we can still see black objects; on another occasion, she unceremoniously dismisses her chemists (ape-men), who cannot give a straightforward definition of the elements of nature (*BW*, 143). Having "imposed a general silence upon them," she concludes vigorously that "nature is but one infinite self-moving body, which by the virtue of its self-motion, is divided into infinite parts, which parts being restless, undergo perpetual changes and transmutations by their infinite compositions and divisions," triumphantly reaching this conclusion by rational speculation, without the aid of animalistic empirical observation or testing (*BW*, 154). The source of the Empress's power is her rational ability and her knowledge; just as Travellia's knowledge outranked the royalty of the cannibals and allowed her to "civilize" them, so the Empress's abstract Cartesian logic renders all others inferior—regardless of their shape, color, or gender.

Asserting this logic as the basis for power allows Cavendish to avoid declaring a belief in either mono- or polygenesis in her romance, just as she avoids declaring a preference for one theory of light above another. When the Empress speculates that a single seed or "seminal principle" might be responsible for the creation of vegetables and minerals (a single origin for all species), the Blazing scientists reply that, although vegetable seeds retain their "species" or character after reproduction, they "increase not barely of themselves, but by joining and commixing with other parts, which do assist them in their productions, and by way of imitation form or figure their own parts into such or such particulars" (*BW*, 152). Paradoxically, Blazing vegetable seeds retain specificity—remain true to their species—but produce various differences in their offspring through a process of grafting rather than, as in the real world, through cloning (cuttings) or sexual reproduction (pollination). Helped by the "art" of "creatures that live within the earth," seeds can even yield "mixed species," which are useless "weeds" to humans; "[g]ardeners and husbandmen" should not, however, interfere in the earth-creatures' mixed grafting, because "'tis a great prejudice to the worms" who are simultaneously sustained and generated from each species of plant (*BW*, 153). Species difference is both essential, in that each "particular" kind of worm is descended from particular flowers, fruits, or roots, and mutable, because "in general . . . like . . . all other natural creatures," the worms derive from "the corporeal figurative motions of nature" and can themselves produce new life forms.

Difference is essential, but it is not essentially hereditary, because reproduction is a collaborative project that can have uncertain outcomes. This erratic reproductive process partly explains the confusion that the Empress elicits when she asks "what opinion [the scientists] had of the beginning of forms?" only to be told that "they did not understand what she meant by this expression": there is no point of origin, "nothing new in nature, nor . . . a beginning of any thing" (*BW*, 152, 153). Later we learn that Blazing human reproduction is based not on sexual relations but upon spontaneous generation, a system that "can project the disabling of patriarchy," as Neely observes, even as it evades the question of where, when, and how all species, and their differences, originate—a question that was intriguing philosophers, and Cavendish herself.[30] Like systematic explanations of light and color, coherent theories of species difference and heredity are out of place in a romance that accepts only the rules of Cartesian logic and timeless, endless, boundless "nature."

The Empress's statements on the nature of nature—infinite, ever changing, self-moving, yet divided into discrete parts whose divisions are always collapsing—could equally well be a statement of Cavendish's views on the "female monarchical self," to borrow Rachel Trubowitz's phrase. Trubowitz observes that Cavendish states outright her belief in the inferiority of women to men in her scientific writings, and suggests that the "female monarchical self" in *Blazing World* allows the possibility of female autonomy but requires the antifeminist exclusion of women from "employment in church or state" in order to preserve the Empress's "imperial singularity."[31]

When the "female monarchical self" is embodied, certain physical characteristics cannot be changed. One of these attributes is color, which Cavendish sees as essential to the body but irrelevant to the mind. The scientists of the Blazing World explicitly deny that color is a superficial or light-dependent characteristic on one of the few occasions when they convince the Empress, instead of being convinced by her:

Why, said the Empress, colour is only an accident, which is an immaterial thing, and has no being of itself, but in another body. Those, replied they, that informed your Majesty thus, surely their rational motions were very irregular; for how is it possible that a natural nothing can have a being in nature? . . . there is no body without colour, nor no colour without body; for colour, figure, place, magnitude, and body, are all but one thing, without any separation or abstraction from each other. (*BW*, 151)

The Empress moves from believing that color cannot exist without light to believing that color is an essential part of physical embodiment. As aspects of physical nature, "color, figure, place, magnitude, and body" are all functions that imprison the soul. Spirits have no permanent or essential colors, as one of these spirits tells the Empress: "colour belongs to body, and as there is no body that is colourless, so there is no colour that is bodiless" (*BW*, 175). When the spirits travel to various worlds, they have to take a material "vehicle," or body, and when they have a vehicle, they have a color. Human beings, in contrast, have not "immaterial spirits" but "material souls." These souls can travel in vehicles "of the purest and finest sort of air" because they are "self-moving, living and self-knowing" (*BW*, 193, 176). Cavendish does not address the question of whether air has a color; since she wrote *Blazing World* before she saw Boyle's experiment with the air pump, she probably considered air to be bodiless, and therefore colorless. It is as "material souls," clothed in air, that the Duchess and the Empress embark upon their travels.

Color can, indeed, *must* be left behind when the soul travels out of the body, but gender is an essential attribute of the soul, and cannot: "they were both females," confirms the narrator (*BW*, 183). What seems at first to be a binary distinction between material/immaterial becomes blurred by the Duchess's and Empress's travels as gendered, "material souls," just as the confusion between materiality/immateriality challenges the Empress's earlier assumptions about the superiority of rational Cartesianism over physical scientific investigation; perhaps the two spheres of intellectual enquiry are not as different as the Empress believes, since souls can be both abstractions and "material" objects clothed in air, all at the same time.

The narrator ironizes the Empress's beliefs further by breaking down another material/immaterial distinction—the difference between "platonic" and earthly love, between friendship and sexual desire. It is not simply the case that "material souls" retain a vague gender identification; they appear to retain the physical possibilities of sex as well. When an "immaterial spirit" suggests that the Empress enlist the Duchess of Newcastle to be her scribe, the Empress agrees, adding,

neither will the Emperor have reason to be jealous, she being one of my own sex. In truth, said the spirit, husbands have reason to be jealous of platonic lovers, for they are very dangerous, as being not only very intimate and close, but subtle and insinuating. You say well, replied the Empress; wherefore I pray send me the Duchess of Newcastle's soul. (*BW*, 181)

The spirit seems to be contrasting the dangers of opposite-sex platonic lovers, whom he characterizes as crafty and "insinuating," with the safety of a female scribe, and the Empress seems to agree. This passage defuses the threat that female friendship or love might supersede the marital tie, but once the Duchess (or rather, the Duchess's "soul") is brought to the Blazing World, the Empress finds that platonic lovers do not have to be male: "truly their meeting did produce such an intimate friendship between them, that they became platonic lovers, although they were both females" (*BW*, 183). Presumably we are meant to keep the spirit's strictures on platonism in mind still: the Duchess is evidently as "subtle and insinuating" as any of the male scientific scribes could have been, but her gender prevents the Emperor from experiencing jealousy. Although the gender of the Duchess's and Empress's souls is fixed, the direction of their erotic desires (their "sexual orientation," to use an anachronism) is not.

We see this dual status of platonic love (as something that both replaces and consolidates opposite-sex marriage) when the souls of the Duchess and the Empress, while visiting the Duke, both leap into his body. The narrator observes that, "Had there been but some such souls more, the Duke would have been like the Grand Signior in his seraglio, only it would have been a platonic seraglio" (*BW*, 194). Kegl analyzes this image in terms of seventeenth-century anxieties about the power of the Ottoman Empire (arguing that Cavendish constructs the Blazing World both in tension with and in collaboration with the Turkish realm), and suggests that Cavendish's denial of sexual activity here "precludes the possibility of sexual contact between women and allows the continued representation of the mobilization of their desire."[32]

The image does both these things, but it also mocks the narrator by highlighting the absurdity of a "platonic seraglio." Critics have tended to underestimate the degree of witty self-consciousness in *Blazing World*; even Kegl's theoretically sophisticated account collapses "Margaret Cavendish" the narrator with the "Duchess of Newcastle" who appears in the text. The hasty "only it would have been a platonic seraglio" destroys not the vision of the harem, but the notion of platonic love, particularly when it is followed by an account of the Duchess's jealousy:

But the Duke's soul . . . afforded such delight and pleasure to the Empress's soul . . . that these two souls became enamoured of each other, which the Duchess's soul perceiving, grew jealous at first, but then considering that no adultery could be committed amongst Platonic lovers, and that Platonism was divine, as being derived from divine Plato, cast forth of her mind that Idea of jealousy. (*BW*, 194–95)

Cavendish is surely satirizing the Duchess's logic as well her own authorial idealism: the slangy phrase, "divine Plato," parodies her own enthusiasm for idealistic philosophy, and points out the inefficacy of ideal, Blazing-World solutions to real-world problems. The narrator writes as though the Duchess has entirely suppressed her jealousy, but this solution to the problems of sexual competition is in every respect imaginary.[33] Only in a platonic world can all three subjects (Duke, Duchess, and Empress) continue to be intimate yet autonomous, connected yet apart, just as only in a "*romancical*" world can Margaret Cavendish become "*Margaret* the *First*" and triumph over "*Alexander* and *Caesar*" (*BW*, 124).

Gallagher characterizes Cavendish as a "Tory feminist," but we might equally call her a "Tory utopianist," for whom freedom depends upon both the subject's own individuality and the suppression of other, lesser ranked subjects. Just as Cavendish argued that science proved that women were essentially different from and weaker than men, so she argued that science proved that black men were essentially different from white ones, who alone were descended from Adam. And just as her model for female subjectivity depended upon an imaginary female monarchy, so her model of racial equality and plurality in *Blazing World* was chimerical, fictionally possible because it seemed historically impossible.

Battigelli suggests that *Blazing World* offers an alternative model for both scientific discovery and subjectivity, one in which fancy, instead of being an unwanted side effect of intellect, takes the central position in defining subjecthood. But Cavendish clearly contrasts her scientific endeavors with her "romancical" ones, and imagines that they have very different purposes:

If you wonder, that I join a work of fancy to my serious philosophical contemplations; think not that it is out of a disparagement to philosophy; or out of an opinion, as if this noble study were but a fiction of the mind; . . . though philosophers may err, . . . this does not prove, that the ground of philosophy is merely fiction . . . since there is but one truth in nature . . . But *fictions* are an issue of man's fancy, framed in his own mind, according as he pleases, without regard, whether the thing he fancies, be really existent without his mind or not. (*BW*, 124)

Despite her disagreements with both the physical means and the philosophical methods of the experimental scientists, Cavendish distinguishes their motives from her own in writing "fiction." Cavendish believes that it is a philosopher's duty to seek out the truth, and many philosophers err because there is "but one truth" to be discovered; those who fail to see this "one truth" are therefore bound to fail. But fiction writers can indulge themselves and their readers. Note that Cavendish has separated the two uses that Sidney attributed to poetry: "philosophy" now has the duty to teach, "fiction," to delight. Part of the delight, for Cavendish, stems from the constant awareness that her Blazing World is imaginary. The Empress's freedom depends upon the subjection of those lower in rank; the ranks in certain ways correspond to the emerging racial classifications of seventeenth-century England; but Cavendish's imagined infinity of worlds also allow the possibility of freedom—not in another's fictional universe, but in one's own.

Thus when Pepys wrote about Cavendish, "The whole story of this Lady is a romance, and all she doth is romantic," his analysis was correct.[34] Cavendish both wrote and lived a romance: willfully presenting herself in frontispieces as eccentric genius and devoted wife to defuse her critics, as James Fitzmaurice argues; deliberately cultivating the appearance of eccentricity with the "antique" appearance and "extravagancies" of clothing that Pepys and others found fascinating; creating romantic versions of herself both in print and in person.[35] A romantic public persona allowed Cavendish to write and publish; a romantic attachment allows her Blazing Empress to become an absolute monarch; and only in and *through* romantic invention can women, and human beings of different colors and shapes, become complete and autonomous subjects. In Restoration England, natural philosophy offers a unified myth of white, masculine superiority, and only fiction can offer multiple mythologies of femininity and color.

Afterword: Nancy Burson's
Human Race Machine

From its very beginnings, the myth of discrete and multiple human races has been used to justify existing hierarchies of power. Cuvier, following Linnaeus, divided human beings into four races, arguing that the white race was not only the most attractive race but also superior to the others in intelligence, courage and energy.[1] The nineteenth century saw the proliferation of races; in 1854 Pickering identified eleven and Bory St. Vincent, fifteen, each thought to have originated from its "own peculiar Adam" and each thought to represent a different step on the developmental ladder.[2] During the late nineteenth and early twentieth centuries, a three-race model replaced earlier schemes, simplifying the human hierarchy but still retaining it.

Today, we encounter a split between geneticists' determination that there is no biological basis for dividing up the human race and the persistence of that division in social life. Thus Bryan Sykes concludes in *The Seven Daughters of Eve* that research on mitochondrial DNA "makes nonsense out of any biological basis for racial classification," but a twenty-first-century physician defends her right to treat her patients differently according to their perceived race.[3] The contemporary artist Nancy Burson's *Human Race Machine*—both as a device and as a process or encounter—seems to enact these contradictions and ambiguities of race in the twenty-first century. The *Machine* aims to emphasize human similarities rather than their differences—an unabashedly optimistic goal for the new millennium (and indeed, her project was originally produced for Britain's Millennium Dome, commissioned like a modern-day masque). Faced with a digital photograph of themselves inside a booth, participants use the computer to measure the distances between their eyes, chin, nose, and other major facial landmarks, and indicate to which "race" they would like to belong: White, Black, South Asian, Asian, and—in response to September 11, 2001—Middle Eastern. At each choice, the viewer reviews her own face: lengthened, broadened, darkened, lightened, oval- or round-eyed, snub-, Grecian- or aquiline-nosed, high-, low- or middle-browed. Since participants do not choose a "default" race with which they already identify before they select which race they would like to be, white people may, if they desire, see themselves whitened, their lips thinned, by checking the white category; black people blackened, their noses flattened; South Asians browned, their foreheads elevated; Asians lightened, their eyes narrowed; Middle Easterners darkened, their brows lowered, and so on. A viewer may also combine her face with that of a companion.

You may have noticed even from my bare description the ways in which the exhibit both loudly proclaims (as in its publicity materials), "There is no gene for race," and yet insistently whispers that race is, must be, real. The machine presents race as an ongoing, willed, and mobile process. Yet the digitized faces that produce that choice come from individuals long ago classified (by themselves or by others) as belonging to a particular "race." The machine asserts sameness, as Burson would wish. Yet it reasserts or exaggerates variation. The machine is highly personal, because it measures individual faces. Yet it is generic, because to generate the racial "types," Burson scanned in thousands of faces. The machine is interactive, requiring a series of decisions from the observer. Yet it is passive, limiting those decisions not only to particular "races" but also to those characteristics already thought, traditionally, to typify them (pigmentation, eye- and nose-shape).

The machine's media are mixed: software, art, genetics, and photography. Yet the final product is static, like a photograph on a billboard (as it was advertised widely in New York). These images, though ephemeral, are haunting, *unheimlich*—seeing one's own, familiar face reframed as a series of strangers'. The machine's methods are innovative: digital image manipulation and complex algorithms. Yet they are also disturbingly archaic, because the machine feeds upon craniofacial measurements, like any nineteenth-century phrenologist. The machine encourages extroversion and identification with others. Yet it fosters a kind of narcissism, as many participants repeat the conclusions of contemporary aesthetics and, especially, female beauty: "Don't I look good with a bit of color!"

I experienced the *Human Race Machine* in Greensboro, North Carolina, just days before I gave birth to my golden-skinned daughter. I couldn't stay away; for one thing, the *Machine* "raced" me (by treating "South Asian" as a separate category) in a way that has been rare in the United States. For another, my goals when I began this project several years ago were similar to Burson's—goals that I soon realized were painfully naïve: to "prove" the social construction of race by exploring the rich mythopoeia of skin color just before the establishment of modern racial hierarchies. At first I responded to the *Human Race Machine* with a bristling irritation. Now, however, I think that the meaning of Burson's artwork lies in its very ambiguity. Its name, at once fleshly and cold, couples *Human* with *Machine* through the medium of "race." And when my partner and I melded our two faces, we produced someone who looked back at us intensely, through my eyes, in Richard's face. Perhaps that virtual child, imaginary sibling of our real infant (whose face and complexion at once solicit ethnic categorizing and complicate it) is as good a metaphor for race as any.

Notes

Introduction

1. OED, "race," sb.,3; v., 3; Towerson, "First Voyage," in Hakluyt, *Principal Navigations (PN)*, 6:184. Hereafter cited within the text.

2. Quotations from Shakespeare's works and from *The Passionate Pilgrim* come from the Riverside edition unless otherwise indicated, and are cited within the text. Plays are cited by act, scene, and line number; longer poems by line number; sonnets by sonnet number and line number.

3. OED, "race," sb., 2.7.

4. Colie, 19.

5. Fowler, 3.

6. OED, "kind," sb., 3c.

7. Colie, 68.

8. Great Britain, Privy Council, *Acts of the Privy Council*, 26:16.

9. OED, "kind," sb., 7a.

10. Raymond Williams, 125.

11. Dollimore, 531.

12. See Jordan; Fryer.

13. See Appiah and Gates.

14. See Allen.

15. See Du Bois; Fanon; Asante.

16. See hooks.

17. See Guinier and Torres, passim.

18. Spivak, "Three Women's Texts."

19. Bhabha, "Of Mimicry and Man."

20. Sinfield; Loomba, "Local-Manufacture."

21. Erickson, "Moment of Race," 33. See Eldred Jones, and G. K. Hunter, for the first wave. For the second, see Loomba, *Gender, Race, Renaissance Drama*; Masten and Wall; Barroll, ed., *Shakespeare Studies*; McGiffert; Hendricks and Parker, eds., *Women, "Race" and Writing*; MacDonald, ed., *Race, Ethnicity, and Power*; Kim Hall, *Things of Darkness*; Bartels, *Spectacles of Strangeness*; Shapiro; Gillies, *Shakespeare and the Geography of Difference*; Habib; Singh, *Colonial Narratives*; Sousa; and Matar.

22. See Baker, Diawara, and Lindeborg; Dabydeen; Ashcroft, Griffiths, and Tiffin; and Dyer.

23. See also Little; Vitkus, *Three Turk Plays*; Callaghan, *Shakespeare Without Women*; Kamps and Singh; Archer; Raman; Gary Taylor, *Buying Whiteness*; Floyd-Wilson, *English Ethnicity*. I thank Gary Taylor for letting me read part of his manuscript.

24. Gould, 353.

25. See Cavalli-Sforza and Cavalli-Sforza for a refutation of racialism on genetic as well as political grounds.

26. See Diamond.

27. Kim Hall, *Things of Darkness*, passim.

28. See Habib.

29. Best, in *PN*, 7; Browne, in *Pseudodoxia Epidemica* (*PE*), 3. Both hereafter cited within the text by volume and page number.

30. Pliny, *Natural History*, 7.12.51. References to Pliny's *Natural History* come from Rackham's translation and will be cited by book, section, and paragraph number.

31. I follow Jonathan Bate in calling this character "Muly" rather than "Muliteus" (see his Arden 3 edition of *Titus Andronicus*). As Francesca Royster argues, black Muly's white baby "both disrupts the notion of the father as the primary agent of reproduction, the mother a mere receptacle, and undermines assumptions about the white race as originary, blackness as secondary" (452).

32. MacDonald, "Subject of Blackness," 59.

33. Kim Hall, *Things of Darkness*, 12–13.

34. Bourne, 5E3r.

35. Ibid., 5E2r.

36. Baron, D2r; Peaps, A3v; Dekker and Middleton, 288.

37. Hendricks, "'Obscured by Dreams.'"

38. Fryer, 133–34.

39. Stuart Hall, 168.

40. Minsheu, "ethnick."

41. Bakhtin, 17.

Chapter 1. Pictures of Andromeda Naked

1. J. R. Morgan puts the *Aithiopika* as late as the fourth century C.E. Modern classical scholars transliterate the author's name as "Heliodoros," but Renaissance texts Latinize the name to "Heliodorus," and I follow their example. Unless otherwise indicated, the modern translation used is by J. R. Morgan, *An Ethiopian Story* (*ES*), hereafter cited within the text. The standard Greek text appears in Heliodorus, *Les Éthiopiques*, ed. Rattenbury and Lumb.

2. All references to these works hereafter appear within the text. Matthews's edition of *The White Ethiopian* reproduces the author's revisions, not the unrevised irregular couplets of the original, so I cite the British Library manuscript. Other copies consulted include the British Library copy of Amyot's *Histoire* (1579) and the British Library copy of Gough's *Strange Discovery* (1640). Underdowne, Lisle, Gough, and the author of *The White Ethiopian* seem not to have influenced each other, although Lisle's *Faire Ethiopian* may have inspired a 1687 prose translation begun by "a Person of Quality" and completed by Nahum Tate.

3. Crooke, *Microcosmographia*, Aa4r. Hereafter cited within the text.

4. Selden, 208.

5. See Dilke.

6. Mary Nyquist, in conversation. Archer argues that "Although human sacrifice is abolished altogether at the end of the tale at the behest of the sages or 'gymnosophists,' its role at court already tarnishes the luster of Ethiopian civility" (35). On the historiography of the gymnosophists, see Archer, 144–47.

7. Heiserman, 192.

8. See Dilke for Philostratus's influence on Heliodorus.

9. Egger, 121.

10. Reardon, quoted in Heliodorus, trans. Lamb, 301.

11. Ibid.

12. See Heliodorus, trans. Hadas.

13. Dilke, 269.

14. Heiserman, 189.

15. Heliodorus, trans. Lamb, 64.

16. Selden, 182; Hilton, 89.

17. Heliodorus, trans. Morgan, "Introduction" to *Ethiopian Story*, xxiii.

18. OED, "mitre," sb., 2d.

19. Origen, 277.

20. Ibid.

21. Ibid, 92. Margo Hendricks has suggested (in conversation) that in the Renaissance there may exist a distinction between Christian "Ethiops," warlike "Moors," and savage "Blackamoors." While I have not found a systematic use of the three terms, it is interesting that the King James Version uses "Ethiopian" where Geneva gives "blackamoor" or "Moor" or "Ethiopian" indiscriminately, and the Bishops' Bible gives "Moor" or "Morien" (compare Jer. 37:7, Num. 12:1).

22. Alvares, ed. and introd. Beckingham and Huntingford, "Introduction," 1:1.

23. Alvares, 1:193.

24. Ibid., 1:294.

25. Ibid., 1:304; 2:393. The historical Ethiopian king identified as Prester John by Alvares was Lebna Dengel, born in 1496, who ascended the throne of his father Na'od when he was only twelve years old. His mother, Queen Na'o Mogasa, and his stepgrandmother Eleni served as regents. After he came to power, the Muslims of Adal began the practice of invading Ethiopia every year (Alvares, ed. and introd. Beckingham and Huntingford, 1:15). Fray Tomas de Padilla translated Alvares's treatise into Spanish in 1557.

26. Mandeville, R3r; Archer, 33.

27. Africanus, trans. Pory, section title and marginal note, A6v. Hereafter cited within the text as *HDA*.

28. Lopez, trans. Hartwell, 2D3v.

29. Ibid.

30. Ovid, trans. Golding, 2:20.

31. Ibid., fo. 22v. See also Ross, A24r–A24v; Fraunce, Kr–Kv; Ovid, trans. Sandys, *Metamorphoses*, 2:66.

32. Ariosto, trans. Harington, 380, 383.

33. *HL*, 1.45–50. Quotations from Marlowe's *Hero and Leander* come from Donno's edition. Hereafter cited within the text by sestiad and line number.

34. All translations from *Histoire* are my own unless otherwise noted. The British Library edition gives "leurs beaux tempes to'deux de blanche enceinte," "their lovely *temples*" in a pun (or perhaps eye-skip error) that compares their brows to the *temple* where they met and alludes to Chariclea's vocation as priestess.

35. I thank Wes Williams for pointing out the pun to me.

36. Webbe, B3v.

37. Knight, E2v. Hereafter cited within the text. Matar offers some statistics: "By the mid-1620s there were between 1200 and 1400 captives in Salee alone; between 1622 and 1642 over 8000 Britons were taken captive; between 1627 and 1640 there were 2828 British captives in Algiers alone" (91).

38. Nicolay, R7v, O8r.

39. Chew, 306–25. On the representation of Islam and the Turks in early modern England, see Matar; Fuchs; Vitkus, "Turning Turk." On the representation of early modern Jews and Judaism, see Shapiro.

40. Hyginus, quoted in Euripides, 150.

41. Pliny, *Natural History*, 7:12.52.

42. Fontanus, 134.

43. Munich, 14.

44. Woodward, 34.

45. Ibid., 84.

46. Ibid., figures 9a, 9b.

47. Ibid., 84, 90.

48. "Candida si non sum, placuit Cepheia Perseo/ Andromeda, patriæ fusca colore suæ" (Ovid, *Heroides*, "Sappho to Phaon," 15.35–36). The Loeb edition translates the lines thus: "If I am not dazzling fair, Cepheus's Andromeda was fair in Perseus's eyes, though dusky with the hue of her native land," but I see no reason to modify the sentiment by adding "though," an interpolation that recalls the controversy over the "black and comely" or "black but comely" bride of the biblical Song of Songs, explored in my next chapter.

49. Otho Vaenius, 172–73.

50. Virgil, *Eclogues*, 2, line 18; Barnfield, *The Teares of an Affectionate Shepheard*, "The Second Day," lines 225–307 and passim. References to Barnfield's *Teares of an Affectionate Shepheard* come from Klawitter's edition. The first and second days' "lamentations" of *The Teares of an Affectionate Shepheard* (*AS*) are designated as 1 and 2 in my text respectively. Hereafter cited within the text by "lamentation" and line number.

51. Otho Vaenius, 172–73.

52. The illustration comes from a French text in better condition than the English.

53. Otho Vaenius, 8–9.

54. Ibid., 152–3.

55. Ovid, *Metamorphoses*, 4.670; "Andromedan Perseus nigris portarit ab Indis"; *Ars Amatoria*, 1.53.

56. "Nec suus Andromedae color est obiectus ab illo, / Mobilis in gemino cui pede pinna fuit." Ovid, *Ars Amatoria*, 2.641.

57. Euripides, 153; Dilke.

58. Ovid, *Metamorphosis*, trans. Florianus.

59. Ovid, *Loves Schoole*, trans. (attrib.) Heywood, A2v, D5v.

60. Baron borrows this tag (without an acknowledgment) for his pastoral *Gripus and Hegio* (1647), itself part of his new "Cyprian Academy," or "Eroto-paignon": "And Perseus among the Negroes sought / And faire Andromade from Inde brought" (C4v).

61. Chapman, *Andromeda Liberata*, Ev. Hereafter cited within the text. The poem proved controversial, judging from Chapman's speedy follow-up apology, *A Free and Offenceles Iustification of a Lately Published and most maliciously misinterpreted Poeme: entituled "Andromeda Liberata"* (1614), a pamphlet disclaiming any political allegory or intention. Apparently some of the "malicious misinterprete[rs]" took umbrage at Chapman's neoplatonic conceit that lovers die and are reborn in their love for one another, and that those who deny love are therefore "Churlish Homicides" (*Andromeda*, Er). Perhaps there were already rumors circulating about Frances Howard's role in the murder of Sir Thomas Overbury (for which a year later she would be tried), and "Homicide" was not a word to

be thrown around this couple casually, even in a Neoplatonic sense. Other readers apparently took the "barraine Rocke" (*Andromeda*, B4v) to which Andromeda was chained to refer to Frances Howard's first husband, an impression that Chapman is at pains to dispel:

as it euer sayd
A man was barraine? Or the burthen layd
Of bearing fruite on Man?

he asks, only to find himself then obliged to clear his Andromeda, too, of the stigma of infertility and to state clearly that she comprised "All beauties" (*Free and Offenceles*, 4).

62. See Cave, *Recognitions*.
63. Heiserman, 198.
64. Crooke, Z3v.
65. Heliodorus, trans. Hadas, 63; *WE*, fo. 34.
66. Sandford, C6r.
67. Hilton, 89.
68. Stephens, 72.
69. Heliodorus, trans. Warschewiczi, Z3r.
70. Hawthorne, 1032.
71. Hilton, 89.
72. On this emblem and its historiography, see Newman.

Chapter 2. Thirteen Ways of Looking at a Black Bride

1. King James Version, Song of Songs, 1:5–6. Hereafter cited as KJV within the text. Other versions of the Bible cited within the text are Geneva, Bishops', and the New Revised Standard Version (NRSV). Translations after and including KJV treat the title, "The song of songs, which is Solomon's," as verse one, chapter one, so that "black but comely" is Song 1:5 in translations after KJV but 1:4 in Geneva and Bishops'.

2. Dove, E2r. Hereafter cited within the text.

3. See Pope for the most detailed commentary on the Song and useful summaries of critical and exegetical interpretation. The Talmudic and Midrashic commentaries on the Song read it as a narrative and identify the male beloved with Solomon and his bride with Israel (Pope, 92–112; Van Norden, 51). An early Christian school of thought interpreted the Song as a paean to the bride's virginity (Methodius, quoted in Van Norden, 55; Pope, 188–92). Alain of Lille argued that the Song itself praised the Virgin Mary (Denys Turner, 291–305). German and French scholars, following a suggestion by Origen, suggested in the nineteenth century that the Song was a drama, or a sequence of wedding songs (Pope, 34–37, 141–45). Following the wedding-song tradition, NRSV treats the Song as a cycle of marriage-songs honoring the consummation of a union between an unspecified king and his foreign bride. Bloch and Bloch, like other recent poets and critics, treat the Song as a coherent, unified poem concerning "the sexual awakening of a young woman and her lover" (Bloch and Bloch, 3; Pope, 192–205). More recently, readers have found the remnants of a female fertility cult and its liturgy (Pope, 145–53), or an anthology of unrelated love lyrics (Pope, 198–99; Falk, 105).

4. Although the four-fold system did not originate with Aquinas, he codified it.

5. Van Norden, 64.

6. See especially Lewalski, *Protestant Poetics*; Hill. Lewalski discusses Beza, Fenner, Finch, Sibbes, Dove, Baldwin, Clapham, Markham, Aylett, and Cotton, but does not consider their treatment of blackness (*Protestant Poetics*, 53–67). Hill evaluates Baldwin, Fenner, Ainsworth, Drayton, Finch, Wither, Quarles, Joseph Hall, Sibbes, Andrewes, Dove, Cotton, Brightman, and Homes specifically with reference to their Puritan (or, occasionally) High Church sympathies (362–70). Kim Hall discusses the Bride's blackness in Baldwin, Brucioli, Joseph Hall, Markham, and Ainsworth (*Things of Darkness*, 107–16). Flinker devotes two chapters to an analysis of allegory in Baldwin and Aylett respectively.

7. Brucioli, B3v.

8. Legh, B6r.

9. Markham, B1v.

10. Ibid., B2r.

11. Erasmus, ed. and introd. Brady and Olin, "Introduction."

12. Origen, 92–93.

13. Van Norden, 56–57.

14. Origen, 91.

15. *The Zohar*, quoted in Van Norden, 51.

16. Pope, 310.

17. Origen, 277. The Latin text,"ut ita dicam, Aethiopici decoris," literally means, "if I may put it like this, you will beautify yourself in the Ethiopian style" (Erasmus, fo. 61v).

18. Origen, 277, original emphasis.

19. Ibid.

20. Erasmus, fo. 61r (emphasis mine).

21. *Biblia Sacra*, Canticum Canticorum. Hereafter cited within the text as Vulgate.

22. Snowden, *Blacks in Antiquity*, 198.

23. New Revised Standard Version, Song 1:5. Hereafter cited within the text as NRSV.

24. Bloch and Bloch, 140.

25. Falk, 168.

26. Bloch and Bloch, 47.

27. I thank Nathan Gilmour for the Hebrew transliteration and Michael Fancher for pointing out to me the high number of hapax legomena in this text.

28. Ainsworth, A3r.

29. Van Norden, 46.

30. Bloch and Bloch, 47; Falk, lyric 2.

31. Pope, 307; Falk, lyric 2.

32. Robotham, M1v.

33. Falk, lyric 2.

34. Ibid.

35. Bloch and Bloch, 140.

36. Ibid.

37. See Said, *Orientalism*.

38. Clapham, A8r. Hereafter cited within the text.

39. Luther, B7r.

40. Kim Hall, *Things of Darkness*, 111.

41. Ainsworth, Cr.

42. Fenner, Br–Bv.

43. Drayton, *The Most Excellent Song*, 15.

44. OED, "notwithstanding," prep., 1, 2.

45. Ibid., "therewithal," adv., 1.

46. Fenner, B4r.

47. Ibid., B4v.

48. Legh, B6v–B7r.

49. On the changing significance of the words "slave" and "villain" in the sixteenth century, see Woodbridge, *Vagrancy*, 230. Fryer suggests that the men were domestic slaves borrowed from an African monarch.

50. Fraser, 255.

51. Great Britain, Privy Council, *Acts of the Privy Council*, 26:16.

52. Ibid., 17.

53. Fryer, 11; Great Britain, Privy Council, *Acts*, 16:20–21.

54. Great Britain, Privy Council, *Acts*, 16:20–21.

55. Great Britain, Sovereign, *Tudor Royal Proclamations*, 3:221–22.

56. Fraser, 259; *Gesta Grayorum*, 12; De Grazia.

57. Kim Hall, *Things of Darkness*, chapter title; Fryer, 22.

58. Knevet, A4v.

59. Lewalski, *Protestant Poetics*, 5–7; Pendergast, 65.

60. Quoted in Hill, 364.

61. Jud Smith, Ar.

62. Quarles, D2r. Hereafter cited within the text.

63. Jelinger, A3v.

64. Ibid., B2v.

65. Sprigg, C3v.

66. Ibid., C5r.

67. Quoted in Pollard, 46.

68. Baldwin, A4r.

69. Ibid., B2r.

70. Quoted in Pollard, 297–98.

71. Hammond, 140.

72. Ibid., 143.

73. Hillebrand, 2:36. Simplifying the debates to such a facile opposition is obviously reductive; in my defense, let me cite Donne, who sarcastically leaves "My faith . . . to Roman Catholiques; / All my good works unto the Schismaticks / Of Amsterdam" ("The Will," lines 19–21).

74. Pendergast, 59–60.

75. Ibid., 65.

76. George Herbert, "The British Church," lines 11, 12, 13–24.

77. Ibid., line 8.

78. Ibid., line 26.

79. Donne, Holy Sonnet 18, lines 3, 13–14.

80. Hillebrand, 2:36.

81. Donne, *Sermons*, 3:368; quoted in Pendergast, 52.

82. On extreme Protestant sects, see George Williams; Baylor. On heresy and the Reformation, see Drees; John Davis. For general information on the history of the church, see Cross and Livingstone; Hillebrand. The Familists, or the Family of Love, were characterized in popular literature (such as Middleton's *The Family of Love*, pub. 1608), as hypocrites who believed that, once elected, they could not

sin and that therefore any acts they committed could not be sinful. The "love" in their chosen name was intended to reflect divine love, but was often willfully misunderstood to mean sexual or earthly indulgence.

83. Kim Hall, *Things of Darkness*, 111, n.41.

84. Clapham, C8r.

85. G. K. Hunter makes this assumption the centerpiece of his argument about *Othello*; Julia Reinhard Lupton's more sophisticated account acknowledges the play's enmeshment in racism even as she argues that Othello reverses the Chametic curse (77).

86. Beza, L2v, L2r, M2r.

87. Ibid., Lr.

88. Ibid., Lr, M2r.

89. On Beza and predestination, see J. S. Bray.

90. Samuel Smith, R4v, Sr.

91. Ibid., Sv.

92. Shapiro, 11.

93. On early modern Jewish conversion narratives and their relationship to tensions between Protestant and Catholic churches, see Shapiro (131–66).

94. Finch, B2v.

95. Ibid., Cr.

96. Ibid., K4v.

97. Sandys, *Paraphrase*, A1v.

98. Ibid.

99. Vitkus, "Trafficking with the Turk," 45.

100. Sandys, *Paraphrase*, A1v, A2v.

101. Ibid., A2v.

102. Homes; Jackson; Sprigg, B3r.

103. Homes, 92.

104. See Cotton.

105. Brightman, *Works*, 7N4r.

106. Homes, 92.

107. Jackson, 7Q3r.

108. Aylett, B3v.

109. Ibid.

110. Origen, 92–93.

111. Baldwin, B3v; Kim Hall, *Things of Darkness*, 113.

112. Ernestus Vaenius, C4v–C5r. I cite the copy in the National Library of Medicine, although I reproduce a clearer illustration from the copy in the Duke University Rare Books and Special Collections.

113. Ibid., C5r. The free translation is my own. The original reads:

Dum sub furenti sedula Sirio,
Phaebique sudat sponsa coloribus:
Formam nigredo fusca vastat,
Et speciem populatur omnem.
Excusat ergo, non ebur aut rosam
Inesse malis, nec teneros sinus.
Quid te molestas, virgo! Regi
Gratior est color iste, luxe. (C5r)

114. Rosseter, Cr. The last line of this song presents a crux. The British Library copy gives "prou d," with a space between the u and the d. Walter Davis's edition gives the final line as "The Sun stil prov'd, the shadow stil disdained," glossing "prov'd" as "approved." It is conceivable that the printer omitted an apostrophe between the u and the d, or that the faint mark visible between the two letters under magnification is the broken tail of an apostrophe that might have appeared in the first copies off the press. But the spacing between letters elsewhere in the book is irregular enough that "prou d" might simply mean "proud." Over the page, in the madrigal "My loue hath vowd hee will forsake mee," stanza two, in the line "When a man alone is wooing" the word "alone" appears as "a lone" (Rosseter, Cv). I have therefore preferred "proud" over "proved," feeling that it gives a more straightforward reading and a better line.

115. See Ryding.

116. Campion, "Umbra," line 343. Hereafter cited within the text by line number.

117. Kim Hall reads "the new alternative" to old poetry "to be to focus on darkness while recognizing that its heterogeneity puts it ultimately beyond poetic control" (*Things of Darkness*, 120), whereas I read the schism between old and new as a converted conversion narrative that consciously evokes a scientific model over a religious one.

118. Edward Herbert, D3v. Hereafter cited within the text by signature.

119. Reprinted in Kim Hall, *Things of Darkness*, 276.

120. Van Norden, 4–6.

121. Aristotle, "De Coloribus," 791a-b.

122. Legh, B6r.

123. Galileo, *Starry Messenger*. I thank Angelica Duran for suggesting that I look at this text.

124. Kim Hall, *Things of Darkness*, 120.

125. Citations of Shakespeare's sonnets come from the Riverside Shakespeare, but I have on occasion modified the editorial punctuation or preferred variant readings.

126. Vendler, 448–50.

127. Shakespeare, ed. Booth, 341.

128. Bach, title.

Chapter 3. Masquing Race

1. Erickson, "Moment of Race," 30–31. References to Jonson's *Blackness* and *GM* come from Orgel's edition of the *Complete Masques* unless otherwise indicated, and will hereafter be cited within the text by line number. References to his *Irish Masque* quote the 1616 Folio, including variant spellings, because Sullivan has recently and convincingly argued that Jonson's command of Irish dialect was excellent and his spellings deliberate. Hereafter cited within the text by signature.

2. Little; Murphy.

3. Little, 122–34.

4. See Ann Jones's "Italians and Others," however, for sustained attention to the link between the black "Moor" Zanche and the wild Irish in John Webster's *The White Devil*.

5. On sixteenth-century Ireland and English representations of the Irish, see Callaghan, *Shakespeare Without Women*; Carey and Carroll; Hadfield, *Spenser's Irish Experience*, "English Colonialism"; Jones and Stallybrass; Maley, "Spenser's Irish English"; Murphy. On early modern representations of Ethiopia, see my Chapters One and Two; Archer. In this chapter I limit myself to a brief overview of both sets of stereotypes.

6. References to Chapman's *Memorable Masque* come from Lindley's edition and will appear within the text, cited by line number.

7. West, 316.

8. Following Orgel, *Jonsonian Masque*, 120.

9. See Kelly.

10. Quoted in Orgel, *Jonsonian Masque*, 68.

11. Andrea's argument parallels my own in its negotiation of Anna's "proto-feminist" blackness and its imbrication in emergent theories of race and color, but I focus upon the connections between the material technologies of physical impersonation within the masque and within the Scottish entertainment that welcomed Anna to Leith. On the masque's water imagery, see Siddiqi; Kelly; Floyd-Wilson, "Temperature"; on its nationalism, see MacDonald, "Subject of Blackness"; Kim Hall, *Things of Darkness*, 128–37; on the queen as patron, see Orgel, "Marginal Jonson."

12. *Accounts of the Lord High Treasurer of Scotland*, 2:318, 97, 106; Edwards, 9–11.

13. *Accounts*, 4:401. For a relation of the Scottish tournament at which a "black lady" presided, see Fradenburg, who, however, argues that the "blak Moir" immortalized in William Dunbar's poem for that occasion was a white woman in sleeves and mask.

14. Ethel Williams prints the following anecdote about James and Anna's wedding in Oslo: "By [James's] orders four young Negroes danced naked in the snow in front of the royal carriage, but the cold was so intense that they died a little later of pneumonia" (21). This story has until recently been taken at face value, but Scottish historian David Stevenson, author of the most recent and detailed account of the wedding, has been unable to find any trace of it prior to 1927 (when it appeared in J. A. Gade's biography of Christian IV), in any of the Scottish accounts of the royal wedding, or in the London reprint of *The Joyfull Receiuing*. I likewise have not unearthed a source for the account. Stevenson suggests that the story arose through confusion with the blacked-up whifflers or ushers who greeted the royals on the entry to Leith. Barroll, Anna's most recent biographer, neither mentions nor refutes the anecdote because, although we cannot verify the story now, he thinks that documentation may possibly exist in Danish (personal communication).

15. For widely varying descriptions of the queen's entry into Edinburgh, see Calderwood; Moysie; Burel, composed in 1590 but unpublished until 1712; *The Joyful Receiving* (1590); and Graves, who in 1997 first translated into English a Danish history presumably written for the absent Christian IV.

16. Ian Smith, "Dressed in Black"; Calderwood, 97; Moysie, 81. I am grateful to Ian Smith for sharing this work at an early stage with a seminar group at the Shakespeare Association of America (2000) and for allowing me to borrow this phrase.

17. Graves, 109.

18. Fryer speculates that this man "could well have been a descendant of the group that had arrived in Scotland some 90 years earlier" (4). Malone suggested that this incident might have inspired Shakespeare's self-deprecating lion, Snug

the joiner in *MND* (*Variorum*, 115). For another reading of this incident and of racialized rhetoric in *MND*, see Kim Hall, *Things of Darkness*, 23–24.

19. Stevenson, 144.

20. Graves, 109.

21. Calderwood; *Joyful Receiving.*

22. Graves; Burel.

23. Lewalski, *Writing Women.*

24. Carleton, quoted in Orgel, *Jonsonian Masque*, 5.

25. Carleton, quoted in Orgel, *Jonsonian Masque*, 68; Barbour.

26. Wroth, 99.

27. Floyd-Wilson, "Temperature," 191.

28. Ibid., 192.

29. Lindley, "Embarrassing Ben," 356.

30. James M. Smith, 299.

31. It is tempting to call this linguistic excess "Irish Blarney," as does Rist, but the term "blarney" or "Irish blarney" does not become current in English until the 1760s.

32. Bach, 168.

33. James M. Smith, 310.

34. Ibid., 308–12.

35. See Bergin: "The supposed 'rise of the bard' is explained by the fact that the word 'bard' came to be used in English, not in Irish, to denote an official Celtic poet" (4, n.1).

36. Shuger, 500.

37. All quotations in this paragraph come from Palmer, I4r.

38. Derricke, 187. I thank Vincent Carey for drawing my attention to this text.

39. Ibid., 187, 194.

40. Ibid., 200.

41. Spenser, *View*, 90, 99, 101, 102. References to Spenser's *View* come from the *Variorum*, unless otherwise noted, and hereafter appear within the text. The Variorum uses the Ellesmere MS (at the Huntington Library) as its copy-text but includes significant collation from *P*, the Public Record Office manuscript. References to *P* come from the Variorum collation.

42. On Irish mantles and glibs, see Jones and Stallybrass.

43. See Jones and Stallybrass; Hadfield, *Edmund Spenser's Irish Experience*, 86, "Race in *Othello*"; Callaghan, *Shakespeare Without Women*, 123–28; Carey and Carroll; Floyd-Wilson, "Temperature," 200–202; Murphy, 67.

44. On the status of *P*, see Renwick, quoted in *Variorum*, 509–11.

45. Pliny, *Natural History*, 6.20.53.

46. Keating, E2r.

47. Quoted in *Variorum*, 320.

48. Quoted in Camden, *Britannia*, 4M6r.

49. Boorde, M4r–M4v.

50. Brereton, ed., *Lusts Dominion* (*LD*), D2v. Hereafter cited within the text. *Lusts Dominion* was first published in 1657, mistakenly attributed to "C. Marloe, gent." Tokson attributes the play to Thomas Dekker, following the general consensus, but Simmonds gives it to Marston, suggesting that the play was "A Showpiece for the Globe." Dekker adherents identify the play with "The spanish mores tragedy" entered in the Stationers Register in 1599. I cite the Louvain University Library transcript, transcribed and edited by J. Le Gay Brereton.

51. Great Britain, Public Record Office, *Calendar Colonial*, 1:328, 401, 407 and

passim. See, however, Pope-Hennessy, Jordan, and Cummins, who argue that from its very inception, American slavery treated dark-skinned Africans differently from light-skinned Irish: black Africans were soon doomed to perpetual servitude, rather than a fixed term.

52. On Native American slavery, see Lauber; Stanwood; Alden T. Vaughan, *Roots of American Racism.* I am grateful to Owen Stanwood for permission to cite his unpublished work. On African American female slavery in early America, see Jennifer Morgan. On the early days of Virginia, see Kupperman; Billings; Gleach.

53. Gordon, 201–2.

54. Gillies, "Shakespeare's Virginian Masque," 675.

55. Council of Virginia, *True Declaration,* 16, 26.

56. Fuller, 55.

57. Lindley, "Courtly Play."

58. Bach; Raman, 221. On the changing currency crisis in the late sixteenth and early seventeenth century, see also Freer. Dubrow uses the trope of "debased" currency (an alloy of gold and silver) deftly to analyze John Collop's "green-sickness" and "yellow beauty" poems, some of which are addressed to a black woman (*Echoes of Desire,* 163–201).

59. Quoted in Matar, 36.

60. Wroth, 99.

61. Gordon, 199.

62. I follow Alden T. Vaughan in calling the episode a "massacre" rather than an uprising. See Vaughan, *Roots,* 105–27.

63. Quoted in Matar, 100.

64. Alden T. Vaughan, *Roots,* 34–54.

65. Matar, 106.

66. Callaghan, 75–96.

67. Beverly, *History of Virginia,* 195.

68. Gleach, 120–21; Kupperman, 94.

69. Montaigne, 91, 93.

70. Gillies, "Shakespeare's Virginian Masque."

71. The identification of Native Americans with one of the Lost Tribes of Israel does not become popular until the 1640s. See Alden Vaughan, *Roots,* 44–54.

Chapter 4. Heroic Blushing

1. Thomas Wright, 82. Hereafter cited within the text.

2. Martin, 5; Braden, 56.

3. OED, "blush," v., 1, 2a, 2b.

4. OED, "embarrassment," sb., 1a.

5. Coeffeteau, 473–94, passim.

6. Ricks, *Keats and Embarrassment.*

7. Ibid., 22–24. References to the works of Milton come from Hughes's edition.

8. Barker, 11–13.

9. Ibid., 31.

10. Ibid., 46.

11. Coeffeteau, 476.

12. Ibid, 488–90.

13. Ibid., 492.

14. Here I employ an anthropological distinction between "shame-" and "guilt-cultures"; a shame-culture is one in which social pressure and stigma are brought to bear upon a transgressor, whereas in a guilt-culture, individuals internalize their own sense of sin. Cognitive psychologists, in contrast, define "shame" as a sense of unworthiness that the subject feels for no apparent reason, while "guilt" is regret for a prior action.

15. Rogers, D2v.

16. Ibid.

17. Ibid.

18. Jobson, F2v. Hereafter cited within the text by signature.

19. Jennifer Morgan argues that Jobson provided his "well-meaning description of African women . . . only when it deviated from what he and his readers expected" (28). While I note his condescension, I believe that his text and his motives deserve further analysis, an objective I attempt in Chapter Eight.

20. Coeffeteau, 492.

21. I try to avoid the tendency that Campbell identifies in critics of "Hero and Leander" to consider Marlowe's and Chapman's minor epics as part of one long poem, although I have retained Chapman's division of Marlowe's poem into "sestiads" for convenience.

22. See Du Bartas, trans. Joshua Sylvester, *Du Bartas His Divine Weekes and Workes* (1605): "Into three Parts he parts this spacious Orbe / 'Twixt Sem, and Cham, and Japheth: Sem the East, / Cham South, and Iapheth doth obtaine the West" (439), and "Japheth, extends from strugling Hellespont" (450).

23. Mason, 56.

24. OED, "orient," adj., 2b.

25. On "poetic geography" in the Renaissance and the influence of the "new geography" on Marlowe and Shakespeare, see Gillies, *Shakespeare and the Geography of Difference*. Most commentators on Marlowe's poem remark upon the cosmic significance afforded the lovers (see Gill; Donno), but fewer suggest that Chapman, too, deifies the lovers; Campbell notes an epic impulse in Chapman's writing but finds it merely "perfunctory and inert" compared to Marlowe's use of metaphor (257).

26. *Liddell-Scott-Jones Lexicon*, "heroes," 2.

27. Martin, 30n.

28. Shakespeare, Sonnet 127.

29. Donno, 19.

30. See Myron Turner.

31. Braden notes that Leander is consumable. "White as Pelops shoulder" seems conventional enough, but contains a mischievous sting in the tail: Pelops lost his fleshly shoulder and gained an ivory one after Demeter unwittingly consumed it (120).

32. Myron Turner, 407; Braden, 121.

33. Braden, 141.

34. Ibid., 142.

35. Lewalski suggests that Chapman's Hero becomes a coded shorthand for seeming chastity and that Shakespeare's Hero owes her name not to the faithful Hero of classical myth but to Chapman's ambiguous priestess ("Hero's Name").

36. Donno, 16.

37. Musaeus, trans. Gelzer, lines 61–62.

38. Martin, 110n.

39. Chapman, "The Shadow of Night," lines 267, 393.
40. Pliny, *History of the World*, 146; *Natural History*, 6.22.70, 7.2.26.
41. Snare, 89.
42. See Huntington.
43. Braden, 122; Donno, 19.
44. Royston, 48.
45. Tuke, B2r; Braithwait, *English Gentlewoman*, 4.

Chapter 5. Blackface and Blushface

1. Tuke; Barnfield, "The Complaint of Matilda Fitzwater," in Barnfield, ed. Klawitter, *Complete Poems*, 107–9. Hereafter cited within the text by line number.
2. All hereafter cited within the text. References to *WD* come from Luckyj's edition.
3. Dawson, 219.
4. R. E. R. Madelaine discusses the motif of the "rotten orange" as a symbol in the period for love that is sweet, but easily and invisibly corruptible. Claudio's complexion of a "civil . . . orange" characterizes him as "neither golden nor blushing, but an unhealthy yellow, . . . neither green nor ripe in love" (491).
5. OED gives the primary meaning of "smear" as "to anoint" or daub with oil, placing the first occurrence of "smear" to mean an ink smudge in the nineteenth century. Consider, however, *King John*, which connects smearing with both painting and writing: "Heaven knows they were besmear'd and overstain'd / With slaughter's pencil—where revenge did paint / The fearful difference of incensed kings" (3.1.236–38).
6. Dawson, 220.
7. See Cook.
8. Ibid., 192.
9. Ibid., 196–97.
10. Paster, *The Body Embarrassed*.
11. Ricks, 184; Little, 108.
12. Ricks, 183.
13. Callaghan, *Shakespeare Without Women*, 75–96.
14. Howard, "Renaissance Antitheatricalism," 181; Clara Claiborne Park, 106.
15. Cook, 200, 196.
16. Lewalski, "Love, Appearance, and Reality," 250. Hays reads neoplatonism in the play as a figure for "mutuality" in love, but she concludes that the Hero-Claudio plot is unsatisfactory without the tempering influence of Beatrice and Benedick.
17. Howard, "Renaissance Antitheatricalism," 181.
18. McEachern, 280.
19. Cook, 200.
20. Howard, "Renaissance Antitheatricalism"; Lewalski, "Love, Appearance, and Reality."
21. Little, 164.
22. For a detailed and elegant reading of the negative value ascribed to Gothic "whiteness" in this play and Tamora's construction as a nonwhite Other, see Royster.
23. For this connection, see Parker, "Fantasies."
24. Neely, *Broken Nuptials*.
25. Woodbridge, *Women in the English Renaissance*, 32; Woodbridge, *Vagrancy*, 50.

26. Drakakis, "Trust," 65; McEwin, 125.

27. I borrow the phrase, "the beauty myth," from Wolf, whose critique, although limited to twentieth-century, European standards of beauty, usefully expresses culturally defined notions of attractiveness and their limitations for women. See also Kim Hall, "Beauty and the Beast."

28. See Drew-Bear; Garner; Dolan.

29. Barnfield, "Complaint," line 14; Lomazzo; Braithwait, *The English Gentleman, A Good Wife.*

30. OED has no entry for "Soliman," but I conjecture that the term refers to the Song of Solomon and the "black and comely" bride who is made "fair."

31. Platt, subtitle; "Sweete Powders," G11v.

32. Drew-Bear, 22.

33. Tuke, K2, Kr.

34. Ibid., Kr.

35. Dolan, 230.

36. Hall, *Things of Darkness*, 87.

37. Ibid., 115.

38. Vickers, 104.

39. Platt, Hr.

40. Braithwait, *English Gentleman*, L13.

41. Ibid., Ev.

42. Barnfield, "Complaint," lines 6–7.

43. Tuke, Dv.

44. Braithwait, *Good Wife*, B8v.

45. Ibid., Kr.

46. *Hic Mulier*, title.

47. Dolan, 229; Kim Hall, *Things of Darkness*, 89.

48. Bulwer, O2v, Q2v, Gg2r. Hereafter cited within the text.

49. Kim Hall, *Things of Darkness*, 88. A Lamarckian *avant la lettre*, Bulwer argues that under certain circumstances human beings inherit acquired characteristics: "thus many Spaniards, and Mediterranean Inhabitants, which are of the Race of Barbary-Moores (although after frequent commixture) have not worn out the Camoyse [chamois] Nose unto this day" (3P4r).

50. Gosson, *Glasse*, A3r, A4v, Br, A4v.

51. Ibid., A4v.

52. Neville Williams, 26.

53. Carroll Camden, 182.

54. I call this example "cross-cultural" under advisement. Of course, as Kim Hall (*Things of Darkness*), Parker ("Fantasies"), and Zhiri ("Leo Africanus") point out, not only does Leo share the Christian prejudice against Muslims and other non-Christians, but John Pory's translation also mediates and frames Leo's narrative to conform to his readers' expectations about African savagery, lust, primitivism and so on.

55. "She paints, which makes me loathe her," writes Pepys on September 16, 1667; see Donne's Paradox 2, "That Women Ought to Paint."

56. Tokson, 42.

57. Drew-Bear, 54–56.

58. Sheryl Stevenson suggests a similar breakdown of *sexual* difference in the play: "men and women define femininity or manliness through a series of projections and imitations *of each other*, making it impossible to separate utterly the two [halves] of any 'differing' pair" (168).

59. Loomba, "Color of Patriarchy," 27.
60. Dena Goldberg, 84.

Chapter 6. Whiteness as Sexual Difference

1. See Shakespeare, ed. Duncan-Jones, "Introduction"; Pequigney.
2. Shakespeare's poem about the lovers seems to have inspired even more interest in the subject; there are 193 references to "Adonis" between 1603 and 1660, and 110 between the Restoration and the end of the century. An electronic search engine is a blunt instrument, however. A Boolean search for "Venus and Adonis" between 1500 and 1603 yields 564 references of which I have isolated only 55 as true references to Shakespeare's poem, using as my criteria date (after 1592, when the theatres closed and it seems likely that *Venus and Adonis* could have been circulating in manuscript) and verbal echoes. The allusions include Drayton's references in *Piers Gaveston*, Edwards's *Narcissus*, Heywood's *Oenone and Paris*, and Weever's *Faunus and Melliflora*. Between 1603 and 1660 there are 626 references to "Venus" with "Adonis" (Boolean search) and 283 between the Restoration and the turn of the century.
3. Shakespeare, ed. Roe, 288; Duncan-Jones, 490; Halpern, 378.
4. Duncan-Jones.
5. Swetnam, A2r; *Schoolhouse of Women*, 152. On the pamphlet wars, see Woodbridge, *Women*; Carroll Camden; Henderson and McManus.
6. Duncan-Jones, 497.
7. Bush, 95.
8. Fraunce, *Countess of Pembroke's Ivychurch*, M2r.
9. Edwards, *Narcissus*, Sonnet 42; Griffin, *Fidessa*, Sonnet 3, B2r; Montreux, trans. Tofte, *Honours Academie*, 35. The microfilm copy of Edwards's *Cephalus and Procris with Narcissus* is incomplete; the only complete surviving copy exists in the Cathedral Library, Peterborough, so I cite Buckley's facsimile edition (1882).
10. Dubrow, "Upon Misprision Growing," 231.
11. Bruce Smith, 136.
12. Halpern, 380.
13. Ibid. Schiffer reads the "absence of the phallus" (364) in Lacanian terms, although he hypothesizes a predominantly male audience for the poem (374n.7). Compare also Catherine Belsey's Lacanian reading, which finds the deferral not just of meaning in the poem but also of specific, controlled, single-object desire.
14. Halpern, 386. Belsey analyses the same image but calls it "love as trompe-l'oeil," a structure of desire that, like Zeuxis's grapes, makes hungry even as it satisfies, by constant and continual deferral.
15. Sasha Roberts, 301. For literary references to *Venus and Adonis*, see *The Shakspere Allusion-Book*. Margaret Cavendish refers to the poem as an aphrodisiac in *Wits Cabal, Part II* (3.12). It seems to me that Cavendish employs the poem in exactly the same way as most of her male contemporaries do—to make fun of an older, highly sexed woman. Suzuki argues, however, that both parts of *Wits Cabal* use irony to criticize the subordination of women in marriage.
16. Middleton, *Mad World*, 1.2.44–46. Hereafter cited within the text.
17. OED, "marrow," sb., 2c., 2d.
18. "Bowdlerization," of course, properly refers to Dr. Thomas Bowdler, whose "family" Shakespeare "omitted [words and phrases] which cannot with propriety be read aloud in a family" (subtitle, 1818).

19. Heywood, *Fair Maide of the Exchange*, 55.

20. Duncan-Jones, 496.

21. Laqueur, *Making Sex*; Maclean, *The Renaissance Notion of Woman*.

22. Paster, *Body Embarrassed*, 167; Katharine Park, "The Rediscovery of the Clitoris."

23. Dubrow, "Upon Misprision," 225.

24. *Schoolhouse of Women*, 148, 149.

25. Ibid., 149.

26. Gosynhill, B2v.

27. Ibid., B4r.

28. Laqueur, 102. On the ancient belief that female orgasm was necessary for conception to occur, see Avicenna, quoted in Bicks, 77–8. Early modern accounts include Jacob Rüff, Lazare Rivière. On early modern gynecology in general, see Eccles, Hilda Smith, "Gynecology and Ideology"; on early modern obstetrics and midwifery, see Bicks.

29. Paré, *Workes*, 889.

30. Bate, "Sexual Perversity," 92.

31. Woodbridge, *Women*, 184. On the feminization of whiteness on stage, see Callaghan, *Shakespeare Without Women*, 80–89.

32. *The Passionate Pilgrim*, Sonnet 9, *Riverside Shakespeare*, 1884.

33. Quoted in Kolin, 15.

34. Donne, "The Extasie, " lines 6, 5, 29; Marvell, lines 34, 45–46.

35. The reading as originally printed in 1681 was "glew," but most editions give "dew" on the grounds that "glew" or "glue" had already acquired its modern meaning. But I see no reason why the modern sense of "glue" should be inadmissible here, especially in the context of Donne's reference to perspiration as a cement-like "balme" that sticks lovers together.

36. Dubrow, *Echoes of Desire*, 163–201.

37. Lange, 488.

38. Starobinski, 459.

39. Varandaeus, A3r. The Latin reads: "nobiliores formosioresque puellas . . . ab omni congressu abstinentes."

40. Culpeper, 400.

41. Hippocrates, quoted in Starobinski, 459; Lange, 489.

42. Culpeper, 403.

43. Paré, *Oeuvres*, 23, c. 63, 3H4r. The original reads: "quand elles deviennent amoureuses, & sentent une chaleur en leurs parties genitales, qui leurs demangent, tittillent, & chatoüllent, qui leur cause de jetter leur semence elles seules: laquelle demeurent aux vaisseaux spermatiques, ou en la matraice, se corrompt, & se tourne en venin . . . d'où provient qui'il s'effleve des vapeurs putredinueeses aux parties nobles."

44. Paré, *Workes*, 950. Emphasis mine.

45. Loughlin, 837.

46. Ibid., 837.

47. See Wack.

48. Neely, "Lovesickness."

49. Sandford, C6r.

50. Culpeper, 401.

51. Traub, "(In)Significance," 77.

52. Ibid.

53. Morris, "Thomas Watson and Abraham Fraunce"; "Richard Barnfield." Barnfield's critical fortunes have waxed and waned according to cultural prejudices

about male homoerotic desire. Nineteenth-century editions include Grosart's (1876) and Arber's (1882), both of which apologize on Barnfield's behalf for his same-sex eroticism and blame the reader for seeing it there. Summers's edition locates Barnfield as a homosexual (his preferred term) poet. Bredbreck's article similarly asserts a self-conscious sexual identity for the poet, while Giant-valley compares Barnfield with Drayton and Marlowe. Morris's monograph (the only one to date) contextualizes Barnfield alongside Spenser and Fraunce. Klawitter's edition is discussed above. Clitheroe's pamphlet is aimed at the common reader. Bruce Smith's excellent, nuanced chapter in *Homosexual Desire* reads the poetry alongside a commonplace book usually, though doubtfully (as Smith acknowledges), attributed to Barnfield. Smith classifies the contents of the commonplace book as explicit, heterosexual pornography. The essays in Borris and Klawitter's recent collection, *The Affectionate Shepherd*, criticize Smith for his use of this commonplace book and for seeing the poet as part of a continuum of masculine desire rather than as an active, engaged, exclusive homosexual (a term that the editors seek to rescue from the charge of anachronism).

54. Bruce Smith, 100.

55. Yen, 133.

56. Barnfield, preface to *Cynthia*, in Barnfield, ed. Klawitter, *Complete Poems*, 116.

57. Virgil, lines 1–2.

58. Ibid., lines 17–18. Fowler translates "uaccinia" as "hyacinth," but most translations give "bilberries" or "berries" (4). Given Daphnis's arguments in favor of the taste of dark berries later in the poem, I assume Barnfield took the phrase "uaccinia nigra" to mean "black berries" rather than "dark hyacinth." See, however, Anne Lake Prescott, who reminds us of the homoerotic overtones in the myth of Hyacinthus (98n.11)

59. Virgil, lines 14–16.

60. Virgil, line 73.

61. H. Hudson, "Penelope Devereux as Sidney's Stella."

62. Morris, *Colin's Child*, 41.

63. Orgel, "Renaissance Homoeroticism."

64. Rawson, 140.

65. Barnfield, ed. Klawitter, 51.

66. On male homoeroticism in the Renaissance, see also Jonathan Goldberg; Bruce Smith, *Homosexual Desire*; Bredbreck. On female homosexuality, see Judith Brown; Traub.

67. Pulton P5v; 25 Hen. VIII 6, 5 Eliz. 17.

68. Spenser, ed. Selincourt, 423.

69. Bredbreck, 46; Morris, *Colin's Child*, 42.

70. Bruce Smith, 101.

71. Spenser, *Amoretti* 16, lines 6–7; 37, lines 1, 6.

72. Boswell, 80–81.

73. Ibid., 86.

74. Ibid., 80.

75. Barnfield, ed. Klawitter, 214n.

76. Bruce Smith, 105.

77. Barnfield, "Complaint," lines 8–14.

78. Ibid., line 37.

79. Ibid., line 15.

80. Ibid., lines 40–41.

81. Compare the praise of blackbirds in Elyot's *The Castel of Helthe* (1539), which claims that "Blacke byrdes or ousyls . . . [A]mong wylde fowle hath the chiefe prayse, for lyghtnesse of digestion, and that they make good nouryshement, and lyttel ordure" (Nv).

82. Elyot, N3v.

83. Legh, B6r-B8v.

84. Ibid., A7v-B2r.

85. Shakespeare, ed. Duncan-Jones, 47–49; Katharine Wilson, 83–90. On the underlying misogyny of the praise of blackness, see also Kim Hall, *Things of Darkness*, 88–91.

86. Quoted in Shakespeare, ed. Duncan-Jones, 48.

87. Barnfield, "Complaint," line 21.

Chapter 7. Artificial Negroes

1. During the Renaissance, the Roma are called "Gypsies" or "Egyptians," and those are the terms I shall use for the remainder of this chapter. All three terms currently in use have raised objections. "Gypsy" implies false links to Egypt and has negative connotations. The term "Romany" did not become popular until the nineteenth century, and it excludes members of the group without Roma ancestry. The preferred term in Britain, "Traveller," ignores Roma ancestry altogether.

2. Lal, 24.

3. See Vesey-FitzGerald, Mayall, and Randall.

4. Dekker, *Lanthorn and Candlelight*, E3v. Hereafter cited within the text.

5. On sea-pirates, see Fuchs.

6. 1 Jac. I c.7. English legal references come, unless otherwise indicated in the text, from Great Britain, Statutes and Laws, *The Statutes of the Realm*. Hereafter cited within the text.

7. Middleton and Rowley, *The Spanish Gypsy* (*SG*). Hereafter cited within the text by signature.

8. On early modern Gypies, see Randall; Timpane; Whitney; Bach, 184–90; Sousa, 129–58; Netzloff; Floyd-Wilson, "Transmigrations," 88–91; Reynolds, 23–63. My reconstruction of anti-Gypsy statutes and rogue literature parallels Sousa's, Netzloff's, Reynolds's, and Whitney's; my suggestion that the figure of Cleopatra foregrounds the sexual and racial technologies of the Renaissance stage parallels Little's important two-chapter discussion of race and sex in *Antony and Cleopatra*, although he does not share my interest in Gypsies. I differ from recent critics in my sustained attention to the rogue literature and its affinities with antitheatricalism, in my reading of *The Spanish Gypsy*, and in my foregrounding the importance of idleness as a mark of Gypsies' ambiguous literary status as agents who resist wage-labor and the hierarchies of rank.

9. Think of the 1572 Vagrancy act, which similarly imposed the death penalty upon third-time offenders. On the harsh laws against vagrants and paupers and the beginnings of poor relief during the Tudor and Elizabethan eras, see Pound, and Woodbridge, *Vagrancy*, especially Appendix A.

10. Hunt, 39.

11. Great Britain, Statutes and Laws, *Anno Quinto*, fo. 55r.

12. Timpane, 268–70.

13. Somerset, 429.

14. Randall, 52.
15. 6 Jac. VI , 74.
16. Scotland, Statutes and Laws, *Lawes and Acts*, 12 Jac. VI, 147.
17. Scotland, Statutes and Laws, *Laws and Acts*, 20 Jac. VI, fo. 850r.
18. Ibid., 21 Jac. VI, fo. 857r.
19. Randall, 53.
20. Woodbridge, *Vagrancy*, 1–37.
21. OED distinguishes between the terms "serf" and "slave" on the grounds that the former is attached to the land, usually held by a particular family or organization, while the latter can be sold to anyone, anywhere (sb., "serf," 2).
22. Hallam finds the "last unequivocal testimony to the existence of villeinage" as late as 15 Jac. I (312).
23. Rymer, 732.
24. Pulton, title.
25. Ibid., 2S5r.
26. Ibid.
27. *Smith v. Browne and Cooper*, Salkeld, 2:666–67.
28. Hunt, 42.
29. Ibid., 44.
30. Mayall, 36.
31. Okely, 14–15.
32. See Netzloff. Two anachronistic parallels come to mind: the so-called "Jewish question" in Germany from the nineteenth century to the Holocaust, and the so-called "Muslim question" in twenty-first century Europe. As we shall see, early modern rogue literature compares the Gypsies to Jews on several occasions.
33. It is also the opposite of, for example, late twentieth-century German legal attitudes towards citizenship, in which ethnic origin first, rather than country of residence, first language, or place of birth determines nationality. Thus, until relatively recently, German-speaking, taxpaying Turks whose families had lived in Germany for three generations were not entitled to become citizens, while Eastern Europeans who had never lived or worked in Germany and spoke no German, but who had a German ancestor, were allowed the full benefits of citizenship. See Scarry, "The Difficulty of Imagining," 48–50.
34. Boorde, A2r.
35. Ibid.
36. Rid, B2r–B2v.
37. Rowlands, G4r.
38. Ibid., G4r.
39. Ibid., G4r; 1 Jac. I c.7.
40. References to Jonson's plays come from Wilkes's edition of the *Complete Plays* unless otherwise noted, and are cited within the text.
41. Rowlands, G4r.
42. "The Braue English Jipsie."
43. For specific verbal parallels of *The Spanish Gypsy* with "La Gitanilla," see Huddlestone.
44. Orgel, *Jonsonian Masque*, 117–18.
45. See Bach for a list of the terms relating to skin color within the masque. She argues that, although the Gypsies are not called "white" within the world of the masque, only in the Epilogue, the construction of the Gypsies as "dark," "olive," "tawny," and so on participates in the creation of an early modern English whiteness (186–87).

46. Randall, 59.

47. Bach, 188.

48. Timpane, 298.

49. Bach, 189.

50. Rowlands, G4r. "Kit Callot" is a tautology; both "kit" and "callet" were slang terms for a harlot.

51. John Taylor; Harman.

52. Randall, 145.

53. Adorno, 254–55.

54. Adelman, *Common Liar*, 188.

55. Charnes, 127; Singh, "Antitheatricality."

56. Loomba, *Gender, Race, Renaissance Drama*; Little, 102–12.

57. Floyd-Wilson, "Transmigrations"; Little, 102–12.

58. Archer, 23–62.

59. Adelman, "'Making Defect Perfection.'"

60. Whitney; Sousa.

61. Sousa, 151.

62. Rowlands, G4r.

63. Since many critics have now commented upon Cleopatra's ambiguous skin color and on the shifting location and valences of her Egypt, my remarks here will be brief. On the one hand, the historical Cleopatra was Greek, as Plutarch knew. Mary Herbert, Countess of Pembroke, imagines the royal Cleopatra marble-pale in her translation of Garnier's *Antonius* (1592), exaggerating her "Allablaster" and "corall" whiteness, and her "faire . . . flaming golde" hair (Garnier, trans. Herbert, I2r). Little finds that most Renaissance visual representations of Cleopatra figure her as white, although Sousa mentions a medieval manuscript that presents her "as a black African" (Little, 170; Sousa, 141). On the other hand, as Weller and Ferguson point out in their introduction to the play, Elizabeth Cary's *Mariam* (1613) characterizes Cleopatra's fairness as relative; she is "black" (5.1.239) or "brown" (1.2.189) in contrast to Mariam, the "Fair Queen of Jewry." George Gascoigne blames not the sun but the soil of Egypt for making his Cleopatra a "nutbrowne Lady": "brown I dare be bolde shee was, for so ye solle [soil] did serve" (Gascoigne, 151). Like Andromeda, Cleopatra is (as Little suggests [170]), darkened by association with her exoticized attendants. Lucan's *Pharsalia* mentions Cleopatra's Ethiopian, Libyan, and Scythian attendants, including the faithful Iras (whose name is a Greek word meaning "tightly-curled hair" [Snowden, 12]). Cleopatra herself, according to Lucan, has "lily skinne" and "snow white" breasts (Lucan, 425–26), yet her Egypt is a place where "Libyan" blackness exists alongside Teutonic pallor. Finally, it would be a mistake to assume that either the historical or the Renaissance Cleopatra were black Africans or tawny Indians simply because they were called "Gypsies"—as I suggested earlier, British Gypsies during the sixteenth and seventeenth centuries could have been, and often were, "white" people in ethnic drag.

64. See, however, Jankowski, who argues that this reported scene is staged by Cleopatra and that it features Antony as the queen's consort rather than coruler, a sign of her conquest of him (153).

65. Rackin; Callaghan, "'Othello was a white man,'" 74–96.

66. Little, 173.

67. Charnes, 132; Little, 149. In contrast, Jankowski reads the arrival at Cydnus as Cleopatra's deliberate exercise of a materialized and willfully sexual

body politic in her capacity as powerful queen and plotting playwright (147–63). Cleopatra may be deliberately using her sexuality to wield power, as Jankowski argues, but in so doing, argues Archer, she enmeshes herself in emergent and imprisoning norms of race and heterosexuality (Archer, 62).

68. Butler, 234.
69. Ibid.; emphasis original.
70. Charnes, 127.
71. Scarry, *Body in Pain*, 290–91.
72. Bullough, 5:316.
73. John Russell Brown, 13.
74. Adorno, 3.

Chapter 8. Suntanned Slaves

1. Munday, Bv.
2. "First Voyage . . . of Sir Iohn Hawkins," in Hakluyt, *Principal Navigations* (*PN*). Hereafter cited within the text by volume and page number.
3. Berkley, 292.
4. See Kim Hall, *Things of Darkness*, for a reproduction of Hawkins's crest (20).
5. Sparke, in Hakluyt, *PN*. Hereafter cited within the text by volume and page number.
6. Great Britain, Privy Council, *Calendar Domestic*, 1:299.
7. Pope-Hennessy, 53.
8. Quoted in Catterall, 1:9.
9. Bragge, fo. 65r; Pinkerton.
10. Ibid., fo. 65v.
11. Fryer, 462n.18; Bragge, fo. 65v. See also Pinkerton.
12. Ibid.
13. Ibid., ff. 65v–66r.
14. Shyllon, 8.
15. Butts v. Penny, Levinz, 2:201. On the etymological connection between "slave" and "Slav," and the progressive "blackening" of Russia or Tartary, see Archer, *Old Worlds*, Chapter Three.
16. *Smith v. Browne and Cooper*, Salkeld, 2:666–67. The plaintiff complained that the defendant owed him £20 for a slave. Justice Holt argued that slaves were free in England (as cited above) but found for the plaintiff, arguing that the latter did indeed owe the former money, but not for the sale of a negro in London, where such a sale was legally impossible, but for the sale of a negro in Virginia. But "[t]hen the attorney-general coming in, said, they were inheritances, and transferrable by deed, and not without: And nothing was done."
17. Chamberlain v. Harvey, Carthew, 396–97.
18. Fraser, 258. See also Catterall, 9–12; Shyllon, 17; Fryer, 113–14. On the status of eighteenth-century Afro-Britons, and the important legal consequences of transatlantic slavery, see also Gerzina.
19. Fryer, 32; Shyllon, 20.
20. Fraser, 258.
21. See Harbage and Schoenbaum.
22. Great Britain, Privy Council, *Calendar Colonial*, 1:18.
23. Bach, 159.

24. OED, "conversation," sb., 1.

25. Munday, Bv.

26. Ibid.

27. Bach, 161.

28. Raman, 221.

29. Ibid., 218.

30. On sugar and slavery, see Sidney W. Mintz.

31. Bartels, "*Othello* and Africa," 60.

32. *TNK*, 3.5.130; Topsell, 11.

33. Cary, 4.7.459–62. On the ape/Africa connection, see Fryer, 133–46; Jordan, 24–36; Kim Hall, "'Mr Moores Revels.'"

34. Eldred Jones, 13; Hawkins, *PN*, 10:65.

35. Manning, 97–98.

36. Guinier and Torres, passim.

37. Gary Taylor suggests intriguingly that Jobson's use of the word "white" to describe himself and his fellow sailors comes not from European explorers but from the Africans who translate for them. See *Buying Whiteness*, Chapter Four.

38. Palmer, K3r–K3v. Hereafter cited within the text.

39. Berkley, 290.

40. See Engels.

41. Jobson's account, although quaint-sounding, may be to some degree based on observation: see Sapolsky for an account of the author's life among baboons, and their elaborate social practices.

42. On the Great Ape Project, see Cavalieri and Singer.

Chapter 9. Experiments of Colors

1. All quotations from *Observations on Experimental Philosophy* come from the first edition, with the exception of the passage on "Blackmoors" cited below, and hereafter appear within the text. Quotations from *Assaulted and Pursued Chastity* (*APC*) and *Blazing World* (*BW*) come from Lilley's edition and hereafter appear within the text. Cavendish's punctuation and grammar are idiosyncratic, but I agree with Lilley that standardizing the text loses the flavor of Cavendish's prose. I have followed Lilley in retaining Cavendish's punctuation except where the sense is hard to decipher.

2. Quoted in Kegl, 135.

3. Ibid.

4. Pepys, 8:243; Samuel Mintz, 175.

5. On Cavendish's life, see her own autobiography, *A True Relation of My Birth*; Douglas Grant; Kathleen Jones; Hilda Smith, *Reason's Disciples*.

6. Jordan, 16.

7. Fryer, 144.

8. La Peyrère, M3v.

9. Ibid.

10. Quoted in Jordan, 93.

11. Ibid., 65.

12. Ibid., 66.

13. Hooke, 101.

14. Ibid., 102.

15. Ibid., 54.

16. Ibid., "Preface," and passim.

17. Pepys, 8:243.

18. Quoted in Mintz, 174.

19. Battigelli, 35.

20. See Wiener's *Dictionary of the History of Ideas* and *Britannica Online* for more detailed accounts of seventeenth-century optical theories.

21. Leslie, "Evading Rape"; Orgel, *Impersonations*, 32–24.

22. Cavendish, ed. and introd. Lilley, xxi.

23. Leslie, "Evading Rape, 192.

24. Ibid., 195.

25. Gallagher, 26.

26. Ibid., 25.

27. Ibid., 28.

28. See Hintz.

29. Kegl, 129.

30. Neely, "Woman/Utopia/Fetish," 83.

31. Trubowitz, 240.

32. Kegl, 134.

33. Trubowitz's molecular metaphor for female friendship in *Blazing World* as "the intimate bond between self-sufficient atoms" (240) is just as apt for the marriage of the Duke and Duchess: expansive yet self-contained, made up of discrete unions (Duke/Duchess, Duchess/Empress, Empress/Duke) that continually dissolve and reform, like chemical bonds.

34. Pepys, 8:163.

35. Fitzmaurice; Pepys, 8:163, 186.

Afterword: Nancy Burson's Human Race Machine

1. Cuvier, 71–75.

2. Quoted in John Wright, 172.

3. Sykes, 295; Satel. I thank Fran Teague for the reference to Sykes.

Bibliography

Aasand, Hardin. "'To Blanch an Ethiop, and Revive a Corse': Queen Anne and *The Masque of Blackness.*" *SEL* 32 (1992): 271–85.

Accounts of the Lord High Treasurer of Scotland [*Compota Thesaurariorum Regum Scotorum*]. Ed. Sir James Balfour Paul. Vol. 2. Edinburgh: HM General Register House, 1900.

Ackroyd, P. R., and C. F. Evans, eds. *From the Beginnings to Jerome.* Vol. 1 of *The Cambridge History of the Bible.* Cambridge: Cambridge University Press, 1970.

Adelman, Janet. *The Common Liar: An Essay on "Antony and Cleopatra."* New Haven, Conn.: Yale University Press, 1973.

———. "Making Defect Perfection: Shakespeare and the One-Sex Model." In Comensoli and Russell, *Enacting Gender,* 23–52.

Adorno, Theodor W. *Aesthetic Theory* [*Ästhetische Theorie*]. Trans. Robert Hullot-Kentor. Minneapolis: University of Minnesota Press, 1997.

Africanus, Leo [al-Hassan Ibn-Mohammed Al-Wezaz Al-fasi]. *The History and Description of Africa.* Trans. John Pory. London, 1600.

———. *The History and Description of Africa.* Trans. and ed. Oumelbanine Zhiri. In Kamps and Singh, *Travel Knowledge,* 249–57.

Ainsworth, Henry. *Solomon's Song of Songs, in English Metre.* London, 1623.

Alciato, Andrea [Andrea Alciati]. *Emblemata.* Lyons, 1550. Ed. Betty I. Knott. Introd. John Manning. Chippenham, UK: Emblem-Scolar, 1996.

Allen, Theodore W. *The Invention of the White Race.* 2 vols. London: Verso, 1994.

Alvares, Francisco. *A True Relation of the Lands of the Prester John.* 1540. Trans. Lord Stanley of Alderley. 1881. Rev. ed. Vols. 114–55 of the Publications of the Hakluyt Society, 2nd ser. Ed. C. F. Beckingham and G. W. B. Huntingford. Cambridge: Cambridge University Press, 1961.

American Association of Physical Anthropologists. "Statement on Biological Aspects of Race." *American Journal of Physical Anthropology* 101 (1996): 569–70.

Anderson, Benedict. *Imagined Communities: Reflections on the Origin and Spread of Nationalism.* London: Verso, 1983.

Andrea, Bernadette. "Black Skin, the Queen's Masques: Africanist Ambivalence and Feminine Author(ity) in the Masques of *Blackness* and *Beauty.*" *ELR* 29 (1999): 246–81.

Andrewes, Bartimaeus. *Certaine Verie Worthie, Godly and Profitable Sermons, upon the Fifth Chapter of the Songs of Solomon.* London, 1583.

Appiah, Kwame Anthony, and Henry Louis Gates, eds. *Africana: The Encyclopedia of the African and African American Experience.* New York: Basic Civitas, 1999.

Archer, John Michael. *Old Worlds: Egypt, Southwest Asia, India, and Russia in Early Modern English Writing*. Stanford, Calif.: Stanford University Press, 2001.

Ariosto, Lodovico. *Orlando Furioso*. Trans. Guido Waldman. Oxford: Oxford University Press, 1991.

———. *Orlando Furioso*. Trans. Sir John Harington. 1591. Ed. Robert McNulty. Oxford: Clarendon Press, 1972.

Aristotle. "De Coloribus [Of Colors]." *Opuscula*. In vol. 6 of *The Works of Aristotle*. Trans. T. Loveday and E. S. Forster, 791a–799b. Oxford: Clarendon, 1913.

———. *The Metaphysics*. Trans. Hugh Tredennick. 2 vols. Cambridge, Mass.: Harvard University Press, 1933–35.

———. *The Physics*. Trans. Philip H. Wicksteed and Francis M. Cornford. 2 vols. London: Heinemann, 1929–35.

———. *Poetics*. Trans. Stephen Halliwell. Cambridge, Mass.: Harvard University Press, 1995.

———. *Problemes of Aristotle*. Edinburgh, 1595.

Asante, Molefi Kete. *The Afrocentric Idea*. Rev. ed. Philadelphia: Temple University Press, 1998.

Ashcroft, Bill, Gareth Griffiths, and Helen Tiffin, eds. *The Empire Writes Back: Theory and Practice in Post-Colonial Literatures*. London: Routledge, 1989.

Ashton, Robert, ed. and introd. *James I: By His Contemporaries*. London: Hutchinson, 1969.

Awdeley, John. *The Fraternity of Vagabonds*. London, 1561.

Aylett, Robert. *The Song of Songs . . . Metaphrased in English Heroiks*. London, 1621.

Ayres, Philip J. "The Revision of 'Lust's Dominion.'" *Notes and Queries* 17 (1970): 212–13.

Bach, Rebecca Ann. *Colonial Transformations: The Cultural Production of the New Atlantic World, 1580–1640*. New York: Palgrave, 2000.

Bacon, Sir Francis. *De Sapientia Veterum Liber*. London, 1609.

———. *The Wisedome of the Ancients*. Trans. Sir Arthur Gorges. London, 1619.

Baker, Houston A., Manthia Diawara, and Ruth H. Lindeborg, eds. *Black British Cultural Studies: A Reader*. Chicago: University of Chicago Press, 1996.

Bakhtin, Mikhail. *Problems of Dostoyevsky's Poetics*. Trans. and ed. Caryl Emerson. Manchester: Manchester University Press, 1984.

Baldwin, William. *The Canticles of Balades of Salomon, phraselyke declared in Englysh*. London, 1549.

Barbour, Richmond. "Britain and the Great Beyond: The Masque of Blackness at Whitehall." In *Playing the Globe: Genre and Geography in English Renaissance Drama*, ed. John Gillies and Virginia Mason Vaughan, 129–53. Madison, N.J.: Fairleigh Dickinson University Press, 1998.

Barker, Francis. *The Tremulous Private Body: Essays on Subjection*. London: Methuen, 1984.

Barnfield, Richard. *The Complete Poems*. Ed. George Klawitter. Selinsgrove, Pa.: Susequehanna University Press, 1990.

Baron, Robert. *Gripus and Hegio, or the Passionate Lovers*. In Εϱοτοπαιγνιον *[Erotopaignion], Or the Cyprian Academy*, Cr-E4v. 1648.

Barroll, Leeds. *Anna of Denmark, Queen of England*. Philadelphia: University of Pennsylvania Press, 2001.

———, ed. "Forum: Race and the Study of Shakespeare." *Shakespeare Studies* 26 (1998).

———. "Theatre as Text: The Case of Queen Anna and the Jacobean Court Masque." *The Elizabethan Theatre* 14 (1996): 175–93.

Bartels, Emily C. "Making More of the Moor: Aaron, Othello, and Renaissance Refashionings of Race." *Shakespeare Quarterly* 41 (1990): 433–54.

———. "*Othello* and Africa: Postcolonialism Reconsidered." In McGiffert, *Constructing Race*, 44–64.

———. *Spectacles of Strangeness: Imperialism, Alienation, and Marlowe.* Philadelphia: University of Pennsylvania Press, 1993.

Barthelmy, Anthony. *Black Face, Maligned Race: The Representation of Blacks in English Renaissance Drama from Shakespeare to Southerne.* Baton Rouge: Louisiana State University Press, 1987.

Bate, Jonathan. "Sexual Perversity in *Venus and Adonis*." *Yearbook of English Studies* 23 (1993): 80–92.

Batman, Stephen. *The Golden Booke of the Leaden Gods.* 1577. Reprint, New York: Garland, 1976.

Battigelli, Anna. "Between the Glass and the Hand: The Eye in Margaret Cavendish's *Blazing World*." *1650–1850* 2 (1996): 25–38.

Baylor, Michael G., ed. and trans. *The Radical Reformation.* Cambridge: Cambridge University Press, 1991.

Beaumont, Francis. *Salmacis and Hermaphroditus.* 1602. In Donno, *Elizabethan Minor Epics*, 281–304.

Beaumont, Francis, and John Fletcher. "The Masque of the Inner Temple and Gray's Inn." In *Complete Works of Beaumont and Fletcher*, ed. Alexander Dyce, 377–82. Boston: Phillips, Sampson, 1854.

Beck, Brandon H. *From the Rising of the Sun: English Images of the Ottoman Empire to 1715.* New York: Lang, 1987.

Bell, Rudolph M. "Renaissance Sexuality and the Florentine Archives: An Exchange." *Renaissance Quarterly* 40 (1987): 485–511.

Belsey, Catherine. "Love as Trompe-l'œil: Taxonomies of Desire in *Venus and Adonis*." *Shakespeare Quarterly* 46 (1995): 257–76. Reprinted in Kolin, "*Venus and Adonis*", 261–85.

Bergin, Osborn, trans. and introd. *Irish Bardic Poetry.* Ed. David Greene and Fergus Kelly. Dublin: Institute for Advanced Studies, 1970.

Berkley, George. *The Naval History of Britain.* Ed. John Hill. London, 1756.

Berlinerbrau, Jacques. *Heresy in the University: The "Black Athena" Controversy and the Responsibilities of American Intellectuals.* New Brunswick, N.J.: Rutgers University Press, 1999.

Bernal, Martin. *Black Athena: The Afroasiatic Roots of Classical Civilization.* New Brunswick, N.J.: Rutgers University Press, 1987.

Bernard of Clairvaux, Saint [S. Bernardus Abbatus Clarae-Vallensis]. Sermons 24 and 25. In Patrologia Latina Database.

Best, George. "Experiences and reasons of the Sphere, to prooue all partes of the worlde habitable, and thereby to confute the position of the fiue Zones." In Hakluyt, *Principal Navigations*, 7:252–68.

Beverly, Robert. *The History of Virginia, in Four Parts.* London, 1722. American Memory. Library of Congress. http://memory.loc.gov/cgi-bin/query/r?ammem/lhbcb:@field(DOCID+@lit(lhbcb06557)):@@@REF (accessed November 24, 2003).

Beza, Theodore [Theodore de Bèze]. *Sermones upon the First Three Chapters of the Canticle of Canticles.* Trans. John Harman. London, 1587.

Bhabha, Homi. "Of Mimicry and Man." *October: Anthology.* Cambridge, Mass.: MIT Press, 1987. Reprinted in Bhabha, *The Location of Culture.* London: Routledge, 1994. 85–92.

The Bible [Bishops' Bible]. London, 1568, 1595.

The Bible [Geneva Bible]. 1560. Facsimile reprint, Madison, Wisc.: University of Wisconsin Press, 1969.

The Bible [King James Version]. 1611. Reprint, London: Penguin, 1974.

The Bible [New English Bible]. *Old Testament.* London: Oxford University Press/ Cambridge University Press, 1970.

The Bible [New Revised Standard Version]. *The Cambridge Annotated Study Bible.* Cambridge: Cambridge University Press, 1990.

The Bible [Rheims-Douai Bible]. Rheims, 1582, and Douai, 1609.

The Bible [Vulgate]. *Biblia sacra.* Ed. Robert Weber. Stuttgart: Wurttembergische Bibelanstalt, 1969.

Bicks, Caroline. *Midwiving Subjects in Shakespeare's England.* Aldershot, UK: Ashgate, 2003.

Billings, Warren M, ed. *The Old Dominion in the Seventeenth Century: A Documentary History of Virginia, 1606–1689.* Chapel Hill: Institute of Early American History and Culture/University of North Carolina Press, 1975.

Bloch, Ariel, and Chana Bloch, trans., eds., and introd. *The Song of Songs: A New Translation and Commentary.* New York: Random House, 1995.

Bloch, Chana. *Spelling the Word: George Herbert and the Bible.* Berkeley: University of California Press, 1985.

Bodin, John [Jean Bodin]. *Method for the Easy Comprehension of History.* 1566. Trans. Beatrice Reynolds. New York: Octagon, 1966.

Boorde, Andrew. *The First Boke of the Introduction to Knowledge.* London, 1542.

Boose, Lynda E. "'The Getting of a Lawful Race': Racial Discourse in Early Modern England and the Unrepresentable Black Woman." In Hendricks and Parker, *Women, "Race," and Writing,* 35–54.

————. "Scolding Brides and Bridling Scolds: Taming the Woman's Unruly Member." *Shakespeare Quarterly* 42 (1991): 179–213.

Borris, Kenneth, and George Klawitter, eds. *The Affectionate Shepherd: Celebrating Richard Barnfield.* Selinsgrove, Pa.: Susquehanna University Press, 2001.

Boswell, John. *Same-Sex Unions in Pre-Modern Europe.* New York: Villard, 1994.

Bourne, William. *A Booke called the Treasure for Traueilers.* London, 1578.

Bowdler, Thomas. *The Family Shakspeare.* London: Longman, 1818.

Bowerbank, Sylvia. "The Spider's Delight: Margaret Cavendish and the 'Female' Imagination." In Farrell, Hageman, and Kinney, *Women in the Renaissance,* 187–203.

Braden, Gordon. *The Classics and English Renaissance Poetry.* New Haven, Conn.: Yale University Press, 1978.

Bradshaw, Brendan. "Geoffrey Keating: Apologist of Irish Ireland." In Bradshaw, Hadfield, and Maley, *Representing Ireland,* 166–90.

Bradshaw, Brendan, Andrew Hadfield, and Willy Maley, eds. *Representing Ireland: Literature and the Origins of Conflict, 1534–1660.* Cambridge: Cambridge University Press, 1993.

Bragge, William. "Bragge's Grievances." Manuscript. British Library Royal 17, BX.

Braithwait, Richard. *The English Gentleman.* London, 1630.

————. *The English Gentlewoman.* London, 1631.

————. *The Good Wife: Or, a Rare One amongst Women.* London, 1618.

Braude, Benjamin. "The Sons of Noah and the Construction of Ethnic and Geographical Identities in the Medieval and Early Modern Periods." In McGiffert, *Constructing Race,* 103–42.

Braudel, Fernand. *The Perspective of the World.* Vol. 3. of *Civilization and Capitalism.* 1979. Trans. Siân Reynolds. New York: Harper, 1984.

"The Brave English Iipsie [Gypsy]." London, 1625.

Bray, Alan. *Homosexuality in Renaissance England.* London: Gay Men's Press, 1982.

Bray, John S. *Theodore Beza's Doctrine of Predestination.* Nieuwkoop: De Graaf, 1975.

Brayne, John. *An Exposition upon the Canticles.* London, 1651.

Bredbreck, Gregory W. "Tradition and the Individual Sodomite: Barnfield, Shakespeare, and Subjective Desire." *Journal of Homosexuality* 23 (1992): 41–68.

Brereton, J. Le Gay, ed. *Lusts Dominion, or the Lascivious Queen.* Materials for the Study of the Old English Drama 2nd ser. 4. Uystpruyst: Louvain Librairie Universitaire, 1930.

Bright, Timothy. *A Treatise of Melancholy.* London, 1586.

Brightman, Thomas. *Commentarium in Cantica Canticorum.* Basel, 1614.

———. *The Works of . . . Thomas Brightman: Together with a Commentary on the Whole Book of Canticles, or Song of Salomon.* London, 1644.

Brown, John Russell, ed. *"Antony and Cleopatra": A Casebook.* London: Macmillan, 1968.

Brown, Judith C. *Immodest Acts: The Life of a Lesbian Nun in Renaissance Italy.* Oxford: Oxford University Press, 1986.

Browne, Sir Thomas. *Pseudodoxia Epidemica.* 1646. Vols. 2–3 of *The Complete Works of Sir Thomas Browne.* Ed. Geoffrey Keynes. London: Faber, 1928.

Bruce, F. F. *History of the Bible in English.* New York: Oxford University Press, 1978.

Brucioli, Antonio. *A Commentary upon the Canticle of Canticles.* Trans. Thomas James. London, 1598.

Bullough, Geoffrey, ed. *Narrative and Dramatic Sources of Shakespeare.* 8 vols. New York: Columbia University Press, 1957–75.

Bulwer, John. *Anthropometamorphosis: Man Transform'd: or, The Artificiall Changling.* London, 1653.

Burel, John. "Discription of the Queenis Maiesties Maist Honorable Entry into the Toun of Edinburgh." 1712. Reprinted in J. T. G Craig, ed., *Papers Relative to the Marriage of King James the Sixth of Scotland, with the Princess Anna of Denmark.* Edinburgh: Bannatyne Club, 1828.

Burton, Robert. *The Anatomy of Melancholy.* 1621. 3 vols. Ed. Thomas Faulkner, Nicolas Kiessling, Rhonda L. Blair. Oxford: Clarendon, 1989–94.

Bush, Douglas. "*Venus and Adonis* and Mythology." In *Mythology and the Renaissance Tradition in English Poetry,* 137–48. Minneapolis: University of Minnesota Press, 1932. Reprinted in Kolin, *"Venus and Adonis,"* 91–102.

Butler, Judith. *Bodies That Matter: On the Discursive Limits of "Sex".* London: Routledge, 1993.

Calderwood, David. *The History of the Kirk of Scotland.* Ed. Rev. Thomas Thomson. 8 vols. Vol. 5. Edinburgh: Wodrow Society, 1844.

Callaghan, Dympna. "'Othello was a white man.'" In *Alternative Shakespeares 2,* ed. Terence Hawkes, 192–215. London: Routledge, 1996. Revised and reprinted in Callaghan, *Shakespeare Without Women,* 75–96.

———. "Re-Reading Elizabeth Cary's *The Tragedie of Mariam, Faire Queene of Jewry.*" In Hendricks and Parker, *Women, "Race," and Writing,* 163–77.

———. *Shakespeare Without Women: Representing Gender and Race on the Renaissance Stage.* London: Routledge, 2000.

Camden, Carroll. *The Elizabethan Woman.* New York: Elsevier, 1952.

Camden, William. *Britannia.* 1586. Reprint, London, 1610.

Campbell, Marion. "'Desunt Nonulla': The Construction of Marlowe's *Hero and Leander* as an Unfinished Poem." *ELH* 51 (1984): 241–68.

Campion, Thomas. *A Booke of Ayres*. London, 1601. In *The Works of Thomas Campion*, ed. Walter R. Davis. New York: Norton, 1969.

———. "Umbra." In *The Works of Thomas Campion*, ed. Walter R. Davis, 378. New York: Norton, 1969.

Carey, Vincent, and Clare Carroll. "Factions and Fictions: Spenser's Reflections of and on Elizabethan Politics." In *Spenser's Life and the Subject of Biography*, ed. Judith H. Anderson, Donald Cheney, and David A. Richardson, 31–44. Amherst: University of Massachussetts Press, 1996.

Carthew, Thomas. *Reports of Cases Adiudged in the King's Bench*. London, 1741.

Cary, Elizabeth, Lady Falkland. *The Tragedie of Mariam, the Fair Queen of Jewry*. 1613. Ed. Margaret Ferguson and Barry Weller. Berkeley: University of California Press, 1994.

Casas, Bartholomé de las. *The Spanish Colonie* [*Brevissima relación de la destruyción de las Indias*. 1552]. Trans. William Brome. London, 1583.

———. *The Tears of the Indians* [*Brevissima relación de la destruyción de las Indias*. 1552]. Trans. John Phillips. London, 1656.

Catterall, Helen Tunnicliff, ed. *Judicial Cases Concerning American Slavery and the Negro*. 5 vols. Vol. 1. Washington, D.C.: Carnegie Institution, 1926. Reprint, Buffalo, N.Y.: Hein, 1998.

Cavalieri, Paola, and Peter Singer, eds. *The Great Ape Project: Equality Beyond Humanity*. New York: St. Martin's, 1994.

Cavalli-Sforza, Luigi Luca, and Francesco Cavalli-Sforza. *The Great Human Diasporas: The History of Diversity and Evolution*. Trans. Sarah Thorne. Reading, UK: Addison-Wesley, 1995.

Cave, Terence. *Recognitions*. Oxford: Clarendon, 1988.

Cavendish, Margaret. *The Blazing World and Other Writings*. Ed. Kate Lilley. London: Penguin, 1994.

———. *Observations upon Experimental Philosophy*. London, 1666.

———. *A True Relation of My Birth, Breeding and Life*. Ed. Sylvia Bowerbank and Sara Mendelson. In *Paper Bodies: A Margaret Cavendish Reader*, 41–63. London: Broadview, 2000.

———. "Wits Cabal." In *Playes*. London, 1662.

Certeau, Michel de. *The Writing of History*. Trans. Tom Conley. New York: Columbia University Press, 1988.

Cervantes, Miguel de [Miguel de Cervantes Saavedra]. "The Little Gypsy Girl" ["La Gitanilla"]. In *Exemplary Stories*. 1613. Trans. C. A. Jones. London: Penguin, 1972.

Chambers, E. K. *The English Folk-Play*. Oxford: Clarendon, 1933.

———. *The Mediæval Stage*. Vol. 1. Oxford: Clarendon, 1903.

Chapman, George. *Andromeda Liberata, or The Nuptials of Perseus and Andromeda*. London, 1614.

———. *A Free and Offenceles Iustification of a Lately Published and Most Maliciously Misinterpreted Poeme: Entituled "Andromeda Liberata."* London, 1614.

———. *Hero and Leander Completed*. 1598. In Donno, *Elizabethan Minor Epics*, 85–126.

———. *The Memorable Masque*. 1613. Ed. David Lindley. *Court Masques: Jacobean and Caroline Entertainments, 1605–1640*, 74–91. Oxford: Clarendon Press, 1995.

———. "The Shadow of Night." *The Poems of George Chapman*. Ed. Phyllis Brooks Bartlett, 20–30. New York: Modern Language Association of America, 1941.

Charnes, Linda. *Notorious Identity: Materializing the Subject in Shakespeare*. Cambridge, Mass.: Harvard University Press, 1993.

Chew, Samuel C. *The Crescent and the Rose: Islam and England During the Renaissance.* New York: Octagon, 1965.

Clapham, Henoch. *Three Partes of Salomon his Song of Songs.* London, 1603.

Clitheroe, Fred. *The Life and Selected Writings of Richard Barnfield, 1574–1627.* Newcastle: Lyme, 1992.

Cluck, Nancy A. "Shakespearean Studies in Shame." *Shakespeare Quarterly* 36 (1985): 141–51.

Coeffeteau, Nicholas. *A Table of Humane Passions.* 1621. Reprint, Ann Arbor, Mich.: University Microfilms International, 1968.

Colie, Rosalie. *The Resources of Kind: Genre-Theory in the Renaissance.* Ed. Barbara K. Lewalski. Berkeley: University of California Press, 1973.

Comensoli, Viviana, and Anne Russell, eds. *Enacting Gender on the Renaissance Stage.* Urbana: University of Illinois Press, 1999.

Conti, Natali [Natalis Comes]. *Mythologiae.* 1551, 1567. London: Garland, 1976.

Cook, Carol. "'The Sign and Semblance of Her Honor': Reading Gender Difference in *Much Ado About Nothing.*" *PMLA* 101 (1986): 186–202.

Coppe, Abiezer [Richard Coppin]. *Some Sweet Sips, of Some Spirituall Wine.* London, 1649.

Cotton, John. *A Brief Exposition of the Whole Book of Canticles.* London, 1642.

Covarrubias, Sebastián de. *Tesoro de la Lengua Castellana.* 1611. Madrid: D. L. Turner, 1979.

Crewe, Jonathan. *Trials of Authorship: Anterior Forms and Poetic Reconstruction from Wyatt to Shakespeare.* Berkeley: University of California Press, 1990.

Croly, David G. *Miscegenation: The Theory of the Blending of the Races, Applied to the American White Man and Negro.* 1863. Upper Saddle River, N.J.: Literature House, 1970.

Crooke, Helkiah. *ΜΙΚΡΟΚΟΣΜΟΓΡΑΦΙΑ [Microcosmographia]: A Description of the Body of Man.* London, 1615.

Cross, F. L., and E. A. Livingstone, eds. *The Oxford Dictionary of the Christian Church.* 3rd ed. 6 vols. Oxford: Oxford University Press, 1997.

Culpeper, Nicholas. *The Compleat Practice of Physick.* London: 1655.

Cummins, Alissandra. "Caribbean Slave Society." In Tibbles, *Transatlantic Slavery,* 51–59.

Cunningham, Bernadette. *The World of Geoffrey Keating.* Bodmin, UK: Four Courts, 2000.

Cuvier, Georges. *Tableau élémentaire de l'histoire naturelle des animaux.* Paris: Baudouin, 1798.

Dabydeen, David, ed. *The Black Presence in English Literature.* Manchester: Manchester University Press, 1985.

Davies, Sir John. "*Nosce Teipsum*: A Critical Edition." 1599. Ed. Clarence Simpson. Ph.D. diss., Stanford University, 1951.

Davis, John F. *Heresy and Reformation in the South-east of England, 1520–1559.* London: Royal Historical Society, 1983.

Dawson, Anthony B. "Much Ado About Signifying." *SEL* 22 (1982): 211–21.

Dekker, Thomas. *Lanthorn and Candlelight.* 1608. London, 1620.

Dekker, Thomas, and Thomas Middleton. *The Magnificent Entertainment.* 1604. In *The Dramatic Works of Thomas Dekker,* 4 vols., ed. Fredson Bowers, 2:229–310. Cambridge: Cambridge University Press, 1953–61.

De Grazia, Margreta. "The Scandal of Shakespeare's Sonnets." *Shakespeare Survey* 46 (1994): 35–49.

Derricke, John. *The Image of Irelande: With a Disoverie of Woodkarne.* London, 1581. Introd. David B. Quinn. Belfast: Blackstaff Press, 1985.

Derrida, Jacques. *Of Grammatology* (*De la grammatologie*. 1967). Trans. Gayatri Chakravorty Spivak. 1976. Baltimore: John Hopkins University Press, 1990.

Di Cesare, Mario A., ed. *George Herbert and the Seventeenth-Century Religious Poets.* New York: Norton, 1978.

Dilke, O. A. W. "Heliodorus and the Colour Problem." *Parola del Passato* 193 (1980): 264–71.

Doebler, John. "The Reluctant Adonis: Titian and Shakespeare." *Shakespeare Quarterly* 33 (1982): 480–90.

Dolan, Frances. "Taking the Pencil out of God's Hand." *PMLA* 108 (1993): 224–39.

Dollimore, Jonathan. "Bisexuality, Heterosexuality, and Wishful Theory." *Textual Practice* 10 (1996): 523–39.

Donnan, Elizabeth, ed. *1441–1700.* Vol. 1 of *Documents Illustrative of the History of the Slave Trade to America.* Washington, D.C.: Carnegie Institution, 1930.

Donne, John. "The Extasie," "The Will," "Aire and Angells." In *Donne: Poetical Works,* ed. Herbert J. C. Grierson. 1929. Reprint, Oxford: Oxford University Press, 1987.

———. "Paradox II: That Women Ought to Paint." In *Iuvenilia, or Certaine Paradoxes, or Problemes.* London, 1633.

———. *The Sermons of John Donne.* Ed. Theodore Gill. New York: Meridian, 1958.

Donno, Elizabeth Story. *Elizabethan Minor Epics.* London: Routledge, 1963.

Dove, John. *The Conversion of Salomon.* London, 1613.

Drakakis, John, ed. *"Antony and Cleopatra": A New Casebook.* London: St. Martin's, 1994.

———. "Trust and Transgression: The Discursive Practices of *Much Ado About Nothing.*" In *Post-Structuralist Readings of English Poetry,* ed. Richard Machin and Christopher Norris, 59–84. Cambridge: Cambridge University Press, 1987.

Drayton, Michael. *The Legend of Piers Gaveston.* London, 1595.

———. "The Most Excellent Song which was Salomons." *The Harmony of the Church.* 1591. Ed. Alexander Dyce. *Early English Poetry,* 7:15–29. London: Percy Society, 1843.

Drees, Clayton J. *Authority and Dissent in the English Church.* Lewiston, N.Y.: Mellen, 1997.

Drew-Bear, Annette. *Painted Faces on the Renaissance Stage.* Lewisburg, Pa.: Bucknell University Press, 1994.

Du Bartas, Guillaume de Salluste. *Du Bartas His Devine Weekes and Works.* [*La Sepmaine; ou, Creation du monde.* 1578. *La Seconde Sepmaine.* 1584]. Trans. Joshua Sylvester. London, 1605. Reprint, Gainesville, Fla.: Scholars' Facsimiles and Reprints, 1965.

Du Bois, W. E. B. *The Souls of Black Folk.* 1903. New York: Signet, 1995.

Dubrow, Heather. *Echoes of Desire: English Petrarchism and Its Counterdiscourses.* Ithaca, N.Y.: Cornell University Press, 1995.

———. "'Upon Misprision Growing': *Venus and Adonis.*" *Captive Victors: Shakespeare's Narrative Poems and Sonnets.* Ithaca, N.Y.: Cornell University Press, 1987. Reprinted in Kolin, *"Venus and Adonis,"* 223–46.

Duncan-Jones, Katherine. "Much Ado with Red and White: The Earliest Readers of Shakespeare's *Venus and Adonis* (1593)." *Review of English Studies,* n.s. 44, 176 (1993): 479–501.

Dusinberre, Juliet. "Squeaking Cleopatras: Gender and Performance in *Antony and Cleopatra.*" In *Shakespeare, Theory and Performance,* ed. James C. Bulman, 46–67. London: Routledge, 1996.

Dyer, Richard. "White." *Screen* 29, 4 (1988): 44–64.

Eccles, Audrey. *Obstetrics and Gynaecology in Tudor and Stuart England.* Kent, Oh.: Kent State University Press, 1982.

Edwards, Paul. *The Early African Presence in the British Isles.* Edinburgh: Centre for African Studies, 1990.

Edwards, Thomas. *Cephalus and Procris, with Narcissus.* 1595. Ed. W. E. Buckley. London: Roxburghe Club/Nichols, 1882.

Egger, Brigitte. "The Role of Women in the Greek Novel: Woman as Heroine and Reader." In Swain, *Oxford Readings,* 108–36.

Elias, Norbert. *The History of Manners.* Vol. 1 of *The Civilizing Process.* Trans. Edmund Jephcott. New York: Urizen, 1978.

Elyot, Sir Thomas. *The Castel of Helthe.* [N.p.], 1539.

Engels, Frederick. "The Part Played By Labor in the Transition from Ape to Man." Marx-Engels Library. http://csf.colorado.edu/psn/marx/Archive/1876–Hands/ (accessed January 11, 2004).

English Poetry Database. Chadwyck-Healey. Literature Online. Stanford Academic Text Service, Stanford University. http://lion.chadwyck.com.

Erasmus, Desiderius. *The Collected Works of Erasmus.* Vol. 61. *Patristic Scholarship: The Edition of St. Jerome.* of Ed. James F. Brady and John C. Olin. Toronto: University of Toronto Press, 1992.

———, trans. "Homiliæ duæ Origenis a Hieronymo versæ." *Divi Eusebii Hieronymii Stridonensis, Opera Omnia.* Vol. 3. Paris, 1534.

Erickson, Peter. "The Moment of Race in Renaissance Studies." In Barroll, "Forum," 27–36.

———. "Representations of Blacks and Blackness in the Renaissance." *Criticism* 35 (1993): 499–528.

Erickson, Peter, and Clark Hulse, eds. *Early Modern Visual Culture: Representation, Race, and Empire in Renaissance England.* Philadelphia: University of Pennsylvania Press, 2000.

Euripides. "Andromeda." *Fragments.* Ed. and trans. François Jouan and Herman Van Looy, 1:147–90. Paris: Belles Lettres/Universités de France/Budé, 1998.

Falk, Marcia. *The Song of Songs: A New Translation and Interpretation.* San Francisco: HarperSanFrancisco/HarperCollins, 1990.

Fanon, Frantz. *Black Skin, White Masks.* Trans. Charles Lam Markmann. New York: Grove, 1967.

Farrell, Kirby, Elizabeth H. Hageman and Arthur F. Kinney, eds. *Women in the Renaissance: Selections from English Literary Renaissance.* Amherst, Mass.: AMS, 1990.

Fenner, Dudley. *The Song of Songs . . . translated out of Hebrue into Englishe meeter.* Middelburgh, 1587.

Ferguson, Margaret W. "Juggling the Categories of Race, Class, and Gender: Aphra Behn's *Oronooko.*" In Hendricks and Parker, *Women, "Race," and Writing,* 209–24.

Ferguson, Moira. "'A Wise, Wittie and Learned Ladie': Margaret Lucas Cavendish." In *Women Writers of the Seventeenth Century,* ed. Katharina Wilson and Frank J. Warnke, 305–18. Athens: University of Georgia Press, 1989.

Finch, Sir Henry. *An Exposition of the Song of Solomon, Called Canticles.* London, 1615.

Fineman, Joel. *Shakespeare's Perjur'd Eye.* Berkeley: University of California Press, 1986.

"The First Voyage of . . . Sir Iohn Hawkins . . . made to the West Indies 1562." In Hakluyt, *Principal Navigations,* 10:7–9.

Firth, C. J., ed. *Memoirs of the Duke of Newcastle.* London: Routledge, 1898.

Fisher, F. J. *London and the English Economy, 1500–1700*. London: Hambledon, 1990.

Fitzmaurice, James. "Fancy and the Family: Self-Characterizations of Margaret Cavendish." *Huntington Library Quarterly* 53 (1990): 199–209.

Fletcher, John. *The Woman's Prize, or The Tamer Tamed*. Vol. 4 of *The Dramatic Works in the Beaumont and Fletcher Canon*. Ed. Fredson Bowers. 10 vols. Cambridge: Cambridge University Press, 1966–96.

Flinker, Noam. *The Song of Songs in English Renaissance Literature: Kisses of Their Mouths*. Ed. John T. Shawcross. Studies in Renaissance Literature 3. Cambridge: Brewer, 2000.

Floyd-Wilson, Mary. "'Clime, Complexion, and Degree': Racialism in Early Modern England." Ph.D. diss., University of North Carolina, 1996.

———. *English Ethnicity and Race in Early Modern Drama*. Cambridge: Cambridge University Press, 2003.

———. "Temperature, Temperance, and Racial Difference in Ben Jonson's *The Masque of Blackness*." *ELR* 28 (1998): 183–209.

———. "Transmigrations: Crossing Regional and Gender Boundaries in *Antony and Cleopatra*." In Comensoli and Russell, *Enacting Gender*, 73–96.

Fonseca, Isabel. *Bury Me Standing: The Gypsies and Their Journey*. New York: Vintage, 1995.

Fowler, Alastair. *Kinds of Literature: An Introduction to the Theory of Genres and Modes*. Cambridge, Mass.: Harvard University Press, 1982.

Fradenburg, Louise Olga. *City, Marriage, Tournament*. Madison: University of Wisconsin Press, 1991.

Fraser, Peter D. "Slaves or Free People? The Status of Africans in England, 1550–1750." In *From Strangers to Citizens: The Integration of Immigrant Communities in Britain, Ireland, and Colonial America, 1550–1750*, ed. Randolph Vigne and Charles Littleton, 254–60. Brighton: Huguenot Society/Sussex Academic Press, 2001.

Fraunce, Abraham. *The Countess of Pembroke's Ivychurch*. London, 1592.

Freer, Coburn. "John Donne and Elizabethan Economic Theory." *Criticism* 38 (1996): 497–520.

Fryer, Peter. *Staying Power*. London: Pluto, 1984.

Fuchs, Barbara. *Mimesis and Empire: The New World, Islam, and European Identities*. Cambridge: Cambridge University Press, 2001.

Fuller, Mary C. "Ralegh's Fugitive Gold: Reference and Deferral in *The Discoverie of Guiana*." In Greenblatt, *The New World*, 42–64.

Fusillo, Massimo. "The Conflict of Emotions: A *Topos* in the Greek Novel." In Swain, *Oxford Readings*, 60–82.

Galileo [Galileo Galilei]. *The Starry Messenger* [*Sidereus Nuncius*]. 1610. In *Discoveries and Opinions of Galileo*, trans. Stillman Drake. 1957. Reprint, New York: Anchor, 1989. 20–58.

Gallagher, Catherine. "Embracing the Absolute: The Politics of the Female Subject in Seventeenth-Century England." *Genders* 1 (1988): 24–29.

Garner, Shirley Nelson. "'Let Her Paint an Inch Thick': Painted Ladies in Renaissance Drama and Society." *Renaissance Drama* n.s. 20 (1989): 123–39.

Gascoigne, George. "In Praise of a gentlewoman who though she were not verye fayre, yet was she as harde favoured as might be." *A Hundreth Sundrie Flowres*. 1573. Ed. Ruth Loyd Miller, et al., 150–51. Port Washington, N.Y.: Kennikat, 1975.

Gates, Henry Louis. *The Signifying Monkey: A Theory of Afro-American Literary Criticism*. Oxford: Oxford University Press, 1988.

Gerzina, Gretchen. *Black London: Life Before Emancipation.* London: John Murray, 1995.

Gesta Grayorum. 1688. Ed. W. W. Greg. Oxford: Malone Society/Oxford University Press, 1914.

Giantvalley, Scott. "Barnfield, Drayton, and Marlowe: Homoeroticism and Homosexuality in Elizabethan Literature." *Pacific Coast Philology* 16, 2 (1981): 9–24.

Gillies, John. *Shakespeare and the Geography of Difference.* Cambridge: Cambridge University Press, 1994.

———. "Shakespeare's Virginian Masque." *ELH* 53 (1986): 673–707.

Gleach, Frederic W. *Powhatan's World and Colonial Virginia: A Conflict of Cultures.* Lincoln: University of Nebraska Press, 1997.

Goddard, Hugh. *A History of Christian-Muslim Relations.* Edinburgh: Edinburgh University Press, 2000; Chicago: New Amsterdam, 2000.

Goldberg, Dena. "'By Report': The Spectator as Voyeur in Webster's *The White Devil.*" *ELR* 17 (1987): 67–84.

Goldberg, Jonathan. *Sodometries: Renaissance Texts, Modern Sexualities.* Stanford, Calif.: Stanford University Press, 1992.

Gordon, D. J. "Chapman's *Memorable Masque.*" In *The Renaissance Imagination,* ed. Stephen Orgel, 194–202. Berkeley: University of California Press, 1975.

Gosson, Stephen. *A Glasse, to View the Pride of Vaineglorious Women.* London, 1595.

———. *The Schoole of Abuse.* London, 1597.

Gosynhill, Edward. *Mulierum Paean.* 1542. London, 1560.

Gouge, William. *An Exposition of the Song of Solomon, Called "Canticles."* London, 1615.

Gough, John. *The Strange Discovery.* London, 1640.

Gould, Stephen Jay. *The Mismeasure of Man.* Rev. ed. New York: Norton, 1996.

Grant, Douglas. *Margaret the First.* London: Rupert Hart-Davis, 1957.

Graves, Peter, trans. "The Danish Account of the Marriage of James VI and Anne of Denmark." In David Stevenson, *Scotland's Last Royal Wedding,* 79–122.

Great Britain, Privy Council. *Acts of the Privy Council of England.* New ser, vol. 26. *1596–97.* Ed. John Roche Dasent. London: HMSO/Mackie, 1902.

Great Britain, Public Record Office. *Calendar of State Papers, Colonial Series.* Vol. 1. *1574–1660.* Ed. W. Noël Sainsbury. London: Longman, 1860.

Great Britain, Public Record Office. *Calendar of State Papers, Domestic Series.* Vol. 4. *Elizabeth, 1595–1597.* Ed. Mary Anne Everett Green. London: Longmans, 1869.

Great Britain, Public Record Office. *Calendar of State Papers, Domestic Series.* Vol. 5. *Elizabeth, 1598–1601.* Ed. Mary Anne Everett Green. London: Longmans, 1869.

Great Britain, Sovereign. *Tudor Royal Proclamations.* Ed. Paul L. Hughes and James F. Larkin. Vol. 3. New Haven, Conn.: Yale University Press, 1969.

Great Britain, Statutes and Laws. *The Statutes of the Realm.* London: Dawsons, 1810–28. Facsimile reprint, London: Record Commission, 1963.

Great Britain. Statutes and Laws. *Anno Quinto Reginæ Elizabethe. At the Parliament holden at Westmynster the xii. of January.* London, 1562.

Greenblatt, Stephen. "Mutilation and Meaning." In Hillman and Mazzio, *Body in Parts,* 221–41.

———, ed. *The New World: Essays in Memory of Michel de Certeau. Representations* 33.

———. *Renaissance Self-Fashioning from More to Shakespeare.* Chicago: University of Chicago Press, 1980.

Greenslade, S. L. "English Versions of the Bible, 1525–1611." In Greenslade, *The West from the Reformation,* 141–74.

————, ed. *The West from the Reformation to the Present Day.* Vol. 3 of *The Cambridge History of the Bible.* Cambridge: Cambridge University Press, 1963.

Griffin, Bartholomew. *Fidessa.* London, 1596.

Guild, William. *Loves Entercours.* London, 1658.

Guillemeau, Jacques. *The Happy Delivery of Women.* London, 1635.

Guilpin, Everard [Edward Guilpin]. *Skialetheia, Or A Shadowe of Truth, in Certaine Epigrams and Satyres.* 1598. Ed. D. Allen Carroll. Chapel Hill: University of North Carolina Press, 1974.

Guinier, Lani, and Gerald Torres. *The Miner's Canary: Enlisting Race, Resisting Power, Transforming Democracy.* Cambridge, Mass.: Harvard University Press, 2002.

Gyffard, George. *Sermons upon the Song of Salomon.* London, 1610.

Habib, Imtiaz. *Shakespeare and Race: Postcolonial Praxis in the Early Modern Period.* Lanham, Md.: University Press of America, 1999.

Hadfield, Andrew. *Edmund Spenser's Irish Experience: Wilde Fruit and Salvage Soyl.* Oxford: Clarendon Press, 1997.

————. "English Colonialism and National Identity in Early Modern Ireland." *Eire-Ireland* 28, 1 (1993): 69–86.

————. "Race in *Othello: The History and Description of Africa* and the Black Legend." *Notes and Queries* 45.3/243 (1998): 336–38.

Häg, Thomas. *The Novel in Antiquity.* Berkeley: University of California Press, 1983.

Hakluyt, Richard, ed. *The Principal Navigations, Voyages, Traffiques and Discoveries of the English Nation.* 3 vols. London, 1598–1600. Reprint, Glasgow: Mac-Lehose, 1903–1905. 12 vols.

Hall, Basil. "Biblical Scholarship: Editions and Commentaries." In Greenslade, *The West from the Reformation,* 37–93.

Hall, Christopher. "The First Voyage of M. Martine Frobisher, to the Northwest . . . made in the yeere of our Lord 1576." In Hakluyt, *Principal Navigations,* 7:204–11.

Hall, Joseph. *Salmon's Divine Arts, With the Song of Songs Paraphrased.* London, 1609.

Hall, Kim F. "Beauty and the Beast of Whiteness: Teaching Race and Gender." *Shakespeare Quarterly* 47 (1996): 461–75.

————. "Sexual Politics and Cultural Identity in *The Masque of Blackness.*" In *The Performance of Power: Theatrical Discourse and Politics,* ed. Sue-Ellen Case, 3–18. Iowa City: University of Iowa Press, 1991.

————. *Things of Darkness: Economies of Race and Gender in Early Modern England.* Ithaca, N.Y.: Cornell University Press, 1996.

————. "'Troubling Doubles': Apes, Africans, and Blackface in *Mr. Moores Revels.*" In MacDonald, *Race, Ethnicity, and Power,* 120–44.

Hall, Stuart. "New Ethnicities." In Baker, Diawara, Lindenborg, *Black British Cultural Studies,* 163–72.

Hallam, Henry. *The Constitutional History of England, from the Accession of Henry VII, to the Death of George II.* London: Murray, 1884.

Halpern, Richard. "'Pining their Maws': Female Readers and the Erotic Ontology of the Text in Shakespeare's *Venus and Adonis.*" In Kolin, "*Venus and Adonis*", 377–88.

Hammond, Gerald. *The Making of the English Bible.* Manchester: Carcanet, 1982.

Harbage, Alfred, and Samuel Schoenbaum. *Annals of English Drama.* London: Routledge, 1989.

Hargreaves, Henry. "The Wycliffite Versions." In Lampe, *The West from the Fathers,* 387–415.

Harman, Thomas. *A Caveat or Warening, for Commen Cursetors.* London, 1567.

Hawkins, John. "The third troublesome voyage . . . to the parts of Guinea, and the West Indies, in the yeeres 1567 and 1568." In Hakluyt, *Principal Navigations,* 10:64–74.

Hawthorne, Nathaniel. "The Birth-mark." 1846. In *The Complete Novels and Selected Tales of Nathaniel Hawthorne,* ed. Norman Holmes Pearson, 1021–33. New York: Random House, 1937. University of Virginia Library Electronic Text Center, 1999. http://etext.lib.virginia.edu/toc/modeng/public/HawBirt. html (accessed December 31, 2003).

Hays, Janice. "Those 'Soft and Delicate Desires': *Much Ado* and the Distrust of Women." In Lenz, Greene, and Neely, *Woman's Part,* 79–99.

Heffernan, Carol Falvo. *The Melancholy Muse: Chaucer, Shakespeare, and Early Medicine.* Pittsburgh: Duquesne University Press, 1995.

Heiserman, Arthur. *The Novel Before the Novel: Essays and Discussions about the Beginnings of Prose Fiction in the West.* Chicago: University of Chicago Press, 1977.

Heliodorus [Heliodorus of Emesa]. *Héliodore: Les Ethiopiques.* Ed. R. M. Rattenbury and T. W. Lumb and trans. J. Maillon. 3 vols. Paris: Les Belles Lettres, 1935.

———. *Histoire Aethiopique.* Trans. Jacques Amyot. Paris, 1559.

———. *An Ethiopian Romance.* Trans. and introd. Moses Hadas. Ann Arbor: University of Michigan Press, 1957. Reprint, Philadelphia: University of Pennsylvania Press, 1997.

———. *Aethiopian Story.* Trans. Sir Walter Lamb. 1961. Ed. and introd. J. R. Morgan. London: Dent, 1997.

———. *An Ethiopian Story.* Trans. J. R. Morgan. In *Collected Ancient Greek Novels,* ed. B. P. Reardon, 349–588. Berkeley: University of California Press, 1989.

———. *An Æthiopian History.* Trans. Thomas Underdowne. London, 1569.

———. *Heliodori Aethiopicae Historiae.* Trans. Stanislao Warschewiczki [Stanislaw Warschewiczi]. Basel, 1552.

———. *An Æthiopian History.* Ed. and introd. Charles Whibley. Trans. Thomas Underdowne. London: Nutt, 1895.

Henderson, Katherine, and Barbara F. McManus, eds. *Half Humankind: Contexts and Texts of the Controversy About Women in England, 1540–1640.* Urbana: University of Illinois Press, 1985.

Hendricks, Margo. "'The Moor of Venice,' or the Italian on the Renaissance English Stage." In *Shakespearean Tragedy and Gender,* ed. Shirley Nelson Garner and Madelon Sprengnether, 193–209. Bloomington: Indiana University Press, 1996.

———. "'Obscured by Dreams': Race, Empire, and Shakespeare's *A Midsummer Night's Dream.*" *Shakespeare Quarterly* 47 (1996): 37–60.

Hendricks, Margo, and Patricia Parker, eds. *Women, "Race," and Writing in the Early Modern Period.* London: Routledge, 1994.

Herbert, Edward, Baron of Cherbury [Lord Herbert of Cherbury]. *Occasional Verses.* Ed. Henry Herbert. London, 1665.

———. *Poems of Lord Herbert of Cherbury.* Ed. John Churton Collins. London: Chatto, 1881.

Herbert, George. "The British Church." In Di Cesare, *George Herbert,* 44–45.

Herford, C. H., Percy Simpson, and Evelyn Simpson, eds. *Jonson's Works.* Oxford: Clarendon, 1952.

Heywood, Thomas. *The Faire Maide of the Exchange.* 1607. *The Dramatic Works of Thomas Heywood.* 1874. Reprint, New York: Russell & Russell, 1964. 2:1–87.

———. *Oenone and Paris*. 1594. In Donno, *Elizabethan Minor Epic*, 127–54.

Hic Mulier, or, The Man-Woman. London, 1620.

Hill, Christopher. *The English Bible and the Seventeenth-Century Revolution*. London: Penguin/Allen Lane, 1993.

Hillebrand, Hans J., ed. *The Oxford Encylopedia of the Reformation*. 4 vols. Oxford: Oxford University Press, 1996.

Hillman, David, and Carla Mazzio, eds. *The Body in Parts: Fantasies of Corporeality in Early Modern Europe*. New York: Routledge, 1997.

Hilton, John. "An Ethiopian Paradox: Heliodorus, *Aithiopika* 4.8." In Hunter, *Studies in Heliodorus*, 79–92.

Hintz, Carrie. "'But One Opinion': Fear of Dissent in Cavendish's *New Blazing World*." *Utopian Studies* 7 (1996): 25–37.

Hippocrates. "Airs, Waters, Places." *Hippocratic Writings*. Ed. G. E. R. Lloyd. Trans. J. Chadwick and W. N. Mann, 148–69. Harmondsworth: Penguin, 1983.

The Historie and Life of King James the Sext. Edinburgh: Bannatyne Club, 1825.

Hobby, Elaine. *Virtue of Necessity: English Women's Writing 1649–88*. Ann Arbor: University of Michigan Press, 1989.

Holinshed, Raphael, and John Hooker, eds. *The First and Second Volumes of Chronicles*. London, 1586.

Hollar, Wenceslas. *Ornatus Muliebris Anglicanus, or, The Severall Habits of English Women from the Nobilitie to the Contry Woman, as they are in these times*. London, 1640.

Homes, Nathanael. "A Commentary Literal or Historical and Mystical or Spiritual, on the whole book of Canticles." *Works*. London, 1652.

Hooke, Robert. *Micrographia*. 1665. Reprint, Lincolnwood: Science Heritage, 1987.

hooks, bell [Gloria Watkins]. *Black Looks: Race and Representation*. Boston: South End, 1992.

Howard, Jean E. "An English Lass amid the Moors: Gender, Race, Sexuality, and National Identity in Heywood's *The Fair Maid of the West*." In Hendricks and Parker, *Women, "Race," and Writing*, 101–17.

———. "Renaissance Antitheatricality and the Politics of Rank and Gender in *Much Ado About Nothing*." In *Shakespeare Reproduced*, ed. Marion F. O'Connor, 163–87. New York: Methuen, 1987.

Huddlestone, Eugene L. "*The Spanish Gipsy* and 'La Gitanilla': An Unnoticed Borrowing." *Notes and Queries* 12 (1965): 103–4.

Hudson, H. H. "Penelope Devereux as Sidney's Stella." *Huntington Library Bulletin* 7 (1935): 93–95.

Hudson, Robert P. "The Biography of Disease: Lessons from Chlorosis." *Bulletin of the History of Medicine* 51 (1977): 448–63.

Hughes-Hallet, Lucy. *Cleopatra: Histories, Dreams, and Distortions*. New York: Harper, 1990.

Hulse, S. Clark. "Shakespeare's Myth of *Venus and Adonis*." *PMLA* 93 (1978): 95–105. Reprinted in Kolin, *"Venus and Adonis"*, 203–22.

Hunt, Maurice. "Slavery, English Servitude, and the *Comedy of Errors*." *ELR* 27 (1997): 31–56.

Hunter, G. K. *Othello and Colour Prejudice*. 1967. Proceedings of the British Academy 53. London: British Academy/Oxford University Press, 1968.

Hunter, Richard, ed. *Studies in Heliodorus*. Cambridge Philological Society, supplemental vol. 21. Cambridge: Cambridge Philological Society, 1998.

Huntington, John. "The Serious Trifle: Aphorisms in Chapman's *Hero and Leander*." *Studies in the Literary Imagination* 11 (1978): 107–13.

Hyginus. *Fabularum Liber.* 1535. London, 1608.

Hyland, Peter. "Boying Greatness: Shakespeare's Venus." *Upstart Crow* 18 (1998): 134–40.

In this Vol. are Conteyned the Statues, made and established from the time of Kinge Henrye The Thirde, until the first yeare of . . . King Henry the viii. London, 1577.

Jackson, Arthur. *Annotations upon the Five Books Immediately Following the Historicall Part of the Old Testament.* London, 1658.

Jankowski, Theodora A. *Women in Power in the Early Modern Drama.* Urbana: University of Illinois Press, 1992.

Jed, Stephanie H. *Chaste Thinking: The Rape of Lucretia and the Birth of Humanism.* Bloomington: Indiana University Press, 1989.

Jelinger, Christopher. *The Excellency of Christ, or the Rose of Sharon.* London, 1641.

———. *A New Canaan.* London, 1664.

Jobson, Richard. *The Golden Trade.* London, 1623.

Jones, Ann Rosalind. "Italians and Others: Venice and the Irish in *Coryat's Crudities* and *The White Devil.*" *Renaissance Drama* n.s. 18 (1987): 101–19.

Jones, Ann Rosalind, and Peter Stallybrass. "Dismantling Irena: The Sexualizing of Ireland in Early Modern England." In *Nationalisms and Sexualities,* ed. Andrew Parker, Mary Russo, Doris Sommer, and Patricia Yaeger, 157–74. New York: Routledge, 1992.

Jones, Eldred. *Othello's Countrymen.* London: Fourah Bay College, University College of Sierra Leone/Oxford University Press, 1965.

Jones, Kathleen. *A Glorious Fame.* London: Bloomsbury, 1988.

Jonson, Benjamin. *Workes.* 2 vols. London, 1616, 1640.

———. *Complete Masques.* Ed. Stephen Orgel. New Haven, Conn.: Yale University Press, 1969.

———. *Complete Plays of Ben Jonson.* Ed. G. A. Wilkes. Oxford: Clarendon Press, 1982.

Jordan, Winthrop. *White over Black.* Chapel Hill: Institute of Early American History and Culture/University of North Carolina Press, 1968.

The Joyfull Receiuing of Iames the Sixt of That Name King of Scotland, and Queene Anne his Wife, into the Townes of Lyeth and Edenborough. London, 1590.

Judges, A. V. *The Elizabethan Underworld.* London: Routledge, 1930.

Kamps, Ivo, and Jyotsna G. Singh, eds. *Travel Knowledge: European "Discoveries" in the Early Modern Period.* New York: Palgrave, 2001.

Kaplan, Sidney. "The Miscegenation Issue in the Election of 1864." *Journal of Negro History* 34, 3 (1949): 274–343.

Keating, Jeoffry [Seathrún Céitinn]. *The General History of Ireland* [*Foras Feasa ar Éirinn*]. Trans. Dermo'd O'Connor. Dublin, 1723.

Kegl, Rosemary. "'This World I have made': Margaret Cavendish, Feminism, and *The Blazing World.*" In *Feminist Readings of Early Modern Culture: Emerging Subjects,* ed. Valerie Traub, M. Lindsay Kaplan and Dympna Callaghan, 119–41. Cambridge: Cambridge University Press, 1996.

Keller, Eve. "Producing Petty Gods: Margaret Cavendish's Critique of Experimental Science." *ELH* 64 (1997): 447–71.

Kelly, Ann Cline. "The Challenge of the Impossible: Ben Jonson's 'Masque of Blackness.'" *College Language Association Journal* 20 (1977): 341–55.

Khanna, Lee Cullen. "The Subject of Utopia: Margaret Cavendish and Her *Blazing World.*" In *Utopian and Science Fiction by Women: Worlds of Difference,* ed. Jane L. Donawerth and Carol A. Komerten, 15–34. Syracuse, N.Y.: Syracuse University Press, 1994.

Kitcher, Philip. *The Lives to Come: The Genetic Revolution and Human Possibilities.* New York: Simon and Schuster, 1996.

K[nevet], R[alph]. *The Canticles or Song of Songs, reduced unto a Decasyllable.* London, 1662.

Knight, Francis. *A Relation of Seaven Yeares Slaverie Vnder the Turkes of Argeire.* London, 1640.

Kolin, Philip C., ed. *"Venus and Adonis": Critical Essays.* New York: Garland, 1997.

Krier, Theresa M. "Sappho's Apples: The Allusiveness of Blushes in Ovid and Beaumont." *Comparative Literature Studies* 25 (1988): 1–22.

Kupperman, Karen Ordahl. *Indians and English: Facing Off in Early America.* Ithaca, N.Y.: Cornell University Press, 2000.

Lal, Chaman. *Gypsies: Forgotten Children of India.* Delhi: Ministry of Information and Broadcasting, 1962.

Lamb, Margaret. *"Antony and Cleopatra" on the English Stage.* Rutherford: Fairleigh Dickinson University Press, 1980.

Lampe, G. W. H., ed. *The West from the Fathers to the Reformation.* Vol. 2 of *The Cambridge History of the Bible.* Cambridge: Cambridge University Press, 1969.

Lange, Johann. "De Morbo Virgineo." 1554. *Epistolarum Medicinalium.* Hanover, 1605. 89–93. Trans. Ralph H. Major. In *Classic Descriptions of Disease*, 3rd ed., 487–89. Springfield, Ill.: Thomas, 1945.

Lanier, Emilia. *Salve Deus Rex Judaeorum.* London, 1611.

La Peyrère, Isaac de. *Men Before Adam.* London, 1656.

Laqueur, Thomas. *Making Sex: Body and Gender from the Greeks to Freud.* Cambridge, Mass.: Harvard University Press, 1990.

Laroque, François. *Shakespeare's Festive World.* Cambridge: Cambridge University Press, 1993.

Lauber, Almon. *Indian Slavery in Colonial Times Within the Present Limits of the United States.* New York: Columbia University, 1913.

Lefkowitz, Mary, and Guy MacLean Rogers, eds. *Black Athena Revisited.* Chapel Hill: University of North Carolina Press, 1996.

Legh, Gerard. *The Accedence of Armorie.* London, 1562.

Leigh, Edward. *Annotations on Five Poetical Books of the Old Testament.* London, 1657.

Lenz, Carolyn Ruth Swift, Gayle Greene, and Carol Thomas Neely, eds. *The Woman's Part: Feminist Criticism of Shakespeare.* Urbana: University of Illinois Press, 1980.

Leslie, Marina. "Evading Rape and Embracing Empire in Margaret Cavendish's *Assaulted and Pursued Chastity.*" In *Menacing Virgins: Representing Virginity in the Middle Ages and Renaissance*, ed. Kathleen Coyne Kelly and Marina Leslie, 179–97. Newark and London: University of Delaware Press/Associated University Presses, 1999.

———. *Renaissance Utopias and the Problem of History.* Ithaca, N.Y.: Cornell University Press, 1998.

Levin, Carole, and Karen Robertson, eds. *Sexuality and Politics in Renaissance Drama.* Lewiston, N.Y.: Mellen, 1991.

Levinz, Creswell. *Reports of Cases Heard and Determined in the Court of King's Bench.* Trans. William Salkeld. London, 1722.

Lewalski, Barbara. "Hero's Name—and Namesake—in *Much Ado About Nothing.*" *English Language Notes* 7 (1970): 175–79.

———. "Love, Appearance, and Reality: Much Ado About Something." *SEL* 8 (1968): 235–51.

———. *Protestant Poetics and the Seventeenth-Century Religious Lyric.* Princeton, N.J.: Princeton University Press, 1979.

———. *Writing Women in Jacobean England.* Cambridge, Mass.: Harvard University Press, 1993.

Liddell-Scott-Jones Lexicon of Classical Greek. Perseus 2.0. http://www.perseus.tufts.edu/ (accessed March 20, 1998).

Lindley, David. "Courtly Play: The Politics of Chapman's *The Memorable Masque.*" In *The Stuart Courts,* ed. Eveline Cruickshanks, 43–58. Stroud: Sutton, 2000.

———. "Embarrassing Ben: The Masques for Frances Howard." *ELR* 16 (1986): 343–59.

———. *Thomas Campion.* Medieval and Renaissance Authors. Leiden: Brill, 1986.

Lisle, William [William L'isle]. *The Faire Ethiopian.* London, 1631.

Little, Arthur L., Jr. *Shakespeare Jungle Fever: National-Imperial Re-Visions of Race, Rape and Sacrifice.* Stanford, Calif.: Stanford University Press, 2000.

Lockyer, Roger. *James VI and I.* London: Longman, 1998.

Lok, John. "The second voyage to Guinea . . . in the yere 1554." In Hakluyt, *Principal Navigations,* 6: 154–77.

Lomazzo, Paolo. *A Tracte Containing the Artes of Curious Painting.* Trans. R[ichard] H[aydocke]. London, 1598.

Loomba, Ania. "The Color of Patriarchy: Critical Difference, Cultural Difference and Renaissance Drama." In Hendricks and Parker, *Women, "Race," and Writing,* 17–34.

———. "'Delicious Traffick': Alterity and Exchange on Early Modern Stages." *Shakespeare Survey* 52 (1999): 201–14.

———. *Gender, Race, Renaissance Drama.* Manchester: Manchester University Press, 1989.

———. "'Local Manufacture Made-in-India Othello Fellows': Issues of Race, Hybridity and Location in Post-Colonial Shakespeares." In *Post-Colonial Shakespeares,* ed. Ania Loomba and Martin Orkin, 143–63. London: Routledge, 1998.

Loughlin, Marie H. "'Love's Friend and Stranger to Virginitie': The Politics of the Virginal Body in Ben Jonson's *Hymenaei* and Thomas Campion's *The Lord Hay's Masque.*" *ELH* 63 (1996): 833–49.

Lopez, Odoardo. *A Report of the Kingdome of Congo.* Trans. Abraham Hartwell. 1597. Amsterdam: Da Capo, 1970.

Lowenstein, Joseph. *Responsive Readings: Versions of Echo in Pastoral, Epic, and the Jonsonian Masque.* New Haven, Conn.: Yale University Press, 1984.

Lucan, M. Annæus. *Pharsalia.* Trans. Sir Arthur Gorges. London, 1614.

Lupton, Julia Reinhard. "Othello Circumcised: Shakespeare and the Pauline Discourse of Nations." *Representations* 57 (1997): 73–89.

Lupton, Lewis. *History of the Geneva Bible.* 24 vols. London: Fauconberg, 1966–.

Luther, Martin. *In Cantica Canticorum, breuis, sed admodum dilucida enarratio.* Wittenberg, 1539.

Lyons, Charles R. "The Serpent, the Sun, and 'Nilus Slime': A Focal Point for the Ambiguity of Shakespeare's *Antony and Cleopatra.*" *Rivista di letterature moderne e comparate* 21 (1968): 13–34.

Mac Craith, Mícheál. "Gaelic Ireland and the Renaissance." In *The Celts and the Renaissance,* ed. Glannor Williams and Robert Owen Jones, 57–89. Cardiff: University of Wales Press, 1990.

MacDonald, Joyce Green. "'The Force of Imagination': The Subject of Blackness in Shakespeare, Jonson, and Ravenscroft." In *Renaissance Papers: Selected Papers from the Southeastern Renaissance Conference,* ed. George Walton Williams and Barbara J. Baines, 53–74. [N.p.]: Southeastern Renaissance Conference, 1992.

———, ed. *Race, Ethnicity, and Power in the Renaissance.* London: Associated University Presses, 1997.

———. "Sex, Race, and Empire in Shakespeare's *Antony and Cleopatra.*" In "Historicizing Shakespeare," ed. Alan Armstrong. Special issue, *Literature and History* 3rd ser. 5 (1996): 60–77.

Maclean, Ian. *The Renaissance Notion of Woman: A Study in the Fortunes of Scholasticism and Medical Science in European Intellectual Life.* Cambridge: Cambridge University Press, 1980.

Madelaine, R. E. R. "Oranges and Lemans: *Much Ado About Nothing,* IV, i, 31." *Shakespeare Quarterly* 33 (1982): 491–92.

Maley, Willy. "How Milton and Some Contemporaries Read Spenser's *View.*" In Bradshaw, Hadfield, and Maley, *Representing Ireland,* 191–208.

———. "Spenser's Irish English: Language and Identity in Early Modern Ireland." *Studies in Philology* 91 (1994): 417–31.

Mandeville, Sir John. *The Voyages and Trauailes of Sir John Mandeuile Knight.* London: [1582].

Manning, Patrick. "The Impact of the Slave Trade on the Societies of West and Central Africa." In Tibbles, *Transatlantic Slavery,* 97–104.

Mannix, Daniel P., and Malcolm Cowley. *Black Cargoes.* New York: Viking, 1962.

Markham, Gervase. *The Poem of Poems, or, Sions Muse.* London, 1596.

Marlowe, Christopher. *Complete Poems of Christopher Marlowe.* Ed. Roma Gill. Vol. 1. Oxford: Oxford University Press, 1987.

———. *Doctor Faustus.* 1604. Ed. Michael Keefer. Peterborough: Broadview, 1991.

———. *Hero and Leander.* 1598. In Donno, *Elizabethan Minor Epic,* 48–69.

———. *Marlowe's Poems.* Ed. L. C. Martin. Vol. 4 of *The Life and Works of Christopher Marlowe.* New York: Gordian, 1966.

———. *The Poems of Christopher Marlowe.* Ed. Millar Maclure. London: Methuen, 1968.

Martz, Louis Lohr. *The Poetry of Meditation.* New Haven, Conn.: Yale University Press, 1954.

Marvell, Andrew. "To His Coy Mistress." In Di Cesare, *George Herbert,* 104–5.

Marx, Karl. *Capital.* 3 vols. Excerpted in *The Marx-Engels Reader.* Ed. Robert C. Tucker. 2nd ed. New York: Norton, 1978.

Mason, John. *The Turke: A Worthie Tragedie.* Ed. Joseph Q. Adams. Materialien zur Kunde des älteren Englischen Dramas, 1st ser. 37. Louvain: Uystpruyst, 1913. Reprint, Vaduz: Kraus, 1963.

Masten, Jeffrey, and Wendy Wall, eds. *Race in the Renaissance.* Special issue, *Renaissance Drama* 23 (1992).

Matar, Nabil I. *Turks, Moors and Englishmen in the Age of Discovery.* New York: Columbia University Press, 1999.

Matthews, Arthur Duncan, ed. "The White Ethiopian: A Critical Edition." Ph.D. diss., University of Florida, 1951.

Maus, Katharine Eisaman. "Horns of Dilemma: Jealousy, Gender, and Spectatorship in English Renaissance Drama." *ELH* 54 (1987): 561–83.

Mayall, David. "The Making of British Gypsy Identities, c. 1500–1980." *Immigrants and Minorities* 11 (1992): 21–41.

McEachern, Claire. "Fathering Herself: A Source Study of Shakespeare's Feminism." *Shakespeare Quarterly* 39 (1988): 269–90.

McEwin, Carole. "Counsels of Gall and Grace: Intimate Conversations Between

Women in Shakespeare's Plays." In Lenz, Greene, and Neely, *Woman's Part*, 117–32.

McGiffert, Michael, ed. *Constructing Race: Differentiating Peoples in the Early Modern World*. Special issue, *William and Mary Quarterly* 3rd ser. 54 (1997).

McLaren, Angus. *Reproductive Rituals: The Perception of Fertility in England from the Sixteenth Century to the Nineteenth Century*. London: Methuen, 1984.

Meitzlitzki, Dorothy. *The Matter of Araby*. New Haven, Conn.: Yale University Press, 1977.

Mela, Pomponius. *The Scituation of the World*. Trans. Arthur Golding. London, 1585.

Meyer, Gerald Dennis. *The Scientific Lady in England 1650–1760*. Berkeley: University of California Press, 1955.

Middleton, Thomas. *A Chaste Maid in Cheapside*. 1630. In *Five Plays*, ed. Bryan Loughrey and Neil Taylor. London: Penguin, 1988.

———. *The Family of Love*. London, 1608.

———. *A Mad World, My Masters*. 1608. Ed. Michael Taylor. Oxford: Oxford University Press, 1995.

———. *The Triumphs of Truth*. 1614. In *The Progresses, Processions, and Magnificent Festivities of King James the First*, ed. John Nichols, 2:679–97. London, 1828.

Middleton, Thomas, and William Rowley. *The Spanish Gipsie*. 1623. London, 1653.

Milton, John. *Complete Poems and Major Prose*. Ed. Merrit Y. Hughes. New York: Odyssey, 1957.

Minsheu, John. *Dictionarie in Spanish and English*. 1599. Early Modern English Dictionaries Database (EMEDD). Ed. Ian Lancashire. Social Sciences and Humanities Research Council of Canada/University of Toronto, 1999. http://www.chass.utoronto.ca/english/emed/html (accessed March 25, 2002).

Mintz, Samuel I. "The Duchess of Newcastle's Visit to the Royal Society." *JEGP* 51 (1952): 168–76.

Mintz, Sidney W. *Sweetness and Power: The Place of Sugar in Modern History*. New York: Viking, 1985.

Montaigne, Michel de. "Des Cannibales." In *Essays and Selected Writings: A Bilingual Edition*, ed. and trans. Donald Frame, 78–116. New York: Columbia University Press, 1963.

Montreux, Nicolas de. *Honours Academie*. Trans. Robert Tofte. London, 1610.

Montrose, Louis Adrian. "'Shaping Fantasies': Figurations of Gender and Power in Elizabethan Culture." *Representations* 1 (1983): 61–94.

———. "The Work of Gender in the Discourse of Discovery." In Greenblatt, *The New World*, 1–41.

Morgan, J. R., and Richard Stoneman, eds. *Greek Fiction: The Greek Novel in Context*. London: Routledge, 1994.

Morgan, Jennifer L. *Laboring Women: Reproduction and Gender in New World Slavery*. Philadelphia: University of Pennsylvania Press, 2004.

Morley, David, and Kuan-Hsing Chen, eds. *Stuart Hall: Critical Dialogues in Cultural Studies*. London: Routledge, 1996.

Morris, Harry. "Richard Barnfield, 'Amyntas,' and the Sidney Circle." *PMLA* 74 (1959): 318–24.

———. *Richard Barnfield, Colin's Child*. Tampa: Florida State University Press, 1963.

———. "Thomas Watson and Abraham Fraunce [Response]." *PMLA* 76 (1961): 152–53.

Moysie, David. *Memoirs of the Affairs of Scotland*. Edinburgh: Bannatyne Club, 1830.

Mullaney, Steven. *The Place of the Stage: License, Play and Power in Renaissance England.* Chicago: University of Chicago Press, 1988.

Munday, Anthony. *Chrysanaleia: The Golden Fishing: Or, Honour of Fishmongers.* London, 1616.

Munich, Adrienne Auslander. *Andromeda's Chains: Gender and Interpretation in Victorian Literature and Art.* New York: Columbia University Press, 1989.

Murphy, Andrew. *"But the Irish Sea Betwixt Us": Ireland, Colonialism, and Renaissance Literature.* Lexington: University of Kentucky Press, 1999.

Musaeus [Grammaticus]. *The Divine Poem of Musæus: Hero and Leander.* Trans. George Chapman. 1616. In Donno, *Elizabethan Minor Epics,* 70–84.

"Hero and Leander." Trans. Cedric Whitman. Ed. and introd. Thomas Gelzer. In *Callimachus, Grammaticus.* 288–389. Cambridge, Mass.: Harvard University Press; London: Heinemann, 1975.

Neely, Carol Thomas. *Broken Nuptials in Shakespeare's Plays.* New Haven, Conn.: Yale University Press, 1985.

————. "Lovesickness, Gender, and Subjectivity: *Twelfth Night* and *As You Like It.*" In *A Feminist Companion to Shakespeare,* ed. Dympna Callaghan, 276–98. Oxford: Blackwell, 2000.

————. "WOMEN/UTOPIA/FETISH: Disavowal and Satisfied Desire in Margaret Cavendish's *New Blazing World* and Gloria Anzaldúa's *Borderlands/La Frontera.*" In *Heterotopia: Postmodern Utopia and The Body Politic,* ed. Tobin Siebers, 58–95. Ann Arbor: University of Michigan Press, 1994.

Neill, Michael. *Putting History to the Question: Power, Politics, and Society in English Renaissance Drama.* New York: Columbia University Press, 2000.

Netzloff, Mark. "'Counterfeit Egyptians' and Imagined Borders: Jonson's *The Gypsies Metamorphosed.*" *ELH* 68 (2001): 763–93.

Newman, Karen. "And Wash the Ethiop White: Femininity and the Monstrous in *Othello.*" In *Fashioning Femininity and English Renaissance Drama,* 71–94. Chicago: University of Chicago Press, 1991.

Newton, Sir Isaac. *Opticks.* 1704. New York: Dover, 1952.

Nicolay, Nicholas. *Nauigations, Peregrinations, and Voyages.* Trans. Thomas Washington. London, 1585.

Okely, Judith. *The Traveller-Gypsies.* Cambridge: Cambridge University Press, 1983.

Oldenburg, Scott. "The Riddle of Blackness in England's National Family Romance." *JEMCS* 1,1 (2001): 46–62.

Orgel, Stephen. *Impersonations.* Cambridge: Cambridge University Press, 1996.

————. *The Jonsonian Masque.* Cambridge, Mass.: Harvard University Press, 1965.

————. "Marginal Jonson." In *The Politics of the Stuart Court Masque,* ed. David Bevington and Peter Holbrook, 144–75. Cambridge: Cambridge University Press, 1998.

————. "Renaissance Homoeroticism." Rev. of *Richard Barnfield: The Poems,* ed. George Klawitter. *Lesbian and Gay Studies Newsletter* (1991): 33–35.

Origen [Origines Adamantius]. *The Song of Songs: Commentary and Homilies.* Trans. R. P. Lawson. Westminster, Md.: Newman, 1957.

Ovid [Publius Ovidius Naso]. [*Ars Amatoria.*] *The Art of Love and Other Poems.* Trans. J. H. Mozley. London: Heinemann, 1929.

————. *Loves Schoole: De Arte Amandi, or, The Art of Love.* Trans. [attrib.] Thomas Heywood. Amsterdam, [1640?].

————. *Heroides and Amores.* Trans. Grant Showerman. 2nd ed. Rev. G. P. Goold. Cambridge, Mass.: Harvard University Press, 1986.

―――. [*Metamorphoses*] *Metamorphosis Dat Is*. Trans. Johannes Florianus. Antwerp, 1615.

―――. [*Metamorphoses*] *The XV Bookes of P. Ovidius Naso, Entytuled Metemorphosis*. Trans. Arthur Golding. London, 1575.

―――. [*Metamorphoses*] *Ovid's Metamorphosis Englished, Mythologiz'd, And Represented in Figures*. Trans. George Sandys. London, 1632.

Padilla, Fray Tomas de. *Historia de las cosas de Etiopia*. Antwerp, 1557.

Palmer, Thomas. *How to Make Our Trauailes . . . Profitable and Honourable*. London, 1606.

Palsgrave, John D. *Lesclarcissement de la langue Francoyse*. 1530. Menston: Scolar, 1969.

Papers Relative to the Marriage of King James the Sixth of Scotland. Edinburgh: Bannatyne Club, 1828.

Paré, Ambroise. *Les Oeuvres d'Ambroise Paré*. Paris, 1579.

―――. *Les Oeuvres d'Ambroise Paré*. 10th ed. Lyons, 1641.

―――. *The Workes of that Famous Chirurgion Ambrose Parey*. Trans. Thomas Johnson. London, 1634.

Park, Clara Claiborne. "As We Like It: How a Girl Can Be Smart and Still Popular." In Lenz, Greene, and Neely, *Woman's Part*, 100–16.

Park, Katharine. "The Rediscovery of the Clitoris." In Hillman and Mazzio, *Body in Parts*, 171–93.

Parker, Henry, Lord Morley, trans. *The Tryumphes of Fraunces Petrarcke*. 1555. Ed. D. D. Carnicelli. Cambridge, Mass.: Harvard University Press, 1971.

Parker, Patricia. "Fantasies of 'Race' and 'Gender': Africa, *Othello*, and Bringing to Light." Hendricks and Parker, *Women, "Race," and Writing*, 84–100.

―――. "Gender Ideology, Gender Change: The Case of Marie-Germain." *Critical Inquiry* 19 (1993): 337–65.

―――. "Literary Fat Ladies and the Generation of Text." In *Literary Fat Ladies: Rhetoric, Gender, Property*, 8–36. London: Methuen, 1987.

Paster, Gail Kern. *The Body Embarrassed: Drama and the Disciplines of Shame in Early Modern England*. Ithaca, N.Y.: Cornell University Press, 1993.

Patrologia Latina Database. CD-ROM. 3 vols. Ed. J. P. Migné. Chadwyck-Healey. 1994. Stanford University (accessed March 13, 1996).

Peaps, William. *Love In its Extasie: Or, The Large Prerogative*. 1649. Ed. and introd. Robert Birley. Ilkley: Roxburghe Club, 1981.

Pendergast, John S. "Pierre Du Moulin on the Eucharist: Protestant Sign Theory and the Grammar of Embodiment." *ELH* 65 (1998): 47–68.

Pepys, Samuel. *Diary*. Ed. Robert Latham and William Matthews. Vol. 8 (1667). Berkeley: University of California Press, 1974.

Pequigney, Joseph. *Such Is My Love*. Chicago: University of Chicago Press, 1985.

Perkins, Judith. "An Ancient 'Passing' Novel: Heliodorus' *Aithiopika*." *Arethusa* 32, 2 (1999): 197–214.

Peterson, Richard S. "Icon and Mystery in Jonson's *Masque of Beautie*." *John Donne Journal* 5 (1986): 169–99.

Pickering, Charles. *The Races of Man; and, Their Geographical Distribution*. Introd. John Charles Hall. London: Bohn, 1854.

Pinkerton, W. "Cats, Dogs and Negroes as Articles of Commerce." *Notes and Queries* 2 3rd ser. (November 1, 1862): 345–46.

Platt, Sir Hugh. *Delightes for Ladies*. London, 1602.

Pliny, the Elder. *The History of the World*. Trans. Philemon Holland. London, 1601.

―――. *Natural History*. Trans. H. Rackham. 10 vols. Loeb Classical Library. Cambridge, Mass.: Harvard University Press, 1938–63.

Pollard, Alfred W. *Records of the English Bible*. London: Frowde, 1911.

Pope, Marvin H. *Song of Songs*. The Anchor Bible. New York: Doubleday, 1977.

Pope-Hennessy, James. *Sins of the Fathers: A Study of the Atlantic Slave Traders, 1441–1807*. London: Weidenfeld, 1967.

Pound, John. *Poverty and Vagrancy in Tudor England*. London: Longman, 1986.

Praz, Mario. *Studies in Seventeenth-Century Imagery*. 2 vols. London: Warburg Institute, 1939.

Prescott, Anne Lake. "Barnfield's Spenser: 'Great Collin' and the Art of Denial." In Borris and Klawitter, *The Affectionate Shepherd*, 84–98.

Price, Hereward T. "Function of Imagery in *Venus and Adonis*." Papers of the Michigan Academy of Science, Arts and Letters 31 (1945): 271–77, 285–92. Reprinted in Kolin, *"Venus and Adonis"*, 107–22.

Prynne, William. *Histrio-mastix*. London, 1633.

Pulton, Fardinando, ed. *An Abstract of all the penal Statutes which be general, in force and vse*. London, 1581.

Quarles, Francis. *Sions Sonets*. London, 1625.

Rabl, Kathleen. "Taming the 'Wild Irish' in English Renaissance Drama." In *Literary Interrelations: Ireland, England, and the World*, 47–59. Vol. 3 of *National Images and Stereotypes*. Tubingen: Narr, 1987.

Rackin, Phyllis. "Androgyny, Mimesis, and the Marriage of the Boy Heroine on the English Renaissance Stage." *PMLA* 102 (1987): 29–41.

Ralegh, Sir Walter. "The Discoverie of . . . Guiana." In Hakluyt, *Principal Navigations*, 10:338–431.

Raman, Shankar. *Framing "India": The Colonial Imaginary in Early Modern Culture*. Stanford, Calif.: Stanford University Press, 2002.

Ranald, Margaret Loftus. "'As Marriage Binds, and Blood Breaks': English Marriage and Shakespeare." *Shakespeare Quarterly* 30 (1979): 68–81.

Randall, Dale B. J. *Jonson's Gypsies Unmasked*. Durham, N.C.: Duke University Press, 1975.

Rawson, Maud Stepney. *Penelope Rich and Her Circle*. London: Hutchinson, 1911.

Reeve, M. D. "Conceptions." *Proceedings of the Cambridge Philological Society: Supplement* n.s. 36, 215 (1989): 81–112.

Relihan, Constance C. "Erasing the East from *Twelfth Night*." In MacDonald, *Race, Ethnicity, and Power*, 80–94.

Reynolds, Bryan. *Becoming Criminal: Transversal Performance and Cultural Dissidence in Early Modern England*. Baltimore: Johns Hopkins University Press, 2002.

Richmond, Hugh M. "Much Ado About Notables." *Shakespeare Studies* 12 (1979): 49–63.

Ricks, Christopher. *Keats and Embarrassment*. Oxford: Clarendon, 1974.

Rid, Samuel. *The Art of Jugling*. London, 1614.

Rist, Thomas C. K. "Religious Politics in Ben Jonson's 'The Irish Masque.'" *Cahiers Élisabéthains* 55 (1999): 27–34.

Rivière, Lazare [Lazarus Rivierus]. *The Universal Body of Physick*. Trans. William Carr. London, 1657.

Roberts, Bleddyn J. "The Old Testament: Manuscripts, Texts and Versions." In Lampe, *The West from the Fathers*, 1–26.

Roberts, Sasha. "Reading the Shakespearean Text in Early Modern England." *Critical Survey* 7 (1995): 299–306.

Robotham, John. *An Exposition of Solomons Song*. London, 1652.

Rogers, Thomas. *The Anatomie of the Minde*. London, 1576.

Rose, Willie Lee. *A Documentary History of Slavery in North America.* 1976. Athens: University of Georgia Press, 1999.

Ross, Alexander. *Mystagogus Poeticus.* 1648. London: Garland, 1976.

Rosseter, Philip [and Thomas Campion]. *A Booke of Ayres.* London, 1601.

R[owlands], S[amuel]. *Martin Markall, Beadle of Bridewell.* London, 1610.

Royster, Francesca T. "'White-Limed Walls': Whiteness and Gothic Extremism in Shakespeare's *Titus Andronicus.*" *Shakespeare Quarterly* 51 (2000): 432–55.

Royston, Pamela. "*Hero and Leander* and the Eavesdropping Reader." *John Donne Journal* 2, 1 (1983): 31–53.

Rüff, Jakob [Jacobus Rueff, Jakob Rueff]. [*De Conceptu.* 1554] *The Expert Midwife.* London, 1637.

Ryding, Erik S. *In Harmony Framed: Musical Humanism, Thomas Campion, and the Two Daniels.* Ann Arbor, Mich.: Sixteenth-Century Journal/Edwards, 1993.

Rymer, Thomas. *Foedera, Conventiones, Literae, et Cujuscunque Generis Acta Publica.* 20 vols. London, 1704–35. Vol. 15. 1713.

Said, Edward. *Orientalism.* New York: Pantheon, 1978.

Salgado, Gamini. *The Elizabethan Underworld.* London: Dent, 1977.

Salkeld, William. *Reports of Cases Adiudged by the King's Bench.* 2 vols. London, 1721.

Sandford, James. *The Amorous and Tragicall Tales of Plutarch.* London, 1567.

Sandys, George. *A Paraphrase upon the Song of Solomon.* London, 1641.

Sapolsky, Robert M. *A Primate's Memoir.* New York: Scribner, 2001.

Sarasohn, Lisa T. "A Science Turned Upside Down: Feminism and the Natural Philosophy of Margaret Cavendish." *Huntington Library Quarterly* 47 (1984): 289–307.

Satel, Sally. "I Am a Racially-Profiling Doctor." *New York Times,* May 5, 2002, national edition, sec. 6.

Scarry, Elaine. *The Body in Pain: The Making and Unmaking of the World.* Oxford: Oxford University Press, 1985.

———. "The Difficulty of Imagining Other Persons." In *The Handbook of Interethnic Coexistence,* ed. Eugene Weiner, 40–62. New York: Continuum/ Abraham Fund, 1998.

Schiebinger, Londa. "The Gendered Ape." In *The Graph of Sex and the German Text: Gendered Culture in Early Modern Germany, 1500–1700,* ed. Lynne Tatlock, 413–42. Amsterdam: Rodopi, 1994.

———. *The Mind Has No Sex.* Cambridge, Mass.: Harvard University Press, 1989.

Schiffer, James. "Shakespeare's *Venus and Adonis:* A Lacanian Tragicomedy of Desire." In Kolin, *"Venus and Adonis,"* 359–76.

The Schoolhouse of Women. London, 1541. 2nd ed. 1560. Abridged in Henderson and McManus, *Half Humankind,* 136–55.

Scotland. Statutes and Laws. *The Lawes and Actes of Parliament, Maid be King James the First, and his Successours Kings of Scotland.* Edinburgh, 1597.

Scotland. Statutes and Laws. *The Laws and Acts of Parliament. Made by King James the First, and his Successors, Kings and Queen of Scotland.* Edinburgh: D. Lindsay, 1682–83.

Scotland. Statutes and Laws. *The Second Volume, Conteininge those Statutes which have beene made in the time of the moste victorious reigne of Kinge Henry the eight.* London, 1575.

Sedgwick, Eve Kosovsky. *Between Men: English Literature and Male Homosocial Desire.* New York: Columbia University Press, 1985.

The Seege or Batayle of Troye: A Middle English Metrical Romance. Ed. Mary Elizabeth Barnicle. Publications of the Early English Text Society, old ser. 72. London: Oxford University Press, 1927.

Selden, Daniel L. "*Aithiopika* and Ethiopianism." In Hunter, *Studies in Heliodorus*, 182–217.

Settle, Dionise. "The second voyage of Master Martin Frobisher, made to the West and Northwest Regions, in the yeere 1577, with a description of the Countrey, and people." In Hakluyt, *Principal Navigations*, 7:211–30.

Shakespeare, William. *A New Variorum Edition of Shakespeare.* Ed. Horace Howard Furness, et al. 27 vols. Philadelphia: Lippincott, 1871–1955.

———. *The Poems.* Ed. John Roe. Cambridge: Cambridge University Press, 1992.

———. *The Riverside Shakespeare.* Ed. G. Blakemore Evans, J. J. M. Tobin, et al. Boston: Houghton Mifflin, 1997.

———. *Shakespeare's Sonnets.* Ed. Stephen Booth. New Haven, Conn.: Yale University Press, 1977.

———. *Shakespeare's Sonnets.* Ed. Katherine Duncan-Jones. The Arden Shakespeare. 3rd ser. N.p.: Thomas Nelson, 1998.

———. *Titus Andronicus.* Ed. Jonathan Bate. The Arden Shakespeare. 3rd ser. London: Routledge, 1995.

The Shakspere Allusion-Book: A Collection of Allusions to Shakspere from 1591 to 1700. 2 vols. Ed. C. M. Ingleby, L. Toulmin Smith, F. J. Furnivall. 2nd ed. Rev. John Munro. London: Humphry Milford/Oxford University Press, 1932.

Shapin, Steven, and Simon Schaffer. *Leviathan and the Air-Pump.* Princeton, N.J.: Princeton University Press, 1985.

Shapiro, James. *Shakespeare and the Jews.* New York: Columbia University Press, 1996.

Shepherd, Geoffrey. "English Versions of the Scriptures Before Wyclif." In Lampe, *The West from the Fathers*, 362–87.

Shuger, Debora. "Irishmen, Aristocrats, and Other White Barbarians." *Renaissance Quarterly* 50 (1997): 494–525.

Shyllon, F. O. *Black People in Britain.* Oxford: Clarendon/Institute of Race Relations, 1977. Rev. ed. of *Black Slaves in Britain*, 1974.

Sibbes, Richard. *Bowels Opened, or, a Discovery of the Neere and Deere Love . . . betwixt Christ and the Church.* London, 1639.

Siddiqi, Yumna. "Dark Incontinents: The Discourse of Race and Gender in Three Renaissance Masques." *Renaissance Drama* n.s. 23 (1992): 139–63.

Simmons, J. L. "*Lust's Dominion*: A Showpiece for the Globe." *Tulane Studies in English* 20 (1972): 11–22.

Sinfield, Alan. "Diaspora and Hybridity: Queer Identities and the Ethnicity Model." *Textual Practice* 10 (1996): 271–94.

Singer, Peter. *Animal Liberation.* 1977. 2nd ed. New York: New York Review of Books/Random House, 1990.

Singh, Jyotsna G. *Colonial Narratives/Cultural Dialogues: "Discoveries" of India in the Language of Colonialism.* London: Routledge, 1996.

———. "Othello's Identity, Postcolonial Theory, and Contemporary African Rewritings of *Othello*." In Hendricks and Parker, *Women, "Race," and Writing*, 287–99.

———. "Renaissance Antitheatricality, Antifeminism, and Shakespeare's *Antony and Cleopatra*." *Renaissance Drama* n.s. 20 (1989): 99–121.

"Sir Isaac Newton: CAREER." *Britannica Online.* (accessed May 9, 1998).

Smith, Bruce R. *Homosexual Desire in Shakespeare's England.* Chicago: University of Chicago Press, 1991.

Smith, Hilda. "Gynecology and Ideology in Seventeenth-century England." In *Liberating Women's History*, ed. Berenice A. Carroll, 97–114. Urbana: University of Illinois Press, 1976.

———. *Reason's Disciples: Seventeenth-Century English Feminists.* Urbana: University of Illinois Press, 1982.

Smith, Ian. "Barbarian Errors: Performing Race in Early Modern England." *Shakespeare Quarterly* 49 (1998): 168–86.

———. "Dressed in Black: Racial Cross-Dressing on the Early Modern Stage." *Renaissance Drama* (forthcoming).

Smith, James M. "Effaced History: Facing the Colonial Contexts of Ben Jonson's *Irish Masque at Court.*" *ELH* 65 (1998): 297–321.

Smith, Jud. *A Misticall Deuise of the Spirituall and Godly Love Betwene Christ the Spouse, and the Church or Congregation.* London, 1575.

Smith, Samuel. *The Great Assize, or, Day of Jubilee.* London, 1633.

Snare, Gerald. *The Mystification of George Chapman.* Durham, N.C.: Duke University Press, 1989.

Snowden, Frank M., Jr. *Blacks in Antiquity.* Cambridge, Mass.: Belknap, 1970.

Somerset, Anne. *Elizabeth I.* London: Weidenfeld and Nicholson, 1991; New York: St. Martin's-Griffin, 1992.

Sousa, Geraldo U. de. *Shakespeare's Cross-Cultural Encounters.* London: Macmillan, 1999.

Sparke, John, the younger. "The voyage made by M. John Hawkins . . . to the coast of Guinea . . . in An. Dom. 1564." In Hakluyt, *Principal Navigations*, 10:9–63.

Spenser, Edmund. *Amoretti.* 1595. In *Poetical Works*, ed. Selincourt and Smith, 561–78.

———. *The Faerie Queene.* 1590–96. Ed. A. C. Hamilton. Rev. ed. London: Longman, 1980.

———. *Poetical Works.* Ed. E. de Selincourt, J. C. Smith. 1912. Oxford: Oxford University Press, 1987.

———. *The Shepherd's Calender.* 1579. In *Poetical Works*, ed. Selincourt and Smith, 415–67.

———. *Spenser's Prose Works.* Ed. Rudolf Gottfried. Vol. 9 of *The Works of Edmund Spenser: A Variorum Edition.* Ed. Edwin Greenlaw, Charles Grosvenor Osgood, Frederick Morgan Padelford and Ray Heffner. 11 vols. Baltimore: Johns Hopkins University Press, 1949.

——— [attrib.]. *A View of the Present State of Ireland.* Ed. W. L. Renwick. Oxford: Clarendon Press, 1970.

Spivak, Gayatri Chakravorty. "Can the Subaltern Speak?" In *The Post-Colonial Studies Reader*, ed. Bill Ashcroft, Gareth Griffiths, and Helen Tiffin, 24–28. London: Routledge, 1995.

———. *A Critique of Post-Colonial Reason: Toward a History of the Vanishing Present.* Cambridge, Mass.: Harvard University Press, 1999.

———. "Three Women's Texts and a Critique of Imperialism." *Critical Inquiry* 12 (1985): 243–61.

Sprigg, Joshua. *Solace for Saints in the Saddest Times . . . Held Forth in a Brief Discourse on the First Words of the Canticles.* London, 1648.

Stanivukovic, Goran V. "Troping Desire in Shakespeare's *Venus and Adonis.*" *Forum for Modern Language Studies* 33 (1997): 289–301.

Stanwood, Owen. "Christian Servants and Indian Slaves: Rethinking the Origins of Chesapeake Slavery." Unpublished paper, presented at the Omohundro Institute of Early American History and Culture, Annual Conference, College Park, Md., June 2002. http://www.wm.edu/oieahc/conferences/8thannual/Session12_Stanwood.pdf (accessed November 17, 2003).

Starobinski, Jean. "Chlorosis—the 'Green Sickness.'" *Psychological Medicine* 11 (1981): 459–68.

Staton, Walter F., Jr. "Thomas Watson and Abraham Fraunce." *PMLA* 76 (1961): 150–52.

The Statutes of the Realm Printed by Command of His Majesty King George the Third. London: Dawsons, 1810–28. Reprint, London: Record Commission, 1963.

Stechow, Wolfgang. "Heliodorus's *Aethiopica* in Art." *Journal of the Warburg and Courtauld Institutes* 16 (1953): 144–52.

Stephens, Walter. "Tasso's Heliodorus and the World of Romance." In *The Search for the Ancient Novel,* ed. James Tatum. Baltimore: Johns Hopkins University Press, 1994.

Sternbold, Thomas, trans. *The Whole Boke of Psalmes.* London, 1585. 2nd ed. London, 1633.

Stevenson, David. *Scotland's Last Royal Wedding: The Marriage of James VI and Anne of Denmark.* Edinburgh: John Donald, 1997.

Stevenson, Sheryl A. "'As Differing as Two Adamants': Sexual Difference in *The White Devil.*" In Levin and Robertson, *Sexuality and Politics,* 159–74.

Strabo, Walafridus. *Glossa Ordinaria.* In Patrologia Latina Database.

Stransky, Eugene. "On the History of Chlorosis." *Episteme* 8.1 (1974): 26–45.

Stubbes, Philip. *The Anatomie of Abuses.* London, 1585.

Sullivan, Jim. "'Language such as men doe vse': The Ethnic English of Ben Jonson's *The Irish Masque at Court.*" *Michigan Academician* 31 (1999): 1–22.

Suzuki, Mihoko. "Margaret Cavendish and the Female Satirist." *SEL* 37 (1997): 483–500.

Swain, Simon, ed. *Oxford Readings in the Greek Novel.* Oxford: Oxford University Press, 1999.

Swetnam, Joseph. *The Arraignment of Lewde, Idle, Froward, and Unconstant Women.* London, 1615. In Henderson and McManus, *Half Humankind,* 189–216.

Sykes, Bryan. *The Seven Daughters of Eve.* New York and London: Norton, 2001.

Takaki, Ronald, ed. *From Different Shores: Perspectives on Race and Ethnicity in America.* Oxford: Oxford University Press, 1987.

Talmon, Shemaryahu. "The Old Testament Text." In Ackroyd and Evans, *From the Beginnings to Jerome,* 159–99.

Tate, Nahum. *The Triumphs of Love and Constancy: A Romance.* 10 vols. Vols. 6–10. 2nd ed. London, 1687.

Taylor, Gary. *Buying Whiteness: Race, Sex, & Slavery from the English Renaissance to the African American Renaissance.* London: Palgrave, forthcoming.

———. "*Hamlet* in Africa 1607." In Kamps and Singh, *Travel Knowledge,* 223–48.

Taylor, John. "A Cove and a Mort Whidling together as they budged upon the Pad." In *Divers Crab-Tree Lectures,* 188–95. London, 1639.

Tempesta, Antonio. *Metamorphoseon . . . Ovidianarum.* 1606. Reprint, New York: Garland, 1976.

Tibbles, Anthony. *Transatlantic Slavery: Against Human Dignity.* Exhibition catalogue. London: HMSO/Merseyside Maritime Museum, 1994.

Timpane, John. "The Rogue as Self-Celebration in *The Gypsies Metamorphosed.*" Chap. 5 of "The Romance of the Rogue," 266–300. Ph.D. diss., Stanford University, 1980.

Todd, Janet. *The Sign of Angellica: Women, Writing, and Fiction, 1660–1800.* London: Virago, 1989.

Tokson, Elliot H. *The Popular Image of the Black Man in English Drama, 1550–1688.* Boston: G. K. Hall, 1982.

Topsell, Edward. *The Historie of Foure-Footed Beasts.* London, 1607.

Towerson, William. "The First Voyage . . . to the coast of Guinea." In Hakluyt, *Principal Navigations*, 6: 177–211.

———. "The Second Voyage . . . to the coast of Guinea." In Hakluyt, *Principal Navigations*, 6: 212–31.

Trapp, John. *Solomonis Πανερετος [Paneretos], or, a Commentarie upon the . . . Song of Songs.* London, 1650.

Traub, Valerie. "The (In)Significance of 'Lesbian' Desire in Early Modern England." In *Queering the Renaissance*, ed. Jonathan Goldberg, 62–83. Durham, N.C.: Duke University Press, 1994.

———. "Response to Richard Levin's "(Re)Thinking Unthinkable Thoughts." *New Literary History* 28 (1997): 539–42.

The Triumphs of Love and Constancy: A Romance. By "A Person of Quality." 2nd ed. 10 vols. Vols. 1–5. London, 1687.

Trubowitz, Rachel. "The Reenchantment of Utopia and the Female Monarchical Self: Margaret Cavendish's *Blazing World*." *Tulsa Studies in Women's Literature* 11 (1992): 229–46.

Tuke, Thomas. *A Discourse Against Painting and Tincturing of Men and Women.* London, 1616.

Turner, Denys. *Eros and Allegory: Medieval Exegesis of the Song of Songs.* Kalamazoo: Cistercian, 1995.

Turner, Myron. "Pastoral and Hermaphrodite: A Study in the Naturalism of Marlowe's *Hero and Leander*." *Texas Studies in Language and Literature* 17 (1975): 397–414.

Unwin, Rayner. *The Defeat of John Hawkins: A Biography of His Third Slaving Voyage.* New York: Macmillan, 1960.

Vaenius, Ernestus. [Ernest Van Veen]. *Tractatus Physiologicus de Pulchritudine.* Brussels, 1662.

Vaenius, Otho. [Otto Van Veen]. *Amorum Emblemata.* Antwerp, 1608. [In Latin, Italian and French.]

———. *Amorum Emblemata: With Verses in the French, English and Italian tongues.* Antwerp, 1608.

Van Norden, Linda. *The Black Feet of the Peacock: The Color-Concept "Black" from the Greeks to the Renaissance.* Ed. John Pollack. Lanham, Md.: University Press of America, 1985.

Varandaeus, Johannes [Jean Varandal]. *De Morbis Mulierum.* 1615. Geneva, 1620.

Vaughan, Alden T. *Roots of American Racism: Essays on the Colonial Experience.* Oxford: Oxford University Press, 1995.

Vaughan, Alden T., and Virginia Mason Vaughan. "Before *Othello*: Elizabethan Representations of Sub-Saharan Africans." In McGiffert, *Constructing Race*, 19–44.

Vendler, Helen. *The Art of Shakespeare's Sonnets.* Cambridge, Mass.: Harvard University Press, 1997.

Vesey-FitzGerald, Brian. *Gypsies of Britain.* Newton Abbot, UK: David and Charles, 1973.

Vickers, Nancy. "'The blazon of sweet Beauty's best': Shakespeare's *Lucrece*." In *Shakespeare and the Question of Theory*, ed. Patricia Parker and Geoffrey Hartman, 95–115. London: Routledge, 1990.

Virgil. "Eclogue II." In *Virgil's Eclogues*, trans. Guy Lee, 12–17. Liverpool: Francis Cairns, 1980.

———. *Vergil's Eclogues.* Trans. Barbara Hughes Fowler. Chapel Hill: University of North Carolina Press, 1997.

Virginia, Council of. *A True Declaration of the Estate of the Colonie in Virginia.* London: 1610. Virtual Jamestown Project. Charlottesville: Virginia Center for Digital History, 2002. http://etext.lib.virginia.edu/etcbin/jamestown-browse?id=J1059 (accessed December 7, 2003).

Vitkus, Daniel J., introd. and ed. *Three Turk Plays from Early Modern England: "Selimus," "A Christian Turned Turk," and "The Renegado."* New York: Columbia University Press, 2000.

———. "Trafficking with the Turk: English Travelers in the Ottoman Empire During the Early Seventeenth Century." In Kamps and Singh, *Travel Knowledge*, 35–52.

———. "Turning Turk in *Othello*: The Conversion and Damnation of the Moor." *Shakespeare Quarterly* 48 (1997): 145–76.

Wack, Mary Frances. *Lovesickness in the Middle Ages: The Viaticum and its Commentaries.* Philadelphia: University of Pennsylvania Press, 1990.

Wall, Wendy. *Staging Domesticity: Household Work and English Identity in Early Modern Drama.* Cambridge: Cambridge University Press, 2002.

Walvin, James. *The Black Presence.* London: Orbach and Chambers, 1971.

Webbe, Edward. *The Rare and Most Wonderfull Things which Edward Webbe . . . hath seene.* London, 1590.

Webster, John. *The White Devil.* 1612. Ed. Elizabeth M. Brennan. London: Ernest Benn, 1966.

———. *The White Devil.* Ed. Christina Luckyj. London: Black/Norton, 1996.

Weever, John. *Faunus and Melliflora.* 1600. In Donno, *Elizabethan Minor Epics*, 253–80.

Welch, Robert, ed. *The Oxford Companion to Irish Literature.* Oxford: Clarendon, 1996.

West, William N. "Gold on Credit: Martin Frobisher's and Walter Ralegh's Economies of Evidence." *Criticism* 39 (1997): 315–36.

Wheeler, Roxann. *The Complexion of Race: Categories of Difference in Eighteenth-Century British Culture.* Philadelphia: University of Pennsylvania Press, 2000.

The White Ethiopian. Manuscript. BM Harleian 7313.

Whitney, Charles. "Charmian's Laughter: Women, Gypsies, and Festive Ambivalence in *Antony and Cleopatra.*" *Upstart Crow* 14 (1994): 67–88.

Wiener, Philip P., ed. "Optics." In *Dictionary of the History of Ideas*, vol. 3. 5 vols. New York: Scribner, 1973–74.

Wilcox, Thomas. *An Exposition uppon the Booke of the Canticles.* London, 1585.

Wilde, Oscar. "Pen, Pencil, and Poison: A Study in Green." In *The Artist as Critic: Critical Writings of Oscar Wilde.* Ed. Richard Ellmann, 320–40. New York: Random House, 1969. Reprint, Chicago: University of Chicago Press, 1987.

Wiles, Maurice F. "Theodore of Mopsuestia as Representative of the Antiochene School." In Ackroyd and Evans, *From the Beginnings to Jerome*, 489–510.

Williams, Ethel Carleton. *Anne of Denmark.* London: Longman, 1970.

Williams, George Huntston. *The Radical Reformation.* Philadelphia: Westminster, 1962.

Williams, Neville. *Powder and Paint: A History of the Englishwoman's Toilet, Elizabeth I to II.* London: Longmans, 1957.

Williams, Raymond. *Marxism and Literature.* Oxford: Oxford University Press, 1977.

Willson, D. Harris. *King James VI and I.* London: Cape, 1956.

Wilson, Dudley. *Signs and Portents: Monstrous Births from the Middle Ages to the Enlightenment.* London: Routledge, 1993.

Wilson, Katharine N. *Shakespeare's Sugared Sonnets.* London: George Allen/ Wilmer, 1974.

Winkler, J. J. "The Mendacity of Kalasiris and the Narrative Strategy of Helio-
   dorus's *Aithiopika.*" In Swain, *Oxford Readings,* 286–350.
Wither, George. *The Hymnes and Songs of the Church.* London, 1623.
Wolf, Naomi. *The Beauty Myth.* New York: Morrow, 1991; New York: Anchor,
   1992.
Woodbridge, Linda. "Black and White and Red All Over: The Sonnet Mistress
   Among the Ndembu." *Renaissance Quarterly* 40 (1987): 247–97.
———. *Vagrancy, Homelessness, and English Renaissance Literature.* Urbana: Uni-
   versity of Illinois Press, 2001.
———. *Women and the English Renaissance: Literature and the Nature of Womankind,
   1540–1620.* Urbana: University of Illinois Press, 1984.
Woodward, Jocelyn M. *Perseus: A Study in Greek Art and Legend.* Cambridge:
   Cambridge University Press, 1937.
Woolf, Virginia. *Orlando: A Biography.* 1928. New York: Harvest, 1992.
———. *A Room of One's Own.* 1929. San Diego: Harvest, 1989.
Worrall, Andrew. "Biographical Introduction: Barnfield's Feast of 'all Varietie.'"
   In Borris and Klawitter, *The Affectionate Shepherd,* 25–38.
Wright, John, ed. *A Natural History of the Globe, of Man, of Beasts, Birds, Fishes,
   Reptiles, Insects, and Plants* [*Buffon's Natural History*]. Boston: Gray, 1831.
Wright, Thomas. *The Passions of the Mind in Generall.* Ed. William Webster
   Newbold. Garland: New York and London, 1986.
Wrigley, E. A. *People, Cities, and Wealth.* London: Blackwell, 1987.
Wrigley, E. A., and R. S. Schofield. *The Population History of England, 1541–1871:
   A Reconstruction.* Cambridge, Mass.: Harvard University Press, 1981.
Wroth, Lady Mary. *Pamphilia to Amphilanthus.* In *Poems,* ed. Josephine A. Roberts.
   Baton Rouge: Louisiana State University Press, 1983.
Wynne-Davies, Marion. "*The Queen's Masque*: Renaissance Women and the
   Seventeenth-Century Court Masque." In *Gloriana's Face: Women, Public and
   Private, in the English Renaissance,* ed. S. P. Cerasana and Marion Wynne-
   Davies, 79–104. New York: Harvester, 1992.
Yen, Julie W. "'If it be sinne to love a sweet-fac'd Boy': Rereading Homoerotic
   Desire in Barnfield's Ganymede Poems." In Borris and Klawitter, *The Affec-
   tionate Shepherd,* 130–48.
Zagorin, Perez. *The Court and the Country.* New York: Atheneum, 1970.
Zhiri, Oumelbanine. "Leo Africanus's *Description of Africa.*" In Kamps and Singh,
   Travel Knowledge, 258–66.

Index

Acknowledgments

A lively and challenging community of scholars at different institutions has helped me by responding to conference papers or article submissions, by sharing work with me, by making pertinent suggestions over tea at libraries and professional meetings, by providing research assistance, and by befriending me. These groups are not mutually exclusive. I therefore thank Esther Arnold, Caroline Bicks, Edmund Campos, Vincent Carey, Christy Desmet, Colleen Donovan, Angelica Duran, Roxanne Eberle, Nancy Felson, Coburn Freer, Barbara Fuchs, Darlene Greenhalgh, Andrew Hadfield, Christine Holbo, Margo Hendricks, Suvir Kaul, Elizabeth Kraft, Tricia Lootens, Anne Mallory, Diana Maltz, Susan Mattern-Parkes, Carla Mazzio, Barbara McCaskill, Lori Newcomb, Eric Oberle, Patricia Parker, Adam Parkes, Leah Price, Paul Saint-Amour, Heather Schell, Laura Smyth, Gary Taylor, Kalpen Trivedi, Kate Washington, Robin Wharton, Jill Whitelock, Anne Williams, and Betsy Wright.

I extend particular thanks to Ania Loomba, Stephen Orgel, David Riggs, Jennifer Summit, and Fran Teague, who read and commented lucidly upon early drafts of several chapters, to Jyotsna Singh for encouragement at a crucial time, to Virginia Mason Vaughan and the anonymous reader from Penn Press, and to my editor, Jerry Singerman.

I am grateful for financial support from the Stanford Institute for Research on Women and Gender, the Mabelle McLeod Lewis Memorial Fund, the Huntington Library, the University of Georgia Research Foundation, the Center for Humanities and Arts at the University of Georgia, and the Sarah H. Moss Foundation. I would also like to thank the librarians and staffs at the Folger Shakespeare Library, the Huntington Library, the Lane Medical Library at Stanford, the Duke University Rare Books, Manuscripts and Special Collections Library, and the Hargrett Rare Books Library at the University of Georgia.

I appreciate permission from the University of Wales press to reproduce a portion of Chapter One that was published (in condensed form) as "An Ethiopian History: Reading Race and Skin Color in Early Modern Versions of Heliodorus's *Aithiopika*" in *Consuming Narratives: Gender and Monstrous Appetite in the Middle Ages and the Renaissance,* ed. Elizabeth Herbert McAvoy and Teresa Walters (University of Wales Press, 2002) and from the Johns Hopkins University Press to include in the Introduction and Chapters Seven and Nine material (again, in different form) from "Royalist, Romancist, Racialist: Rank, Gender, and Race in the Science and Fiction of Margaret Cavendish" in *ELH* 69.3 (Fall 2002). I also thank the Folger Shakespeare Library for permission to include in Chapters Two, Seven, and Eight material that appeared (in different form and for a different readership) as "The Tolerance and Persecution of Africans in Early Modern Britain," in the catalog for the exhibition "Voices of Tolerance in an Age of Persecution," curated by Vincent Carey.

Finally, I thank my family for their support, love and interest: my father, Dr. E. N. Iyengar; my mother, Dr. Mythili Iyengar; my sister, Harini Iyengar, and her son, Chandrasekhar Iyengar; my husband, Richard Menke; and my daughter, Kavya Iyengar Menke.